AF244496

Christ Crucified

On the Resurrection
and the Life

Julian Gress

All Scripture quotations from the King James Version of the Bible.

Cover design by Dissect Designs.

ISBN
978-1-950436-03-3 (paperback)
978-1-950436-04-0 (hardback)
978-1-950436-05-7 (ebook)

Library of Congress Control Number: 2024913391

First printing edition

Julian Gress
Lynnwood, WA
julianrgress@gmail.com

TABLE OF CONTENTS

The purpose of this work is to prove that Jesus is the Christ, the Son of God; that by faith in his name men are enabled to repent, and by the promise of the divine likeness they are persuaded to believe; and that by his life and resurrection they are saved from their sins, and God is glorified in their salvation.

A proposition exhibits the union of a concept and an intuition. A doctrine is a proposition necessary to keep the moral law.[1] God is an inwardly lawful being, three persons in one; his blessedness is identical in distinction to his righteousness. Therefore, the intuitions of the fundamental doctrines are distinct from them, yet in identity with them, yield doctrines. As there are doctrines for the concepts, so also for the intuitions. The concepts contain within themselves the ground of their intuitions; likewise, the intuitions produced contain the concepts within themselves, and both are necessary to obey the moral law: the former, for the possibility of repentance, the latter, for the knowledge of this possibility, or faith.[2] The first I call *fundamentals*, the second, *historicals*.

The intuitions produced are distinct from the concepts that produce them, and belong to sensibility, yet are they identified with them, and yield knowledge of things in themselves, even of the divine nature manifest in the flesh. And the intuition of God lies in the person of the Son. There is therefore a body of doctrine peculiar to the Son, in whom person lies the ground of an intuition distinct from the concept, wherein the power of God to save sinners is actualized in space and time.

The production of an intuition through a concept is a form of causality, and the spontaneous causality of a person within the world of sense is life. The intuition distinct from the concept is, in identity therewith, grounded therein.

---

[1] Thomas Aquinas, *Summa Theologica* 1.1.1; Immanuel Kant, *Critique of Practical Reason*, ed. by Mary Gregor, trans. by Mary Gregor (Cambridge: Cambridge University Press, 1997), 5:132-141.

[2] Heb. 11:1.

Accordingly, the divine persons reveal themselves in the life of Christ, in his virgin birth, death, burial, resurrection, ascension, and second coming.

Historical doctrine is the history, not of the world, but of the Son. The creation of the world and the fall of mankind belong to historical doctrine in an order different from the history of the world. Christ indeed comes into the land of Israel, at the end of the sixth age, under the reign of Imperial Rome, yet the time and place thereof belong to him, not as the ground of the world, but as a member thereof, and their full exposition belongs to a work on prophetic history.

The moments of quantity express thoughts of the thinking subject; of modality, the relation of objects to the thinking subject. Therefore, the object of intuition is not revealed in particular doctrines under either heading, because the thoughts of a thinking subject are always universal. Quality and relation, however, both contemplate an object, and may be represented with particularity. Thus, the fundamental doctrines are revealed in six historical events. There are historical doctrines for the moments of quantity and modality, but they do not have events. Those of quantity pertain to Christ's headship over mankind, namely, the original righteousness of Adam, the original sin of many, and the divine headship of Christ; those of modality are offices, and explain the way in which Christ's headship pertains to us, namely, his prophetic, priestly, and kingly offices. They belong universally to his person, and to periods of his life, first on earth, then in heaven, then in heaven on earth.

The fundamental doctrines are concepts that contain within themselves the ground of their intuitions. The historical doctrines are the intuitions yielded by the concepts and contain the concepts within themselves. Nevertheless, the intuitions are identical in distinction to the concepts, and therefore conceptual, and for these intuitions conceptual, intuitions distinct may be given. The former I call the event, the latter, the sign. There are twelve historical doctrines, and therefore twelve signs.

Whether an event should be classified as a sign must be taught in Scripture, and with difficulty they are discovered and assigned to their peculiar doctrine. A few are expressly given, with or without the doctrine they adjoin. Some are so significant that they cannot fail of this signification. Nevertheless, the unmistakable quality of a sign is that it is not understood at the time, either by the disciples or by others, because as intuitions for concepts, they must be understood through the doctrines, yet are they given before them.[3]

The exposition of historical doctrine first states the doctrine itself, philosophically explained and Scripturally defended; then, the history of the doctrine from the narrative of Scripture; lastly, the sign of the doctrine in the life of Christ.

The former work demonstrated the possibility of salvation through the Incarnation and the Trinity. The divine persons are conditions of the transition from condemnation to justification. However, the possibility thereof is not the work itself. Nevertheless, as the blessedness of God is identical in distinction to his righteousness, so the actuality of the work rests in the possibility thereof. Accordingly, the salvation of sinners is accomplished prior to the coming of Christ,[4] as though he had already come, being signified by laws, promises, figures, and types.[5] And because the work is possible, God also produces an intuition thereof in the person of Jesus Christ, and in the kingdom of God, the church. The latter I reserve to its own place; here, I content myself with the former.

---

[3] John 2:18-22.
[4] 1 Pet. 1:19-21; Rev. 13:8.
[5] *Westminster Confession of Faith* 8.6.

The Act of Creation

Creation is the transition from non-existence to existence, whether in the beginning of time, or in the eternal ground of the world.[6]

God is an inwardly lawful being, perfectly happy in his own perfect righteousness: whatsoever he wills necessarily comes to pass. If God wills the world to exist, it exists, and howsoever he wills it to be, so it is. If he wills it to exist from eternity, it exists from eternity; or from nothing, then from nothing; and if not, then not.

> And God said, Let there be light: and there was light. Genesis 1:3

> But our God *is* in the heavens: he hath done whatsoever he hath pleased. Psalm 115:3

> Yea, before the day *was* I *am* he; and *there is* none that can deliver out of my hand: I will work, and who shall let it? Isaiah 43:13, cf. Is. 40:26, 41:20

The world exists, and therefore God wills the existence of the world. God is an inwardly lawful being; therefore, the creation of the world is good.

> And God saw the light, that it *was* good. Genesis 1:3-4

> Let them praise the name of the LORD: for he commanded, and they were created. Psalms 148:5

---

[6] Aquinas, *Summa* 1.46.2.

> Thou art worthy, O Lord, to receive glory and honour and power: for
> thou hast created all things, and for thy pleasure they are and were
> created. Revelation 4:11, cf. Is. 42:5-6, 43:15, 45:12-13, 18-19

God is all powerful. Whatsoever is possible, is possible for God, and all things come to pass according to his will.[7]

God wills nothing but what is right. This forms no limitation of his power. Howsoever lawful, the act is known to be lawful through its actuality. That it should rain or shine, God wills as he pleases. This is known to be right because it rains or shines, not otherwise. God has power to do either, yet he knows beforehand that one or the other is right, and wills accordingly.[8]

God cannot sin, yet this forms no limitation of his power, for it is precisely because he is perfectly righteous that he is able to do all things, and that all things come to pass according to his will.

The first antinomy of pure reason posits either a beginning in time or an infinite past. Kant has proved this problem insoluble. A beginning in time is preceded by a time of nothing, indistinguishable from any other, but an eternity past cannot have been elapsed. Neither is adequate to experience, which gives the progression alone to past time, through the sequence of alterations.[9]

Neither of these is possible according to theoretical reason, yet there is nothing in them that contradicts it. A beginning in time is conceivable, though it is impossible to produce through successive synthesis. Likewise an eternal world may be thought, but the infinite series of alterations can never be completed.[10]

The world must therefore be preceded not by a past time, but by the pure representation of a past time. Every past time is represented by a cause, but a cause without any past is a purpose, for every cause precedes its effect in time, but the means is the cause, and the end precedes the means, as the cause of the

---

[7] Aquinas, *Summa* 1.19.6.

[8] Job 36:22-42:6; Ps. 104; Matt. 5:45.

[9] Kant, *Critique of Pure Reason*, trans. by Werner Pluhar (Indianapolis: Hackett Publishing Company, 1996), B432-595.

[10] *Critique*, B458-462.

desired effect.[11] Therefore, the antinomy of practical reason asks whether the world began, and time with it, or both time and the world are infinite.[12]

The world is not preceded by a time but by a purpose, and through this representation alone the successive synthesis of representations in time may be regarded as complete. The beginning of time represents a ground of the world before time itself; an eternity past represents a ground within the series of events.[13] If then time began, and the world with it, the reason for the world lies outside the world, but if time has no beginning, and the world is eternal, then its purpose lies solely in itself, and the world has no purpose but what it has in itself.[14]

The world exists for the will of God. God is the supreme being, for whose sake all things exist. The world has no purpose of itself, but what God gives it. The moral law prescribes to man his purpose, and the fulfillment thereof belongs to God. Therefore, to represent the eternal purpose of the Creator, practical reason requires that the world have a beginning.

> In the beginning God created the heaven and the earth. Genesis 1:1, cf. Job 38:4; Eph. 1:4; 2 Tim. 1:9

> For the invisible things of him from the creation of the world are clearly seen, being understood by the things that are made, even his eternal power and Godhead; so that they are without excuse. Romans 1:20

Nevertheless, man is free to disobey the law, wherein he ascribes to the world a purpose of its own, and an infinite past; nor is there anything in theoretical reason to deny him this ephemeral refuge, because for any series of events one may inquire into the former state, even if that past state is not to be

---

[11] Kant, *Critique of Judgment*, trans. by Werner Pluhar (Indianapolis: Hackett Publishing Company, 1987), Ak. 220, 408.
[12] Augustine, *City of God*, 11.4-6.
[13] Kant, *Critique*, B481-488.
[14] *Critique*, B490-504.

represented as actual, so that even in the darkness of sin, the Lord reigns forever from his throne in heaven.

> Thy throne *is* established of old: thou *art* from everlasting. Psalm 93:2

> Thus saith the Lord, The heaven *is* my throne. Isaiah 66:1

The divine purpose of the world is a secret. The supreme being is the end of all things, but not yet an end in himself. The divine persons are not known to man in the state of creation.[15] Man grasps only the possible purpose of the world in himself. There remains a purpose conceivable, yet not known, and by speculation thereon, rational beings fall into sin. Nevertheless, their sin is the very means God uses to accomplish his eternal purpose.

> It *is* the glory of God to conceal a thing: but the honour of kings *is* to search out a matter. Proverbs 25:2

> Now to him that is of power to stablish you according to my gospel, and the preaching of Jesus Christ, according to the revelation of the mystery, which was kept secret since the world began, But now is made manifest, and by the scriptures of the prophets, according to the commandment of the everlasting God, made known to all nations for the obedience of faith: To God only wise, *be* glory through Jesus Christ for ever. Amen. Romans 16:25-27, cf. Deut. 29:29; Job 15:8; 1 Cor. 2:7; Eph. 1:9, 3:3, 6:19; Col. 1:26

> According as he hath chosen us in him before the foundation of the world, that we should be holy and without blame before him in love. Ephesians 1:4

---

[15] Aquinas, *Summa* 1.32.1; *Westminster* 1.1.

Who hath saved us, and called *us* with an holy calling, not according to our works, but according to his own purpose and grace, which was given us in Christ Jesus before the world began. 2 Timothy 1:9

Original Righteousness

Creation requires the consent of the creature. The law requires that every person consent to the purpose for which he is used as a means. A person is an end in itself, not to be used as a means, but with his consent. God is the supreme end of all things; therefore, the creation of a person is a means to God's ends. As an end in itself, the existence of a person is an end of the law, and creation is lawful for the sake of the creature, but as a means to God's ends, creation requires the consent of the creature.

Nevertheless, the creature cannot consent to his own creation before he exists. God must therefore be the author of his consent through the very act of creation. This consent may only lawfully be given through the law.[16] Therefore, all rational creatures must be made in original righteousness.[17]

And God saw every thing that he had made, and, behold, *it was* very good. Genesis 1:31

Lo, this only have I found, that God hath made man upright; but they have sought out many inventions. Ecclesiastes 7:29

Even God, who quickeneth the dead, and calleth those things which be not as though they were. Romans 4:17

The thinking subject is conscious of itself through an object, and contains within its consciousness the ground of the intuition of an object, which is the concept of the moral law. And through his conception of the law, he is conscious

---

[16] 1 Tim. 1:8; 2 Tim. 2:5.
[17] *Westminster* 4.1-2; *Westminster Larger Catechism* Q.15-17.

of its goodness, and of the goodness of his own conception thereof. Wherefore, he spontaneously consents unto the law, that it is good;[18] so he binds himself to keep the law, and keeps it by consent. The thinking subject is a person, an end in itself, good in itself, and in its original self-consciousness.

And because the law of God requires rational beings to have no other gods before the Lord, every man and angel implicitly consents to the purpose for which he is made, whether unto honor or dishonor.[19]

> Woe unto him that striveth with his Maker! *Let* the potsherd *strive* with the potsherds of the earth. Shall the clay say to him that fashioneth it, What makest thou? Or thy work, He hath no hands? Woe unto him that saith unto *his* father, What begettest thou? or to the woman, What hast thou brought forth? Isaiah 45:9-10

> Then the word of the LORD came to me, saying, O house of Israel, cannot I do with you as this potter? saith the LORD. Behold, as the clay *is* in the potter's hand, so *are* ye in mine hand, O house of Israel. *At what* instant I shall speak concerning a nation, and concerning a kingdom, to pluck up, and to pull down, and to destroy *it*; If that nation, against whom I have pronounced, turn from their evil, I will repent of the evil that I thought to do unto them. And *at what* instant I shall speak concerning a nation, and concerning a kingdom, to build and to plant *it*; If it do evil in my sight, that it obey not my voice, then I will repent of the good, wherewith I said I would benefit them. Jeremiah 18:5-10

> Thou wilt say then unto me, Why doth he yet find fault? For who hath resisted his will? Nay but, O man, who art thou that repliest against God? Shall the thing formed say to him that formed *it*, Why hast thou made me thus? Hath not the potter power over the clay, of the same

---

[18] Rom. 7:16; cf. James 1:25.
[19] Ex. 20:3.

lump to make one vessel unto honour, and another unto dishonour?
Romans 9:19-21

Hath not the potter power over the clay, to destroy those who sin, to save those who repent, and to create each one to his predestined end.

The Essences of Creatures

To every rational creature reason belongs in common, and to each a rational nature peculiar to themselves. There is nothing in the concept of a person to distinguish one person from another, besides that portion of the common nature allotted to them.[20] This I call the essence, whether a concept, as of angels, or an intuition, as of men.

There is no universal concept, neither intuition so conceived, that does not refer to a particular person, that the thought thereof may be an end in itself. The moral law affirms the intuition of the concept, and the ground of the intuition lies in the particular to which the universal refers. All persons are summoned by the moral law, and called into being by the Creator, that each one should contemplate the others in all things, and the Lord of all above all.

An angel rules over a concept, and the concept of each angel is his essence.[21] God is the spirit of affirmation, the devil is the spirit of negation, and all other pure concepts have their angels, for if it is lawful to think a concept, there ought to be a person thought thereby, that the contemplation thereof may be an end in itself.[22]

There are then two divisions of spirits: transcendental and ideal. The former are entirely subjective; the latter fulfill the concept of an object. The two transcendental spirits are God and the devil.[23]

---

[20] Ps. 16:6.
[21] Aquinas, *Summa* 1.50.2, 4.
[22] Ps. 104:4; 2 Cor. 10:3-5.
[23] John 8:38.

The Lord rules over all, over all concepts and intuitions. He is the universal spirit, the spirit of affirmation.[24] All other spirits rule over concepts in particular. What is thought particularly in them is found universally in God, and what is thought identically in God is distributed to his angels, to each one a certain calling, to show forth the glory of God, who is all in all.[25]

The devil is the spirit of negation. Negation is a transcendental concept. The devil does not rule over any particular object, but over the distinctions between creatures, and between creature and Creator. Within him lies the pattern of all things made.

The devil is the opposite of God. God is the ground of all that is, and therefore his opposite is the ground of nothing at all. A genus is a universal under which stand several particulars, but nothing stands under the particular *negation*. Therefore, while God and the devil both belong to the same genus, all that is thought in that genus belongs to God. Thus, according to the reality of things, God does not belong to a genus and has no opposite, but he does and has, according to pure logic.[26]

The classes of ideal spirits are three: the unconditional, the conditional, and the mutually conditional, according to the relations of an object. The first class thinks the concepts of objects; the second thinks the intuition through the concept; the third thinks the concept through the intuition. Wherefore, the first class rules over theoretical objects, the second over practical objects, and the third over aesthetic objects. Scripture calls them *Seraphim*, *Teraphim*, and *Cherubim*.[27]

Man is made in the image of God. His essence is not a concept, but an intuition. Men are either male or female. The essence of a man is the union of a universal with a particular; the essence of a woman is the union of a universal with a singular; the essence of their union is the identity thereof.[28] The essence

---

[24] 1 John 1:5, 4:8, 16.

[25] Rom. 12:1-8; 1 Cor. 12; Eph. 4:1-10. Aquinas, *Summa* 1.44.1, 3, 4.

[26] *Summa* 1.3.5.

[27] Gen. 3:24; Ex. 25:19, 37:8; 2 Sam. 22:11; 1 Kings 6:24-27; 2 Chron. 3:11-12; Ps. 18:10; Is. 6:1-3; Judg. 17:5 cf. Deut. 32:17 & 1 Cor. 10:20; Ezek. 1, 9-10, 41:18.

[28] 1 Cor. 11:7-12.

of an object is the union of a particular and a singular, wherein lies the particular of intuition.

The Fall

All these are made in original righteousness, according to the rational nature common to all, and the free conception of the moral law in them; the essence of each applying the law, through which they think their own selves, to their own persons. And yet some fall into sin. Whence then is sin?

The rational nature common to all is universal, and commands each one to obey the moral law; and the essence of each, though particular to the nature, is universal to the person, and so applies the law to the person; but the particular person, in whom dwells both the essence and the common nature, either obeys or disobeys, according as the essence of each indwells him. According to the essence of each, not in itself, but insofar as it dwells within a particular person, a person falls into sin.[29]

Whence then arises the thinking subject, the particular to a universal concept? For it must arise from the concept itself, in that the moral law commands an intuition for the concept, but the particular is distinct from the universal. It is the moral law that conceives a person, and God gives him being. In the moral law itself, and in every concept thought through it, lies the ground of an intuition in agreement with the concept, but the ground thereof is a person. Thus, the moral law summons a person to be the particular of a universal concept, or of an intuition.

And according to the essence of each, a creature either perseveres in righteousness or falls into sin, for the essence of each person is that object whereby he is conscious of himself, wherein he finds his peculiar happiness. Every creature sins so far as he conceives his happiness apart from the law, for all seek to be happy, whether by law or apart from it. Therefore, according to the essence of each, a person either stands or falls. Thus it is written,

---

[29] Aquinas, *Summa* 1.49.1-3.

> Why doth thine heart carry thee away? and what do thy eyes wink at,
> That thou turnest thy spirit against God, and lettest *such* words go out
> of thy mouth? Job 15:12-13, cf. Ps. 5:9, 7:8, 9:17, 10:3-5, 26:1-11, 33:13-15,
> 36:4; Prov. 17:24, 19:3, 24:7, 28:18

Though his heart carry him away, yet is a man guilty before God, because he turns his own spirit against him.

> Do good, LORD, unto *those that be* good, and *to them that are* upright in
> their hearts. As for such as turn aside unto their crooked ways, the
> LORD shall lead them forth with the workers of iniquity: *but* peace *shall
> be* upon Israel. Psalm 125:4-5

As for such as turn aside unto their crooked ways, for they sin, each one according to his own essence.

The devil is the spirit of negation. Negation is thought through affirmation, and the spirit of negation is the person in whom this concept dwells, that the thought thereof may be an end in itself. Negation is thought through affirmation,[30] and the spirit of negation is bound to obey the law of God. And because he conceives the law in his own person, he acknowledges the goodness of the law, and so binds himself to the law, and keeps it by consent.

The devil is made in original righteousness, yet it is written that *he was a murderer from the beginning* (John 8:44). Although made in original righteousness, and completely happy therein, nevertheless in the day of his creation he spontaneously contemplated the distinction between himself and his creator, and the limitation of his own happiness before God, and in pursuit of the divine likeness, he sinned and fell short of the glory of God.[31]

> How art thou fallen from heaven, O Lucifer, son of the morning! *how*
> art thou cut down to the ground, which didst weaken the nations! For

---

[30] Kant, *Critique*, B595-612.
[31] Rom. 3:23; Aquinas, *Summa* 1.63.3; Anselm, *On the Fall of the Devil*, Ch. 4.

thou hast said in thine heart, I will ascend into heaven, I will exalt my
throne above the stars of God: I will sit also upon the mount of the
congregation, in the sides of the north: I will ascend above the heights
of the clouds; I will be like the most High. Yet thou shalt be brought
down to hell, to the sides of the pit. Isaiah 14:12-15

The devil is the spirit of negation. The intuition he produces of himself, grounded solely in his person, is nothing. He ought to have been the humblest of all God's creatures, though greater than them all. Nevertheless, he conceived distinction in God when he saw only identity, for he sought to combine negation in himself with affirmation in God, whereby he willed an intuition distinct from the concept, without any ground in the concept. So he fell from heaven to earth,[32] and lost the vision of God,[33] and became the god of this world.[34]

What he sought and found not is this: the Trinity of divine persons revealed in the Lord Jesus Christ, wherein lies the identity in distinction of God's righteousness and his blessedness; for without the knowledge of the divine persons, in whom lies the ground of an intuition identical in distinction to the concept, the conception thereof contains within itself the negation of its own intuition. The devil sought to produce an image of the invisible God, distinct from the concept, yet not from God, but in himself. He had neither ground nor faculty to conceive identity in distinction, but pried curiously into divine mysteries, to wrest the hidden the purpose of God. Thus he turned from identity to distinction, and from God to himself, to whom he ascribed the divinity. Though the greatest of God's creatures, yet by his greatness he fell so far short of God's glory.

Moreover the word of the LORD came unto me, saying, Son of man, take
up a lamentation upon the king of Tyrus, and say unto him, Thus saith
the Lord GOD; Thou sealest up the sum, full of wisdom, and perfect in

---

[32] Luke 10:18.
[33] Jas. 2:19.
[34] 2 Cor. 4:4.

beauty. Thou hast been in Eden the garden of God; every precious stone *was* thy covering, the sardius, topaz, and the diamond, the beryl, the onyx, and the jasper, the sapphire, the emerald, and the carbuncle, and gold: the workmanship of thy tabrets and of thy pipes was prepared in thee in the day that thou was created. Thou *art* the anointed cherub that covereth; and I have set thee *so*: thou wast upon the holy mountain of God; thou hast walked up and down in the midst of the stones of fire. Thou *wast* perfect in thy ways from the day that thou wast created, till iniquity was found in thee. By the multitude of thy merchandise they have filled the midst of thee with violence, and thou hast sinned: therefore I will cast thee as profane out of the mountain of God: and I will destroy thee, O covering cherub, from the midst of the stones of fire. Thine heart was lifted up because of thy beauty, thou hast corrupted thy wisdom by reason of thy brightness: I will cast thee to the ground, I will lay thee before kings, that they may behold thee. Thou hast defiled thy sanctuaries by the multitude of thine iniquities, by the iniquity of thy traffick; therefore will I bring forth a fire from the midst of thee, it shall devour thee, and I will bring thee to ashes upon the earth in the sight of all them that behold thee. All they that know thee among the people shall be astonished at thee: thou shalt be a terror, and never *shalt* thou *be* any more. Ezekiel 28:11-19

Thou sealest up, he is not the sum itself, neither the ground, but a singular representation of the whole; *the sum,* the unity of the many, that is, the world, whose ground lies in God; *full of wisdom,* understanding the whole creation; *perfect in beauty,* encompassing the agreement of the world with man's moral purpose. *Every precious stone was thy covering,* ten stones for the whole law. *Thou art the anointed cherub that covereth;* who distinguishes all things from one another and from God, by their distinction under a common universal, for cherubim rule over the concepts of community and reciprocity, and there is one anointed cherub, negation itself, through which all particulars are distinguished; *thou hast walked up and down in the midst of the stones of fire,* to prosecute the judgment of God upon any who might transgress. *Thou was perfect in thy ways from the day that thou wast created,* made in original righteousness; *till iniquity was found in thee.* He sinned because of who he is, from the very essence of his person; wherefore he is solely to blame, and worthy of hell. *By the multitude of thy merchandise they,* his angels; *have filled the midst of thee with violence, and thou hast sinned:* to rule over angels; *therefore I will cast thee as profane out of the mountain of God:* out of heaven and away from the presence of God; *and I will destroy thee, O covering cherub, from the midst of the stones of fire,* from the very judgment he ought to have executed upon the disobedient. *Thine heart was lifted up because of thy beauty, thou hast corrupted thy wisdom by reason of thy brightness:* of all creatures nearest to God, yet so far to be like God himself, for of all creatures he alone is numbered with him.

> Ye are of *your* father the devil, and the lusts of your father ye will do. He was a murderer from the beginning, and abode not in the truth, because there is no truth in him. When he speaketh a lie, he speaketh of his own: for he is a liar, and the father of it. John 8:44

He was a murderer from the beginning, because he sinned from himself, not through any other creature, but from himself, in the very moment of his creation. *He abode not in the truth,* no, not for any duration;[35] *because there is no truth in him,* for although the concept of negation is very truth, the intuition thereof is nothing.

> And he said unto them, I beheld Satan as lightning fall from heaven. Luke 10:18

He fell in a flash of light, in the moment of his creation. In the very instant that the devil conceived the law in his own person, and bound himself to the goodness thereof, he sinned and fell. Through his own conception of the law, he

---

[35] Aquinas, *Summa* 1.63.6.

conceived distinction in the divine nature, and became the spirit of contradiction.

This conception he communicated to a third of the angels, who fell with him in his sin.[36] This is the second class of ideal spirits, who are causal, and follow negation, for they agree with negation as their unconditional condition, and within them only lies an intuition thought distinctly from the concept. These are called Teraphim, for the idols worshipped by the heathen are devils.[37] This third the devil brought down with his tail, that peculiar essence of his, which ought to have been subjected to his maker.

> And his tail drew the third part of the stars of heaven, and did cast them to the earth. Revelation 12:4

This same conception he communicated to men, and brought down the whole of humanity with him in his fall. Nevertheless, the sin of the devil harmonizes with the eternal purpose of God, to reveal himself to reasonable creatures in the form of man. The devil gained nothing by his sin, but became the instrument of God's most holy purpose. By the revelation of the divine persons in the humanity of our Lord Jesus Christ, the seed of the woman bruised the head of the serpent and put him to confusion,[38] in righteousness revealing what the devil could never by sin attain.

> And the light shineth in darkness; and the darkness comprehended it not. John 1:5

The End of Creation

The purpose of God is to save men from their sins, that they might partake of the divine nature in heaven forever, together with the elect angels, through

---

[36] Aquinas, *Summa* 1.63.8.
[37] Judg. 17:5, 18:14-20, cf. Deut. 32:16-17; 1 Cor. 10:18-21.
[38] Gen. 3:15.

the knowledge of God's holiness, for in that the blessedness of God is identical in distinction to his righteousness, the rational creature is, through the knowledge of the Trinity, free to conceive of his own righteousness and blessedness as identical, though distinct, because God is the holiness of his creatures in obedience to the moral law. Therefore, whoever sees God in Christ finds his happiness perfectly united to his lawfulness, and by faith in the promise of God partakes of the divine nature.[39]

> And one cried unto another, and said, Holy, holy, holy, *is* the LORD of hosts: the whole earth *is* full of his glory. Isaiah 6:3

Holy, holy holy, three times predicated of God, because predicated of three divine subjects, whose glory is manifest in the earth.

> They shall not hurt nor destroy in all my holy mountain: for the earth shall be full of the knowledge of the LORD, as the waters cover the sea. Isaiah 11:9, cf. Hab. 2:14

As the waters cover the sea, an apodictic truth of identity in distinction.[40]

> But we all, with open face beholding as in a glass the glory of the Lord, are changed into the same image from glory to glory, *even* as by the Spirit of the Lord. 2 Corinthians 3:18

God desires all men to be saved,[41] yet some remain in their sin, even unto death and hell. Whence then is this difference between men?

Man's essence consists of two distinct concepts that combine to form an intuition. The intuition yields an object for the universal concept, grounded in

---

[39] 2 Pet. 1:4.

[40] This was first suggested to me by a Facebook post, which is no longer available to me. I have searched in vain for a scholarly source to cite, even with the use of artificial intelligence.

[41] 1 Tim. 2:4; 2 Pet. 3:9.

the thinking subject, who contains within himself the very conception formed. This intuition is either identical to the universal concept or distinct, because the particular thought within the intuition either lies under the universal concept or outside it. If identical, there is no distinction whereby the concepts united may be identified in distinction; if however they are distinct, they may be identified in distinction, and the person represented may partake of the divine nature. Thus, the essences of men are divided between the reprobate and the elect.

Although all men are free to repent and believe, they are not therefore able to receive the fullness of salvation and participate in the divine beatitude, but only those to whom it is given. Thus it is that they neither repent nor believe, because the end of their sin is to attain the divine likeness, and this they cannot receive. Those in whom the divine bliss may dwell, whose essences are thought distinctly, and may be identified in distinction: these are chosen by God for salvation, and do come unto God to attain the divine likeness.

> *Even* the Spirit of truth; whom the world cannot receive, because it seeth him not, neither knoweth him: but ye know him; for he dwelleth with you, and shall be in you. John 14:17

> Wherefore he is able also to save them to the uttermost that come unto God by him. Hebrews 7:25

The essences of the reprobate show within them the identity thought in the divine nature, and reflect the glory thereof in sensible intuition. They "have their portion in this life" (Psalm 17:13-14); they are *fitted to destruction,* even as they are made *unto dishonor,* because they are not of God, but of the world.[42]

> And he said unto them, Ye are from beneath; I am from above: ye are of this world; I am not of this world. I said therefore unto you, that ye shall die in your sins: for if ye believe not that I am *he,* ye shall die in your sins. John 8:23-24

---

[42] John 8:42-47.

Hath not the potter power over the clay, of the same lump to make one vessel unto honour, and another unto dishonour? *What* if God, willing to shew *his* wrath, and to make his power known, endured with much longsuffering the vessels of wrath fitted to destruction: And that he might make known the riches of his glory on the vessels of mercy, which he had afore prepared unto glory…? Romans 9:21-23

(For many walk, of whom I have told you often, and now tell you even weeping, *that they are* the enemies of the cross of Christ: Whose end *is* destruction, whose God *is their* belly, and *whose* glory *is* in their shame, who mind earthly things.) Philippians 3:18-19

The essences of the elect are weaker and less glorious, that the glory of God may be manifest in them.

Blessed *are* the poor in spirit: for theirs is the kingdom of heaven. Matthew 5:3

At that time Jesus answered and said, I thank thee, O Father, Lord of heaven and earth, because thou hast hid these things from the wise and prudent, and hast revealed them unto babes. Even so, Father: for so it seemed good in thy sight. All things are delivered unto me of my Father: and no man knoweth the Son, but the Father; neither knoweth any man the Father, save the Son, and *he* to whomsoever the Son will reveal *him*. Matt. 11:25-27, cf. Luke 10:21-22

And Jesus said, For judgment I am come into this world, that they which see not might see; and that they which see might be made blind. John 9:39, cf. Matt. 11:25-27; Luke 10:21-22

He that loveth his life shall lose it; and he that hateth his life in this world shall keep it unto life eternal. John 12:25, cf. Matt. 10:39, 16:24-26; Mark 8:35-36; Luke 9:23-25, 17:33

I have given them thy word; and the world hath hated them, because they are not of the world, even as I am not of the world. John 17:14

For ye see your calling, brethren, how that not many wise men after the flesh, not many mighty, not many noble, *are called*: But God hath chosen the foolish things of the world to confound the wise; and God hath chosen the weak things of the world to confound the things which are mighty; And base things of the world, and things which are despised, hath God chosen, *yea*, and things which are not, to bring to nought things that are: That no flesh should glory in his presence. But of him are ye in Christ Jesus, who of God is made unto us wisdom, and righteousness, and sanctification, and redemption: That, according as it is written, He that glorieth, let him glory in the Lord. 1 Corinthians 1:26-31

Hearken, my beloved brethren, Hath not God chosen the poor of this world rich in faith, and heirs of the kingdom which he hath promised to them that love him? James 2:5

Why then did God create the reprobate? For they are ends in themselves, but every end must harmonize with the supreme end. He did not create them for sin, neither for destruction, but *that he might make know the riches of his glory on the vessels of mercy, which he had afore prepared unto glory.*

For thou *art* not a God that hath pleasure in wickedness: neither shall evil dwell with thee. Psalm 5:4

For thus saith the Lord GOD, the Holy One of Israel; In returning and rest shall ye be saved; in quietness and in confidence shall be your strength: and ye would not. Isaiah 30:15

Have I any pleasure at all that the wicked should die? saith the Lord GOD: *and* not that he should return from his ways, and live? ... For I have no pleasure in the death of him that dieth, saith the Lord GOD: wherefore turn *yourselves*, and live ye. Ezekiel 18:23, 32

O Jerusalem, Jerusalem, *thou* that killest the prophets, and stonest them which are sent unto thee, how often would I have gathered thy children together, even as a hen gathereth *her* chickens under her wings, and ye would not! Matthew 23:37

The punishment of the wicked is mercy to the elect, that they might depart from wickedness.

The righteous shall rejoice when he seeth the vengeance: he shall wash his feet in the blood of the wicked. So that a man shall say, Verily *there is* a reward for the righteous: verily he is a God that judgeth in the earth. Psalm 58:10-11

Ye have said, It *is* vain to serve God: and what profit *is it* that we have kept his ordinance, and that we have walked mournfully before the LORD of hosts? And now we call the proud happy; yea, they that work wickedness are set up; yea, *they that* tempt God are even delivered. Then they that feared the LORD spake often one to another: and the LORD hearkened, and heard *it*, and a book of remembrance was written before him for them that feared the LORD, and that thought upon his name. And they shall be mine, saith the LORD of hosts, in that day when I make up my jewels; and I will spare them, as a man spareth his own son that serveth him. Then shall ye return, and discern between the righteous and the wicked, between him that serveth God and him that serveth him not. Malachi 3:14-18

And the wicked themselves know the Lord by fire and by judgment.

All *they that be* fat upon earth shall eat and worship: all they that go down to the dust shall bow before him: and none can keep alive his own soul. Psalms 22:29

The LORD hath made all *things* for himself: yea, even the wicked for the day of evil. Proverbs 16:4

He made them, each according to his essence, according to which they sinned, according to which God appointed them to destruction, not for its own sake, but for the elect, whom he has saved from such destruction.

But now thus saith the LORD that created thee, O Jacob, and he that formed thee, O Israel, Fear not: for I have redeemed thee, I have called *thee* by thy name; thou *art* mine. When thou passest through the waters, I *will be* with thee; and through the rivers, they shall not overflow thee: when thou walkest through the fire, thou shalt not be burned; neither shall the flame kindle upon thee. For I *am* the LORD thy God, the Holy One of Israel, thy Saviour: I gave Egypt *for* thy ransom, Ethiopia and Seba for thee. Since thou wast precious in my sight, thou hast been honourable, and I have loved thee: therefore will I give men for thee, and people for thy life. Fear not: for I *am* with thee: I will bring thy seed from the east, and gather thee from the west; I will say to the north, Give up; and to the south, Keep not back: bring my sons from far, and my daughters from the ends of the earth; *Even* every one that is called by my name: for I have created him for my glory, I have formed him; yea, I have made him. Isaiah 43:1-7

The Heavenly Body

The devil and his angels are ends in themselves, that the concepts of their essences may be lawfully contemplated through their persons, the fullness whereof is only possible in their obedience to God. If the end lies in a person, that the contemplation thereof may be an end in itself, yet it is required that the contemplation thereof be lawful, and lawfully contemplated, through the obedience of their persons to God.[43] Therefore, the offices vacated by fallen angels must be filled by others, like them in essence, even the elect,[44] who in the resurrection are as the angels of heaven.[45]

> *And* having spoiled principalities and powers, he made a shew of them openly, triumphing over them in it. Colossians 2:15

Having spoiled them, that is, taken their domains and given them to his own, who war against them.

> For though we walk in the flesh, we do not war after the flesh: (For the weapons of our warfare *are* not carnal, but mighty through God to the pulling down of strong holds): casting down imaginations, and every high thing that exalteth itself against the knowledge of God, and bringing into captivity every thought to the obedience of Christ. 2 Corinthians 10:3-5

Every thought, that is, every concept, not in itself, but in the fallen angels.

> But unto every one of us is given grace according to the measure of the gift of Christ. Wherefore he saith, When he ascended up on high, he led captivity captive, and gave gifts unto men. (Now that he ascended,

---

[43] 1 Tim. 1:8; 2 Tim. 2:5.
[44] Aquinas, *Summa* 1.108.8; Anselm, "Cur Deus Homo," in *Basic Writings*, 1.16-17.
[45] Matt. 22:30; Mark 12:25; Luke 20:36.

what is it but that he also descended first into the lower parts of the earth? He that descended is the same also that ascended up far above all heavens, that he might fill all things.) Ephesians 4:7-10

He ascended, to give them gifts from heaven, even the offices of fallen angels, whom he had conquered in hell, that he might be glorified in all things.

> For we wrestle not against flesh and blood, but against principalities, against powers, against the rulers of the darkness of this world, against spiritual wickedness in high *places*. Ephesians 6:12

> And there was war in heaven: Michael and his angels fought against the dragon; and the dragon fought and his angels, And prevailed not; neither was their place found any more in heaven. And the great dragon was cast out, that old serpent, called the Devil, and Satan, which deceiveth the whole world: he was cast out into the earth, and his angels were cast out with him. Rev. 12:7-9

According to the saying,

> Let his days be few; *and* let another take his office. Psalm 109:8

God is the spirit of unity and affirmation; therefore, the essence of Jesus Christ must be unity-totality, affirmation-limitation. These are identical in intellectual intuition as Christ is God, but distinct in sensible intuition as Christ is man, for Christ is the image of God, identical in distinction to the concept. The identity thought therein is glorified in the elect men, in whom lies the union of a universal and a particular, that is, the identity of universal and singular, but the distinction is glorified in the women, in whom lies the union of a universal and a singular, that is, their distinction.

For a man indeed ought not to cover *his* head, forasmuch as he is the image and glory of God: but the woman is the glory of the man. 1 Corinthians 11:7

So are women to be silent in the church.

Let your women keep silence in the churches: for it is not permitted unto them to speak; but *they are commanded* to be under obedience, as also saith the law. And if they will learn any thing, let them ask their husbands at home: for it is a shame for women to speak in the church. 1 Corinthians 14:34-35

The relation of each class of angels is thought originally in the divine persons; therefore, each divine person rules over one class of angels. The Father rules over Seraphim; the Son rules over Teraphim, the fallen angels, whose offices he gives to his elect; the Holy Spirit rules over Cherubim. [46] Every angelic triad forms an image of the Trinity revealed in the Lord Jesus Christ.[47]

That they all may be one; as thou, Father, *art* in me, and I in thee, that they also may be one in us: that the world may believe that thou hast sent me. And the glory which thou gavest me I have given them; that they may be one, even as we are one: I in them, and thou in me, that they may be made perfect in one; and that the world may know that thou hast sent me, and hast loved them, as thou hast loved me. Father, I will that they also, whom thou hast given me, be with me where I am; that they may behold my glory, which thou hast given me: for thou lovedst me before the foundation of the world. O righteous Father, the world hath not known thee: but I have known thee, and these have known that thou hast sent me. And I have declared unto them thy

---

[46] Ex. 25:17-22; Ps. 91:11; Ezek. 9; Matt. 26:53; Rev. 12:7-8.
[47] Ps. 90:17; John 1:51.

name, and will declare *it*: that the love wherewith thou hast loved me may be in them, and I in them. John 17:21-26, cf. Ps. 90:17; John 1:51

As for the office of the devil, it is given unto two men, "the two anointed ones, that stand by the LORD of the whole earth" (Zech. 4:14). These are unity-plurality, and affirmation-negation.

> Verily I say unto you, Among them that are born of women there hath not risen a greater than John the Baptist: notwithstanding he that is least in the kingdom of heaven is greater than he. Matthew 11:11

John the Baptist is unity-plurality.

> There was a man sent from God, whose name *was* John. The same came for a witness, to bear witness of the Light, that all *men* through him might believe. He was not that Light, but *was sent* to bear witness of that Light. John 1:6-8

So close was he to that light, that John says, *he was not that light*.

The least in the kingdom of heaven is affirmation-negation; for he is the greatest, and also the least, because he is nothing. Negation includes plurality; therefore, the devil may be called the spirit of negation, rather than the spirit of plurality. Accordingly, the least in the kingdom of heaven is called greater than John the Baptist.

The same transcendental concepts may perhaps be united with ideal concepts, but in no other persons may two transcendental concepts be so united, than in John the Baptist and the least in the kingdom of heaven, for unity combines with plurality, and affirmation with negation, the particular under each, to form intuitions distinct from the concepts.

The offices of the devil are given unto these two men. The matter of a spirit is identical to its form, but the matter of a man is distinct; therefore, because quantity and quality are distinguished as formal and material principles of the understanding, it is necessary to distinguish two men, who are purely transcendental in their essence. The devil is one, the spirit of plurality and negation, but the anointed ones are two, one of plurality, the other of negation.

The devil rules over the distinctions between creatures, and between creature and Creator, but the purpose of God is to bestow the divine likeness upon men and angels. John the Baptist represents, *first*, the unity of the person of Christ, *second*, the plurality of members united in his body. *The same came for a witness, to bear witness of the Light, that all men through him might believe.* Likewise, he that is least in the kingdom of heaven represents: *first*, the divine nature of which the members partake; *second*, the distinction of creatures from God. Together, they represent the unity of the body in Christ, whereby the church partakes of the divine nature. Wherefore, they sit on his right hand and on his left in his kingdom.

Then came to him the mother of Zebedee's children with her sons, worshipping *him*, and desiring a certain thing of him. And he said unto her, What wilt thou? She saith unto him, Grant that these my two sons may sit, the one on thy right hand, and the other on the left, in thy kingdom. But Jesus answered and said, Ye know not what ye ask. Are ye able to drink of the cup that I shall drink of, and to be baptized with the baptism that I am baptized with? They say unto him, We are able. And he saith unto them, Ye shall drink indeed of my cup, and be baptized with the baptism that I am baptized with: but to sit on my right hand, and on my left, is not mine to give, but *it shall be given to them* for whom it is prepared of my Father. And when the ten heard *it*, they were moved with indignation against the two brethren. But Jesus called them *unto him*, and said, Ye know that the princes of the Gentiles exercise dominion over them, and they that are great exercise authority upon them. But it shall not be so among you: but whosoever will be great among you, let him be your minister; And whosoever will be chief among you, let him be your servant: Even as the Son of man came

not to be ministered unto, but to minister, and to give his life a ransom
for many. Matthew 20:20-28

Not mine to give, for though they are saved by his blood, their offices are given them unconditionally, according to their essences, by the Father of spirits; not by the Son but by the Father; nor do they take the place of Teraphim, but belong to the class of transcendental beings.

Jesus Christ rules over all angels,[48] chiefly over his own, but also over Seraphim and Cherubim, for he is greater than all; yet not in his own person, but in his divine nature he rules over them together with the other divine persons. Therefore, the anointed ones must represent his reign over the other angels, as he himself rules over his own. This is not a representation of his divine rule, but of his human rule, so far as the divine is manifested in the human; nor do they themselves rule over angels, but represent the rule of Christ, because the angels are also represented together with the divine in the human, and partake of one and the same glory with the elect.[49]

John comes before the Lord, as a prophet and a priest, to proclaim his coming, for he is the son of a priest, to anoint the Lord to his ministry. Likewise, he that is least in the kingdom of heaven comes before the millennium,[50] to inaugurate the reign of the anointed one, together with all his saints and holy martyrs,[51] for he proclaims the coming of Christ formed in his people.[52] But of the second coming, there is no forerunner, but Jesus Christ himself shall suddenly appear to all.[53]

---

[48] Col. 2:10; Aquinas, *Summa* 3.8.4.
[49] Matt. 20:23; Mark 10:40; Rev. 11:3; Rev. 12:7.
[50] Mal. 4:5-6; Matt. 17:11.
[51] Rev. 11:3; Zech. 6:10-15; Luke 1:5-17.
[52] Rev. 12:5, cf. Gal. 4:19.
[53] 2 Peter 3:10.

Nature Reveals the Moral Purpose of the World

God formed the earth to be inhabited.

> For thus saith the LORD that created the heavens; God himself that formed the earth and made it; he hath established it, he created it not in vain, he formed it to be inhabited: I *am* the LORD; and *there is* none else. Isaiah 45:18

The existence of a person is an end in itself. A person ought to be happy in obedience to God's commandments, blessed for his righteousness by a holy lawgiver and judge. Moral purposes belong to the world of intellect, yet a human person finds his happiness in the world of sense, and these must be combined; therefore, man's moral purpose requires that nature harmonize with freedom, that the visible world agree with the one prescribed by reason, and that the objects of man's earthly happiness symbolize the heavenly.

> Because that which may be known of God is manifest in them; for God hath shewed *it* unto them. For the invisible things of him from the creation of the world are clearly seen, being understood by the things that are made, *even* his eternal power and Godhead; so that they are without excuse. Romans 1:19-20, cf. Job 37; Ps. 8, 19, 65, 103

Manifest in them; for God hath shewed it unto them. The world shows them the moral purpose that lies within them, whereby the necessary conditions of this end are verified,[54] *so that they are without excuse.*

---

[54] Cf. Gress, *Christ Condemned: On the Incarnation and the Trinity* (Lynnwood, WA: Julian Gress, 2019), 63-65.

The World is a System of Natural Purposes

Man's moral purpose must be represented visibly in the world, but the moral law lies outside the realm of sense. There must therefore be a mediate representation in the world of sense, which belongs to both, and permits the transition from one to the other. Herein theoretical reason is applied to practical, and practical is subsumed under theoretical. Theoretical reason applies concepts to intuitions, practical reason produces intuitions through concepts. They agree in this, that their judgments are only possible through an act of the imagination combining concepts and intuitions within the thinking subject, who perceives itself in time, the form of inner sense. Therefore, the transition from theoretical reason to practical depends upon an aesthetic representation in the feeling of pleasure he derives from the beauty and sublimity of the natural world.[55]

Furthermore, as the world shows to man the pattern of righteousness, so also it possesses the sensible form thereof. The beautiful and the sublime follow the course of theoretical reason, as much as they symbolize the ends of practical. As the world shows to man the symbols of his moral purpose, so also the world contains within itself a multitude of natural purposes, connected as means to ends, and comprehensible to the understanding. This is called teleological judgment.[56]

The System of the World is Grounded in the Fundamental Concepts of the Understanding

The ground of creation rests in concepts, for it is the work of God, whose work is right, and the righteousness of things lies in their concepts. Of fundamental concepts for the ground of an intuition, there are twelve: unity, plurality, totality; reality, negation, limitation; substance, causality, community;

---

[55] Kant, *Judgment*, Ak. 176-179, 195-198, 286-291, 338-346; Julian Gress, *The Harmony of Reason and the Possibility of Man's Final End in Kant's Critique of Judgment*, (B.A. thesis, St. John's College, Santa Fe, NM, 2010, revised 2017). https://juliangress.mywriting.network/essay-on-kant/.

[56] Kant, *Judgment*, Ak. 192-194, 232'-237', 362-485; cf. Gress, *Christ Condemned*, 84.

possibility, actuality, necessity. There are therefore twelve sayings or blessings. Of these, two are omitted from the forms of judgment, yielding ten commandments. Six of the twelve refer to the subject, six to the object. However, the object of creation is invisible; therefore, the objective conditions are united with the subjective to yield six representations of man's moral purpose in the world of sense. And because the natural world reveals the invisible through feeling, and feeling is in the subject, who perceives itself in time, each pair belongs to a different time. Furthermore, because the invisible objects are here represented visibly, in intuitions distinct, their completeness must also be represented in a distinct time, for though as concepts they have their completeness in themselves, yet as intuitions they have it beside them. There are therefore seven days of creation, ten commandments, and twelve sayings.

The humanity of Jesus Christ reveals his divinity. God is invisible, yet he has appeared to us in Jesus Christ. There are therefore six historical events in the life of Christ, the objective conditions of the representation of an object merging with the subjective conditions. Yet because God does actually appear to us in Jesus Christ, the invisible made visible, there is no seventh time, for the completeness of the system is everywhere present in the system itself.

The Fundamental Concepts Represented in Time

Thus, day one: unity and reality; day two: plurality and negation; day three: totality and limitation; day four: substance and possibility; day five: causality and actuality; day six: community and necessity. These are divided into two triads, and the third of each triad is both the category and the sum of the three; thus, the third and sixth days each have two works. Likewise, the completeness of the work is thought through the agreement of the sums, the first being appointed as food for the second, and then, by the distinction of the sums, and of all the parts, in a seventh day of rest.

The works are distinguished by days, for although the concepts cohere in the unity of a system, the intuition contains within itself a particular in time. The work represents the invisible world to our senses, and that through feeling, in the form of inner sense, which is time. So it is written, *the first day, the second day, the third day,* and etc.

The seventh day is distinct from the six, because the intuition of the completeness of the work is distinct from the particular work of each day. Though it is thought in each, it is never intuited by itself. And the seventh contains within itself the distinction of the third and the sixth in a day distinct from either. The completeness of the work lies in the universal concept, and the intuition of the distinction of its parts is nothing; hence, the seventh day is a day of universal moral purposes, and nothing in particular, as to labor for profit, or recreation for pleasure. This is a holy day of worship.

> This *is* the day *which* the LORD hath made; we will rejoice and be glad in it. Psalm 118:24

Not the day on which the Lord made this or that, but the day which he made unto itself.

> If thou turn away thy foot from the sabbath, *from* doing thy pleasure on my holy day; and call the sabbath a delight, the holy of the LORD, honourable; and shalt honour him, not doing thine own ways, nor finding thine own pleasure, nor speaking *thine own* words: Then shalt thou delight thyself in the LORD; and I will cause thee to ride upon the high places of the earth, and feed thee with the heritage of Jacob thy father: for the mouth of the LORD hath spoken *it.* Isaiah 58:13-14

Because this day represents the universality of moral purposes, there is also the possibility of a sabbath on the first day, which is accomplished through the resurrection of Christ: a work of rest, whose rest lies in the work itself.[57]

On the first day God made light, the division between day and night; therefore, the work of the first day is itself the dawn of creation, and every day being modelled after the first, the work of each day is its dawn. The second

---

[57] Heb. 4.

works of the third and sixth days are their evenings, while on the other days God rested in the evening or gave blessings, to show forth the completeness of the work of each day, whether in work or in rest.

Apart from the work of each day, a blessing is added whenever a concept of the moral law is thought together with a particular, to yield an intuition of the good. Blessedness belongs first to persons, who desire happiness. Hence there are blessings on the fifth, sixth, and seventh days.

The blessings take the form of commandments, of which there are ten. The order of the commandments is: unity, totality; affirmation, limitation; substance, causality, community; possibility, actuality, necessity. Totality takes the place of plurality, and limitation of affirmation, because creation respects an object made, not a subject commanded. An object is thought through intuition, the matter through its combination with the form; whereas in the subject, the matter is thought distinctly from the form, and contains the ground of the intuition. Plurality and negation are therefore omitted from the commandments, but included in the sayings, as declarations of things made. The first observes the natural appointment of the fruits of the earth for man's nourishment; the second observes the completeness of the work, and is silent, because it represents negation.

The order of commandments and sayings differs from that of natural purposes; therefore, it comes to pass that the same work may be understood through different concepts, according to the mode of its conception, whether theoretical, practical, or aesthetic. Creation is a system of natural purposes, the symbols of moral purposes: a system of things, twelve; of commandments, ten; and of natural beauties and purposes, seven; a system of systems, showing forth things in themselves.[58]

The Moral Purposes Symbolized by the Work

The moral purposes symbolized are righteousness, blessedness, holiness, personal righteousness, personal blessedness, personal holiness. These

---

[58] Rom. 1:18-20; Kant, *Judgment*, Ak. 176-179, 195-198, 286-291, 338-346.

particular purposes arise from the application of the concept of a moral purpose to each pair of categories. The unity and reality of man's moral purpose is a concept that contains the ground of an intuition, or righteousness; its plurality and distinction lies in an intuition, which is blessedness; then follows the agreement between the concept and the intuition, which is holiness. And because the concept of a person is the root of all moral purposes, these moral purposes are successively combined with the concept of a person. Thus, the whole purpose of man is to be blessed in obedience to a holy God.

The End of Creation is the Glory of God

The first three days symbolize righteousness, blessedness, and holiness; the second triad symbolizes these in persons: personal righteousness, personal blessedness, and personal holiness; to which a day of nothing is added, because to them nothing is to be added, but we are to rest therein as the final end of all things. And God himself is one in three; righteous, blessed, holy; Father, Son, and Holy Spirit.

The supreme end of the world is the glory of the Trinity. Creation is the work of the divine persons, to reveal them in the things made. The inner emptiness of the world is given purpose through the persons, who are ends in themselves: God, the Word, and the Spirit of God. The Spirit is the breath of God, by which the Word of God is spoken, for to produce an intuition of God that is itself divine, it must be thought of as identical in distinction to the concept.

Yet the Trinity is not known to man in the state of creation, because man is not witness to the creative act, therefore neither to the persons; because man is not the image of God, but made in the image of God; because God made all things very good, and he himself is not made; and because God rested on the seventh day, for he is invisible.

Nevertheless, the three who are one made man in their own image, in the image of the Word, for the Word of God is his image; wherefore, God made man in his own image, after his own likeness, that the Word of God might become flesh, and make known the persons. Adam indeed is made in the image of the one God, but Jesus Christ is the image of the Triune God,[59] and through him man becomes the image of God.[60]

THE DAYS OF CREATION

Day One

In the beginning, not a beginning in time, but the beginning of time, preceded not by a natural cause, but by a purpose divine; *God created*, the one in three, righteous, blessed, and holy; *the heaven and the earth*, all things visible and invisible, phenomena and noumena, by him for whom they are identical in distinction.[61] *And the earth was without form, and void;* without dry land or plant, covered in water; *and darkness was upon the face of the deep*. It lacked purpose of itself, neither was there any visible purpose, or purpose visible. *And the Spirit of God*, the breath of God, by which the word is spoken;[62] *moved upon the face of the waters*, as if, had you been there, you might have felt him. *And God said*, as if, had you been there, you might have heard him; *Let there be light*, the commandment; *and there was light*, the commandment fulfilled. Moses does not write, *and it was so*, as on other days, but, *and there was light*, because light is an intuition that represents a pure concept, and all that is thought under it lies within it.[63] *And God saw the light*, as a thing visible, yet in itself, for light makes all things visible, yet is not visible in itself, but all things are visible to God who made them, both appearances and things in themselves; *that it was good:* a thing to be made, and to behold; good, and a symbol of goodness; *and God divided the light from the darkness*, both in itself, because light distinguishes itself from darkness, and also in time, by the succession of light and darkness, whereby the passage of time becomes visible. *And God called the light Day*, a symbol of a

---

[59] Col. 1:15; Heb. 1:3.
[60] 1 Cor. 11:3, 7.
[61] Ps. 139:1-6, 11-12.
[62] Ps. 33:6.
[63] Kant, *Critique*, B39, B47.

symbol, a word for an image; *and the darkness he called Night,* and the darkness also, not in itself, but through the light. *And the evening and the morning were the first day,* to bring forth light out of darkness again every day thereafter. The first day dawns with the creation of light, and ends when the darkness returns; thus, the end of the first day is the beginning of the second.

This first day is the measure of all, and its work is the measure of the whole, a symbol of symbols, that through which all things are visible, and all visible things real, "for whatsoever doth make manifest is light" (Ephesians 5:13). This is the symbol of righteousness, the unity and reality of moral purposes.

The Second Day

And God said, on the second day; *Let there be a firmament in the midst of the waters,* the plurality of concept in the midst of the plurality of intuition; *and let it divide the waters from the waters,* an expanse, as of nothing, to distinguish sensible intuition from intellectual. *And God made the firmament,* made, not created, as a form without matter; *and divided the waters which were under the firmament from the waters which were above the firmament:* God divided, and made the firmament to divide. The light divides itself immediately from the darkness because the division of concepts is twofold; but the division of waters is mediated by the firmament, because it divides between the plurality of intuition. Light symbolizes righteousness; the waters below symbolize happiness, to be joined with lawfulness above, for the grace of heaven is communicated through earthly symbols.[64] The light divides between universal and particular; the firmament between universal and singular. The first belongs to heaven and earth; the second belongs to earth; *and it was so,* a form not without matter, a real object. The particular work is first described, and then the refrain, *and it was so,* because the actuality of the firmament lies in the concept itself, to symbolize intellectual intuition. *And God called the firmament Heaven.* The firmament is a symbol of heaven, which is neither visible nor sensible, yet are men to partake of the blessedness of heaven through things sensible, because they are symbols of the

---

[64] Is. 55:10-13.

happiness rewarded to those who obey. Moses does not say, *and God saw that it was good,* because the firmament is not seen, nor was it as yet united with righteousness in the earth; nor did God give names to the waters below, for as yet they were formless, but the firmament represents a pure form.

And the evening and the morning were the second day. The work of the first day divides time, the work of the second divides space. The morning of the second day is the creation of the firmament, and in the evening God rested therein, as an end of nature. Space is the second measure of all things visible, to symbolize freedom and blessedness, and the expanse is its measure.[65]

The Third Day

And God said, Let the waters under the heaven be gathered together unto one place, a totality; *and let the dry land appear:* limitation, for the earth is limited by the privation of water, and the dry land sets a boundary upon the waters.[66] The appearance of dry land limits the waters: happiness unto the law, that is, holiness in obedience to God's commandments;[67] *and it was so,* the intuition in agreement with the concept, the existence of an object. *And God called the dry land Earth;* the symbol of appearances in general; *and the gathering together of the waters called he Seas:* the symbol of sensation in general; *and God saw that it was good,* the intuition in agreement with the concept. The seas form a totality in quantity, but the earth limits and bounds sensation through its quality; therefore, the seas represent sensation, but the earth, the object of sensation, for the object of sensation lies in a quality beyond sensation. *And God said, Let the earth bring forth grass, the herb yielding seed, and the fruit tree yielding fruit after his kind, whose seed is in itself, upon the earth:* the earth symbolizes the object of sensation; therefore, it brought forth on the same day sensible objects, to reveal the particular ends of the moral law. There are three kinds of plants for the three days, distinguished by the manner of seed, because they symbolize all the virtues of

---

[65] Is. 40:12, 44:12.
[66] Job 38:8-11; Ps. 104:6-9.
[67] Ex. 3:5; Josh. 5:14-5.

righteousness, blessedness, and holiness; *and it was so,* this is said before the description of the work, because the concepts of these objects come to us through intuition. *And the earth brought forth grass, and herb yielding seed after his kind, and the tree yielding fruit, whose seed was in itself, after his kind:* the actuality of these objects is particularly described, because they are the particular symbols of the moral law. The earth and seas represent intuitions; wherefore Moses writes, *and God saw that it was good,* after God gave them names, to show that their intuitions represent pure concepts, for they receive their goodness from their concepts. Of them he says, *and it was so,* for they are intuitions. Of the vegetation, the order of the second day is reversed, because the actuality of vegetation lies in intuition, for they are empirical concepts. Hence Moses first writes, *and it was so,* and then says, *And the earth brought forth grass,* etc. It is once stated to show the concept of totality, and a second time to show the totality of concepts, because these are distinguished in intuition, and show forth the completeness of the work of the first three days. *And the evening and the morning were the third day,* for the works of that day are its morning and its evening, and end in the morning of the fourth day.

The morning of the third day is the gathering of the waters and the appearance of dry land, for this is the beginning and measure of things earthly: of matter, that which fills space and time. And the evening of the third day brings forth plants, the natural purposes measured by the earth and the seas, their fullness.

The Fourth Day

And God said, Let there be lights, light substances, the forms of light embodied, the grounds of its possibility; *in the firmament of the heaven,* for to heaven belong those things thought through pure concepts; *to divide the day from the night;* to divide purpose from emptiness, and form from the void; *and let them be for signs, and for seasons, and for days, and years:* to measure time, and to show the symbols of heavenly things upon the earth; *And let them be for lights in the firmament of the heaven to give light upon the earth:* that light should be given through a body, to be received by bodies; likewise ought righteousness to subsist in persons. The lights symbolize angels, who are made in the idea of God, after his concept, who have not their life in this world, but in heaven; *and it was so*, according to the universal concept of light substances, not particularly divided. *And God made two great lights*; because division by concepts is twofold; *the greater light to rule the day, and the lesser light to rule the night*: because affirmation is greater than negation, and prior to it. Affirmation rules over all things; negation, over the distinctions of things; but there is no distinction in affirmation, neither any darkness in light, yet by it all distinctions are affirmed, and the darkness is not hidden;[68] *he made the stars also*, visible only in their distinction from the greater light, and from one another. *And God set them in the firmament of the heaven to give light upon the earth*, to illuminate earthly purposes, and to be visible in themselves for contemplation; *And to rule over the day and over the night*, to continue until the end of the world, upheld by natural laws, rather than God's immediate work; *and to divide the light from the darkness*: that light should dwell in bodies, as righteousness in persons, that light should be a natural purpose of the world; *and God saw that it was good*, for if the concept is good, then the subsistence thereof in a body is also good. *And the evening and the morning were the fourth day*, the measure, not of time, but of substances in time, which lies in their permanence, for which reason their history extends indefinitely into the past, to show forth the depths of God's eternity.[69]

The Fifth Day

And God said, Let the waters bring forth abundantly the moving creature that hath life, and fowl that may fly above the earth in the open firmament of heaven. From the plurality of sensation comes a plurality of objects, distinguished by the property of motion, based on the concept of causality, and symbolizing freedom. In them the symbols of happiness and blessedness inhere, for if a person ought to be

---

[68] Ps. 139:11-12; John 1:5.
[69] Ps. 93:2; Is. 66:1-2

righteous, then he also ought to be blessed for his righteousness.[70] The property of motion refers to causality, not to living creatures as such, but to, *the moving creature that hath life*, and they are free to swim in the waters, or fly in the open firmament. *And God created great whales*, a plurality in quality as well as in quantity; *and every living creature that moveth*, living, though not distinguished by life, but by motion; *which the waters brought forth abundantly*; yet not after the manner of a totality, but of a plurality; *after their kind*, after the concepts of happiness, to be joined with righteousness, and of blessedness, which is their union; *and every winged fowl after his kind*: for wings symbolize the identity of concept and intuition;[71] *and God saw that it was good. And God blessed them, saying,* they are blessed because they are symbols of personal blessedness. It is only on account of persons, who desire happiness, that happiness should be united to obedience. Hence the phrase, *and God saw that it was good*, is omitted from the second day, but included here together with a blessing; *Be fruitful, and multiply*, because the concept contains within itself the ground of an intuition distinct from the concept, and the concept inheres in the creature; therefore, within them lies the ground of intuitions distinct from themselves, and they reproduce according to their kinds; *and fill the waters in the seas*, that the blessedness of the world should be made full by the abundance of individuals of all kinds; *and let fowl multiply in the earth*, because their reproduction belongs to them as objects of sensible intuition, though they are symbols of the intelligible. *And the evening and the morning were the fifth day*, the morning of the fifth day fills the waters, the measure of substances in space, and of their causality in the world, and in the evening they are blessed, because they symbolize the blessedness of persons in obedience to God's commandments.

The Sixth Day

And God said, Let the earth bring forth the living creature after his kind, cattle, and creeping thing, and beast of the earth after his kind: and it was so. The living

---

[70] Matthew 5:3-12.
[71] Gen. 15:10; Lev. 1:17, 5:8.

creatures, by their life distinguished, are brought forth from the earth, and symbolize holiness in persons. *And God made the beast of the earth after his kind, and cattle after their kind, and every thing that creepeth upon the earth after his kind:* three divisions of living creatures, according to the work of these three days; *and God saw that it was good.* If the concept is good, and the intuition is good, then their agreement is also good. *And God said, Let us make man in our image, after our likeness:* to be blessed in obedience to God's commandments; to show forth, in an intuition distinct from the concept, the holiness of his maker; *and let them have dominion over the fish of the sea, and over the fowl of the air, and over the cattle, and over all the earth, and over every creeping thing that creepeth upon the earth,* for in man is summed up every good thing made by God; every virtue elsewhere distributed is present altogether in man. *So God created man in his own image, in the image of God created he him;* the words, *and it was so,* are here joined to the thing itself, because the creation of man is an end in itself: *so God created man in his own image, in the image of God created he him.* This is stated twice, with the order of subject and object reversed, because it has two different meanings. In the second statement, *the image of God,* takes the place of the subject in the first, for man indeed is made in the image of God, but Jesus Christ is the image of God; *male and female created he them.* Man is made in the image of God's righteousness, woman in the image of his blessedness, and their union in the image of his holiness. *And God blessed them, and God said unto them, Be fruitful, and multiply, and replenish the earth, and subdue it:* blessed above every creature on earth; *and have dominion over the fish of the sea, and over the fowl of the air, and over every living thing that moveth upon the earth,* over all things in the earth, because all the virtues of all things therein are summed up in man, and these things are altogether symbols of his moral purpose. *And God said, Behold, I have given you every herb bearing seed, which is upon the face of all the earth,* to show that blessedness is everywhere to be met with in the world, as the reward of man's righteousness; *and every tree, in the which is the fruit of a tree yielding seed; to you it shall be for meat; And to every beast of the earth, and to every fowl of the air, and to every thing that creepeth upon the earth, wherein there is life, I have given every green herb for meat: and it was so.* An act whereby nothing new is made, but what has been made already is appointed for their nourishment. *Behold,* a declaration; *I have given you,* then the refrain, *and it was so,* because the plants made on the third day are not only ends of nature, but also good for man's food, since mankind ought to be nourished by the symbols of his moral purpose. *And God saw every thing that he had made, and, behold, it was very good,* for it is summed up in man by his dominion over the earth, and by the appointment of food for his preservation. *And the evening and the morning were the sixth day,* though there is nothing further for this day, or for the work itself, yet time continues.

The morning of the sixth day is the creation of beasts, the measure of material substances, the symbols of holiness in the world; the creation of man is its evening, who is measured by them, the measure of all things, in whom all the diverse virtues of living creatures are united, wherein he is blessed with dominion, and plants are appointed for his food, because therein lies the completeness of the system of natural purposes.

The Seventh Day

Thus the heavens and the earth were finished, and all the host of them, the contemplation whereof belongs to the seventh day. *The host of them,* all things in heaven and earth, even the angels of heaven.[72] *And on the seventh day God ended his work which he had made;* the end of the work requires a separate day, to consider the completeness of the work, whose parts are represented distinctly in intuition; *and he rested on the seventh day from all his work which he had made.* He rested and made no more, but hallowed the time. *And God blessed the seventh day, and sanctified it: because that in it he had rested from all his work which God created and made,* wherein lies the complete and final purpose of man. All the works of God do show that man ought to be blessed in obedience to a holy God, and he ought to observe this day in remembrance thereof, for it is three times said that he ended his work and rested, because on that day his righteousness, blessedness, and holiness are fully manifest.

---

[72] Gen. 32:1-2; Ps. 148:2.

The Unity of Man

God made man in his own image, an intuitive representation of the divine nature. God is one, therefore man is also one.

By "image" I understand an intuition distinct from the concept, for that there is another kind of rational creature made in the idea of God, after his concept,[1] is evident from the lights made on the fourth day, yet not under man's dominion.

Angels are creatures of intellectual intuition; therefore, the angelic nature is simple. In man, the intuition is distinct from the concept; therefore, the nature of man is complex: a part made after the concept, a part made after the intuition. These are *soul* and *body*.[2] The soul is, as the concept of man's nature, simple, but the body is particular, and is made of parts.

The soul is the ground of man's rationality, the universality of his nature; therefore, the soul also contains within itself the ground of its union with the body, for the union of the soul with the body is the intuition thereof. As ground of its union with the body, the soul is called *spirit*.[3]

> And the very God of peace sanctify you wholly; and *I pray God* your whole spirit and soul and body be preserved blameless unto the coming of our Lord Jesus Christ. 1 Thessalonians 5:23

Your whole spirit, for it is identical to the soul, yet within it lies the ground of the soul's union with the body.

This union, whereby man accomplishes his purposes in the sensible world, is *life*.

---

[1] Aquinas, *Summa* 1.93.3.
[2] *Summa* 1.75.2, 76.1; *Larger Catechism* Q.17.
[3] Aquinas, *Summa* 1.76.4, 7.

And the LORD God formed man *of* the dust of the ground, and breathed into his nostrils the breath of life; and man became a living soul. Genesis 2

And the LORD God formed man of the dust of the ground, his body; *and breathed into his nostrils the breath of life,* his spirit; *and man became a living soul.*

The lawfulness of man lies in his soul,[4] his happiness lies in the objects of sense.[5] Their union is man's blessedness, which is distinct from his righteousness, and so its identity therewith, required by the moral law, depends upon the existence of God. Man is not holy in himself, but in obedience to God's commandments. Man is holy and happy before God as long as he perseveres in original righteousness. And in the righteousness of his soul lies the ground of its union with the body, and he lives.

Sin distinguishes man's blessedness from his righteousness, seeking the one without the other. Therefore, sin distinguishes the spirit of man from his soul, and divides the body from the soul, and the parts of the body from one another.[6] In death the body returns to the dust, the spirit goes to God who gave it, and the soul departs to its forever abode.[7]

The body represents the person's subjective desire for happiness; within the soul lies the ground of his duty to obey the moral law. Again, the body is visible, the soul is invisible. The body is the appearance of a person; the soul is the person as a thing in itself.

Man is made in the image of God's righteousness, for the law contains within itself the ground of an intuition in agreement therewith, but the woman is made in the image of his blessedness, as the intuition produced agrees with the concept. And their union is made in the image of his holiness, for these are one in God, so united, though distinct.

---

[4] Ezek. 18:4.
[5] Ezek. 24:15-18; Deut. 12:15, 20; 14:26.
[6] Heb. 4:12.
[7] Gen. 3:19; Job 34:14-15; Eccl. 12:5-7.

Blessed *is* every one that feareth the LORD; that walketh in his ways. For thou shalt eat the labour of thine hands: happy *shalt* thou *be*, and *it shall be* well with thee. Thy wife *shall be* as a fruitful vine by the sides of thine house: thy children like olive plants round about thy table. Behold, that thus shall the man be blessed that feareth the LORD. The LORD shall bless thee out of Zion: and thou shalt see the good of Jerusalem all the days of thy life. Yea, thou shalt see thy children's children, *and* peace upon Israel. Psalm 128, cf. 1 Cor. 11:1-12

The essence of a man is the union of a universal and a particular, to yield an intuition of the righteousness of God. The essence of a woman is the union of a universal and a singular, wherein lies an intuition of his blessedness. The essence of their union is the identity thereof, for these are one, though distinct: the universal, the particular, and the singular; and the universal, the singular, and their identity; for the identity thought in the woman first distinguishes them, and that identity already lies within the man, in whom the singular is thought through the universal concept. "And did not he make one? Yet had he the residue of the spirit" (Malachi 2:15). The former pertains to things in themselves, the latter to appearances. Man represents the thing in itself, woman, the appearance of the thing in itself, because the woman is the glory of the man, and the man is the glory of God.[8] And from the joy of their union proceed the objects of man's happiness, for as the essences of men include every possible intuition of an object, man's happiness is lawfully contemplated in his children.

Lo, children *are* an heritage of the LORD: *and* the fruit of the womb *is his* reward. As arrows *are* in the hand of a mighty man; so *are* children of the youth. Happy *is* the man that hath his quiver full of them: they shall not be ashamed, but they shall speak with the enemies in the gate. Psalm 127:3-5

---

[8] 1 Cor. 11:7.

The body of a man is particular, and the spirit is singular, but the body of a woman is singular, and contains within itself the particular, and the spirit of a woman is the identity of the universal and the singular.

Adam is an intuitive representation of the divine unity. The unity of man lies in the soul, and the man ensouled is alive.

> And the Lord God formed man *of* the dust of the ground, and breathed into his nostrils the breath of life; and man became a living soul. Genesis 2:7

In this essence of his lies the ground of his headship over all humanity, for life is the causality of the thinking subject, and man's life contains within itself the ground of other men's lives.

His wife, Eve, is a singular representation of the living soul. The singular of the soul is the soul that bears life, having the particular within itself. This is motherhood.

> And Adam called his wife's name Eve; because she was mother of all the living. Genesis 3:20

Thus, Adam and Eve are the man and the woman through whom all other human persons have their life in this world.

> And Adam knew Eve his wife; and she conceived. Genesis 4:1

As one essence knew the other, so she also conceived others by him: Cain, *possession*; Abel, *breath*; Seth, *appointed*: Body, spirit, and soul.

God is the spirit of affirmation. The essence of the Lord Jesus Christ is unity-totality, affirmation-limitation. Affirmation and limitation are identical in intellectual intuition as Christ is God, distinct in sensible intuition as Christ is man, for he is the image of God, identical in distinction to the concept.

A man is the union of a universal and a particular; a woman is the union of a universal and a singular. Wherefore, elect men represent the divine nature of Christ, as the singular is identical to the universal, and the particular under the universal; elect women represent the human nature of Christ, wherein the singular is distinguished from the universal, yet contains within itself a particular under his authority. Together they form an intuition of the Incarnation of the Son, and together with the holy angels, the heavenly body forms an image of the Trinity.[9]

> For a man indeed ought not to cover *his* head, forasmuch as he is the image and glory of God: but the woman is the glory of the man. 1 Corinthians 11:7, cf. 14:35

He is the image and glory of God, of the divine nature of Christ; *but the woman is the glory of the man,* of the human nature of Christ.

Scripture Proof

Genesis 2:4-25

These are the generations of the heavens and of the earth when they were created, begotten, though made, created by the Father through the Son, "who is the image of the invisible God, the firstborn of every creature" (Colossians 1:15); "Hath the rain a father? Or who hath begotten the drops of dew? Out of whose womb came the ice? And the hoary frost of heaven, who hath gendered it?" (Job 38:28-29); *in the day that the* LORD *God made the earth and the heavens,* for every seven days is one day, as of the one day that contains the whole, and by which it is called;[10] and the history of the world is divided into periods, like unto the days of creation, because it is the work of a new creation. Wherefore, in what follows the works of the seven days are treated simultaneously, as of one day;

---

[9] John 17:20-26; Eph. 1:10; Heb. 12:22-24.
[10] John 20:1.

And every plant of the field before it was in the earth, and every herb of the field before it grew: the plants of the field did not yet overspread the earth; the herb of the field overspread without growth, for these are the objects of man's labor: the one, to plant in holiness, the other, to cultivate in righteousness; *for the LORD God had not caused it to rain upon the earth, and there was not a man to till the ground.* That growth depended on two things: the blessing of God from heaven, and the work of man's hands in righteousness. *But there went up a mist from the earth, and watered the whole face of the ground,* that the earth might be preserved by its own means, because man's prosperity depended upon his perseverance in original righteousness. *And the LORD God formed man of the dust of the ground,* a rational being of sensible intuition, to be holy in obedience to God's commandments; *and breathed into his nostrils the breath of life,* a creature blessed with life; *and man became a living soul,* consenting unto righteousness. *And the LORD God planted a garden eastward in Eden;* the place of one man; *and there he put the man whom he had formed,* to show that he ought first to be righteous, that he might afterward be blessed. *And out of the ground made,* on that first of all days; *the LORD God to grow every tree that is pleasant to the sight, and good for food; the tree of life also in the midst of the garden, and the tree of knowledge of good and evil.* God gave him the fruits of the earth, that he should be holy in obedience to God's commandments. *And a river went out of Eden to water the garden; and from thence it was parted, and became into four heads,* after the four heads of concepts. *The name of the first is Pison: that is it which compasseth the whole land of Havilah, where there is gold; And the gold of that land is good: there is bdellium and the onyx stone. And the name of the second river is Gihon: the same is it that compasseth the whole land of Ethiopia. And the name of the third river is Hiddekel: that is it which goeth toward the east of Assyria. And the fourth river is Euphrates,* that through Adam the whole world should be populated, and the whole earth subdued. *And the LORD God took the man, and put him into the garden of Eden to dress it and to keep it,* that he should receive life through his work. *And the LORD God commanded the man, saying, Of every tree of the garden thou mayest freely eat:* because man is free to do good or evil, to live by his works, or die for his sin; *But of the tree of the knowledge of good and evil, thou shalt not eat of it:* for that knowledge, though good, is peculiar to divinity; *for in the day that thou eatest thereof thou shalt surely die*. Though man was free to eat thereof, he ought not to do evil, lest he be punished; but that he should not tempt the man, God does not speak of the divine likeness, to which the man by eating thereof might aspire. *And the LORD God said, It is not good that the man should be alone;* for he should be blessed for his righteousness; *I will make him an help meet for him.* God is one, but man ought not to be alone, because his intuition is distinct from his concept. *I:* God did not reveal his persons to man before he gave him a companion, that it might afterward be to them a symbol of the divine community. "But I would have you know, that the head of every man is Christ; and the head of the woman is the man; and the head of Christ is God" (1 Corinthians 11:3); "This is a great mystery: but I speak concerning Christ and the church" (Ephesians 5:32); *And out of the ground the LORD God formed every beast of the field, and every fowl of the air;* all the blessed and holy creatures; *and brought them unto Adam to see what he would call them:* God himself named the elements and domains, according to the divine nature revealed, but Adam is a person, and ought to name the symbols of persons, that he might afterward receive another person to himself, to be blessed by her, and with her holy; *and whatsoever Adam called every living creature, that was the name thereof,* because he had authority, and his wife should be subject to him. *And Adam gave names to all cattle, and to the fowl of the air, and to every beast of the field;* to learn from the symbols of things in themselves what is blessed and holy; *but for Adam there was not found an help meet for him,* no, not one to show Adam the whole blessedness of his obedience to God, for none of these were equal to Adam's righteousness. *And the LORD God caused a deep sleep to fall upon Adam, and he slept:* that he should not be eyewitness to an act of creation. He slept for tiredness, not without pain, but always outweighed by pleasure, and the remedy of rest, and the reward soon to come, and in sleep he formed an obscure conception of his helpmeet, for God even took her out of his dreams; yet that he should still have need of revelation: *and he took one of his ribs,* as of the heart, to guard it; *and closed up the flesh instead thereof;* that he might still be a whole person, and she also, joined together in love; *And the rib, which the LORD God had taken from man, made he a woman, and brought her unto the man.* That he might do him no harm, he gave much more than he took, and with Adam's consent, bestowed on him the object of his desire, for God first revealed to Adam his need, that he might afterward recognize its fulfillment. *And Adam said, This is now bone of my bones, and flesh of my flesh:* the same, though distinct; *she shall be called Woman, because she was taken out of Man.* As man is made in the image of God's righteousness, and blessedness comes out of righteousness, God also took the woman out of the man, to form their union after the image and likeness of his holiness. *Therefore shall a man leave his father and his mother, and shall cleave unto his wife: and they shall be one flesh,* a sensible representation of God's holiness. *And they were both naked, the man and his wife, and were not ashamed,* for they had their righteousness from themselves, and blessedness therewith, and were holy and altogether happy in obedience to God's commandments.

The Four Gospels

The Gospels record the life of Christ. There are four heads of concepts; consequently, the life of Christ has a fourfold distinction, according to the divine nature revealed in his humanity. Matthew treats of him as an inwardly lawful being; Mark, as the spirit of affirmation; Luke, as the Son of God; and John, as the blessedness of God.

Every man has his lawful existence in this world by generation from his parents. Wherefore, Matthew traces the lineage of Christ from Abraham and David, to show that he is the promised seed, the heir to the throne of David, and the legitimate son of Joseph and Mary. In this Gospel the Lord explains the law, and the faith to its fulfillment; he fulfills the law through his death and resurrection; and as king of the church, he tells us of the kingdom of God in parables.

Mark treats chiefly of what pertains to the preaching of the Gospel, beginning with John the Baptist. He records the miracles of Jesus, whereby the Gospel is signified and confirmed, especially the casting out of demons, to prove that he is the spirit of affirmation, and rules over all, even over angels. Mark's gospel ends with the ascension of Christ into heaven, to show the apodictic certainty of the Gospel preached by the church in all ages.

Luke begins with the virgin birth, tracing the lineage of Christ from Joseph to Adam, even to God. Luke gives a thorough account of the end of Christ's ministry,[11] and of the resurrection, whereby he proves that Jesus Christ is the Son of God; and ends with the ascension, whereby he is glorified in the fulfillment of his work.[12]

John speaks particularly of Christ's testimony concerning himself,[13] because he writes of Christ in the character of his own person. Christ performs miracles unto man's life and happiness, makes known the Father who sent him, and fulfills his purpose, to save men by his death and resurrection, and withal bestow his blessedness on the church.

The difference in John's Gospel has its ground in the structure of concepts. This will be illuminated by the analogy of space. There are four directions in space, but only three dimensions: the first dimension is unconditional, the second is conditioned by the first, and the third is conditioned by the first and the second together. The third is the community and reciprocity of space, whereby space forms a totality, to which no addition can be made. Because space is a form of intuition, and belongs to the mode of apprehending appearances, the relations of directions, which express the quality of a magnitude, can only be thought through pure a priori relations, of which there are three and only three. The third relation contains the totality, not in itself, but in a relation that determines the whole by the interdependence of its parts.

This is identical to the proof that there are only three divine persons. And because the pure a priori relations are the grounds of every possible object, analogies of the Trinity are found everywhere in nature. The divine nature is absolutely unique: nothing can be compared to it; nevertheless, an analogy requires only that the same function of thought be present in each, not that the object represented be the same. Therefore, there are true analogies of the Trinity,

---

[11] Luke 9:51, cf. 8:1, 9:1.
[12] John 17:5.
[13] John 8:12-14.

as has already been proven in the prequel, and such analogies are even met with in Scripture.[14]

The whole itself is signified by totality and limitation. However, in sensible intuition, each of these categories is itself distinct from the two prior moments; therefore, the whole is also thought through the combination of all three categories together. This is not itself a fourth category, but is already present within the third, not in thought, but in intuition. Totality and limitation already think the completeness of their moments; therefore, their completeness is either threefold in concept, or fourfold in intuition. Likewise, there are two works on each of the third and sixth days, one for the concept, the other for the intuition. Thus, the completeness of quantity or quality may be expressed either by three or by four.

> Thus saith the LORD; For three transgressions of Damascus, and for four, I will not turn away *the punishment* thereof. Amos 1:3, cf. Proverbs 30:15, 18, 21, 24, 29; Amos 1:6, 9, 11, 13; 2:1, 4, 6

The four directions in space form a totality. The two directions that together make up the third dimension are not included, because in them lies, not the concept of a totality, but its relation. When the four directions are given, the third dimension is straightway given also, because it is determined by the former. The second dimension, together with the first, determines the third; therefore, the second must be set off independently from the third, in dependence on the first. Thus, the positive perpendicular signifies completeness according to the concept of direction. It thinks every possible quality of direction, because it contains a rule for producing all directions, but the negative perpendicular expresses the whole of directions in an intuition distinct from the concept. It is determined by the combination of the three, each of which is thought distinctly. And after it is given, it determines the other directions in space, and therefore all directions in space are represented by the negative perpendicular, because it contains within itself a relation, not only to the former

---

[14] John 8:38; 1 Cor. 2:11, 11:3; Eph. 5:22-32; Gal. 5:22; Rev. 16:8-9.

directions, but also to the latter ones. Therefore, it comes to pass that the number four symbolizes completeness in intuition.

> And he shall set up an ensign for the nations, and shall assemble the outcasts of Israel, and gather together the dispersed of Judah from the four corners of the earth. Isaiah 11:12, cf. Jer. 49:36; Ezek. 7:1-3, 37:9; Dan. 8:8, 11:4; Zech. 2:6; Matt. 24:31; Mark 13:27; Rev. 7:1

The four directions coincide with the four headings of categories. The universal and the particular think the form and the matter of concepts, their quantity and quality. The third category is the form of intuition, which thinks the relation of concepts, because an intuition is the combination of concepts, and contains within itself their relation to one another. And these three are all together present in modality, because modality thinks the concept of an object through the object itself.[15] Thus, the object conceived of through quantity, quality, and relation becomes the ground of the whole concept of the object. Relation thinks the form of an object, modality thinks the matter. Relation thinks the whole quantity and quality of concepts; therefore, modality also thinks the whole of quantity, quality, and relation. And the four heads of categories coincide with the four directions in space, because the same function of thought is present in each. The first direction thinks quantity; the second, quality or direction, for it is opposite to the first; the third concerns the relation of the first two, a quantity opposite to both; and the fourth thinks all the former three directions through an object distinct from them all.

> And had a wall great and high, *and* had twelve gates, and at the gates twelve angels, and names written thereon, which are *the names* of the twelve tribes of the children of Israel: On the east three gates; on the north three gates; on the south three gates; and on the west three gates. Revelation 21:12-13, cf. Num. 2

---

[15] Cf. Gress, *Christ Condemned*, 67-75.

The four Gospels may therefore be explicated either according to the four headings, or according to the fourfold quantity of objects, or the fourfold quality of objects. Matthew is the Gospel of Jesus Christ; Mark is the Gospel of the preaching of Jesus Christ; Luke is the Gospel of the Son of God; John is the Gospel of the preaching of the Son of God. The vast difference between John and the other Gospels arises because it is the combination of everything present in the first three, in an intuition distinct from them all, the word of the Word, the image of the Image.

Agony in the Garden

Jesus suffered his whole life, "a man of sorrows, and acquainted with grief" (Isaiah 53:3). Nevertheless, the condemnation of the Father manifests itself particularly at the end of his life. This empirical passion is necessary to produce a sensible intuition distinct from the concept, in agreement therewith.

The passion of Christ begins with his agony in the garden, where he suffers, not for anything done to him by men, but for the things imminently to be done to him by God. He suffered through the mere conception of what he must soon suffer.[16] Yet Christ not only suffered, but endured; he persevered in righteousness, patiently bearing the wrath of God, and was sanctified beyond temptation.

There is one God, and man is one, so also the Lord Jesus Christ. The unity of the divine nature lies in the identity of righteousness and blessedness; the unity of man lies in their agreement, though distinct. The unity of Christ consists of the identity in distinction of his righteousness and his blessedness, manifest in his submission to death. Because in him dwells the fullness of the divine nature,[17] he delights in the moral law of God, by the agony of all things besides, even unto death.[18] Wherefore, the unity of man in Christ is given in a sign: the beginning of his passion in the garden of Gethsemane.

---

[16] Prov. 17:10; Is. 28:18-19.
[17] Col. 1:19.
[18] Ps. 40:8, 12.

This event is omitted from the Gospel of John. Christ's agony in the garden ought to be recorded, because by it he is sanctified; and all things negation are transformed into affirmation; and therein he submits to the will of the Father. Nevertheless, because his happiness lies solely in the law, it was not meet for his agony to be described by the one who speaks of his blessedness. Yet even John records this saying, "The cup which my Father hath given me, shall I not drink it?" (John 18:11), to show that by his own blessedness he resolved to bear the wrath of the Father.

Matthew 26:36-46

Then cometh Jesus with them unto a place called Gethsemane, from the Mount of Olives, after the Lord's supper, to show that he suffered in the fullness of joy, to be sanctified therein, for the sake of his seed; *and saith unto the disciples, Sit ye here, while I go and pray yonder,* for he ought to suffer alone what he alone could bear. *And he took with him Peter and the two sons of Zebedee,* Peter, the apostle of unity, James, of totality, and John, of affirmation, to represent the identity in distinction of his righteousness and blessedness; *and began to be sorrowful and very heavy,* for the time was at hand, and he knew what things he would suffer, and for the greatness of his passion, the very thought thereof put him to grief. *Then saith he unto them, My soul is exceeding sorrowful, even unto death:* that suffering was in his soul, in the body also from the soul; *even unto death,* his sorrow exceeded the ground of life, to put a division between the body and the soul, so greatly he rejoiced in the law of God, to bear the torments of hell; *tarry ye here, and watch with me.* His passion begun, continued, because he persevered in righteousness; yea, he was sanctified therein. *And he went a little further,* for as near to his sufferings as they were, they could not suffer with him, unless he first suffered without them; *and fell on his face,* he gave himself up to God, and in the obedience of his soul he gazed into the depths of hell; *and prayed,* by words he drew near to God;[19] *saying, O my Father, if it be possible, let this cup pass from me: nevertheless not as I will, but as thou wilt.* That he prayed, *let this cup pass from*

---

[19] Hos. 14:2.

me, shows how greatly he suffered, in that he suffered righteously, because he bore a burden he neither sought nor deserved; and by his very submission to condemnation, his prayer is answered; the cup of God's wrath passed away from him because he drank it fully to the end. Mark says, "And he went forward a little, and fell on the ground, and prayed that, if it were possible, the hour might pass from him" (Mark 14:35). He exceeded time itself, yet was subject to it, for time itself shall not pass, but by the will of the Father. "My times *are* in thy hand" (Psalm 31:15). "And there appeared an angel unto him from heaven, strengthening him," the Holy Spirit, in a visible form, to give strength to his flesh (Luke 22:43). "And being in an agony he prayed more earnestly," sanctified by suffering (Luke 22:44); "and his sweat was as it were great drops of blood falling down to the ground," for he labored for our lives (Luke 22:44). "In the sweat of thy face shalt thou eat bread" (Genesis 3:19). *And he cometh unto the disciples, and findeth them asleep,* they did not understand the sign, neither took heed; *and saith unto Peter, What, could ye not watch with me one hour?* They would not yet partake of his agony, but Christ must first suffer for them, that they might suffer with him. *Watch and pray, that ye enter not into temptation:* for by producing within himself an intuition contrary to sin, a man is delivered from temptation;[20] *the spirit indeed is willing, but the flesh is weak.* He was condemned in the flesh, and by that condemnation, his flesh could not submit thereunto, but by the Holy Spirit. "The sacrifice of the wicked *is* an abomination to the LORD: but the prayer of the upright *is* his delight" (Proverbs 15:8). Yea, the condemned are not received by God, though they do nothing wrong. "The sacrifice of the wicked *is* abomination: how much more, *when* he bringeth it with a wicked mind?" (Proverbs 21:27). Nevertheless, by the divine nature dwelling in him, he submitted himself to condemnation, that he should be justified by the Holy Spirit; by whom he willed in the flesh what could not be willed through the flesh. τὸ μὲν πνεῦμα πρόθυμον: *the spirit is spirited,* an apodictic truth of identity in distinction. *He went away again the second time, and prayed,* to show his perseverance therein, while his disciples slept; *saying, O my Father, if this cup may not pass away from me, except I drink it, thy will be done.* The wrath of God is

---

[20] Gal. 5:16-18.

satisfied by the submission of the Son. *And he came and found them asleep again: for their eyes were heavy,* as though his agony was a great a burden to look upon. *And he left them, and went away again, and prayed the third time, saying the same words.* He resolved to bear the wrath of God, even to death, for this was only the beginning of his torment. *Then cometh he to his disciples, and saith unto them, Sleep on now, and take your rest: behold, the hour is at hand, and the Son of man is betrayed into the hands of sinners,* condemned by God the Father to bear their sins. *Rise, let us be going: behold, he is at hand that doth betray me.* His sufferings begin immediately after he is prepared for them by the Father.

Plurality of Man

Man is one; from one man, many. Man is an intuitive representation of the divine nature. The unity of man's nature manifests itself empirically, and may be repeated,[21] according to the multitude of essences thought thereby, and the particular distribution of divine virtues. And because of the unity of the divine nature represented therein, all men proceed from one, and the righteousness of the one stands for many, because every man has his lawful existence in this world through the first. One concept is thought through another, and one intuition is given through another; one angel rules over another, and one man is begotten of another. Yea, though all souls are of God, nevertheless, in the appearances of things the souls of men proceed from others,[22] and inherit their innocence or guilt, for every man coming into the world through the first, bears the image and likeness of the first.[23] By his life Adam is the cause of other lives, and by his person they are affirmed or negated, for as one man lives, and produces an intuition in agreement with his essence, so one man begets another, and produces an essence in agreement with his own.

By the plurality of men, I understand not the many members of the human race, but rather the doctrine of original sin, whereby men seek out the blessedness of the divine nature, and falling short thereof, freely sell themselves into slavery to sin. Man is made in the image of God, but God is invisible. Man is not the image of God, but the pattern[24] for producing an image of God in obedience to his commandments. The image itself requires a righteousness greater than that of man, above the law and before it; wherefore, for the glory of God, mankind must fall into sin, that the Lord Jesus Christ may be revealed.

The doctrine of the Trinity gives apodictic certainty to the fall. Without the fall, God cannot be glorified in the salvation of sinners, yet neither God is the author of sin. Therefore, the necessity of redemption must contain the fall of mankind within itself as an actual consequence of creation. The fall is not a

---

[21] Gress, *Christ Condemned*, 8-9.
[22] Ex. 1:5.
[23] Gen. 5:3; Aquinas, *Summa* 1.100.1, 2.1.81.1.
[24] Kant, *Critique*, B176-181.

necessity of creation, as though deducible beforehand, neither a mere possibility, never coming to pass, but an actual consequence thereof, whose deduction is only possible a posteriori.

Man's blessedness is distinct from his righteousness, and he is free by nature to do good or evil.[25] His happiness is not perfectly united to his lawfulness, and he may seek his happiness elsewhere than in obedience to the law; nor does he take pleasure in the law itself, but in the things of this world, whereby he contemplates the goodness of his maker. And God made man, not that he should sin, but that he should do good, and for the sake of the good commanded, he also suffered the possibility of evil, and ordained it for his glory.[26]

Evil is a concept that contains within itself the negation of its own intuition. Nevertheless, a person is an end in itself; therefore, whoever wills to sin may sin, for that there lies within each one the ground of an intuition in agreement with the concept of the will. Accordingly, God suffers rational beings to sin.

> But when I speak with thee, I will open thy mouth, and thou shalt say unto them, Thus saith the LORD God; He that heareth, let him hear; and he that forbeareth, let him forbear: for they *are* a rebellious house. Ezekiel 3:27

> He that is unjust, let him be unjust still: and he which is filthy, let him be filthy still: and he that is righteous, let him be righteous still: and he that is holy, let him be holy still. Revelation 22:11

Nevertheless, the one who sins produces an intuition contrary to the law. Therefore, to bring that intuition into agreement with the law, sin must be punished. The intuition produced is a negation of the law, and contains within itself the ground of the negation of the person, that is, of their happiness, for

---

[25] Aquinas, *Summa* 1.83.1; *Westminster* 9.1-2.
[26] Aquinas, *Summa* 1.23.3; *Westminster* 3.1, 6, 7.

they are cursed. Wherefore, in righteousness God both suffers men to sin, and punishes them for it, having foreordained it for his glory.

> *Art* thou not from everlasting, O LORD my God, mine Holy One? we shall not die. O LORD, thou hast ordained them for judgment; and, O mighty God, thou hast established them for correction. *Thou art* of purer eyes than to behold evil, and canst not look on iniquity: wherefore lookest thou upon them that deal treacherously, *and* holdest thy tongue when the wicked devoureth *the man that is* more righteous than he? Habakkuk 1:12-13

Wherefore? It is certain that God ordains sin and its punishment, but how it harmonizes with the divine purpose is only revealed in Jesus Christ.

Neither does God tempt anyone,[27] but having made them all in original righteousness, he bestows upon them their happiness, whether in himself, or in the world. And they, being made completely happy in righteousness, have no desire to anything more, and no motive to sin.

Men indeed are made with the hope of heaven, for if they had persevered in righteousness, they should have enjoyed the Lord himself forever, being confirmed therein, together with the angels, but this hope man could not conceive, and formed no diminution of his happiness.[28]

The fall indeed comes to pass of necessity, but of necessity also sin enters the world without consciousness of the divine purpose, for to sin against this end is to overturn it. Thus, the fall must be deducible from the creation of the world, but not by those in the state of creation, whereby they might infer the purpose of their sin, and be tempted by the holy purpose. The fall must only be deducible after it has occurred. This requires that the conception whereby it may be deduced is also the conception whereby men fall into sin.

The knowledge of good and evil is to know good and evil, not in commandments and prohibitions, but in themselves; to find one's happiness

---

[27] Jas. 1:13; Aquinas, *Summa* 1.49.2, 2.1.79.1.
[28] Gen. 5:21-24; Ps. 8:4-5.

perfectly united to the good, for though evil itself is evil, the concept thereof is good: to avoid evil is good, and evil forbids itself. Thus, the knowledge of good and evil is peculiar to the divine nature. To know what man ought rather to do, to make a piece of fruit the measure of good and evil, to worship an idol, and to do that which is right in his own eyes, this is not to man, but to sin.[29]

A completely happy creature has all that he desires. God made man in original righteousness, completely happy. Although man did not have all pleasure within himself, he had everything he desired, for a man may only desire what he conceives, and whatsoever he conceives, and in righteousness desires, that God gives him as the reward of his obedience, lest he fall into sin.

> For the lot of the wicked shall not rest upon the righteous, lest the righteous put forth their hands unto iniquity. Ps. 125:3

God made man completely happy in original righteousness, yet not so happy as God himself, for God is holy. God has his joy in the law, and his happiness is to do what is right. He is perfectly righteous, and being perfectly happy in his own perfect righteousness, whatsoever he wills necessarily comes to pass, for that his joy never fails. The law is universal, and rules over all things, and God's happiness is as the law itself, encompassing every conceivable desire.

God also made the devil happy in righteousness, yet the devil spontaneously conceived of the limitation of his own happiness before God, and of the divine likeness, whereby he fell into sin. Though the spirit of negation saw identity in God, he speculated on the divine nature, that God's righteousness and blessedness might be identical in distinction, that his own may be identical, though distinct. The devil combined the identity he saw in God with the distinction in himself, to will both in the unity of his person. He willed an intuition not grounded in himself, nor in the law itself without the divine persons, but in a conception of the divine nature that contains within itself the ground of its own negation.

---

[29] Deut. 12:8, 13:18; Judg. 17:6, 21:25; Prov. 12:15, 21:2.

The devil is the spirit of negation. Through him man contemplates negation, a concept necessary for man's existence. If then the devil turns negation against his maker, he ought not to be restrained from communicating his conception to other rational creatures, for he is an end in himself, who rules over other ends in themselves. An end in itself exists in relation to other ends in themselves, and a thing in itself contains within itself its relation to other things in themselves. If by the influence of the devil, man should fall into sin, man is not therefore guiltless, since by nature he is liable to his influence, and freely chooses to follow him in his sin. Man is as guilty for his sin as he is innocent for his righteousness, because he is free by nature to do good or evil.

The devil, then, because he was nigh unto God, spontaneously conceived the divine likeness, and envied the divine felicity, and he is solely to blame for his sin, because it arises solely from his own person, that is, from the fact that he is such a person with such an essence. Nevertheless, man does not see God, nor does he spontaneously conceive the divine likeness, for he seeks to produce an intuition, not of the divine nature itself, but in agreement with its concept. And because God made man in original righteousness, and forbade him to eat of the fruit of the tree of knowledge of good and evil, he neither speculates thereon, nor seeks any addition to his happiness.

Therefore, *the tree of knowledge of good and evil* signified to Adam a thing whereof he knew nothing; a name, the meaning of which he ought not to inquire, for it was forbidden even to touch that fruit, let alone taste it, lest he be tempted. This prohibition arose not from his own reason, but from divine revelation. He was free indeed to eat of that fruit, and knew not by nature but that he might, for as he is not conscious of the divine likeness, neither is he conscious of the prohibition, but through the commandment of God; nor did the commandment in any way make him conscious thereof, but expressly forbade it, and morally prevented it; and lest haply he eat of that fruit, and desire to be like God through his sensible nature, and God be found to have tempted him, having left him to his own devices,[30] the LORD forbade him to eat thereof. This prohibition was effectual to preserve man in a state of innocence, besides the

---

[30] Eccl. 7:29.

influence of any other rational being. Their eyes were closed, and they were naked, and they were not ashamed.[31] Adam was conscious of the divine nature, but not of the divine likeness. He knew that God is holy, and that God is one, but his conception of the divine nature did not encompass the idea that he himself might be as holy as God, for what might be thought is just as soon denied. Though the law made it possible for man to think upon this end, the law also restricted him by his very own conception of the divine nature, as absolutely unique, and transcending every representation of sensibility. This only Adam knew, that by eating of the fruit of that tree, he would violate the express commandment of God, and die. Now the threat of death encompasses, first, the natural consequence of man's conception of the divine likeness; second, the punishment for disobedience to God.

Nevertheless, man conceives of the divine nature, and is therefore able to think the holiness of God together with the distinction in himself, if only presented therewith by another, for if he conceives identity in distinction in God, he may also will that the holiness of God be present in his sensible nature. This is a possible object of man's will, though not actual. It lay dormant, until proposed to man's consciousness by the devil.

And although the end itself is lawful, the means to that end is sin, because through his own righteousness man could never attain to the righteousness of God. The divine nature is good, and so for creatures to desire it, as an end, but he who wills the end, wills also the means, and since there is no way for a creature to attain the divine likeness through his own righteousness, this end, which is lawful, requires sinful means, that is, sin as a means, and the necessary condition of the end willed.

Whoever wills the end wills the means, for to will any end, one must be conscious of the means proper to that end, because the means are included in the end, as the cause of the desired effect.[32] The will is the power of the thinking subject to produce an intuition in agreement with its representation. If then the

---

[31] Gen. 2:25, 3:7.
[32] Kant, *Groundwork of the Metaphysics of Morals*, ed. by Mary Gregor, trans. by Mary Gregor (Cambridge: Cambridge University Press, 1998), 4:417.

causality of the will is through means, he who wills the end, wills also the necessary means. This principle belongs to the actuality of the will, so that it neither makes men evil by nature, as a condition of its possibility, nor binds men to sin, as condition of its necessity, but as a condition of its actuality, constitutes a fact of the will itself, which is free.

The means are not present in the possibility of the end, but solely in the actuality of the thing willed. When therefore the devil brought this end from potentiality to actuality, man willing the end, willed also the means. Since by his own righteousness man could never be as God, he chose rather to sin, for though he knew not that he would be as God, he knew that without sin, never could he be partaker of the divine nature. Man would not acquire the righteousness of God by his sin, but neither could he acquire the divine likeness without it. Therefore, for the sake of the divine likeness man fell into sin.

> Is it not lawful for me to do what I will with mine own? Is thine eye evil, because I am good? Matthew 20:15

> For all have sinned and come short of the glory of God. Romans 3:23

> For the wrath of man worketh not the righteousness of God. James 1:20

The end does not justify the means.

> For if the truth of God hath more abounded through my lie unto his glory; why yet am I also judged as a sinner? And not *rather*, (as we be slanderously reported, and as some affirm that we say,) Let us do evil, that good may come? whose damnation is just. Romans 3:7-8, cf. 2 Sam. 6:6-7; 1 Kings 2:36-46; 20:35-36

There is therefore an act of the will both good and evil. A moment includes before and after. In the act of original sin, the will before is good with respect to the end, but evil after with respect to the means. Herein lies the possibility of a transition from good to evil.

The means lies in the actuality of the will, and pertains not to the form of the will, but to the matter. There is therefore no sin in the natural state of man, wherein this end is merely possible. Nevertheless, when the devil brought this end into man's consciousness, for the sake of that end man fell into sin, but God is blameless.

The divine likeness is a lawful end, but the means to that end is sin. It is a lawful end, for it is holiness itself, to will the law as one's own happiness. Yet to do so not for the sake of the law, but for the sake of one's own happiness, this is to fall short of the end willed. It is impossible to will the divine likeness for the sake of righteousness, except when the ground of this desire lies in the divine persons; nor is it possible for one to be holy who is bound by the law, whether by it, or without it. Adam knew not the grace of God, nor our Lord Jesus Christ, nor did God reveal unto man what would tempt him to sin.[33] Adam willed this end not for righteousness, but for happiness. Although God made man perfect, man is not made perfectly righteous; though he lacks nothing proper to the concept of man,[34] he does not by nature attain to the righteousness of God.

Nor does the influence of the serpent excuse man for his sin, for though he sinned through the influence of the devil, he chose to be influenced by him. And God permitted the devil to influence man, because through the spirit of negation man contemplates negation, a concept necessary for his existence, and not for him only, but for every rational creature in heaven and earth. Man is by nature liable to the influence of the devil, if he should fall into sin thereby, just as if he should fall by his own personal defect.

God is not the author of sin. He neither sins, nor tempts any one to sin, either by the creation of the devil, or of man, or of the tree of knowledge of good and evil, and the prohibition to eat therefrom, or by permitting the devil to tempt man, or by saving men from their sins, and bestowing his righteousness upon them. In all cases sin arises from the person of man or angel, through his

---

[33] Prov. 25:2.
[34] Kant, *Critique*, B595-611.

free conception of the divine likeness, and the great distance between himself and his Creator.

> Let no man say when he is tempted, I am tempted of God: for God cannot be tempted with evil, neither tempteth he any man: But every man is tempted, when he is drawn away of his own lust, and enticed. Then when lust hath conceived, it bringeth forth sin: and sin, when it is finished, bringeth forth death. James 1:13-15

His own lust, to be like God.

Now by one sin Adam corrupted his whole person, and became guilty of the law.[35]

> For whosoever shall keep the whole law, and yet offend in one *point*, he is guilty of all. For he that said, Do not commit adultery, said also, Do not kill. Now if thou commit no adultery, yet if thou kill, thou art become a transgressor of the law. James 2:10-11, cf. Ex. 15:26; Lev. 26:14-15; Num. 15:22; Deut. 5:29; Mark 10:21; Luke 18:22

The law is universal, and the subject of the law is an absolute unity. He who denies the law in one particular denies the universality thereof, for the universality of the law is the law itself, and the absolute unity of a person cannot be torn asunder.[36]

> Jesus answered them, Verily, verily, I say unto you, Whosoever committeth sin is the servant of sin. John 8:34

---

[35] *Westminster* 6.2.

[36] Kant, *Religion*, 6:18-26; Immanuel Kant, *Metaphysics of Morals*, ed. by Mary Gregor, trans. by Mary Gregor (Cambridge: Cambridge University Press, 1996), 6:278

Adam through sin became a sinner, and sold himself into slavery, and became the servant of sin. And although men are unable to repent, yet they remain free, and God does not cease to require of them that which is due.[37]

> And if thou say in thine heart, Wherefore come these things upon me? For the greatness of thine iniquity are thy skirts discovered, *and* thy heels made bare. Can the Ethiopian change his skin, or the leopard his spots? *then* may ye also do good, that are accustomed to do evil. Therefore will I scatter them as the stubble that passeth away by the wind of the wilderness. This *is* thy lot, the portion of thy measures from me, saith the Lord; because thou hast forgotten me, and trusted in falsehood. Therefore will I discover thy skirts upon thy face, that thy shame may appear. I have seen thine adulteries, and thy neighings, the lewdness of thy whoredom, *and* thine abominations on the hills in the fields. Woe unto thee, O Jerusalem! wilt thou not be made clean? when *shall it* once *be?* Jeremiah 13:22-27

Can the Ethiopian change his skin, or the leopard his spots? then may ye also do good, that are accustomed to do evil. Therefore will I scatter them, because they have sinned, and refuse to repent.

> Now therefore go to, speak to the men of Judah, and to the inhabitants of Jerusalem, saying, Thus saith the LORD; Behold, I frame evil against you: return ye now every one from his evil way, and make your ways and your doings good. And they said, There is no hope: but we will walk after our own devices, and we will every one do the imagination of his evil heart. Therefore thus saith the LORD; Ask ye now among the heathen, who hath heard such things: the virgin of Israel hath done a very horrible thing. Will *a man* leave the snow of Lebanon *which cometh* from the rock of the field? *Or* shall the cold flowing waters that come from another place be forsaken? Because my people hath forgotten me,

---

[37] Kant, *Practical Reason*, 5:89-106.

they have burned incense to vanity, and they have caused them to stumble in their ways *from* the ancient paths, to walk in paths, *in* a way not cast up; To make their land desolate, *and* a perpetual hissing; every one that passeth thereby shall be astonished, and wag his head. I will scatter them as with an east wind before the enemy; I will shew them the back, and not the face, in the day of their calamity. Jeremiah 18:11-17

And they said, There is no hope: but we will walk after our own devices, and we will every one do the imagination of his evil heart. They are unable to repent, because they have freely sold themselves to do iniquity.[38]

And not only that, but the children of Adam inherit his guilt, and fall with him and in him.[39] Though they are different persons, they are personally united to him, because through him they have their lawful existence in this world. Man is made in the image of God. God is one; therefore, man is also one, but man is many. And because the many proceed from the one, the guilt of the one is imputed to the many, just as they should have inherited his righteousness, for the one represents the many, as much as the many represent the one. The children inherit the guilt of the father, and the father brings guilt upon the children.

The moral quality of a person is good or evil, and pertains to his nature, but his legal state is his relation to the law, and belongs to his person.[40] One person is related to another as cause to effect, and when the subject varies, the cause is represented in the effect, as the universal in the particular.[41] Therefore, the children of Adam share in his relation to the law, and the guilt of original sin is imputed to them.

Every man bears the guilt of his own iniquity; yet the guilt of original sin is imputed to all Adam's children; for the guilt of their father Adam is their own guilt, because they sin with him and in him. Therefore God says that every man

---

[38] 1 Kings 21:20, 25.

[39] *Westminster* 6.3.

[40] Cf. Gress, *Christ Condemned*, 37.

[41] Cf. *Christ Condemned*, 48-49.

shall be put to death for his own sin;[42] nevertheless, he shall execute the punishment of the fathers upon the sons,[43] for when the son commits the iniquity of the father, he brings upon himself the guilt and punishment of the father. Likewise, the sin of Adam's children justifies the imputation of his guilt, for indeed if they would not have sinned, the guilt of Adam would not have been imputed to them, without their consent. And as men are free to repent, so likewise they are free to persevere in righteousness.

Every man comes into the world through the head. The moral law requires that every man obey the law, to live thereby. Man is by nature a unity; therefore, the covenant of works requires the whole of humanity to obey the moral law, the head on behalf of the members, the members through the head.[44] By the failure of Adam to keep the covenant of works, that covenant is broken, not only in the head, but also in the members. The covenant for all, broken in one, is broken in all. To them God imputes the guilt of Adam's sin, in whom lies the ground of their existence in this world. And because they are guilty, they do follow Adam in his sin, for the same predilection that abides in Adam, abides in all his children, and they are liable by nature to his guilt, as he himself is liable to the influence of the devil.

> Behold, I was shapen in iniquity; and in sin did my mother conceive me. Psalm 51:5

> Thy first father hath sinned, and thy teachers have transgressed against me. Isaiah 43:27

> Ye are of *your* father the devil, and the lusts of your father ye will do. John 8:44

Notwithstanding, every man's sin is his own.

---

[42] Deut. 24:16; Ezek. 18.
[43] Ex. 20:5.
[44] Aquinas, *Summa* 2.1.81.1; *Westminster* 7.1-2.

> Behold, all souls are mine; as the soul of the father, so also the soul of
> the son is mine: the soul that sinneth, it shall die. Ezekiel 18:4

The sin itself is not imputed, but the guilt thereof.

> Against thee, thee only, have I sinned, and done this evil in thy sight:
> that thou mightest be justified when thou speakest, and be clear when
> thou judgest. Behold, I was shapen in iniquity; and in sin did my
> mother conceive me. Psalm 51:4-5

For the judgment *was* by one to condemnation. Romans 5:16

And through the guilt of original sin, men become conscious of the end of Adam's sin, and willing the same end, fall with him and in him into sin, for everyone begotten of the father is as the father, made in his image and likeness.

> And Adam lived an hundred and thirty years, and begat *a son* in his
> own likeness, after his image. Genesis 5:3

Every man is born with the guilt of original sin, and dies for his own sin, and is born into death.[45] Nevertheless, the Lord Jesus Christ, born of a virgin, consents to bear the guilt of original sin, and he, persevering in the original righteousness of Adam, overcomes the temptation of the devil, as the rightful head of humanity, forgiving men their sins, and withal bestowing his blessedness upon his people. By the same rule that God condemns, by that rule also he saves.

Man is an outwardly lawful being of sensible intuition; an angel, of intellectual intuition. It is not in man to fall, but through the influence of devil. The devil and his angels know things in themselves, and reject the law in itself. They sin for the sake of sin, the intuition willed in identity with the concept.

---

[45] *Westminster* 6.2-3.

Wherefore, they are neither free nor able to repent;[46] having seen the divine nature and rejected it, they also reject it in the person of Jesus Christ. Angels are simple unities; their sin is one, forever. An angel sins with the knowledge that, though without sin he shall never be as God, yet neither by it shall he ever be as God. He sins contemptuously and with a high hand,[47] for the sin of angels is itself the means whereby they aspire to the divine likeness. The sin of men is the means necessary to that end; the sin of angels is the means whereby they seek its fulfillment, for the matter of an angel is within the form, but the matter of a man is in an intuition besides. An angel's righteousness and blessedness are in the Lord, identical; an angel sees God and finds his happiness in him; wherefore by sin he rejects the whole of his own happiness, without hope of redemption. Therefore is the fall of angels irrevocable.[48]

> For if God spared not the angels that sinned, but cast *them* down to hell, and delivered *them* into chains of darkness, to be reserved unto judgment. 2 Peter 2:4

> And the angels which kept not their first estate, but left their own habitation, he hath reserved in everlasting chains under darkness unto the judgment of the great day. Jude 6

Nevertheless, fallen man may be redeemed. Though he is a unity, he is also a plurality. He sins not with his soul only, but with his body ensouled, and his soul embodied, save when the two are separated; thus while he lives, he may yet repent. Though he has turned away from righteousness, by sin he seeks happiness not against the law, but apart from it; he has not rejected God unconditionally, but only for the sake of his happiness, nor does he find his happiness immediately in God, but in the things of this world, whereby he contemplates the goodness of his maker.[49] He has not seen God, so he does not

---

[46] Num. 15:30-31; Aquinas, *Summa* 1.64.2.
[47] Job 1:6-12, 2:1-6.
[48] *Larger Catechism* Q.19.
[49] Ps. 34:12.

sin wholly against God, but only against what God has revealed, and he may be saved according to that which is kept secret.

Although man may be redeemed, he cannot of himself repent, and if indeed man had fallen of his own accord, without the influence of the devil, he would be as little free to repent as the fallen angels, but because he fell through the influence of the devil, he may also be saved by the grace of God. Though man is free, yet by his sin he has freely sold himself into slavery, and freely continues in service to sin. Only the truth of God revealed to him in the Son may set him free.[50] Because he sinned to be like God, he may also be saved to be like God, for he knew not but that he might be like God, and God knew that he would freely make man like himself.

A rational being cannot sin against what he cannot conceive. The moral law obliges through its conception; without the conception, there is no obligation.[51] Sin is as the conception of the law therein. Man does not see the divine nature, nor can he sin against the sight of it. Wherefore, God may yet save man by revealing himself in the likeness of sinful flesh.

> For what the law could not do, in that it was weak through the flesh, God sending his own Son in the likeness of sinful flesh, and for sin, condemned sin in the flesh: That the righteousness of the law might be fulfilled in us, who walk not after the flesh, but after the Spirit. Romans 8:3-4

What man sinfully sought, God freely gives; through the promise of a savior, God makes men partakers of the divine nature.

> Grace and peace be multiplied unto you through the knowledge of God, and of Jesus our Lord, According as his divine power hath given unto us all things that *pertain* unto life and godliness, through the knowledge of him that hath called us to glory and virtue: Whereby are

---

[50] John 8:31-36.

[51] Rom. 2:12-16, 5:13; Kant, *Groundwork*, 4:446-458; *Practical Reason*, 5:27-41.

given unto us exceeding great and precious promises: that by these ye might be partakers of the divine nature, having escaped the corruption that is in the world through lust. 2 Peter 1:2-4

By forgiveness of sins, a man is made perfectly righteous before God, because the law is one, for that same unity of law that renders men unable to repent of their sin, also renders them unable to fall from Christ's righteousness, if they partake of his righteousness in deed and in truth.[52]

Though men are free to repent, yet are they unable. The ability to repent comes from the ability to save. As man sinned through the influence of the devil, so he may be saved by the influence of God. And the sight of God in Christ, who bears the sins of men, is the means whereby God saves sinners from their sin, because in him they see the possibility of repentance, and are persuaded to believe, that they might be like Christ.

There is another conception of God that a man may have, through the knowledge of the divine persons, according to which his righteousness and blessedness are identical in distinction, a conception valid for man through their distinction, and for God through their identity.[53] According to this conception, a man may yet choose to repent and believe the Gospel, and so be like God in Christ, but an angel cannot, for he is made with the intuition of their identity, and in sin he distinguishes them, and falls into contradiction. Having once rejected the identity of God, he cannot turn back to it; having rejected the sight of the divine nature, he also rejects God manifest in the flesh.

Man sinned to be like God. This God permitted that he might make man like himself. Adam sinned for the glory of God, not to glorify God, but to attain his glory, and though God rejects the means, he approves so highly of the end, that he freely gives them salvation through his only begotten Son,

Who, being in the form of God, thought it not robbery to be equal with God, But made himself of no reputation, and took upon him the form

---

[52] 1 John 3:18.
[53] Gress, *Christ Condemned*, 92.

of a servant, and was made in the likeness of men: And being found in fashion as a man, he humbled himself, and became obedient unto death, even the death of the cross. Wherefore God also hath highly exalted him, and given him a name which is above every name: That at the name of Jesus every knee should bow, *of things* in heaven, and *things* in earth, and *things* under the earth; And *that* every tongue should confess that Jesus Christ *is* Lord, to the glory of God the Father. Philippians 2:6-11

He *thought it not robbery to be equal with God,* for men sought to rob God of his glory, but he thought it not robbery to be equal with God, that he might bestow his glory on the elect.

> Now then we are ambassadors for Christ, as though God did beseech *you* by us: we pray *you* in Christ's stead, be ye reconciled to God. For he hath made him *to be* sin for us, who knew no sin; that we might be made the righteousness of God in him. 2 Corinthians 5:20-21

Now the righteousness of man is in his soul, but his happiness is in the body. These are distinct, though united; therefore, by sin man brings death upon himself, through the separation of body and soul.

The death is as the sin. If man sins unconditionally, as the angels who fell, that death is immediate; if however man sins not for the sake of sin, but for the sake of the divine nature, neither through himself, but through the subtlety of the serpent, the sentence of immediate death is commuted to mortality. And though he is dead in sin,[54] he yet lives in the body, that he may be redeemed by the Son, whom God promises to man in the day of his sin, that the lie of the devil should abound to God's truth.

The devil is the spirit of negation. He rules not over any one kind of thing, but over the distinctions between creatures, and between creature and creator. His office therefore includes the prosecution of sin in creatures. He was to be

---

[54] Eph. 2:5; Col. 2:13.

the minister of death to those who disobeyed. Although he himself brought about that disobedience, it remains true that through him there is death for sin.

The devil became unto man the instrument of death itself, by tempting him to sin. This does not make void the office, because it remained true that he who was to inflict death for sin, inflicted sin for death, and that sinfully; it was yet true that only sinners would die for their sins. But God overcame this subtlety by sending his Son, who was by the devil betrayed,[55] that the offices of the fallen angels might be taken from them, and given to others in righteousness, whom he redeemed from the world.

> Forasmuch then as the children are partakers of flesh and blood, he also himself likewise took part of the same; that through death he might destroy him that had the power of death, that is, the devil; And deliver them who through fear of death were all their lifetime subject to bondage. Hebrews 2:14-15

> *And* having spoiled principalities and powers, he made a shew of them openly, triumphing over them in it. Colossians 2:15

The devil was therefore confounded and bruised in the head,[56] when his schemes were lawfully usurped, God turning that which was meant for evil into good:[57] bestowing on men the divine likeness, which the devil deceitfully promised; and revealing in his Son the Trinity, which the devil sought by speculation.

> In the beginning was the Word, and the Word was with God, and the Word was God. The same was in the beginning with God. All things were made by him; and without him was not any thing made that was

---

[55] Luke 22:3; John 13:2, 27.
[56] Matt. 27:3-5.
[57] Gen. 50:20.

made. In him was life; and the life was the light of men. And the light
shineth in darkness; and the darkness comprehended it not. John 1:1-5

Scripture Proof

The devil sinned, and a third of the angels with him, and the whole of
humanity was brought down by him in his fall, for the sake of the divine
likeness. How then did the evil one cause man to fall into sin?

The possible is actual under a condition. The condition of the fall is the
temptation of the devil, whereby he represents to man the end of the divine
likeness in the form of a legitimate claim, for although the end is lawful, the
means thereunto is sin. This claim the woman received, according to the
dependence of her nature, for the blessedness therein promised, and gave also
to her husband, who received the fruit at her hand, according to the union he
enjoyed with her, and the happiness of her person.

The fall of man requires that the devil implant this end into the mind of
man in the form of a legitimate claim, for man can receive nothing except it be
lawfully given to him. A legitimate claim consists of facts, disputes, and
remedies. A fact is commonly agreed; a dispute is the matter of the claim; and a
remedy is what the law provides upon proof of the claim.

What is legitimate from one perspective may be found illegitimate from
another. It is often a question of facts formerly unknown, or the application of
laws difficult to comprehend. That man should be like God is an end willed both
by God and man. Nevertheless, God forbade man to eat of that tree upon pain
of death. There is therefore no lawful remedy to the devil's claim.

However, to enter into the mind of man, that claim need not be legitimate,
but only presented in the form thereof. To consider once whether it is legitimate,
it must first be received according to its form, to judge of it according to the
matter. Once conceived, man willing the end, wills also the means.

Man is made in the image of God's righteousness, impervious to the
temptation of the devil, for he receives nothing but what is from God, according
to a legitimate claim. The woman, however, is subject to the man, and employs

a lower standard of proof. Where the man requires a legitimate claim, the woman accepts a claim thereunto, as worthy of trial, to bring to her husband. And the husband receives the claim of his wife, to judge of it.

Woman is made in the image of God's blessedness; the scope of her soul is happiness united to lawfulness. She depends upon the man, as the intuition upon the concept, and is under his authority. And those under authority employ a standard of proof one degree lower than the authority, which they apply both to the authority, and to the claim itself. Thus, where a legitimate claim suffices for Adam, a claim alone suffices for Eve. The devil presented his claim to Eve in the form of legitimacy, without the matter. Accordingly, Eve submitted this claim to the judgment of her husband. The devil's words savored nothing of lawfulness, but of happiness, perchance of blessedness, to which nothing wanting is outside the view of woman. And where Eve for blessedness received the claim of the devil, Adam for righteousness judged the matter brought to him by his wife.

God is perfectly happy because he is perfectly holy. By seeking to be as happy as God himself, Adam sinned through his union with his wife. She represents the union of lawfulness and happiness, and therefore in the matter of original sin she represents the sought after end of happiness. She was beguiled, because in her was the union thereof, and she knew not which to direct her action, nor in sin distinguished them. Once she conceived the end, she immediately imputed lawfulness to it. Man, on the other hand, knew the unlawfulness thereof, without any consideration of his own happiness, yet because he was united to his wife, he sinned for her sake, that they might be like God. Though he knew that by sin they could neither be perfected in righteousness, nor made as happy as God, yet because he willed the end, being conscious thereof through his wife, he also willed the means.

> For Adam was first formed, then Eve. And Adam was not deceived, but the woman being deceived was in the transgression. 1 Timothy 2:13-14

This is the devil's claim: the fact that man, though forbidden, was free to eat of the fruit of that tree, for he was free to eat of every tree of the garden, to do good or evil; the dispute, that he was forbidden from eating of all the trees in the garden, and so his happiness was limited to the trees of which he might lawfully eat; the remedy, that God withholding from man what man might will for his own happiness, man should eat thereof, that he might be like God.

The devil presented himself to the woman in the form of a serpent. This ruse, though illegitimate, was sufficient to present his claim to the woman, requiring only that he could talk. Spirits are things in themselves; before the fall, they could not present themselves to men in a rational likeness. God and angels appear to men only after the fall, through the revelation of the Son, in whose Spirit phenomena and noumena are identified in distinction.[58] Wherefore, the devil could not have appeared to Eve in any rational likeness, but one like unto it, a sensible likeness, for having confounded the two he made himself like a serpent, that being most like unto himself, of single body and forked tongue, and so partook of its curse.

Genesis 3:1-8

Now the serpent was more subtil than any beast of the field which the LORD *God had made,* for the devil conceived distinction in God, in whom he saw only identity. *And he said unto the woman, Yea, hath God said, Ye shall not eat of every tree of the garden?* The devil identified what God distinguished: the freedom to eat of all, and the prohibition to eat of one. *And the woman said unto the serpent, We may,* the union of freedom and permission; *eat of the fruit of the trees of the garden:* a general statement, not universal. The scope of her person was open to beguiling claims, not because she was unrighteous, but because her righteousness was more intuitive than conceptual; *But of the fruit of the tree which is in the midst of the garden, God hath said, Ye shall not eat of it, neither shall ye touch it, lest ye die.* She now distinguishes the prohibition of God from the freedom of the will, for she had as clear a conception of this as Adam, because she knew the word of God

---

[58] 1 Cor. 11:13-15; 2 Thess. 1:7.

from her husband, who also instructed her to avoid temptation. *And the serpent said unto the woman, Ye shall not surely die:* a lie, but because the devil had already laid forth the facts and the dispute, the woman also contemplated the remedy proposed; *For God doth know that in the day ye eat thereof, then your eyes shall be opened, and ye shall be as gods, knowing good and evil.* The devil now propounds his contradiction, identifying what is distinct: because man was free to eat of that tree, though forbidden, nevertheless by it he might be as happy as God. This lie God was pleased retroactively to fulfill by the promise of a savior, that men should be forgiven their sins, and partake of the divine nature. *And when the woman saw,* for she considered the end of the matter given to her in the form of a legitimate claim; *that the tree was good for food, and that it was pleasant to the eyes,* from the sensible to the spiritual; *and a tree to be desired to make one wise,* for the end is good; *she took of the fruit thereof, and did eat, and gave also unto her husband with her; and he did eat.* The man, in whom lies the unity of man, partook of the identity in distinction showed him by the woman. *And the eyes of them both were opened, and they knew that they were naked; and they sewed fig leaves together, and made themselves aprons.* Their eyes were opened because they saw the end proposed to them by the devil; and they knew that they were naked because they desired to be clothed with the divine likeness; and because they found something to be lacking in their own nature, they were covered with shame, and made clothes for themselves. *And they heard the voice of the* LORD *God walking in the garden in the cool of the day:* revealed to them now in a visible form; *and Adam and his wife hid themselves from the presence of the* LORD *God,* even the Holy Spirit, who is distinguished from the Lord who is present in a particular place, that is, the Son. From the beginning God revealed himself graciously to them; *amongst the trees of the garden.* They hid themselves, because they clothed themselves with the symbols only, and not with the divine likeness itself. Nor did they sin contemptuously, and with a high hand, but afterward were ashamed. *And the* LORD *God called unto Adam, and said unto him, Where art thou?* God calls him to mind his place, and to stand before him, though he has sinned. *And he said, I heard thy voice in the garden, and I was afraid, because I was naked; and I hid myself.* He confesses the facts. *And he said, Who told thee that thou wast naked?* To discover the cause. *Hast thou eaten of the tree, whereof I commanded thee that thou shouldest not eat?* Though the end is lawful, and accordant with his own purpose, God yet condemned the sin, for the commandment of God is unconditional. *And the man said, The woman whom thou gavest to be with me, she gave me of the tree, and I did eat.* He confesses his sin, and owns the cause of it. *And the LORD God said unto the woman, What is this that thou hast done? And the woman said, The serpent beguiled me, and I did eat.* She also confesses her sin, because the grace of God was upon them in his word, for he spoke not to condemn them, but that they might be saved, and they themselves knew that their sin was not committed at their own behest, but through the subtlety of the serpent, the consciousness whereof shows the possibility of redemption. When therefore the Lord had established the facts of the case from the mouths of our first parents, he proceeded to judgment.

Temptation in the Wilderness

Adam yielded to the subtlety of the serpent. Jesus Christ was tempted forty days in the wilderness, yet he overcame the temptation of the devil, and was sanctified beyond measure. Jesus is born a man, free by his human nature to sin, and subject to temptation, yet by the manifestation of the divine nature in his humanity, he can do nothing but what is right,[59] and through many trials his human nature is conformed to the divine. This is he who came to make true the devil's promise, because the lies of the devil are nought for whom they are no lies at all. *Ye shall not surely die,* for there is salvation in Christ; *For God doth know that in the day ye eat thereof, then your eyes shall be opened, and ye shall be as gods, knowing good and evil,* for the promise of a savior is given them the very same day that they sinned, and through him men partake of the divine nature.

The sign of original sin is the part of original sin that pertains to Christ. This is the temptation in the wilderness. There are three temptations.

---

[59] John 5:19; Aquinas, *Summa* 3.7.1, 18.4, 41.1; *Westminster* 8.2.

For all that *is* in the world, the lust of the flesh, and the lust of the eyes, and the pride of life, is not of the Father, but is of the world. 1 John 2:16

As the devil tempted Eve, so he tempted Christ, yet the temptations are here distinguished, where at the first they were united. The devil knowing the coming of our Lord Jesus Christ, tempted not man, but the image of the Triune God. The devil tempted Christ to prove his divinity by turning stones into bread; then, by casting himself off the temple; and then, with power over the nations; that is, by hunger, by proof, and by power.

The temptation in the wilderness immediately follows his baptism, for the baptism illustrates the virgin birth. Born of a woman, he is tempted like us, but born of the Father, he overcomes all temptation, to show that in him dwells the Spirit of holiness, by whom he speaks and works miracles. Thus he is sanctified to his ministry, having proved himself the rightful head of the human race.

Mark's account is brief, to show the preparation of Christ to preach the Gospel. John omits the temptation altogether, because these temptations proved futile against the blessed one, saving only to sanctify his flesh.

Matthew 4:11-11

Then was Jesus led up of the Spirit into the wilderness to be tempted of the devil. He did not tempt himself, nor God, but the devil; and the Spirit led him into the wilderness, by whom he should not succumb to temptation, but being justified by the Spirit, he should also be sanctified by the Spirit. Luke says, "And Jesus being full of the Holy Ghost returned from Jordan, and was led by the Spirit into the wilderness" (Luke 4:1). *And when he had fasted forty days and forty nights, he was afterward an hungred,* that he should see the face of God by the perfection of his obedience,[60] for God brought him to the limit of his strength. "Jesus saith unto them, My meat is to do the will of him that sent me, and to finish his work" (John 4:34). When all his strength was spent, he hungered, that he might be purified all the more above every earthly desire. *And when the tempter,* the spirit

---

[60] Ex. 24:18, 34:28.

of negation, who at the first tempted Eve; *came to him, he said, If thou be the Son of God, command that these stones be made bread,* to satisfy his hunger. *But he answered and said, It is written, Man shall not live by bread alone, but by every word that proceedeth out of the mouth of God.* Though weak, he yet lived, persevering in righteousness. *Then the devil taketh him up into the holy city, and setteth him on a pinnacle of the temple, And saith unto him, If thou be the Son of God, cast thyself down: for it is written, He shall give his angels charge concerning thee: and in their hands they shall bear thee up, lest at any time thou dash thy foot against a stone.* To sin for the glory of God, to condemn himself, if God would deliver him. *Jesus said unto him, It is written again, Thou shalt not tempt the Lord thy God.* The devil tempted Jesus to tempt the Father, yet Jesus should not condemn himself, but the Father only. Luke ends with this temptation to show that Christ by his perfect obedience proves himself to be the blessed Son of God. *Again, the devil taketh him up into an exceeding high mountain, and sheweth him all the kingdoms of the world, and the glory of them; And saith unto him, All these things will I give thee, if thou wilt fall down and worship me.* The devil tempted Christ with his own inheritance, which he should receive by the work of the Holy Spirit. *Then saith Jesus unto him, Get thee hence, Satan: for it is written, Thou shalt worship the Lord thy God, and him only shalt thou serve.* That glory and power belongs to him only through righteousness divine. *Then the devil leaveth him, and, behold, angels came and ministered unto him.* After he had proven his divinity without the help of angels, he received their assistance graciously, that they also might partake of his glory.[61] Luke adds, "And Jesus returned in the power of the Spirit into Galilee: and there went out a fame of him through all the region round about. And he taught in their synagogues, being glorified of all," for he was now about his ministry (Luke 4:14-15).

---

[61] Ps. 16:2-3.

Totality of Man

The totality of mankind consists of the unity of its many members. The unity of man represents the divine unity; the plurality thereof represents God's invisibility; the totality of man in Christ forms a representation of the divine nature through the many members of the human race. Whereas the first Adam is a pattern[62] for producing the image of God by obedience to his commandments, the second is the image[63] of God himself, blessed and holy, by whom the likeness of God is imprinted onto all humanity.

Anthropology studies the universality of sin and death in mankind, together with the distribution of divine virtues to men. The former is not distinct from the unity; rather, the unity of the many already lies within the one from whom the many proceed. There is therefore no distinct totality pertaining to man, but a logical one, for if there is no totality of the divine nature, then neither of the human.[64]

Theology is not the study of man, but of God, yea, of God manifest in the flesh. Accordingly, the totality of man consists of an intuition of the divine unity in the many members of the human race. This belongs not to Adam, but to Christ. Adam represents the unity of God itself; the many are not one, but the one; the many do not represent the unity of God, but his invisibility; nor are the many contained within Adam's person, but only in relation to it. Their essences are not thought within his, nor under his, but only their intuitions.

All the essences of men are thought through the person of Jesus Christ.[65] The Lord Jesus is the unity of many persons in one, because the sins of the world are imputed to him. In any totality the unity is not only repeated in the plurality, but the plurality in the unity. The unity of Adam encompasses the many members, but God imputes the guilt of many to the righteous one. Through the Lord Jesus Christ, in whom lies the harmony of diverse judgments, the human race forms an image of the divine nature, for the totality of man necessarily

---

[62] Kant, *Critique*, B176-181.
[63] *Critique*, B595-599.
[64] Cf. Gress, *Christ Condemned*, 18.
[65] 1 Cor. 12:13-15, 27; Gal. 3:26-29; Col. 2:10, 3:11.

refers to a single man in whom those judgments are found, because he bears the guilt of Adam's sin in righteousness.

Wherefore, *first*, there is one Lord Jesus Christ, the second Adam, the rightful head of the human race;[66] *second*, there is a division amongst men between just and unjust, the seed of the woman and the seed of the serpent; *third*, notwithstanding, they are all gathered together in Christ, reconciled to God, and freely offered the Gospel, and in due time profess Jesus Christ as Lord, to the glory of God the Father, whether unto life or death.[67]

Every historical doctrine consists of the combination of a fundamental doctrine with intuition. The headship of the Lord Jesus Christ arises from the harmony of diverse judgments executed upon him, yet it is also formed from the combination of original righteousness and original sin, because these are intuitive representations of the unity and invisibility of the divine nature. The difference lies in the order of combination; first, with one another, and then with intuition; second, with intuition, and then with one another; lastly, the identity of the combination.

Jesus Christ is unconditionally condemned by the Father, not for any sin he committed, but for the glory of God. Yet the law of God requires that wherever there be guilt, there also be sin. If not for his own sin, then for the sin of others. Those whose sins are imputed to Christ are chosen in him by the Father, his the guilt, theirs the sin, and because they are personally united to Christ, they also bear his righteousness, as beloved children.

> Yet it pleased the Lord to bruise him; he hath put *him* to grief: when thou shalt make his soul an offering for sin, he shall see *his* seed, he shall prolong *his* days, and the pleasure of the Lord shall prosper in his hand. He shall see of the travail of his soul, *and* shall be satisfied: by his knowledge shall my righteous servant justify many; for he shall bear their iniquities. Isaiah 53:10-11

---

[66] Aquinas, *Summa* 3.8.3; *Westminster* 3.3.

[67] Ps. 22:29; Matt. 25:31-46; Acts 17:30-31; Rom. 5:18; 1 Cor. 3:12-15; Phil. 2:9-11; Col. 1:20; Aquinas, *Summa* 3.8.1-3; *Westminster* 33.2.

According as he hath chosen us in him before the foundation of the world, that we should be holy and without blame before him in love: Having predestinated us unto the adoption of children by Jesus Christ to himself, according to the good pleasure of his will, To the praise of the glory of his grace, wherein he hath made us accepted in the beloved. Ephesians 1:4-6

The rest are passed over and appointed to destruction, and that unconditionally, for if some are passed over, it is manifest that they have sinned who are passed over. Wherefore, all sin is ordained by God through the condemnation of Christ, for the glory of the Father.

> For the love of Christ constraineth us; because we thus judge, that if one died for all, then were all dead: And *that* he died for all, that they which live should not henceforth live unto themselves, but unto him which died for them, and rose again. 2 Corinthians 5:14-15, cf. Ps. 51:4, Rom. 3:4

The Father condemns the Son, not for any sin he committed, but for the sins of others, yet so this condemnation is unconditional, because the sins of men are unconditionally imputed to Christ in the condemnation of the Father. Therefore, the necessity of sin for condemnation is not a fundamental doctrine, but historical, and its application to individuals is derivative.

Christ died for mankind: *universally*, for the whole world, that whosoever believes on him should be saved; *particularly*, for those individual persons whose sins are imputed to Christ. The former God reveals, the latter he conceals. It does not appear for whom Christ died, but it does appear to all that he died, and therefore that he died for all. He is a law of salvation to all, to be saved by faith in his name. Those for whom Christ died believe by the universal promise; those who are passed over are yet bound by it, and condemned for their unbelief.

These words spake Jesus, and lifted up his eyes to heaven, and said,
Father, the hour is come; glorify thy Son, that thy Son also may glorify
thee: As thou hast given him power over all flesh, that he should give
eternal life to as many as thou hast given him. John 17:1-2

He has power to save all who believe, for he died for all, that whosoever believes
should be saved, and he died for the elect, that they should believe, and so be
saved.

For it pleased *the Father* that in him should all fulness dwell; And,
having made peace through the blood of his cross, by him to reconcile
all things unto himself; by him, *I say,* whether *they be* things in earth, or
things in heaven. And you, that were sometime alienated and enemies
in *your* mind by wicked works, yet now hath he reconciled In the body
of his flesh through death, to present you holy and unblameable and
unreproveable in his sight: If ye continue in the faith grounded and
settled, and *be* not moved away from the hope of the gospel, which ye
have heard, *and* which was preached to every creature which is under
heaven; whereof I Paul am made a minister. Colossians 1:19-23

That God rewards obedience with happiness, shows that he desires all men
to obey, and that he commands all men to obey, shows that he loves all men,
and desires their happiness. And that he loves all men, he desires all to be
saved;[68] so he sent his Son into the world, that whosoever believes in him may
be saved.[69] Insofar as it depends on him, he is at peace with all men, reconciling
all things to himself by the blood of his cross.[70]

Faith is certainty in the objects of practical reason.[71] The objects of faith may
only be known through the free choice of a person to obey the moral law,
whereby he consents to the ends of practical reason, and all the conditions of his

---

[68] 1 Tim. 2:4; 2 Pet. 3:9.
[69] John 3:16.
[70] Rom. 12:18.
[71] Heb. 11:1.

moral purpose receive their objective reality. Therefore, saving faith consists in the consent of the individual to his own salvation. God saves no man without his consent. Hope is the expectation of the object through the certainty of the promise.[72]

Man consents unto the law, that it is good; wherefore also implicitly to the law manifest in the flesh. As man is bound to keep the law in his original conception thereof, so also he is bound to keep it in its divine manifestation. And because Christ is manifest to all, so all are bound to believe and be saved.

Accordingly, Christ is the head of the human race, in whom all are gathered together, some unto salvation, others unto damnation.[73] Those who are not found in Christ are yet reconciled to the purpose of God through the knowledge of the Trinity, for the divine persons are the supreme ends in themselves: knowledge of them is the supreme end of creation.

The divine image requires that man be subject both to wrath and to mercy, according to the plurality thought within the unity. Those who bear the wrath of God show forth his eternal hatred of sin, and the sufferings of Christ, and the mercy of God to those who believe;[74] and by their profession of the Lord Jesus, they glorify God the Father, who has power to save and to destroy.[75]

> And the Egyptians shall know that I *am* the Lord, when I have gotten me honour upon Pharaoh, upon his chariots, and upon his horsemen. Exodus 14:18

> If any man's work shall be burned, he shall suffer loss: but he himself shall be saved; yet so as by fire. 1 Corinthians 3:15, cf. vs. 17

For they are burned, because he judges every man according to his work.

Let us now make a new beginning from historical doctrine.

---

[72] Rom. 4:18; 5:5, 8:24-25, 15:4; 1 Cor. 13:13; Aquinas, *Summa* 2.1.40.1; 2.2.17.
[73] Matt. 25:31-46.
[74] Rom. 9:23.
[75] Phil. 2:9-11; James 4:12.

By *rightful* headship, I mean headship lawfully exercised. God created Adam to bear children in righteousness; this office he vacated by sin. Nevertheless, he continues to be the head of humanity according to the flesh, and the guilt of his sin is imputed to all his children by law, for that same unity whereby God imputes Adam's innocence to his children remains the ground of the imputation of his guilt. Nor is there any other through whom men may lawfully come into the world, but the first man, a living soul, the father of us all.

Since then righteousness comes through the head, and the first head is fallen, another must take his place. Through Adam mankind might have persevered in righteousness, but through the Lord Jesus Christ only do men repent of their sins. The fallen angels are not bound by time, neither are they free to repent, but are bound in everlasting chains under darkness, reserved unto judgment.[76] Wherefore, the moral law does not prescribe them to repent, but never to have sinned. Man, however, is a creature of space and time, and is free to repent, as the law commands him; wherefore, having fallen through the first Adam, he is able to repent through faith in the second.

Adam's children inherit the guilt of original sin, whereby they become conscious of the end for which he fell, and fall with him and in him for the same. Yet because they sin freely, it is conceivable that one of Adam's children should consent to bear the guilt of original sin, and persevere in his original righteousness. And because he recovers the righteousness of Adam, he is called the second Adam.

This man is righteous, all else are fallen. He is therefore one, "Jesus Christ, the righteous," yet he bears the guilt of original sin (1 John 2:1). He is condemned, not for any sin of his own, but unconditionally by the Father, and in righteousness he submits unto condemnation, and is justified by the Holy Spirit. He is condemned for the sin of those whose guilt he bears: of the whole of humanity, as the head; and of the elect, whose sins are imputed to him in the condemnation of the Father.

Through Christ God offers righteousness to the children of men, and those whom God has chosen are conformed to the image of his Son. Because he bears

---

[76] 2 Pet. 2:4; Jude 1:6.

their sins, he is personally united to them; and being personally united to him, they also bear his righteousness. And because he is their righteousness, he not only justifies them, but also makes them partakers of the divine nature.[77]

Christ is born of Adam, yet righteous. His righteousness is original, and because he proceeds from Adam, he inherits Adam's original righteousness; yet as the Son of God, Christ has his righteousness from the Father. Therefore, the sin of Adam taking away his righteousness, has ever been preserved in the Son who precedes him. Through him the human race, having been made righteous, is made righteous again, a new creation. As Jacob supplanted Esau, and David Saul, so Jesus Christ supplanted Adam, and became the rightful head of humanity.[78]

> John bare witness of him, and cried, saying, This was he of whom I spake, He that cometh after me is preferred before me: for he was before me. John 1:15

> For since by man *came* death, by man *came* also the resurrection of the dead. For as in Adam all die, even so in Christ shall all be made alive. 1 Corinthians 15:21-22

> I Jesus have sent mine angel to testify unto you these things in the churches. I am the root and the offspring of David, and the bright and morning star. Revelation 22:16

Accordingly, if the human race forms an image of God, not merely a pattern for producing an image through obedience to the moral law, but the very image of his holiness: the human race must form a totality, in which lies the unity of one, and the guilt of the many imputed to him. The head is the one in whom all are gathered; the plurality thereof is the elect, divided from the reprobate; the totality thereof is humanity, by him reconciled to God.

---

[77] Is. 53:10-12; 2 Cor. 5:21.
[78] Gen. 25:19-34, 27:1-41; 1 Sam. 15:27-29, 18:12-16.

God elects part of humanity to salvation, and appoints the rest to destruction, for the divine likeness comes not through sin, but through the gift of God. Why then are some chosen to faith, and others left in unbelief? God is no less able to save those whom he destroys, but it does not follow that through him all might partake of the divine nature. Those whom God saves, he not only restores to righteousness, but endows them with the blessedness of his Son, for in that they are forgiven, they are also holy. A single offense makes void the law, but by forgiveness of sins the law is restored, and sin is no more. That same unity of law that renders sinners the servants of sin, also renders the repentant the servants of righteousness.

> For I *am* the LORD that bringeth you up out of the land of Egypt, to be your God: ye shall therefore be holy, for I *am* holy. Leviticus 11:45

> Know ye not, that to whom ye yield yourselves servants to obey, his servants ye are to whom ye obey; whether of sin unto death, or of obedience unto righteousness? But God be thanked, that ye were the servants of sin, but ye have obeyed from the heart that form of doctrine which was delivered you. Being then made free from sin, ye became the servants of righteousness. I speak after the manner of men because of the infirmity of your flesh: for as ye have yielded your members servants to uncleanness and to iniquity unto iniquity; even so now yield your members servants to righteousness unto holiness. For when ye were the servants of sin, ye were free from righteousness. What fruit had ye then in those things whereof ye are now ashamed? for the end of those things is death. But now being made free from sin, and become servants to God, ye have your fruit unto holiness, and the end everlasting life. Romans 6:16-22, cf. 2 Pet. 1:4

Those who are unable to bear the divine likeness are left in their sins, justly to be punished, for the end of their sin is to attain the divine likeness, and this they cannot receive; wherefore, neither do they believe, that they might be made like Christ.

> He that is of God heareth God's words: ye therefore hear *them* not, because ye are not of God. John 8:47

> *Even* the Spirit of truth; whom the world cannot receive, because it seeth him not, neither knoweth him: but ye know him; for he dwelleth with you, and shall be in you. John 14:17

Those whom God has chosen he saves in the same way they fell. They sinned that they might be like God; they are also persuaded to believe, that they might be like Christ. This they choose not for their own happiness, but as a necessary condition thereof, that they might repent for righteousness, as they find the end of their sin attained in Christ. Accordingly, those persons with whom lies the possibility of being clothed with the divine likeness find this end included in their sin, the end having been hidden therein, and as they have fallen into sin, so also they freely choose to believe. God restores men to righteousness by giving them the very blessedness that they sought by sin.

This is the difference between Adam and Christ: the totality of man in Adam is not distinct from the unity. The totality of man requires not only that the unity be thought within the plurality, but also the plurality within the unity. Hence Paul says, "And not as *it was* by one that sinned, *so is* the gift: for the judgment *was* by one to condemnation, but the free gift *is* of many offences unto justification" (Romans 5:16). Christ calls himself "the Son of man" because he is born of the whole human race, to bear the guilt of original sin.[79] It is a free gift, not the righteousness which is owed, but the righteousness of the Son, who overcomes all sin.[80] Though a Son, he came as a servant, for as a servant he was

---

[79] Is. 9:6.
[80] John 8:34-36.

under the law, and obeyed it; as a Son he was above it, and bore the sins of his people through the condemnation of the Father.[81]

Adam indeed is made in the image of God, but Jesus Christ is the image of God. Adam is a pattern for producing the image, Jesus Christ is the image itself. A pattern is a rule for producing an image.[82] The rule is the moral law. Man is blessed in his obedience to God's commandments. The image itself is the intuition of God's righteousness, identical in distinction: the Lord Jesus Christ, into whom all are gathered.[83]

There is another, the second Adam, the Lord Jesus Christ. As God is one, and as Adam, so also Jesus Christ is one.

> For *there is* one God, and one mediator between God and men, the man Christ Jesus; who gave himself a ransom for all, to be testified in due time. 1 Timothy 2:5-6

As Adam reveals the unity of the divine nature, Christ reveals the Trinity of divine persons.

> Let us make man in our image, after our likeness. Genesis 1:26

Let us, not only that man should be made in the image of the one God, but also that he should be made in the image of the Triune God.

Adam indeed is made in the image of God, but Jesus Christ is the image of God. Adam is the head of the human race by law and by flesh, because the absolute unity of the divine nature may not be torn asunder. Jesus Christ is the rightful head of humanity by grace, for that in him lies the ground of the transition from condemnation to justification, men are enabled to repent of their sins through faith in his name.

---

[81] Isaiah 53:6, 10.
[82] Kant, *Critique*, B176-187.
[83] Eph. 1:10-11.

The guilt of original sin is common to all men. Christ bears the guilt of original sin, yea, the very guilt of Adam, and of all his children, for so he is the seed of Abraham.

> Now to Abraham and his seed were the promises made. He saith not, And to seeds, as of many; but as of one, And to thy seed, which is Christ. Galatians 3:16

He says not, *as one*, but *as of one*, ως εφ ενός, for as Adam is one from whom many come, Christ is also one, and in him all his seed; not as Adam, whose guilt is imputed to all, but as Messiah, to whom the guilt of all is imputed, for the seed of Abraham is not blessed on account of Abraham, but Abraham is blessed on account of his seed. Neither does he say, "his children," but "his seed," for the seed is not the many, but the ground of the many in the one.

> Yet it pleased the LORD to bruise him; he hath put *him* to grief: when thou shalt make his soul an offering for sin, he shall see *his* seed, he shall prolong *his* days, and the pleasure of the Lord shall prosper in his hand. He shall see of the travail of his soul, *and* shall be satisfied: by his knowledge shall my righteous servant justify many; for he shall bear their iniquities. Therefore will I divide him *a portion* with the great, and he shall divide the spoil with the strong; because he hath poured out his soul unto death: and he was numbered with the transgressors; and he bare the sin of many, and made intercession for the transgressors. Isaiah 53:10-11

> Whosoever is born of God doth not commit sin; for his seed remaineth in him: and he cannot sin, because he is born of God. 1 John 3:9

Though deducible from the former doctrines, the appearance of our savior cannot be derived from human reason alone, because it presupposes sin, which has no interest therein.

That the headship of Christ derives from two distinct sources concerns the order of combination. In the first, the concepts are first combined and then represented in intuition; in the second, the concepts are first represented in intuition and then combined. The latter is only possible through former, the intuition through the concept. The significance whereof is this: Jesus Christ is a secret, a mystery, hidden of God, in the bosom of the Father.[84] No one can find Christ, save those to whom he reveals himself.[85] Nevertheless, man is free to conceive of his need of savior, and so repent of his sin, yet he cannot do so because he is unwilling. Having rejected righteousness, men implicitly reject Christ, and God may by degrees withhold from them the hearing of the Gospel, according to his wisdom.[86]

Nevertheless, if only they would recognize their sin and seek righteousness, they may yet search for a second Adam, and perhaps find him, through whom they may be saved. God has not left any without testimony, even by the commutation of immediate death, as also by the signs of his goodness, imbued with divine mercy for the sake of repentance, and by those practices which can only be lawful for the sake of a savior, as the sacrificing of animals throughout the world from time immemorial,[87] and the eating of meat.[88]

> Doth not wisdom cry? and understanding put forth her voice? She standeth in the top of high places, by the way in the places of the paths. She crieth at the gates, at the entry of the city, at the coming in at the doors. Proverbs 8:1-3

> Or despisest thou the riches of his goodness and forbearance and longsuffering; not knowing that the goodness of God leadeth thee to repentance? Romans 2:4

---

[84] Is. 49:2; John 1:18; Eph. 1:9-10, 3:8-11.
[85] Matt. 11:27; Luke 10:22.
[86] Prov. 9:7-9; Acts 17:30.
[87] Herodotus.
[88] Gen. 8:20-9:3.

Sirs, why do ye these things? We also are men of like passions with you, and preach unto you that ye should turn from these vanities unto the living God, which made heaven, and earth, and the sea, and all things that are therein: Who in times past suffered all nations to walk in their own ways. Nevertheless he left not himself without witness, in that he did good, and gave us rain from heaven, and fruitful seasons, filling our hearts with food and gladness. And with these sayings scarce restrained they the people, that they had not done sacrifice unto them. Acts 14:15-18

God that made the world and all things therein, seeing that he is Lord of heaven and earth, dwelleth not in temples made with hands; Neither is worshipped with men's hands, as though he needed any thing, seeing he giveth to all life, and breath, and all things; And hath made of one blood all nations of men for to dwell on all the face of the earth, and hath determined the times before appointed, and the bounds of their habitation; That they should seek the Lord, if haply they might feel after him, and find him, though he be not far from every one of us: For in him we live, and move, and have our being; as certain also of your own poets have said, For we are also his offspring. Forasmuch then as we are the offspring of God, we ought not to think that the Godhead is like unto gold, or silver, or stone, graven by art and man's device. And the times of this ignorance God winked at; but now commandeth all men every where to repent: Because he hath appointed a day, in the which he will judge the world in righteousness *by that* man whom he hath ordained; *whereof* he hath given assurance unto all *men*, in that he hath raised him from the dead. Acts 17:24-28

For even without a knowledge of the Gospel, men are commanded to repent, and promised life; howsoever unable, yet are they free.

But if the wicked will turn from all his sins that he hath committed,
and keep all my statutes, and do that which is lawful and right, he shall
surely live, he shall not die. All his transgressions that he hath
committed, they shall not be mentioned unto him: in his righteousness
that he hath done he shall live. Have I any pleasure at all that the
wicked should die? saith the Lord GOD: *and* not that he should return
from his ways, and live? Ezekiel 18:21-23, cf. 33:10-20

On Scripture

Christ is head of all men, yet is he only one man, born in the land of Israel,
under the reign of Imperial Rome. A universal representation of his person is
required, whereby all men may come to know of his salvation, in all times and
places. This is the doctrine of the word, for words are images of men, and of the
inner thoughts of the person.

For the word of God *is* quick, and powerful, and sharper than any
twoedged sword, piercing even to the dividing asunder of soul and
spirit, and of the joints and marrow, and *is* a discerner of the thoughts
and intents of the heart. Neither is there any creature that is not
manifest in his sight: but all things *are* naked and opened unto the eyes
of him with whom we have to do. Hebrews 4:12-13

This word is given in sensible intuition; it is an empirical doctrine, and
therefore not strictly universal. God may save whosoever he pleases, howsoever
he pleases, without the ordinary means, by regeneration and revelation of his
Son, who is the Word of God, immediately to the person;[89] and the human
person is able to receive this revelation and believe in Jesus Christ, according to
his reasonable need for a savior.[90]

---

[89] Matt. 11:27; Luke 10:22.
[90] Jas. 1:21.

The fundamental doctrines are absolutely certain; their truth proceeds from the concepts themselves. Therefore, the book that reveals them must also be the word of God. If there is a doctrine that may not be discovered by human reason, or by any reason but that of God, yet being revealed may be known through the very concept, then the revelation thereof must be from God.[91] Such is the problem of sin, that it may only be resolved through the divine persons revealed in the Lord Jesus Christ. Therefore, the word that reveals Christ is the word of God: the Scriptures of the Old and New Testaments.

The Scriptures of old were given to Israel and reserved to them, that all men might seek the Lord in the place that he should come;[92] but are now given to all men, that all might know that Jesus Christ has come in the flesh.[93]

Scripture Proof

In the work of redemption God makes men partakers of the divine nature, promising them to enter into the joy of their lord.[94] Though the church, and every member thereof, sinned in eating of the tree of knowledge of good and evil, and so brought death upon themselves, nevertheless they should not surely die, but rather be redeemed, and be as gods, knowing good and evil. The lies of the devil are retroactive promises of God to the church, to bring forth good from evil. Though the serpent meant them for evil, Christ fulfills them for their good.[95] It is Jesus Christ, the second Adam, who hearkened unto the voice of his wife, sinlessly took on her sins, and redeemed her by the blood of his face, following her unto hell, that he might bring her into heaven, of whose sufferings the church partakes until she is perfected, and Christ is formed in her children.[96]

---

[91] Ps. 92:5, 119:18; Is. 55:8-9; Jer. 33:3; Dan. 2:22.
[92] Matt. 2.
[93] 1 Tim. 2:4-6; *Westminster* 1.8.
[94] Matt. 25:21-23.
[95] Gen. 50:20.
[96] Gal. 4:19.

Genesis 3:14-24

And the LORD *God said unto the serpent,* the Lord does not inquire of the serpent, because he, being an angel, cannot repent of his sin; *Because thou hast done this, thou art cursed above all cattle, and above every beast of the field;* not because they were cursed before, but being blessed with man, they were also cursed with him. The serpent is cursed above them all, because through him the curse comes to all, for he represents wisdom and negation;[97] *upon thy belly shalt thou go, and dust shalt thou eat all the days of thy life:* the devil and his angels, though of superior intelligence, were deprived of their lawful offices, and live now by their appetite for men, and subsist in dependence on sensible intuition: *And I will put enmity between thee and the woman, and between thy seed and her seed;* yet are they opposed by those whom God has chosen out of mankind; the serpent himself is opposed; *it shall bruise thy head, and thou shalt bruise his heel.* The devil is broken and confounded by the mystery of salvation, because he brought death upon an innocent,[98] for the Lord Jesus Christ would suffer condemnation of God, and death at the hands of men, and bear the sin and curse of the world, and overcome the devil, to redeem for himself a people unto God, zealous for good works.[99] *Unto the woman he said, I will greatly multiply thy sorrow and thy conception;* because she conceives and bears children in sin; *in sorrow thou shalt bring forth children; and thy desire shall be to thy husband, and he shall rule over thee.* In many afflictions and persecutions the church brings forth children to God, to be conformed to the image of his Son. *And unto Adam he said, Because thou hast hearkened unto the voice of thy wife, and hast eaten of the tree, of which I commanded thee, saying, Thou shalt not eat of it:* he judges them for their disobedience, but not for the end thereof, to attain the divine likeness; *cursed is the ground for thy sake;* that symbol of holiness in obedience to God became the symbol of misery for sin; *in sorrow shalt thou eat of it all the days of thy life;* that he should willingly bear the curse of the land through the Lord Jesus Christ; *Thorns also and thistles shall*

---

[97] Matt. 10:16; 2 Cor. 11:3; Rev. 12:9-10, 20:2.
[98] Heb. 2:14-15.
[99] Tit. 2:14.

it bring forth to thee; it would bring forth evil as well as good, that we should receive both at the hand of God;[100] *and thou shalt eat the herb of the field;* to be to him a lesson of the law throughout the land;[101] *In the sweat of thy face shalt thou eat bread, till thou return unto the ground;* man's works would not yield to him life, but by bearing of the curse and obedience unto death; *for out of it wast thou taken:* having sinned not for its own sake, but at the behest of the devil; *for dust thou art, and unto dust shalt thou return.* Christ labored under many sorrows, to redeem man by the blood of his face, returning unto the dust, yet without corruption,[102] that he might rise again, the firstborn of a new creation. *And Adam called his wife's name Eve; because she was the mother of all living,* even of the Lord Jesus Christ, who lives, and was dead, and is alive forevermore, through whom all live to God and rise again.[103] *Unto Adam also and to his wife did the LORD God make coats of skins, and clothed them,* to clothe them with divine righteousness through the sacrifice of Christ. *And the LORD God said, Behold, the man is become as one of us, to know good and evil:* this forms no part of his judgment upon man, but of his wisdom for edification; *and now, lest he put forth his hand, and take also of the tree of life, and eat, and live for ever:* which he should not do by himself, but by Jesus Christ the Lord; *Therefore the LORD God sent him forth from the garden of Eden, to till the ground from whence he was taken,* that they should live, not by their own works, but by the one who bore the curse of their sin. *So he drove out the man;* against his will: having hid himself from the Lord, he now desired to stay, for he was made willing by Christ, through whom men both seek and attain the divine likeness; *and he placed at the east of the garden of Eden Cherubims, and a flaming sword which turned every way, to keep the way of the tree of life,* to show that whosoever seeks life by works should die and suffer hell. The way of life was not altogether cut off, but preserved for the one worthy to pass by the flaming sword, and to walk with angels.

---

[100] Job 2:10.
[101] Ex. 12:8.
[102] Ps. 16:10.
[103] Rev. 1:18, cf. Luke 20:38; 1 Cor. 15:20-22.

Romans 5:12-21

Paul is the last of the apostles, "not meet to be called an apostle, because [he] persecuted the church of God" (1 Corinthians 15:9). He shows forth the necessity of conversion from sin to righteousness, which is only possible through faith in Christ, and therefore it pertains to him to speak of Christ's headship over the whole human race, as "the gospel of the uncircumcision" was committed to him (Gal. 2:7).

Wherefore, as by one man sin entered into the world, and death by sin; and so death passed upon all men, for that all have sinned: though every man sins for himself, yet because of the unity of the human race, the sin of Adam passes to all through the imputation of his guilt. ἐφ ᾧ: "in whom all have sinned," (Geneva Bible). *(For until the law sin was in the world: but sin is not imputed when there is no law,* for there is a law whereby all in Adam partake of his guilt, and by that same law they are redeemed in Christ. *Nevertheless death reigned from Adam to Moses, even over them that had not sinned after the similitude of Adam's transgression, who is the figure of him that was to come.* Without the law of Moses there is the moral law instituted in the covenant of works, which requires that Adam's descendants partake of the guilt of original sin, though they ate not of the forbidden fruit. *But not as the offence, so also is the free gift,* not a debt, but a gift. *For if through the offence of one many be dead, much more the grace of God, and the gift by grace, which is by one man,* in whom lies the harmony of diverse judgments; *Jesus Christ, hath abounded unto many,* to take away their sins, and to bestow upon them a righteousness greater than all sin, and also to angels. *And not as it was by one that sinned, so is the gift: for the judgment was by one to condemnation, but the free gift is of many offences unto justification.* God imputed the guilt of Adam's sin to his descendants, but to Christ the sins of the elect, that he might also impute to his righteousness. *For if by one man's offence death reigned by one; much more they which receive abundance of grace and of the gift of righteousness shall reign in life by one, Jesus Christ.)* By the same rule that they are condemned, by that rule also are they saved. *Therefore as by the offence of one judgment came upon all men to condemnation;*

even so by the righteousness of one the free gift came upon all men unto justification of life, for by grace Christ is the head of the human race, as Adam by the flesh, that all may be saved, whosoever believes in him. *For as by one man's disobedience many were made sinners, so by the obedience of one shall many be made righteous*, because Christ submitted himself to the condemnation of the Father, wherein the sins of the elect are imputed to him. *Moreover the law entered, that the offence might abound.* If through the law sin offends, then through the revelation of the law sin is aggravated. *But where sin abounded, grace did much more abound:* because the law was not given to condemn us, but that we might be saved, for grace covers sin, and adds righteousness divine. *That as sin hath reigned unto death, even so might grace reign through righteousness unto eternal life by Jesus Christ our Lord.* Because Christ is as much and more the head of mankind by grace, as Adam is by the flesh.

The Betrayal of Judas

Judas is the last of the twelve apostles; therefore, he must represent necessity. The apostles and prophets are the foundation of the church, Jesus Christ himself being the chief cornerstone.[104] They represent the whole foundation of the church in the person of Jesus Christ, and stand in his place.[105] There being twelve apostles, their names given in order,[106] each one must represent a category, and the last of all categories is necessity.

God is glorified in the salvation of sinners, but the necessary condition thereof is sin. Therefore, Judas represents the necessity of sin for the glory of God. That sin being taken away, Matthias is chosen in his place, and Paul is added, to show the necessity of conversion from sin to righteousness, illustrated by the salvation of the Gentiles.[107]

---

[104] Eph. 2:20.
[105] Matt. 10:40; John 13:20; Gal. 4:14; 2 Cor. 5:20.
[106] Matt. 10:2-4; Luke 6:13-15.
[107] Eph. 2:11-18; Col. 2:11-15.

By God the Father Christ is unconditionally condemned, wherein there lies a division between those whose sins are imputed to Christ, and those who are passed over. Wherefore, the divine image in man requires that one part of the race be damned, to show forth the wrath of God for sin, and his mercy to the elect. Thus he puts a difference between the seed of the woman and the seed of the serpent.

They are all the seed of Adam, but some are the seed of the woman, others the seed of the serpent. Because the guilt of original sin is transmitted from father to son, the devil tempting the father tempts also the son, bringing both to ruin, and those foreordained to persevere in their sin are called his seed.[108] Nevertheless, those who sin for the sake of the divine likeness, not with invisible contempt, but with a secret and transcendent hope to be like God,[109] these are the seed of the woman, having as it were a cloak for their sin, which is Christ.[110]

The head of Satan is his rule and authority, his reason and rational nature, which is confounded by the mystery of salvation, for what the devil sought by sin, God reveals in righteousness. The heel of Christ is his weaker part, upon which he walks, his essence, for he should be sanctified by sufferings. Accordingly, the reprobate are destroyed, but the elect are lifted up. This is signified by the person of Judas. Judas hanged himself, but the Lord Jesus Christ

---

[108] John 8:44, 47.
[109] 2 Tim. 1:9.
[110] John 15:22, 18:37.

was crucified. Judas condemned himself; Jesus was condemned by the Father, and justified by the Holy Spirit.

"Yea, mine own familiar friend, in whom I trusted, which did eat of my bread, hath lifted up *his* heel against me" (Ps. 41:9; John 13:18). *His heel*, that peculiar essence of his, which ought to have been subjected to his maker. Having walked with Christ, he sitting with him would not be at rest, but plotted against him, and the wrestlings of his conscience betrayed themselves in his body.

The beloved is condemned by the lover, and this is signified by the betrayal of Judas. It is not lawful in the unity of his person, but only in the three who are one. Nor did Judas act of himself, but of the devil, and so the devil himself was bruised in the head, condemning himself, and justifying Christ.

> For *it was* not an enemy *that* reproached me; then I could have borne *it*: neither *was it* he that hated me *that* did magnify *himself* against me; then I would have hid myself from him: But *it was* thou, a man mine equal, my guide, and mine acquaintance. We took sweet counsel together, *and* walked unto the house of God in company. Psalm 55:12-14

Thus, the betrayal of Judas signifies the whole of Christ's sufferings on our behalf. That agony, having begun in the garden, comes to pass through the hand of Judas, who gave the Lord into the hands of the rulers, and because they unlawfully arrested the Son of man, the whole of his trial, religious and civil, lies in the righteous hand of God, for the sins of others, even of those who sought his life.

> All we like sheep have gone astray; we have turned every one to his own way; and the LORD hath laid on him the iniquity of us all. Isaiah 53:6

The betrayal of Judas signifies the condemnation of the Father, wherein some men's sins are imputed to Christ, and others not imputed to Christ, because Christ was not condemned for his own sin, but for the sins of others.

Christ is freely offered to all, yet he puts a division between those who believe, and those who do not believe.

Again, the betrayal of Judas signifies the division between the righteous and the wicked: the righteous in Christ their head, and the wicked in the devil, their head. Judas is called "the son of perdition," because he is born to destruction, yet is he a son, and he is the head of all the wicked, because in him is wickedness made perfect (John 17:12; cf. Matt. 26:24),[111] for that same name is given unto the Antichrist.[112]

The unity and invisibility of God are doctrines accessible to human reason. Christ inherits both the righteousness of the one and the guilt of the many through his mother. Accordingly, there is no historical event to manifest these doctrines distinctly in the Lord Jesus Christ, but in Adam only, whom the Lord, though prior, succeeds. Therefore, neither is there any historical event for the totality of man in Christ Jesus, for what is lacking to the elements of the combination is also lacking to the combination itself.

Nevertheless, there are signs illustrative of these doctrines, because the intuition contains within itself the particular, for the intuition remains particular to the concept. To the unity of the human nature, Christ adds the unity of the divine; though common in concept with Adam, it is distinguished in intuition. Accordingly, the Gospels record the beginning of Christ's agony in the garden of Gethsemane, whereby he is prepared for death. Likewise, they reveal the temptation in the wilderness, whereby he is sanctified for his ministry. Lastly, they record the betrayal of Judas, wherein the whole ground of Christ's torments on our behalf is signified.

The sufferings of Christ show the identity in distinction of his righteousness and blessedness. They contain, first, the identity, demonstrated in his agony in the garden; second, the distinction, shown forth in his temptation; third, the identity in distinction, manifested in the betrayal of Judas, for the condemnation of the Father is nought but the pouring out of his love upon the Son, that he might be like himself.

---

[111] Aquinas, *Summa* 3.8.7-8.
[112] 2 Thess. 2:3.

This sign is recorded in every Gospel because it is the ground of the whole of Christ's suffering for us, for the condemnation of the Father is the fount of every grace given us in Christ: the law embodied, affirmation from negation, the only begotten Son, the blessedness of God.

The betrayal of Judas consists of the opportunity, whereby the chief priests sought to apprehend Christ secretly, lest there be an uproar among the people; the motive, money; the occasion, when he saw the ointment of great value poured out upon Christ, for he was a thief; the allegiance betrayed, which, besides the whole of Judas' discipling with Christ, is expressed chiefly in his partaking of the passover, but not of the Lord's Supper; of the means, his knowledge that Christ oft resorted to the garden of Gethsemane with his disciples; of the sign, which is the kiss; and of the act, when he came with many to arrest Christ secretly in the garden.

The sign itself is divided into intention and act, for these are the elements of the crime. The other aspects are distributed amongst the signs, to be discussed in their places, but these are given places of their own. After Judas partook of the passover, he went out from the midst of the disciples, and that by the permission of Christ, because the condemnation of the Father is propitiated by the submission of the Son. Then follows the Lord's Supper, because it is the will of God to save sinners through the sacrifice of Christ.

John 13:18-35

I speak not of you all: I know whom I have chosen: but that the scripture may be fulfilled, a moral necessity; *He that eateth bread with me hath lifted up his heel against me. Now I tell you before it come, that, when it is come to pass, ye may believe that I am he,* a sign. *Verily, verily, I say unto you, He that receiveth whomsoever I send receiveth me;* the apostles and prophets being the foundation of the church; *and he that receiveth me receiveth him that sent me,* "Jesus Christ himself being the chief corner stone" (Ephesians 2:20). *When Jesus had thus said, he was troubled in spirit, and testified, and said, Verily, verily, I say unto you, that one of you shall betray me,* for it must be so, to bring forth salvation from sin. *Then the disciples looked one on another, doubting of whom he spake. Now there was leaning on Jesus' bosom one of his disciples,* for the disciples of Christ lean on his bosom, and he leans on the bosom of the Father, and his disciples with him;[113] *whom Jesus loved,* the one distinguished by this mark, for he loved them all. *Simon Peter therefore beckoned to him, that he should ask who it should be of whom he spake. He then lying on Jesus' breast saith unto him, Lord, who is it? Jesus answered, He it is, to whom I shall give a sop, when I have dipped it.* To show them in a sign, which they did not understand, though it be told them. *And when he had dipped the sop, he gave it to Judas Iscariot, the son of Simon. And after the sop Satan entered into him,* by the special permission of God, that Satan himself should be bruised in the head by the seed of the woman. *Then said Jesus unto him, That thou doest, do quickly,* that the will of God be fulfilled without delay. *Now no man at the table knew for what intent he spake this unto him,* a sign. *For some of them thought, because Judas had the bag, that Jesus had said unto him, Buy those things that we have need of against the feast; or, that he should give something to the poor. He then having received the sop went immediately out: and it was night,* in the darkness of condemnation. *Therefore, when he was gone out, Jesus said, Now is the Son of man glorified, and God is glorified in him,* glorified in his submission to the condemnation of the Father. *If God be glorified in him, God shall also glorify him in himself, and shall straightway glorify him.* They shall be glorified in one another by the justification of the Holy Spirit. *Little children, yet a little while I am with you. Ye shall seek me: and as I said unto the Jews, Whither I go, ye cannot come;* which the disciples have in common with the world; *so now I say to you. A new commandment I give unto you,* identical in distinction to the old; *That ye love one another; as I have loved you, that ye also love one another,* yet do they know him by obedience to his commandments. *By this shall all men know that ye are my disciples, if ye have love one to another,* and the world itself knows him by the obedience of his people, for he afterward ascended into heaven, to work his salvation in their hearts. *Simon Peter said unto him, Lord, whither goest thou? Jesus answered him, Whither I go, thou canst not follow me now; but thou shalt follow me afterwards.* Christ must first suffer alone, that his disciples might suffer with him, that he should lead them into the holy place. *Peter said unto him, Lord, why cannot*

---

[113] John 1:18.

I follow thee now? I will lay down my life for thy sake, within him lay the will to obey, but not the power to fulfill his intention. *Jesus answered him, Wilt thou lay down thy life for my sake? Verily, verily, I say unto thee, The cock shall not crow, till thou hast denied me thrice*, because Christ alone is righteous, and he must suffer alone for his people, that they might partake of his righteousness.

Matthew 26:47-58

And while he yet spake, the immediate judgment of God, whereunto he had been prepared by his agony in the garden; *lo, Judas, one of the twelve*, a friend and a lover; *came, and with him*, at the head; *a great multitude*, not of the whole people, but of a part only; *with swords and staves from the chief priests and elders of the people*, who ruled Israel of old by the will of God. *Now he that betrayed him*, for there is but one traitor; *gave them a sign*, of his own design, to show the will of God; *saying, Whomsoever I shall kiss, that same is he*: for he knew him even in the darkness of night; *hold him fast*. In Mark, he says "Whomsoever I shall kiss, that same is he; take him, and lead *him* away safely," for he was not without natural affection to him, and Jesus would submit himself to the condemnation of the Father (14:44). *And forthwith he came to Jesus, and said, Hail, master; and kissed him*, for in love the Father condemns the Son; *And Jesus said unto him, Friend, wherefore art thou come?* Judas knew not the mystery of God to be accomplished through himself. Luke reads, "But Jesus said unto him, Judas, betrayest thou the Son of man with a kiss?" for he understood not the sign (22:48). *Then came they, and laid hands on Jesus, and took him*, for he was not condemned by himself, nor lawfully by man, but by God the Father only. *And, behold, one of them which were with Jesus stretched out his hand*, to act by his own power, whose name is withheld for grace, because it was not his hour; *and drew his sword, and struck a servant of the high priest's, and smote off his ear*, to judge their deafness. *Then said Jesus unto him, Put up again thy sword into his place*: for there is indeed a place for the sword; *for all they that take the sword shall perish with the sword*, but neither Jesus nor his apostles ought to have died in lawful combat, but in persecution for the glory of God. Luke: "And Jesus answered and said, Suffer ye thus far." Not by the will of man, but of God. "And he touched his ear, and healed him," that no harm be done, nor vengeance sought, nor that Christ should be taken for the zeal of Peter,[114] but that even the enemies of Christ should hear the word of salvation (22:51). *Thinkest thou that I cannot now pray to my Father, and he shall presently give me more than twelve legions of angels?* for by his work he should procure the sons of men to be angels of his own. *But how then shall the scriptures be fulfilled, that thus it must be?* That he should submit to the condemnation of the Father, for he himself is the Word of God, whose glory is manifest. *In that same hour said Jesus to the multitudes, Are ye come out as against a thief with swords and staves for to take me?* "Who thought it not robbery to be equal with God" (Philippians 2:6), but they sought to rob God of his likeness, and for envy slew his only begotten Son. *I sat daily with you teaching in the temple, and ye laid no hold on me,* that Christ should be condemned in private, by divine privilege. *But all this was done, that the scriptures of the prophets might be fulfilled,* that the moral law should be fulfilled in him. In Luke, "When I was daily with you in the temple, ye stretched forth no hands against me," for they feared the people, without whom no crime may be prosecuted, "but this is your hour, and the power of darkness" (22:53). He suffers their sin, not for their sake only, but for the glory of God above. *Then all the disciples forsook him, and fled,* that Christ alone should be glorified therein, for they could not submit with him, unless after him. *And they that had laid hold on Jesus led him away to Caiaphas the high priest, where the scribes and the elders were assembled,* the will of the Father fulfilled by his appointed instruments. In John, "Then the band and the captain and officers of the Jews took Jesus, and bound him, And led him away to Annas first; for he was father-in-law to Caiaphas, which was the high priest that same year" (John 18:12-13). They went to one who might influence the high priest, that Christ should be put to death for the sake of a woman, even his church, the bride of the true high priest. "Now Caiaphas was he, which gave counsel to the Jews, that it was expedient that one man should die for the people" (John 18:14). By him his own prophecy comes to pass, to show that the true prophet and the end of all prophecy is also the true high priest. Caiaphas is here named to show that it is not of man, but of God,

---

[114] John 18:10.

for the high priest is anointed by the Lord.[115] *But Peter followed him afar off unto the high priest's palace, and went in, and sat with the servants, to see the end*, that he might truly confess, not himself, but Christ, whose servant he is.

---

[115] Ex. 28:43-29:1, 29-31, 44, 40:9, 12-16; Lev. 21:10-12.

The legal states conceptualize Christ's relation to the law. Each one thinks an intuition manifesting a relation. These intuitions are subjective, and inhere in the divine persons, whose judgments they are, yet there remains within each the ground of an intuition distinct from the concept. The intuition for the concept of a human person lies in the union of the soul with the body. Therefore, the judgments of the divine persons are manifested in the life of Christ. To his innocence belongs life and resurrection; to his condemnation, death; and to his nonlegal righteousness, burial.

The condemnation of Christ abides forever, yet by his submission thereunto, the wrath of God passes away from him, and the guilt of original sin is dissolved, because he is simultaneously justified by the Holy Spirit,[188] through whom the condemnation of the Father is transformed into a crown of glory and honor.[189] By the temporal schema,[190] the divine persons are represented distinctly in sensible intuition, and the historical intuitions are ordered in time: death, burial, resurrection.

To the actuality of a thing belongs, *first*, the knowledge of its possibility; *second*, the causality whereby it comes to pass; for by the causality of a thing its substance is revealed, and by its effects it is known. For his obedience unto death, God rewards Jesus with life, whereby he reveals the possibility of salvation to men, and so saves men by his work, for therein the righteous demands of God's law are satisfied in the head on behalf of all the members.

---

[188] Ps. 30:3, 5, 11; Matt. 26:39.
[189] Heb. 2:9.
[190] Kant *Critique,* B176-187.

The Resurrection of Jesus

Reality is plurality within unity. The plurality of man's nature belongs to the body; the unity thereof, to the soul; and in the righteousness of the soul lies the ground of their union. This union is of God, who gives to man his spirit. *Life* is therefore the union of the soul with the body, the causality of the thinking subject to produce an intuition in agreement with his essence. Angels have a life transcendent;[191] animals, purely natural; but in men, the one naturally expresses the other.[192] And the life of Christ manifests the life of God.

The life of man contains the affirmation of his person, that is, of his innocence. The person is the subject of thought, the ground of the concept of an object. Therefore, the life of man is that whereby he brings to pass the object of his will; it is the causality of the will itself. However, because the life of Jesus contains within itself the identity in distinction of God's righteousness and blessedness, Jesus not only lives, but rises from the dead.

> Concerning his Son Jesus Christ our Lord, which was made of the seed of David according to the flesh; And declared *to be* the Son of God with power, according to the spirit of holiness, by the resurrection from the dead. Romans 1:3-4

The innocence of Christ simultaneously represents his human and divine righteousness: affirmation and infinity, identical in distinction. Therefore, their union must also be represented through their separation: the intuition of their identity, together with the intuition of their distinction. They must form a plurality through separation of the parts, that in their reunion they may represent identity in distinction, because the resurrection contains within itself, in past time, the intuition of their distinction. Hence he says,

---

[191] Aquinas, *Summa* 1.50.1-2, 5.
[192] *Summa* 1.50.1.

I *am* he that liveth, and was dead, and behold, I am alive forevermore. Revelation 1:18

O LORD my God, I cried unto thee, and thou hast healed me. O LORD, thou hast brought up my soul from the grave: thou hast kept me alive, that I should not go down to the pit. Psalm 30:2-3

If the just shall live, and Christ obeys unto death, then life from death is his reward.[193] This joy exceeds the first, wherein all sorrow is turned into joy.

I have set the LORD always before me: because *he is* at my right hand, I shall not be moved. Therefore my heart is glad, and my glory rejoiceth: my flesh also shall rest in hope. For thou wilt not leave my soul in hell; neither wilt thou suffer thine Holy One to see corruption. Thou wilt shew me the path of life: in thy presence *is* fulness of joy; at thy right hand *there are* pleasures for evermore. Psalm 16:8-11

Thou hast turned for me my mourning into dancing: thou hast put off my sackcloth, and girded me with gladness; To the end that *my* glory may sing praise to thee, and not be silent. O Lord my God, I will give thanks unto thee forever. Psalm 30:11-12

In the resurrection, the divinity of Christ manifests itself fully in his humanity. His human will, perfectly sanctified in death, is bodily realized in the resurrection, and he receives the full reward of his work, the salvation of his people, so that by his life eternal, he raises up the dead. In his obedience unto death, he bore the sins of humanity, and proved himself to be their rightful head,[194] that they might partake of his life.[195]

-----

193 Aquinas, *Summa* 3.53.1.
194 1 Cor. 15:20.
195 Phil. 3:10-11; 1 Pet. 1:3, 3:21.

> I am the resurrection, and the life: he that believeth in me, though he were dead, yet shall he live: And whosoever liveth and believeth in me shall never die. John 11:25-26

> I *am* he that liveth, and was dead; and, behold, I am alive for evermore, Amen; and have the keys of hell and of death. Revelation 1:18

The resurrection is absolutely certain because it is manifests the glory of the Triune God in the salvation of sinners.

> Then he said unto them, O fools, and slow of heart to believe all that the prophets have spoken: Ought not Christ to have suffered these things, and to enter into his glory? Luke 24:25-26

> And he said unto them, These *are* the words which I spake unto you, while I was yet with you, that all things must be fulfilled, which were written in the law of Moses, and *in* the prophets, and *in* the psalms, concerning me. Then opened he their understanding, that they might understand the scriptures, And said unto them, Thus it is written, and thus it behoved Christ to suffer, and to rise from the dead the third day: And that repentance and remission of sins should be preached in his name among all nations, beginning at Jerusalem. And ye are witnesses of these things. Luke 24:46-48

Jesus Christ is the rightful head of humanity, to be glorified in all its members, for because he reveals the divine nature to men, yea, he himself is God manifest in the flesh, he is their divine head, through whom they have righteousness. Therefore, as Christ is raised from the dead, so also the whole of humanity, because in him lies the union of every man's soul with his body,[196] and the distinction in man is ever enveloped in identity: even in the wicked, and how much more in the righteous?

---

[196] Aquinas, *Summa* 3.56.2, Supp. 75.1-2, 76.1.

Marvel not at this: for the hour is coming, in the which all that are in the graves shall hear his voice, And shall come forth; they that have done good, unto the resurrection of life; and they that have done evil, unto the resurrection of damnation. John 5:28-29

For as in Adam all die, even so in Christ shall all be made alive. 1 Corinthians 15:22

In him is "justification of life" to all, even to those who are damned, "*that every tongue should confess that Jesus Christ is Lord, to the glory of God the Father*" (Rom. 5:18, Phil. 2:11).

For in death *there is* no remembrance of thee: in the grave who shall give thee thanks? Psalm 6:5

All *they that be* fat upon earth shall eat and worship: all they that go down to the dust shall bow before him: and none can keep alive his own soul. Psalm 22:29

What profit *is there* in my blood, when I go down to the pit? Shall the dust praise thee? shall it declare thy truth? Psalm 30:9

For the grave cannot praise thee, death can *not* celebrate thee: they that go down into the pit cannot hope for thy truth. The living, the living, he shall praise thee, as I *do* this day: the father to the children shall make known thy truth. The LORD *was ready* to save me: therefore we will sing my songs to the stringed instruments all the days of our life in the house of the LORD. Isaiah 38:18-20

The sufferings of the damned show forth the condemnation of sin, not for the sake of sin, but for the glory of the Father, who has passed over them in the condemnation of his beloved Son, and the knowledge of the Trinity gives life to their bodies.

> Verily, verily, I say unto you, The hour is coming, and now is, when the dead shall hear the voice of the Son of God: and they that hear shall live. For as the Father hath life in himself; so hath he given to the Son to have life in himself; And hath given him authority to execute judgment also, because he is the Son of man. Marvel not at this: for the hour is coming, in the which all that are in the graves shall hear his voice, And shall come forth; they that have done good, unto the resurrection of life; and they that have done evil, unto the resurrection of damnation. John 5:25-29

That their damnation should not only be for their sin, but to show forth the punishment deserved by all, and his mercy to the elect, and the sufferings of Christ on their behalf.[197]

> The wicked *shall be* a ransom for the righteous, and the transgressor for the upright. Proverbs 21:18

> For I *am* the LORD thy God, the Holy One of Israel, thy Saviour: I gave Egypt *for* thy ransom, Ethiopia and Seba for thee. Since thou wast precious in my sight, thou hast been honourable, and I have loved thee: therefore will I give men for thee, and people for thy life. Isaiah 43:3-4

> Even as the Son of man came not to be ministered unto, but to minister, and to give his life a ransom for many. Matthew 20:28, cf. Mark 10:45

The resurrection is the beginning of a new creation. The old creation is life from the dust; the new is life from death, for in death the body returns to the dust, whence also it is raised. Wherefore, in the resurrection God makes man

---

[197] Rom. 9:23.

anew, and for him a new creation to inhabit. Having made men in original righteousness, he makes them again when he restores them to righteousness and adds to them righteousness divine.[198]

> And the sea gave up the dead which were in it; and death and hell delivered up the dead which were in them: and they were judged every man according to their works. And death and hell were cast into the lake of fire. This is the second death. And whosoever was not found written in the book of life was cast into the lake of fire. And I saw a new heaven and a new earth: for the first heaven and the first earth were passed away; and there was no more sea. Revelation 20:13-21:1

For this reason also, there is a change of the Sabbath to the first day, because he is "the light of life," the light of a person, giving life (John 8:12, cf. 1:4). In his life lies the whole purpose of man, for he lives unto God,[199] and in his resurrection he rests in his work.[200]

Scripture Proofs

The office of an apostle is to bear witness to the resurrection, for this is the foundation of the church.

> Wherefore of these men which have companied with us all the time that the Lord Jesus went in and out among us, Beginning from the baptism of John, unto that same day that he was taken up from us, must one be ordained to be a witness with us of his resurrection. Acts 1:21-22

---

[198] 2 Pet. 1:4.
[199] Rom. 6:10-11.
[200] Heb. 4.

> And are built upon the foundation of the apostles and prophets, Jesus
> Christ himself being the chief corner *stone*; Ephesians 2:20, cf. Acts 2:32-
> 36

The life of man is not a specific event, but a general truth of his existence; it is a universal doctrine of his nature: the reward for his obedience. Life is the causality of a rational being, inhering in the person, who is permanent. Nevertheless, the resurrection is an event because it contains within itself, in past time, the state of death, and the transition to life. The resurrection is the life of Christ itself, whereby he rises from the dead, and shows us the way of eternal life.

Matthew 28:1-20

In the end of the sabbath, as the end of the old creation; *as it began to dawn toward the first day of the week*, as the beginning of the new; *came Mary Magdalene and the other Mary to see the sepulchre*, from virgin birth to death, from death to burial, and from burial to resurrection. *And, behold, there was a great earthquake:* the removal of the old; *for the angel of the Lord descended from heaven*, as Christ himself, for in him the angels are revealed; *and came and rolled back the stone from the door, and sat upon it*, as the judgment of God, who rules over death and hell. *His countenance was like lightning, and his raiment white as snow*: like unto Christ, for the angels are glorified with Christ through the knowledge of the divine persons and their ministry to the saints;[201] *And for fear of him the keepers did shake, and became as dead men.* The living shall praise God, though dead. *And the angel answered and said unto the women, Fear not ye*: for the grace of God relieves the fear that it inspires in the hearts of sinners; *for I know that ye seek Jesus, which was crucified*, his resurrection containing, in past time, the state of death. *He is not here: for he is risen*, the angels are witnesses of the resurrection, which no man was fit to see;[202] *as he said*, that they might believe after. *Come, see the place where*

---

[201] Heb. 2:14.

[202] Aquinas, *Summa* 3.55.2.

the Lord lay. God buries the old creation in Christ with honor, for a testimony to his resurrection. *And go quickly, and tell his disciples that he is risen from the dead;* that the faithful women should be the first to testify to the resurrection, that the apostles should walk by faith, not by sight,[203] as the women who saw in him the blessedness of God, and received the testimony from angels; *and, behold, he goeth before you into Galilee; there shall ye see him:* as he lived there, so there they should see him raised; *lo, I have told you. And they departed quickly from the sepulchre with fear and great joy;* being overwhelmed with the good news, and trembling for joy;[204] *and did run to bring his disciples word.* They eagerly obeyed for joy. *And as they went to tell his disciples, behold, Jesus met them, saying, All hail.* As they believed the angel with their ears, so they saw Christ with their eyes, that they should bear witness to his majesty. *And they came and held him by the feet, and worshipped him,* his divine nature fully manifest in the flesh. *Then said Jesus unto them, Be not afraid: go tell my brethren,* who are to be raised with him;[205] *that they go into Galilee, and there shall they see me,* who is the beginning and the end, that they should see him at the last, as they saw him at the first. *Now when they were going, behold, some of the watch came into the city, and shewed unto the chief priests all the things that were done,* their hearts not being transformed by grace. *And when they were assembled with the elders, and had taken counsel, they gave large money unto the soldiers, Saying, Say ye, His disciples came by night, and stole him away while we slept.* They knew the facts, but not the truth, and so denied the facts for the truth revealed, to their own condemnation. *And if this come to the governor's ears, we will persuade him, and secure you.* One sin begets another. *So they took the money, and did as they were taught: and this saying is commonly reported among the Jews until this day,* whereby even they testify to his resurrection by their manifest falsehoods. *Then the eleven disciples went away into Galilee, into a mountain where Jesus had appointed them,* there to reveal his holiness. *And when they saw him, they worshipped him: but some doubted.* They ought not to believe by sight, but by word, that they might preach to others what they themselves having seen, doubted. *And Jesus came and spake*

---

[203] 2 Cor. 5:7.
[204] Jer. 33:9.
[205] Rom. 8:29.

unto them, saying, All power is given unto me in heaven and in earth. The second Adam, the Lord from heaven.[206] *Go ye therefore, and teach all nations,* that they might be the children of Abraham;[207] *baptizing them in the name of the Father, and of the Son, and of the Holy Ghost:* because in Christ all the divine persons are revealed to men; *Teaching them,* teaching those who are baptized, and baptizing those who are taught; *to observe all things whatsoever I have commanded you:* that he should be with us in our obedience; *and, lo, I am with you alway,* for he is ever with us in his Spirit; *even unto the end of the world,* for as he would soon ascend into heaven, so also he would quickly return from heaven to earth, delayed only by the mercy of God to men, that they might repent.[208] *Amen.* That from his resurrection the church should receive life through the Gospel.

Mark 16:1-14

And when the sabbath was past, Mary Magdalene, and Mary the mother of James, and Salome, had bought, beforehand, to keep the sabbath; *sweet spices, that they might come and anoint him,* they thought to anoint him again,[209] to consecrate his burial in their hearts, for his burial shows forth his perfect sanctification in the flesh, and this is repeated in his resurrection. *And very early in the morning the first day of the week, they came unto the sepulchre at the rising of the sun.* They came as early as the commandment of God permitted, and the light allowed, for they were eager to do his will. *And they said among themselves, Who shall roll us away the stone from the door of the sepulchre?* They came in faith, not knowing how it should be, nor his resurrection already accomplished. *And when they looked, they saw that the stone was rolled away: for it was very great.* It came to pass as they trusted in God, to do his will. *And entering into the sepulchre, they saw a young man sitting on the right side, clothed in a long white garment;* an angel, a witness to the resurrection, and a fellow partaker of glory; *and they were affrighted,* the Gospel calls to mind our sins, that they may be washed away by the blood of Christ.

---

[206] 1 Cor. 15:47.
[207] Gen. 17:4-5.
[208] 2 Pet. 3:8-9; Rev. 22:20.
[209] John 19:39-40.

And he saith unto them, Be not affrighted: Ye seek Jesus of Nazareth, they sought not the body of the Lord, but the Lord himself; *which was crucified: he is risen; he is not here: behold the place where they laid him,* that by steps they might believe that God had raised him from the dead, and that as a necessary consequence of his burial. *But go your way, tell his disciples and Peter,* whom he names specifically, to show that he is included in his mercy, that he should not despair; *that he goeth before you into Galilee: there shall ye see him, as he said unto you,* that the faith of the apostles might rest in the blessedness of the Son. *And they went out quickly, and fled from the sepulchre; for they trembled and were amazed: neither said they any thing to any man; for they were afraid,* for the grace of God is astonishing to the senses. *Now when Jesus was risen early,* immediately to fulfill the will of God; *the first day of the week,* the beginning of a new creation, wherein there is rest from the old; *he appeared first to Mary Magdalene, out of whom he had cast seven devils,* that the resurrection might be sure to those who are saved thereby. *And she went and told them that had been with him, as they mourned and wept,* for they yet believed in Jesus. *And they, when they had heard that he was alive, and had been seen of her, believed not,* yet they ought to have believed the word of witnesses for the glory revealed. *After that he appeared in another form unto two of them, as they walked, and went into the country. And they went and told it unto the residue: neither believed they them,* to test them, if they should believe the word of two of their men. *Afterward he appeared unto the eleven as they sat at meat, and upbraided them with their unbelief and hardness of heart, because they believed not them which had seen him after he was risen,* for how should they convince others, if they believed not the word of witnesses? Nevertheless, our faith rests not on the faith of the apostles, but on the blessedness of Christ, whom they saw and preached.

Luke 24:1-49

Now upon the first day of the week, very early in the morning, they came unto the sepulchre, bringing the spices which they had prepared, beforehand, to keep the sabbath, that they might anoint the body afterward; *and certain others with them. And they found the stone rolled away from the sepulchre,* the gates of death being shattered. *And they entered in, and found not the body of the Lord Jesus,* to show them their need for revelation. *And it came to pass, as they were much perplexed thereabout, behold, two men stood by them in shining garments:* in works of light, for they are angels: witnesses of the resurrection, and fellow partakers of his glory; *And as they were afraid, and bowed down their faces to the earth, they said unto them, Why seek ye the living among the dead?* They understood not through their own reason, yet once revealed to them, they knew the resurrection of Jesus through its apodictic truth. *He is not here, but is risen: remember how he spake unto you when he was yet in Galilee, Saying, The Son of man must be delivered into the hands of sinful men, and be crucified, and the third day rise again.* It was told them beforehand, that they might understand its necessity afterward. *And they remembered his words, And returned from the sepulchre, and told all these things unto the eleven, and to all the rest,* the blessedness of God testified by the image of his blessedness. *It was Mary Magdalene, and Joanna, and Mary the mother of James, and other women that were with them, which told these things unto the apostles,* that they might have opportunity to believe for the sake of the Son, the very blessedness of God. *And their words seemed to them as idle tales, and they believed them not.* The gospel is, to the natural man, neither comprehensible nor relevant;[210] it must be received by practical reason, for the necessity of salvation from sin. *Then arose Peter, and ran unto the sepulchre,* for he had the seed of faith; *and stooping down, he beheld the linen clothes laid by themselves,* the old creation put away as a garment;[211] *and departed, wondering in himself at that which was come to pass.* He must see it for himself, to understand and believe, that he should be the first to confess that Jesus is the Christ, the Son of God.[212] *And, behold, two of them went that same day to a village called Emmaus, which was from Jerusalem about threescore furlongs,* as the fulfillment of the law in the Son of man. *And they talked together of all these things which had happened.* Before he reveals himself to us, he shows us our need of revelation. *And it came to pass, that, while they communed together and reasoned, Jesus himself drew near, and went with them,* for he reveals himself to those who seek him. *But*

---

[210] 1 Cor. 2:14.
[211] Ps. 102:26.
[212] Matt. 16:13-23.

their eyes were holden that they should not know him, that they should believe, not because they saw him alive, but through the testimony of God, according to the reason within them, and the word of God in their souls. *And he said unto them, What manner of communications are these that ye have one to another, as ye walk, and are sad?* He came not in answer but in inquiry, to cure their unbelief. *And the one of them, whose name was Cleopas, answering said unto him, Art thou only a stranger in Jerusalem, and hast not known the things which are come to pass there in these days?* It was common knowledge. *And he said unto them, What things?* He established what they already knew, that he might build upon the foundation. *And they said unto him, Concerning Jesus of Nazareth, which was a prophet mighty in deed and word before God and all the people:* they spoke according to the measure of their faith; *And how the chief priests and our rulers delivered him to be condemned to death, and have crucified him.* They considered not that he was condemned by the Father, that he, being justified by the Spirit, might also be raised from the dead. *But we trusted that it had been he which should have redeemed Israel: and beside all this, to day is the third day since these things were done.* They were in perplexity because of the promise of his resurrection. *Yea, and certain women also of our company made us astonished, which were early at the sepulchre; And when they found not his body, they came, saying, that they had also seen a vision of angels, which said that he was alive,* which report confounded their reason. *And certain of them which were with us went to the sepulchre, and found it even so as the women had said: but him they saw not.* Though corroborated, they did not yet believe, because it was not yet given unto them by the Father. *Then he said unto them, O fools, and slow of heart to believe all that the prophets have spoken: Ought not Christ to have suffered these things, and to enter into his glory?* That they should believe, according to its apodictic truth and practical necessity, for the glory of the Father in the condemnation of the Son. *And beginning at Moses and all the prophets, he expounded unto them in all the scriptures the things concerning himself,* that the necessity thereof might be revealed to them through the voice of truth, the matter together with the form. *And they drew nigh unto the village, whither they went: and he made as though he would have gone further,* for there are yet many Scriptures that speak of him. *But they constrained him, saying, Abide with us:* for the saints live both by their knowledge of God and by his presence; *for it is toward evening, and the day is far spent.* They would have Christ abide with them in their present knowledge. *And he went in to tarry with them.* He obliged them according to the degree of their faith. *And it came to pass, as he sat at meat with them, he took bread, and blessed it, and brake, and gave to them.* After he had instructed them, he offered them the food of his own body. *And their eyes were opened, and they knew him;* that they might believe in the one whose righteousness sustained them; *and he vanished out of their sight,* that they should bear witness to him who, having been raised, also ascended unto the Father, being invisible. *And they said one to another, Did not our heart burn within us, while he talked with us by the way, and while he opened to us the scriptures?* They felt their need of Christ, and the heat of his light. *And they rose up the same hour, and returned to Jerusalem, and found the eleven gathered together, and them that were with them, Saying, The Lord is risen indeed, and hath appeared to Simon. And they told what things were done in the way, and how he was known of them in breaking of bread,* in that common activity, whereby God is glorified in obedience to the moral law. *And as they thus spake, Jesus himself stood in the midst of them, and saith unto them, Peace be unto you,* for we know the Lord by his peace. *But they were terrified and affrighted,* they were afraid for their sins, because grace calls to mind the need for mercy; *and supposed that they had seen a spirit,* for they truly saw the spirit of affirmation in the flesh. *And he said unto them, Why are ye troubled? and why do thoughts arise in your hearts? Behold my hands and my feet, that it is I myself:* for the body shows the soul; *handle me, and see; for a spirit hath not flesh and bones, as ye see me have.* A spiritual body.[213] *And when he had thus spoken, he shewed them his hands and his feet.* The wounds of the cross remained in him, and in the resurrection God preserved the glory of his death.[214] *And while they yet believed not for joy, and wondered,* because that joy exceeded their senses; *he said unto them, Have ye here any meat? And they gave him a piece of a broiled fish, and of an honeycomb,* as happiness, and the sweetness of holiness. *And he took it, and did eat before them.* They ought to partake of his flesh, as he partook of theirs. *And he said unto them, These are the words which I spake unto you, while I was yet with*

---

[213] 1 Cor. 15:44-49.

[214] Aquinas, *Summa* 3.54.4.

you, that all things must be fulfilled, which were written in the law of Moses, and in the prophets, and in the psalms, concerning me. Then opened he their understanding, that they might understand the scriptures, And said unto them, Thus it is written, and thus it behoved Christ to suffer, and to rise from the dead the third day: these things coming to pass to fulfill the moral law; *And that repentance and remission of sins should be preached in his name among all nations, beginning at Jerusalem,* for the necessity of salvation from sin. *And ye are witnesses of these things,* that the church might believe through witnesses, the Spirit testifying through the history. *And, behold, I send the promise of my Father upon you: but tarry ye in the city of Jerusalem, until ye be endued with power from on high.* That not they, but Christ in them should preach the Gospel to the world, to seal their testimony by his Spirit.

John 20:1-30

The first day of the week, μιᾷ τῶν σαββάτων, the first of the sabbaths. The week is yet called by the sabbath, because the sabbath is perpetual; and the day of the resurrection is identified, because it is the sabbath of the new creation,[215] for it is to be identified by us, and remembered, because on that day Christ rested from his work. *The first day of the week cometh Mary Magdalene early, when it was yet dark,* for the light shines in the darkness;[216] *unto the sepulchre, and seeth the stone taken away from the sepulchre. Then she runneth,* she did not yet look inside, but brought the matter to the men; *and cometh to Simon Peter, and to the other disciple, whom Jesus loved, and saith unto them, They have taken away the Lord out of the sepulchre, and we know not where they have laid him,* thus she reasoned. *Peter therefore went forth, and that other disciple, and came to the sepulchre. So they ran both together: and the other disciple did outrun Peter, and came first to the sepulchre,* for the perfections of Christ are distributed by measure to his people. *And he stooping down, and looking in, saw the linen clothes lying;* because the righteousness of Christ remains in his burial; *yet went he not in. Then cometh Simon Peter following him, and went into the sepulchre, and seeth the linen clothes lie,*

---

[215] Ex. 20:8-11; Deut. 5:14-15; Is. 65:17.
[216] John 1:5.

And the napkin, that was about his head, not lying with the linen clothes, but wrapped together in a place by itself, as the divine righteousness of the head. *Then went in also that other disciple, which came first to the sepulchre, and he saw, and believed.* Mary saw the stone taken away and believed; John believed when he saw the empty tomb. *For as yet they knew not the scripture, that he must rise again from the dead.* They believed the word of Mary, that the body of Jesus was taken away. *Then the disciples went away again unto their own home.* They went no further than to verify this fact. *But Mary stood without at the sepulchre weeping:* that by her devotion she might be the first to see Jesus raised from the dead; *and as she wept, she stooped down, and looked into the sepulchre,* receiving no satisfaction from men, but from the Lord only; *And seeth two angels in white sitting,* because God reveals himself to those who seek him earnestly; *the one at the head, and the other at the feet, where the body of Jesus had lain,* the elect angels encompass the church, seraphim at the head,[217] cherubim at the feet.[218] *And they say unto her, Woman, why weepest thou?* They appeared to her because of her love for Jesus.[219] *She saith unto them, Because they have taken away my Lord, and I know not where they have laid him.* She professed him as Lord, but not yet his resurrection. *And when she had thus said, she turned herself back,* for she sought the Lord only; *and saw Jesus standing,* wherefore he appeared to her; *and knew not that it was Jesus.* She knew him by faith, but not yet by sight. *Jesus saith unto her, Woman, why weepest thou? whom seekest thou? She, supposing him to be the gardener,* that is, Adam, for Jesus is the rightful head;[220] *saith unto him, Sir, if thou have borne him hence, tell me where thou hast laid him, and I will take him away.* She honored his body. *Jesus saith unto her, Mary.* Christ is known to his disciples because he calls them by name. *She turned herself, and saith unto him, Rabboni; which is to say, Master;* and they know him because he is their Lord. *Jesus saith unto her, Touch me not; for I am not yet ascended to my Father:* that she should believe not by touch, nor by sight, but by the hearing of faith; *but go to my brethren, and say unto them, I ascend unto my Father, and your Father; and to my God, and your God,* to appear before God on our

---

[217] Is. 6:2.
[218] Ezek. 1:26, 10:1.
[219] John 14:21
[220] Gen. 2:15.

behalf. *Mary Magdalene came and told the disciples that she had seen the Lord,* to be testified by his blessedness; *and that he had spoken these things unto her,* for the blessedness of God is his Word. *Then the same day at evening, being the first day of the week,* here again identified, because the church ought to observe this day in remembrance of the resurrection, for what is identified in Scripture ought to be identified by us through obedience to his commandments; *when the doors were shut where the disciples were assembled for fear of the Jews, came Jesus and stood in the midst, and saith unto them, Peace be unto you,* for he is our peace. *And when he had so said, he shewed unto them his hands and his side,* because through his life from death our warfare is accomplished.[221] *Then were the disciples glad, when they saw the Lord. Then said Jesus to them again, Peace be unto you: as my Father hath sent me, even so send I you,* to be witnesses of his resurrection. *And when he had said this, he breathed on them, and saith unto them, Receive ye the Holy Ghost: Whose soever sins ye remit, they are remitted unto them; and whose soever sins ye retain, they are retained. But Thomas, one of the twelve, called Didymus, was not with them when Jesus came.* Though perhaps he despaired, yet is he not judged. *The other disciples therefore said unto him, We have seen the Lord. But he said unto them, Except I shall see in his hands the print of the nails, and put my finger into the print of the nails, and thrust my hand into his side, I will not believe.* This he said of faith, for as an apostle he must bear witness to the resurrection with his own eyes. *And after eight days again his disciples were within, and Thomas with them:* to see Jesus for himself; *then came Jesus, the doors being shut,* because to him all doors are open, even the gates of hell;[222] *and stood in the midst, and said, Peace be unto you. Then saith he to Thomas, Reach hither thy finger, and behold my hands; and reach hither thy hand, and thrust it into my side: and be not faithless, but believing.* By degrees Christ resolves all his doubts. *And Thomas answered and said unto him, My Lord and my God.* The word of the Lord sufficed, as though he had done so, and for all those who hear and believe. *Jesus saith unto him, Thomas, because thou hast seen me, thou hast believed: blessed are they that have not seen, and yet have believed.* Those who believe through the testimony of history, yet not for the sake of history, but for the blessedness

---

[221] Is. 40:2.

[222] Matt. 16:18, cf. Is. 43:2.

of God revealed therein: these are blessed; for by the hearing of Christ raised from the dead, men do see Christ in their need of him, yea, they touch the imprint of the nails, and the hole in his side. *And many other signs truly did Jesus in the presence of his disciples,* for he often gives us signs sufficient for our need; *which are not written in this book: But these are written, that ye might believe that Jesus is the Christ, the Son of God; and that believing ye might have life through his name,* because in righteousness he bore the guilt of original sin, "being put to death in the flesh, but quickened by the Spirit," to be our head (1 Peter 3:18).

The Cleansing of the Temple

The resurrection reveals the innocence of Christ, even under the burden of our guilt, and the righteousness of Christ cleanses away all our sins. Wherefore, consumed by zeal, he cleansed the temple, as a sign of his life and resurrection. The temple is the dwelling place of God, the man who delights in his law. Having sanctified himself, he also sanctifies his people. By his presence in the heart of man, Christ gives life to the body and the soul.

> Thus saith the LORD, The heaven *is* my throne, and the earth *is* my footstool: where *is* the house that ye build unto me? and where *is* the place of my rest? For all those *things* hath mine hand made, and all those *things* have been, saith the LORD: but to this *man* will I look, *even* to *him that is* poor and of a contrite spirit, and trembleth at my word. Isaiah 66:1-2

> Sanctify them through thy truth: thy word is truth. As thou hast sent me into the world, even so have I also sent them into the world. And for their sakes I sanctify myself, that they also might be sanctified through the truth. John 17:17-19

> For it became him, for whom *are* all things, and by whom *are* all things, in bringing many sons unto glory, to make the captain of their salvation perfect through sufferings. Hebrews 2:10

Christ has a righteousness not earthly, but heavenly; he delights to obey the law that dwells within him.[223] Wherefore, Christ cleansed the temple, not only of what is sinful, but also of what is ordinarily lawful, yet unlawful in the worship of God. This he did not by his own will, but by the Holy Spirit, the zeal of the Lord of hosts.[224]

He is the Son, who must about his Father's business, wholly dedicated to the things of God.[225] By his life he consecrates all things to God,[226] and by his resurrection he makes the church partaker of heavenly blessings.[227] In his death the form of the world passes away,[228] and all earthly purposes being buried with him,[229] are also raised with him in righteousness,[230] set apart to God in the new creation,[231] for he is dedicated to God and his kingdom, and his kingdom is not of this world.[232]

There are two cleansings recorded in the Gospels: first by John, at the beginning of his ministry, after Jesus' baptism and temptation in the wilderness; second, at the end of his ministry, after the triumphal entry. The first signifies his life, the second his resurrection, for these are one, though distinct, because his life is the life of his resurrection, and by his life eternal he rises from the dead.[233] By the first, he is sanctified to God; by the second, he sanctifies the world to God, for he sanctifies himself, that the world may be sanctified to God. By his presence in the temple and appearance before men, he cleanses the dwelling

---

[223] Ps. 40:8.
[224] Is. 9:7.
[225] Luke 2:49.
[226] John 3:35; Eph. 1:10.
[227] Rom. 6:4; Eph. 2:6.
[228] Rom. 6:6, cf. 1 Cor. 3:21-23, 2 Cor. 4:15; 1 John 2:15-17.
[229] Ps. 102:26, cf. John 20:5-7; Rom. 6:4.
[230] Col. 3:1-4.
[231] Is. 65:17-25; Rev. 21:5.
[232] John 18:36.
[233] Ps. 30:3.

place of God on earth, casting out those who used it for civil purposes, and dedicating it to prayer.

The life of Christ is one. To this John looks when he writes of the first cleansing. Jesus is the blessedness of God, and has all life within himself, and in his resurrection he takes up what he laid down.

> Therefore doth my Father love me, because I lay down my life, that I might take it again. No man taketh it from me, but I lay it down of myself. I have power to lay it down, and I have power to take it again. This commandment have I received of my Father. John 10:17-18, cf. 11:25

The second cleansing is recorded in Matthew, Mark, and Luke. The life of Christ appears fully in his resurrection from the dead, to show the fulfillment of his ministry. As an inwardly lawful being, Christ must not only live, but rise from the dead; this is the word of the Gospel preached, life from death; by it, the Son glorifies the Father.

John 2:13-22

And the Jews' passover was at hand, and Jesus went up to Jerusalem, to observe the feast commanded by God; *And found in the temple those that sold oxen and sheep and doves, and the changers of money sitting:* he did not seek them out, but found them in his way; *And when he had made a scourge of small cords,* for he should be sanctified by sufferings; *he drove them all out of the temple, and the sheep, and the oxen;* all the animals, not fit for holy use, because defiled by the civil;[234] *and poured out the changers' money, and overthrew the tables;* all the contraband he set at naught; *And said unto them that sold doves, Take these things hence;* he dealt gently with the doves, to do no harm to the weak, and because they were for the poor; *make not my Father's house an house of merchandise.* They are not here called thieves, as in the other Gospels, because that inference is to show that they

---

[234] Lev. 19:30, 26:2, cf. Neh. 13:15-22.

sought the divine likeness through sin, but here it is shown only that they drew no distinction between the common and the holy. The life of Christ, though dedicated to God, is not yet sufficient ground for the mercy bestowed on the elect, except he be raised from the dead. The first cleansing represents his life, which they sought, the second represents his resurrection, through which they might receive. *And his disciples remembered that it was written, The zeal of thine house hath eaten me up,* wholly devoted to God, and sanctified by his Spirit, "for God giveth not the Spirit by measure *unto him*" (John 3:35). *Then answered the Jews and said unto him, What sign shewest thou unto us, seeing that thou doest these things?* His authority, for he is priest and king. *Jesus answered and said unto them, Destroy this temple, and in three days I will raise it up,* for by his resurrection he would cleanse the temple of God. The cleansing of the temple is the sign of his resurrection; therefore, the promise of his resurrection is the sign of his authority to cleanse the temple. *Then said the Jews, Forty and six years was this temple in building, and wilt thou rear it up in three days?* They thought he spoke of the temple, not knowing that the temple spake of him. *But he spake of the temple of his body,* whereby he produces an intuition in agreement with the concept. *When therefore he was risen from the dead, his disciples remembered that he had said this unto them; and they believed the scripture, and the word which Jesus had said.* It was a sign, that they should believe after, for the signs are given first, but understood after, through the historical doctrines that they signify.

Matthew 21:12-16

And Jesus went into the temple of God, the holy place; *and cast out all them that sold and bought in the temple, and overthrew the tables of the moneychangers,* the common activities, however lawful on earth, but unfit for the service of God; *and the seats of them that sold doves,* that the life of Christ should be given without price for his people; *And said unto them, It is written, My house shall be called the house of prayer;* dedicated to that purpose; *but ye have made it a den of thieves.* They sought to profit from the holy things, and partake of the divine blessedness by sin. *And the blind and the lame came to him in the temple; and he healed them.* After he cleansed the temple, he glorified the Father through the salvation of sinners. Mark says, "And would not suffer that any man should carry *any* vessel through the temple," for the body is the vessel,[235] that it should be raised unto God. "And he taught, saying unto them, Is it not written, My house shall be called of all nations the house of prayer? but ye have made it a den of thieves. And the scribes and chief priests heard *it*, and sought how they might destroy him:" that through death for sin he should receive life again, and sanctify the world to God; "for they feared him, because all the people was astonished at his doctrine. And when even was come, he went out of the city," to preserve his life until the appointed time (Mark 11:16-19). *And when the chief priests and scribes saw the wonderful things that he did,* working new life from the old; *and the children crying in the temple,* for all the happiness is the Lord's, for he is holy;[236] *and saying, Hosanna to the Son of David; they were sore displeased, And said unto him, Hearest thou what these say? And Jesus saith unto them, Yea; have ye never read, Out of the mouth of babes and sucklings thou hast perfected praise?* That being made perfectly holy in his resurrection, he should also be perfectly happy forever, and with him all the children of God.[237]

---

[235] 1 Pet. 3:7.
[236] Cf. Lev. 3:16.
[237] Ps. 16:2-3, 10-11; Heb. 12:1-3.

The Death of Christ

Negation is the quality thought in the particular that distinguishes it from every other particular under a common universal. The intuition of negation is separation, wherein each particular lies in a distinct intuition.

Sin is a concept that contains within itself the ground of the negation of an intuition in agreement therewith, that is, the separation of body and soul, and the parts of the body from one another.

> In the sweat of thy face shalt thou eat bread, Till thou return unto the ground; for out of it wast thou taken: for dust thou *art*, and unto dust shalt thou return. Genesis 3:19

Unto dust, the dissolution of the parts.

> Behold, all souls are mine; as the soul of the father, so also the soul of the son is mine: the soul that sinneth, it shall die. Ezekiel 18:4

> The body without the spirit is dead. James 2:26

God punishes sin with death, to put a distinction between the righteous and the wicked, that men might seek the Lord.

> For the rod of the wicked shall not rest upon the lot of the righteous; lest the righteous put forth their hands unto iniquity. Psalm 125:3, cf. Ps. 136:10, 15, 17-20

> The way of life *is* above to the wise, that he may depart from hell beneath. Proverbs 15:24

The spirit and the soul are divided, the essence from the nature, by the righteous judgment of God; and the body from the soul, and the parts of the body from one another.

> For the word of God *is* quick, and powerful, and sharper than any twoedged sword, piercing even to the dividing asunder of soul and spirit, and the joints and marrow, and *is* a discerner of the thoughts and intents of the heart. Hebrews 4:12

In death the body returns to the dust, the spirit to God who gave it, and the soul departs to its forever abode.

> Remember now thy Creator in the days of thy youth, while the evil days come not, nor the years draw nigh, when thou shalt say, I have no pleasure in them; While the sun, or the light, or the moon, or the stars, be not darkened, nor the clouds return after the rain: In the day when the keepers of the house shall tremble, and the strong men shall bow themselves, and the grinders cease because they are few, and those that look out of the windows be darkened, And the doors shall be shut in the streets, when the sound of the grinding is low, and he shall rise up at the voice of the bird, and all the daughters of musick shall be brought low; Also *when* they shall be afraid of *that which is* high, and fears *shall be* in the way, and the almond tree shall flourish, and the grasshopper shall be a burden, and desire shall fail: because man goeth to his long home, and the mourners go about the streets: Or ever the silver cord be loosed, or the golden bowl be broken, or the pitcher be broken at the fountain, or the wheel broken at the cistern. Then shall the dust return to the earth as it was: and the spirit shall return unto God who gave it. Ecclesiastes 12:1-7

To negate the law, one need only violate it in one particular. The law commands universal obedience. Failure to keep the law in one instance constitutes rejection of the whole. And because the soul of man is immortal, rejection of the law is forever, and in death the sinner is tormented for eternity.

> The sinners in Zion are afraid; fearfulness hath surprised the hypocrites. Who among us shall dwell with the devouring fire? who among us shall dwell with everlasting burnings? Isaiah 33:14

> For their worm shall not die, neither shall their fire be quenched. Isaiah 66:24

> And these shall go away into everlasting punishment: but the righteous into life eternal. Matthew 25:46

A person is an absolute unity. Whether he choose good or evil, he is wholly devoted to his choice. And one who is wholly devoted to sin deserves total misery: the complete destruction of the will itself, and all its desires. This is death. Therefore, the wicked choose death for sin.

> But he that sinneth against me wrongeth his own soul: all they that hate me love death. Proverbs 8:36

Nevertheless, the destruction of the will can never be achieved if it is the very end sought. Therefore, there must be something worse than death, which the wicked can neither seek nor imagine, in which their immortal souls suffer for eternity.

> Her house *is* the way to hell, going down to the chambers of death. Proverbs 7:27

> And I looked, and behold a pale horse: and his name that sat on him was Death, and Hell followed with him. Revelation 6:8

Fire breaks down and destroys, but the form of a thing can never be destroyed. Therefore, by hell I understand the destruction of the form, the consciousness of the contradiction of the will against itself. This is thinkable, though unimaginable, nor is it possible to seek out or desire, but is ever opposed to the will itself, their rational nature forever contending against them, together with the saints in heaven, the holy angels, and the divine persons.[238]

Nevertheless God, who promised man life for obedience, and death for sin, did not threaten man with hell, but only with death, for Adam surely knew that hell should follow, except he be saved from his sin. Adam's sin exposed him to the certainty of death and the danger of hell.

Yet suppose the punishment of death were born by a righteous man. The justice of God might then be satisfied, because the just do not seek death, but life. Wherefore, in the day that Adam sinned, God promised him a savior, who should hearken to the voice of his church, and bear the punishment of the curse, and redeem men by the blood of his face.

The human will of Christ possesses a degree, and Christ is tempted by the agony that pertains not to the righteous, but to the wicked. Howsoever righteous a man, howsoever great a temptation endured, what might he do if he were faced with a greater? Yet Christ bore the greatest of all possible trials, and endured. Having submitted himself to the wrath of God, he is sanctified above measure, unto the full manifestation of his divine nature in the flesh. The more he suffered, the holier he became, and the holier he became, all the more he suffered, until in death he suffered perfectly, and became perfectly holy.

Christ is sanctified by sufferings, and the Holy Spirit justifies him in his submission to condemnation; wherefore, Christ is sanctified by the Spirit, who vindicates the condemnation of the Father, and so he suffers even by the Spirit who justifies him, that the innocence of Christ might show forth his nonlegal righteousness.

For thine arrows stick fast in me, and thy hand presseth me sore. Psalm 38:2

---

[238] Rev. 14:9-11.

Remove thy stroke away from me: I am consumed by the blow of thine hand. Psalm 39:10

Wherefore Christ, fully suffering the wrath of God, in that he suffered righteously, not for himself but for others, proves himself to be his Son, and the justice of God satisfied in his death is imputed to all who believe, who see in him the righteousness of their head, yea, of God with us.

Who in the days of his flesh, when he had offered up prayers and supplications with strong crying and tears unto him that was able to save him from death, and was heard in that he feared; Though he were a Son, yet learned he obedience by the things which he suffered; And being made perfect, he became the author of eternal salvation unto all them that obey him. Hebrews 5:7-9

Christ died, that he might be the head of all who die.

For to this end Christ both died, and rose, and revived, that he might be Lord both of the dead and living. Romans 14:9

For the love of Christ constraineth us; because we thus judge, that if one died for all, then were all dead: And *that* he died for all, that they which live should not henceforth live unto themselves, but unto him which died for them, and rose again. 2 Corinthians 5:14-15

Christ indeed endured all the torments of hell,[239] whereby he raises up even the wicked, to glorify God in their damnation, to show forth his mercy to the elect, whom he has saved from such destruction.[240] He does not leave the souls of the wicked in hell, but casts them, body and soul, into the lake of fire, whereby he glorifies his own suffering in theirs. He has paid for them, and bought

---

[239] Aquinas, *Summa* 3.5-8.
[240] Rom. 9:22-23.

them,[241] that they should live, that they should glorify God with their bodies, and their torments are an eternal memorial to the agony of our Lord.

> For this *is* the day of the Lord GOD of hosts, a day of vengeance, that he may avenge him of his adversaries: and the sword shall devour, and it shall be satiate and made drunk with their blood: for the Lord GOD of hosts hath a sacrifice in the north country by the river Euphrates. Jeremiah 46:10, cf. Is. 43:3-4

> And the third angel followed them, saying with a loud voice, If any man worship the beast and his image, and receive *his* mark in his forehead, or in his hand, The same shall drink of the wine of the wrath of God, which is poured out without mixture into the cup of his indignation; and he shall be tormented with fire and brimstone in the presence of the holy angels, and in the presence of the Lamb: And the smoke of their torment ascendeth up for ever and ever: and they have no rest day nor night, who worship the beast and his image, and whosoever receiveth the mark of his name. Revelation 14:9-11

But those who die with Christ shall also live with him.

> Know ye not, that so many of us as were baptized into Jesus Christ were baptized into his death? Therefore we are buried with him by baptism into death: that like as Christ was raised up from the dead by the glory of the Father, even so we also should walk in newness of life. Romans 6:3-4, cf. Col. 3:3-4

Scripture Proof

God gives the tree of the field for the life of man, even the tree of life, and the tree of the knowledge of good and evil, which by avoiding man should live.

---

[241] 2 Pet. 2:1.

Yet in eating of that tree, he lifted himself up to be like God, and fell. Wherefore, he that hangs upon a tree is accursed of God, because he has lifted himself up against the Lord.[242]

Christ showed himself to be the Son of God by bearing the curse of our sin; wherefore, he is hanged on a tree, to which he is nailed by nails of iron, because he submitted himself to the condemnation of the Father.[243]

Judas hanged himself, but Christ was crucified. Judas condemned himself, and his head was bruised for his sin, and he bore his own guilt. Christ bore the sins of others, and was bruised in the heel, and pierced in his hands and feet. Though he bore the curse, he bore it in his hands and feet, that he might walk with God, and perform divine works, that he might both walk and work, the Father working in him and with him.[244] He was bruised in his essence and in his works, but not in his nature. He obeyed unto death, and was sanctified therein.

In crucifixion the legs are nailed together, but the hands are stretched out. Thus in the death of Christ, affirmation and infinity are identified in distinction, but the two natures are fully distinguished in his works, because he performs divine works on behalf of his people. The hands of Christ are like the anointed ones; one represents his headship over humanity, the one over the many; the other represents the divine likeness, whereby humanity, though distinct from God, yet partakes of his holiness.[245]

Matthew 27:27-54

Then the soldiers of the governor took Jesus into the common hall, and gathered unto him the whole band of soldiers, to make war against him who conquers all by his blood. *And they stripped him,* fully exposed to the wrath of God, righteous and unashamed;[246] *and put on him a scarlet robe,* covered with the wrath of God for sin. *And when they had platted a crown of thorns, they put it upon his head,*

---

[242] Deut. 20:19-20, 21:22-23.
[243] Ps. 2:9; Dan. 2:40.
[244] John 5:17.
[245] Cf. Aquinas, *Summa* 3.46.4.
[246] Gen. 2:25.

crowned the king of suffering by the sinners for whom he died; *and a reed in his right hand*: whereby he sends forth the Spirit of sanctification to all those who suffer righteously; *and they bowed the knee before him, and mocked him, saying, Hail, King of the Jews!* They acknowledged him king, because the truth thereof follows from the saying of it, for although they mocked him, yet it is by bearing their mockery that he is their king. *And they spit upon him*, for he is their bone and their flesh,[247] and he bore their shame; *and took the reed, and smote him on the head*, sanctified by the Spirit of the Father. *And after that they had mocked him, they took the robe off from him, and put his own raiment on him, and led him away to crucify him*, for his patience under agony they gave him back what was his. *And as they came out, they found a man of Cyrene, Simon by name: him they compelled to bear his cross.* They would not bear it themselves, but a foreigner. After Christ had spent all his strength, he persevered through righteousness divine. *And when they were come unto a place called Golgotha, that is to say, a place of a skull*, of the death of the head; *They gave him vinegar to drink mingled with gall: and when he had tasted thereof, he would not drink*, for it was not yet the time, but when once he had tasted death, he would not remain under its power.[248] *And they crucified him, and parted his garments, casting lots:* his glory divided to the sons of men; *that it might be fulfilled which was spoken by the prophet*, not by theft but by grace; *They parted my garments among them, and upon my vesture did they cast lots.* Christ is crucified for the whole world, especially for those chosen by God, to be clothed with his righteousness. *And sitting down they watched him there*; for he died visibly for all. *And set up over his head his accusation written, this is Jesus the King of the Jews*, they acknowledged the legitimacy of his claim, putting him to death for its sake, proving him to be the Messiah. *Then were there two thieves crucified with him, one on the right hand, and another on the left.* Men sought to rob God of his likeness, but what belongs to the Son by nature, God gives to them by his grace. *And they that passed by reviled him, wagging their heads, And saying, Thou that destroyest the temple, and buildest it in three days, save thyself*, as if he had condemned himself, that he should also save himself. *If thou be the Son of God, come down from the cross*, for

---

[247] Gen. 29:14; Judg. 9:2; 2 Sam. 5:1, 19:13; 1 Chron. 11:1.
[248] Matt. 25:29; Mark 14:25; Luke 22:18.

they understood not the mystery revealed before their eyes, that is, his obedience unto death. *Likewise also the chief priests mocking him, with the scribes and elders, said, He saved others; himself he cannot save*, for he should be saved by the Holy Spirit. *If he be the King of Israel, let him now come down from the cross, and we will believe him.* They believed according to their eyes, according to their sinful flesh and fleshly minds. *He trusted in God; let him deliver him now, if he will have him: for he said, I am the Son of God*, so he suffered, forsaken of God.[249] *The thieves also, which were crucified with him, cast the same in his teeth*, as men ready to perish mock their hope of salvation. *Now from the sixth hour there was darkness over all the land unto the ninth hour.* The heavens bore witness to the judgment of God, the angels looking on. *And about the ninth hour Jesus cried with a loud voice, saying, Eli, Eli, lama sabachthani? that is to say, My God, my God, why hast thou forsaken me?* Because in him was no ground of forsaking. *Some of them that stood there, when they heard that, said, This man calleth for Elias*, as if to save him from death by one who had ascended, who yet spoke of the one in whom lies eternal life. *And straightway one of them ran, and took a spunge, and filled it with vinegar, and put it on a reed*, to taste death by the Holy Spirit;[250] *and gave him to drink*, to taste of God's mercy in judgment.[251] *The rest said, Let be, let us see whether Elias will come to save him. Jesus, when he had cried again with a loud voice, yielded up the ghost.* He submitted to the Father in the very moment of his death. *And, behold, the veil of the temple was rent in twain from the top to the bottom;* because the sacrifice of Christ opens the way to the Father;[252] *and the earth did quake, and the rocks rent;* the old creation passes away, the hiding places are destroyed, and the gates of hell are opened;[253] *And the graves were opened; and many bodies of the saints which slept arose, And came out of the graves after his resurrection, and went into the holy city, and appeared unto many*, for the death of Christ gives life to men. *Now when the centurion, and they that were with him, watching Jesus, saw the earthquake, and those things that were done, they feared greatly, saying, Truly this was the Son of God.* In his

---

[249] Is. 53:4-6.
[250] Heb. 2:9.
[251] Prov. 27:7.
[252] Heb. 10:19-20.
[253] Is. 2:20-21; Heb. 12:25-27; Rev. 1:18; 6:15-17; 20:12-14.

obedience unto death they saw the righteousness of the Father. *And many women were there beholding afar off,* for they saw in him the blessedness of God; *which followed Jesus from Galilee, ministering unto him:* the blessedness of God sustained by the image thereof; *Among which was Mary Magdalene, and Mary the mother of James and Joses, and the mother of Zebedee's children.* The Father blessed our Lord Jesus Christ abundantly with the company of women, who saw in him the very blessedness of God.

Mark 15:16-41

And the soldiers led him away into the hall, called Praetorium; to be vindicated in the place of judgment, before he is sacrificed outside the city; *and they call together the whole band,* to make war against him. *And they clothed him with purple, and platted a crown of thorns, and put it about his head, And began to salute him, Hail, King of the Jews!* He came a king not to do, but to be done unto. *And they smote him on the head with a reed, and did spit upon him, and bowing their knees worshipped him.* They owned him as king, not by righteous consent, but by the very sin they committed against him, which he so patiently bore. *And when they had mocked him,* blasphemously confessing the one who bore their sins; *they took off the purple from him, and put his own clothes on him, and led him out to crucify him.* They clothed him with divine honor, to glorify him as king, and now they returned to him his own clothes, that he might fulfill the work of his priesthood, to die for their sins. *And they compel one Simon a Cyrenian, who passed by, coming out of the country, the father of Alexander and Rufus, to bear his cross,* because the Father bears the cross of the Son.[254] *And they bring him unto the place Golgotha, which is, being interpreted, The place of a skull. And they gave him to drink wine mingled with myrrh: but he received it not,* for he drank already with his disciples; he drank the cup given him by his Father. *And when they had crucified him, they parted his garments, casting lots upon them, what every man should take. And it was the third hour,* for on that day he labored for men's souls; *and they crucified him. And the superscription of his accusation was written over, the King of the Jews,* affirmed by all, even in their sin.

---

[254] John 5:19.

And with him they crucify two thieves; the one on his right hand, and the other on his left. And the scripture was fulfilled, which saith, And he was numbered with the transgressors, reckoned by God a sinner, not for any sin he committed, but because he partook of their guilt.[255] *And they that passed by railed on him, wagging their heads, and saying, Ah, thou that destroyest the temple, and buildest it in three days,* because he is put to death that he might be raised; *Save thyself, and come down from the cross.* They did not understand that he should be saved by the Holy Spirit, even as he was put to death by the Father. *Likewise also the chief priests mocking said among themselves with the scribes, He saved others; himself he cannot save.* They minded not the things of God, but of men, that he should glorify himself, and not rather be glorified by the one who sent him.[256] *Let Christ the King of Israel descend now from the cross, that we may see and believe.* They tempted him, whom they acknowledged to be God. *And they that were crucified with him reviled him. And when the sixth hour was come, there was darkness over the whole land until the ninth hour,* the darkness of day, that is, unconditional condemnation. *And at the ninth hour Jesus cried with a loud voice, saying, Eloi, Eloi, lama sabachthani? which is, being interpreted, My God, my God, why hast thou forsaken me?* because in him was no ground of forsaking. *And some of them that stood by, when they heard it, said, Behold, he calleth Elias.* They did not understand his speech, for he spoke to the Hebrews, the people of God.[257] *And one ran and filled a spunge full of vinegar, and put it on a reed, and gave him to drink, saying, Let alone; let us see whether Elias will come to take him down,* they acknowledged Jesus to be a prophet. *And Jesus cried with a loud voice, and gave up the ghost,* even his spirit to God. *And the veil of the temple was rent in twain from the top to the bottom,* the Old Testament fulfilled from heaven to earth. *And when the centurion, which stood over against him, saw that he so cried out, and gave up the ghost,* by the very manner of his death, wherein he was perfected; *he said, Truly this man was the Son of God,* obedient unto death. *There were also women looking on afar off: among whom was Mary Magdalene, and Mary the mother of James the less and of Joses, and Salome; (Who*

---

[255] 2 Cor. 5:21.
[256] Matt. 16:21-23; John 7:16-19.
[257] John 8:47; 18:37.

also, when he was in Galilee, followed him, and ministered unto him;) and many other women which came up with him unto Jerusalem, by whom the church testifies to the death of the blessed one.

Luke 23:26-49

And as they led him away, they laid hold upon one Simon, a Cyrenian, coming out of the country, and on him they laid the cross, that he might bear it after Jesus, a stranger, that the kingdom of God should come to the Gentiles, that after him they should bear his cross. *And there followed him a great company of people, and of women, which also bewailed and lamented him,* who had seen his miracles, and would have made him king.[258] *But Jesus turning unto them said, Daughters of Jerusalem, weep not for me, but weep for yourselves, and for your children,* for they should bear the punishment of their sin against him. *For, behold, the days are coming, in the which they shall say, Blessed are the barren, and the wombs that never bare, and the paps which never gave suck,* for in that day the blessedness of women shall be a curse. *Then shall they begin to say to the mountains, Fall on us; and to the hills, Cover us. For if they do these things in a green tree,* when they safely looked upon the judgment of Christ; *what shall be done in the dry?* when they are in danger of judgment. *And there were also two other, malefactors, led with him to be put to death,* for he is the head of a sinful race. *And when they were come to the place, which is called Calvary,* outside the city, to bear the wrath of God; *there they crucified him, and the malefactors, one on the right hand, and the other on the left,* before whom the sheep and the goats are divided.[259] *Then said Jesus, Father, forgive them; for they know not what they do.* It is the mystery of God, to condemn the righteous, that sinners might be forgiven their sins. *And they parted his raiment, and cast lots. And the people stood beholding,* crucified in the sight of all men. *And the rulers also with them derided him, saying, He saved others;* they acknowledged his miracles; *let him save himself, if he be Christ, the chosen of God,* by these words they confessed him. *And the soldiers also mocked him, coming to*

---

[258] John 6:15.
[259] Matt. 25:31-46.

him, and offering him vinegar, tempting him; *And saying, If thou be the king of the Jews, save thyself,* for he should be saved by the Holy Spirit proceeding from him. *And a superscription also was written over him in letters of Greek, and Latin, and Hebrew, this is the King of the Jews,* for the King of the Jews inherits all nations. *And one of the malefactors which were hanged railed on him, saying, If thou be Christ, save thyself and us,* he sought a worldly salvation. *But the other answering rebuked him, saying, Dost not thou fear God, seeing thou art in the same condemnation? And we indeed justly; for we receive the due reward of our deeds: but this man hath done nothing amiss.* He saw Christ in his need of him. *And he said unto Jesus, Lord, remember me when thou comest into thy kingdom.* He owned him as king. *And Jesus said unto him, Verily I say unto thee, Today shalt thou be with me in paradise. And it was about the sixth hour,* about noon; *and there was a darkness over all the earth,* for the light shines in the darkness;[260] *until the ninth hour,* three hours for the full testimony of his righteousness; *And the sun was darkened,* because in his light even the sun is dark; *and the veil of the temple was rent in the midst,* the way to the Father being opened by his death. *And when Jesus had cried with a loud voice, he said, Father, into thy hands I commend my spirit:* His spirit he gave up to God, to be justified by God, even by his Spirit; *and having said thus, he gave up the ghost.* This is his dying testimony, righteous to his last breath. *Now when the centurion saw what was done, he glorified God, saying, Certainly this was a righteous man,* even to the end. *And all the people that came together to that sight, beholding the things which were done, smote their breasts, and returned.* They were moved, but not to repentance. *And all his acquaintance, and the women that followed him from Galilee, stood afar off, beholding these things.* They were witnesses, not only in the flesh, but chiefly by faith.

John 19:16-37

And they took Jesus, and led him away. The hands of the wicked lead the righteous to glory.[261] *And he bearing his cross,* because he freely submitted himself

---

260 Ps. 139:11-12; John 1:5.
261 Ps. 17:13-14.

to the wrath of the Father; *went forth into a place called the place of a skull,* as the death of the head; *which is called in the Hebrew Golgotha: Where they crucified him, and two other with him, on either side one, and Jesus in the midst. And Pilate wrote a title, and put it on the cross. And the writing was, Jesus of Nazareth the King of the Jews.* He was acknowledged by the deputy of the Roman government, who had justified him. *This title then read many of the Jews: for the place where Jesus was crucified was nigh to the city:* a public place; *and it was written in Hebrew, and Greek, and Latin,* because he is king of all nations. *Then said the chief priests of the Jews to Pilate, Write not, The King of the Jews; but that he said, I am King of the Jews.* They being more subtle did not understand the apodictic truth of the matter. *Pilate answered, What I have written I have written,* the written word of God. *Then the soldiers, when they had crucified Jesus, took his garments, and made four parts, to every soldier a part; and also his coat: now the coat was without seam,* perfectly united; *woven from the top throughout,* as heavenly works. *They said therefore among themselves, Let us not rend it, but cast lots for it, whose it shall be: that the scripture might be fulfilled, which saith, They parted my raiment among them, and for my vesture they did cast lots. These things therefore the soldiers did,* for all partake of his mercy, whether on earth only or also in heaven. *Now there stood by the cross of Jesus his mother, and his mother's sister, Mary the wife of Cleophas, and Mary Magdalene,* for by the cross of Christ the church stands in the grace of God.[262] *When Jesus therefore saw his mother, and the disciple standing by, whom he loved, he saith unto his mother, Woman, behold thy son! Then saith he to the disciple, Behold thy mother! And from that hour that disciple took her unto his own home.* To fulfill all righteousness, he gave her a son in place of himself, for men are born to live, but he was born to die, and raised to ascend unto the Father. *After this, Jesus knowing that all things,* even the whole work of redemption; *were now accomplished,* the time appointed by the Father made manifest; *that the scripture might be fulfilled, saith, I thirst.* At the end of his power, he suffered want, to be sanctified to the utmost. *Now there was set a vessel full of vinegar: and they filled a spunge with vinegar, and put it upon hyssop,* a visible token of the blessing of God's wrath, to perfect him in his death; *and put it to his mouth,* "that he by the grace of God should taste

---

262 Rom. 5:1-2.

death for every man" (Hebrews 2:9). *When Jesus therefore had received the vinegar,* for the time was at hand: in that moment he was in the kingdom of heaven with his own, and alive by his righteousness; *he said, It is finished:* being fully sanctified to the end, the justice of God satisfied in his death; *and he bowed his head,* in submission to God the Father; *and gave up the ghost,* to the Holy Spirit.[263] *The Jews therefore, because it was the preparation, that the bodies should not remain upon the cross on the sabbath day,* that the body of Christ might rest; *(for that sabbath day was an high day,),* even the perfect rest of God; *besought Pilate that their legs might be broken, and that they might be taken away,* because the image of God is marred in death by a sinful walk of life. *Then came the soldiers, and brake the legs of the first, and of the other which was crucified with him,* as the common lot of mankind. *But when they came to Jesus, and saw that he was dead already,* for he hastened to perfection; *they brake not his legs:* because he ran perfectly, and in his death the image of God is preserved; *But one of the soldiers with a spear pierced his side,* to confirm his death, he offered violence to his body, to show forth in death the perfect submission of the Son; *and forthwith came there out blood and water,* for his blood is as water to drink, and his death issues forth in life. *And he that saw it bare record, and his record is true:* the Spirit speaking through the history; *and he knoweth that he saith true, that ye might believe,* spoken by witnesses who believed, who also testified by their manner of life; *For these things were done, that the scripture should be fulfilled, A bone of him shall not be broken,* that the divine form of his body be not marred. *And again another scripture saith, They shall look on him whom they pierced,* even with their own sins, that the matter should issue forth to their salvation.

The Trial of Jesus

The trial of Jesus signifies his death. This sign is clearer than any other because it is the cause of the event. He was tried that he might be put to death, not by the law of God, but by the form of law, that is, the law of the Father. All the institutions of ancient Israel governed by the special appointment and

---

[263] Ps. 31:5.

providence of God. Thus, the judgment of the elders and the people signifies the divine judgment, which the rulers of this world did not understand, nor his disciples at the time.[264]

The trial of Christ shows that he died not for any sin he committed, but for the glory of the Father, and that in an intuition distinct from the person of the Father, through the men who unjustly put him to death. And because these men worked by offices divinely ordained, wherein God himself resides, they also show forth the divine truth of the Gospel to the world.[265]

> And David said unto him, How wast thou not afraid to stretch forth thine hand to destroy the LORD's anointed? 2 Samuel 1:14

> A divine sentence *is* in the lips of the king: his mouth transgresseth not in judgment. Proverbs 16:10

In his trial it appears that Christ, though condemned, did nothing worthy of death; that he had a righteousness outside the law; and that he was justified by Pilate, and by all those who through Pilate condemned him.

Matthew 26:59-27:26

Now the chief priests, and elders, and all the council, sought false witness against Jesus, to put him to death, they sought to legitimize their purpose, to condemn the righteous, lawful only in the singular will of the Triune God; *But found none: yea, though many false witnesses came, yet found they none.* No one condemned him to death, but God the Father only, because their falsehood was apparent to all. *At the last came two false witnesses, And said, This fellow said, I am able to destroy the temple of God, and to build it in three days.* They imputed to him that sin of their own, in one person both to justify and condemn. *And the high priest arose, and said unto him, Answerest thou nothing? what is it which these witness against thee?*

---

[264] Matt. 23:2; 1 Cor. 2:6-8.
[265] Jer. 21:1-10, 24, 29:7, 32:28, 38:2, 17-23; Dan. 2; Matt. 23:2; Rom. 13:1-7.

The high priest would not prove the charge, but demanded that Jesus defend himself. *But Jesus held his peace,* for he submitted himself to the wrath of God. *And the high priest answered and said unto him, I adjure thee by the living God, that thou tell us whether thou be the Christ, the Son of God.* However unlawful according to the form of the oath imposed, yet Christ answered for the sake of his testimony. *Jesus saith unto him, Thou hast said:* for the question answers itself; *nevertheless I say unto you, Hereafter shall ye see the Son of man sitting on the right hand of power, and coming in the clouds of heaven.* Though for the time he was under their power, yet he foretold his ascension and second coming, that they should mind their sins and repent. *Then the high priest rent his clothes, saying, He hath spoken blasphemy;* they rejected even the possibility of salvation through the Messiah; *what further need have we of witnesses? behold, now ye have heard his blasphemy. What think ye? They answered and said, He is guilty of death,* for he bore the guilt of original sin. *Then did they spit in his face, and buffeted him; and others smote him with the palms of their hands, Saying, Prophesy unto us, thou Christ,* whom they confessed; *Who is he that smote thee?* They humiliated him contrary to law, and he suffered their indignities, to bear the fullness of man's sin. *Now Peter sat without in the palace:* Jesus suffered alone, to bring his disciples into his heavenly palace; *and a damsel came unto him,* gently to rebuke him and call him to his place; *saying, Thou also wast with Jesus of Galilee,* she did not accuse him of any wrongdoing, but only stated the fact of his association, that by the least means possible God might call him to repentance. *But he denied before them all, saying, I know not what thou sayest.* His denials savored of nonsense rather than contrariety. *And when he was gone out into the porch, another maid saw him, and said unto them that were there, This fellow was also with Jesus of Nazareth. And again he denied with an oath, I do not know the man,* the fervency of his denials showed the truth of the matter. *And after a while came unto him they that stood by, and said to Peter, Surely thou also art one of them; for thy speech bewrayeth thee,* even the enemies of Christ are given for the good of his church, by whom God calls them to maintain their profession. *Then began he to curse and to swear, saying, I know not the man. And immediately the cock crew,* to wake him from his sin. *And Peter remembered the word of Jesus, which said unto him, Before the cock crow, thou shalt deny me thrice. And he went out, and wept bitterly*, that his faith might be manifested not by words but by repentance. *When the morning was come, all the chief priests and elders of the people took counsel against Jesus to put him to death:* having condemned him by night, they sought to execute their sentence by day. *And when they had bound him, they led him away, and delivered him to Pontius Pilate the governor*, to condemn him now in public, as they had before in private, but rather to be justified by the representative of the Roman government. *Then Judas, which had betrayed him, when he saw that he was condemned*, because he partook of the sin of those who condemned the Lord; *repented himself*, his own rational nature working against him; *and brought again the thirty pieces of silver to the chief priests and elders, Saying, I have sinned in that I have betrayed the innocent blood*. Not an innocent only, but the innocent one. Judas' own nature worked against him, and compelled him to confess the righteousness of Christ. *And they said, What is that to us? see thou to that*. Neither the chief priests nor the elders could atone for sin. *And he cast down the pieces of silver in the temple, and departed, and went and hanged himself*. He condemned himself. *And the chief priests took the silver pieces, and said, It is not lawful for to put them into the treasury, because it is the price of blood,* for the worship of God lies in obedience to his commandments.[266] *And they took counsel, and bought with them the potter's field, to bury strangers in*. The profit of Jesus' blood is salvation for all, whosoever believes, both Jew and Gentile, for in Christ every man is buried unto the resurrection of the dead, that God may be glorified in them all, both the righteous and the wicked.[267] *Wherefore that field was called, The field of blood, unto this day. Then was fulfilled that which was spoken by Jeremy the prophet, saying, And they took the thirty pieces of silver, the price of him that was valued, whom they of the children of Israel did value; And gave them for the potter's field, as the Lord appointed me,* for it must have been so, because God gathers all of humanity in Christ, and divides between the righteous and the wicked. *And Jesus stood before the governor: and the governor asked him, saying, Art thou the King of the Jews? And Jesus said unto him, Thou sayest,* for that is a Messianic title. *And when he was accused of the chief priests and elders, he answered nothing*, as before to

---

[266] 1 Cor. 7:19.
[267] Jer. 18:1-10; Rom. 9:21-24.

bear their condemnation, so now to be justified therein. *Then said Pilate unto him, Hearest thou not how many things they witness against thee?* For the multitude of sins imputed to him. *And he answered him to never a word,* he bore it all in righteousness; *insomuch that the governor marvelled greatly,* for by his human righteousness he manifested his righteousness divine. *Now at that feast the governor was wont to release unto the people a prisoner, whom they would,* to ensure that only the guilty are punished, and that the benefit of justice outweighs the harm. *And they had then a notable prisoner, called Barabbas.* Pilate chose a man known to the multitude, that by his exceeding guilt he might deliver an innocent, yea, the innocent one.. *Therefore when they were gathered together, Pilate said unto them, Whom will ye that I release unto you? Barabbas, or Jesus which is called Christ?* He sought to deliver Jesus, not by his own power, but with their consent, so that if they released not Christ, they must release a notorious criminal, because Christ died for sinners, even the worst of them. *For he knew that for envy they had delivered him,* for in their sin they sought to be like God. *When he was set down on the judgment seat, his wife sent unto him, saying, Have thou nothing to do with that just man: for I have suffered many things this day in a dream because of him.* The innocence of Christ is attested to Pilate, not only by his own conscience, but also by the image of God's blessedness, that it should be to his misery to meddle with one whose righteousness so far exceeded princes and powers. *But the chief priests and elders persuaded the multitude that they should ask Barabbas,* whom they chose for their head, through whom came death; *and destroy Jesus,* that Christ should bear the sin of many at the hand of the Father. *The governor answered and said unto them, Whether of the twain will ye that I release unto you? They said, Barabbas.* Through the death of Christ the guilty receive pardon. *Pilate saith unto them, What shall I do then with Jesus which is called Christ? They all say unto him, Let him be crucified. And the governor said, Why, what evil hath he done? But they cried out the more, saying, Let him be crucified.* Through the condemnation of the Father, Christ bore the guilt of many. *When Pilate saw that he could prevail nothing, but that rather a tumult was made, he took water,* as though it might cleanse his sin; *and washed his hands before the multitude,* for his guilty conscience; *saying, I am innocent of the blood of this just person:* He professed Christ righteous, yet not himself a sinner; *see ye to it.* Pilate acquits Christ, yet suffers him to be punished, which ought not to proceed from one and the same person. *Then answered all the people, and said, His blood be on us, and on our children,* that salvation might come to the whole world, and return unto the Jews. *Then released he Barabbas unto them: and when he had scourged Jesus, he delivered him to be crucified,* that by the testimony of his innocence, Christ might be sanctified above the measure of the law.

Mark 14:54-15:15

And Peter followed him afar off, even into the palace of the high priest: to bear witness to his trial, without yet partaking of his suffering; *and he sat with the servants, and warmed himself at the fire,* a servant of the Lord, comforted by his sacrifice. *And the chief priests and all the council sought for witness against Jesus to put him to death; and found none,* that he should be condemned to death for the glory of God alone, in the private dwelling place of the high priest. *For many bare false witness against him, but their witness agreed not together.* An object is that to which thought is particular; therefore, two or three witnesses are required to establish a fact, whether they agree, that they may be cross-examined.[268] *And there arose certain, and bare false witness against him, saying, We heard him say, I will destroy this temple that is made with hands, and within three days I will build another made without hands.* The mere statement of which fails to establish guilt.[269] *But neither so did their witness agree together.* They did not understand that he must be put to death that he might be raised. *And the high priest stood up in the midst, and asked Jesus, saying, Answerest thou nothing? what is it which these witness against thee?* Though his accusers had not met the burden of proof, the high priest called Jesus to account, as the Father holds the Son accountable for the sins of the world. *But he held his peace, and answered nothing.* He rested in his innocence, nor did he defend himself when condemned by God, but trusted in God, that he would also justify him.[270] *Again the high priest asked him, and said unto him, Art*

---

[268] Deut. 17:2-7; 19:15-21.
[269] 1 Kings 21:13.
[270] 1 Pet. 2:21-23.

thou the Christ, the Son of the Blessed? The very blessedness of God, whom they knew of, but knew not. *And Jesus said, I am:* Jesus confessed himself, preaching the Gospel to the whole council of priests and elders, that he should be put to death for that only; *and ye shall see the Son of man sitting on the right hand of power, and coming in the clouds of heaven,* that they might know that all their schemes accomplished nothing but what God himself had ordained from everlasting.[271] *Then the high priest rent his clothes, and saith, What need we any further witnesses?* He held him in contempt, as though he had blasphemed in the presence of the court, because they despised their hope of salvation. *Ye have heard the blasphemy: what think ye? And they all condemned him to be guilty of death.* Jesus Christ is not put to death for the law, but for the glory of the Father, who laid on him the sins of the world, to bear the false accusations of many. *And some began to spit on him, and to cover his face, and to buffet him, and to say unto him, Prophesy: and the servants did strike him with the palms of their hands.* They multiplied the injustices of his trial, that he might patiently bear all their sins, whereby he prophesied of the Father. *And as Peter was beneath in the palace, there cometh one of the maids of the high priest:* gently to call him to himself; *And when she saw Peter warming himself,* the Lord did not berate him with his sins, but comforted him with his mercy; *she looked upon him, and said, And thou also wast with Jesus of Nazareth,* the disciples of Christ are conspicuous among men. *But he denied, saying, I know not, neither understand I what thou sayest,* he denied by evasion, lying, yet refusing to be numbered among them. *And he went out into the porch; and the cock crew,* that he might by a sign be brought to repentance, and awoken from his sinful slumber. *And a maid saw him again, and began to say to them that stood by, This is one of them. And he denied it again. And a little after, they that stood by said again to Peter, Surely thou art one of them: for thou art a Galilaean, and thy speech agreeth thereto.* God uses even ordinary qualities to mark his own, to distinguish them from the world. *But he began to curse and to swear, saying, I know not this man of whom ye speak. And the second time the cock crew,* to awaken him from his sin. *And Peter called to mind the word that Jesus said unto him, Before the cock crow twice, thou shalt deny me thrice. And when he thought thereon, he wept.* He wept for the words of Jesus, with godly

---

[271] Acts 2:23, 4:28.

feeling. *And straightway in the morning,* for they were intent; the divine purpose being unconditional, is fulfilled without delay; *the chief priests held a consultation with the elders and scribes and the whole council,* the will of all the leaders of the Jews, as of the divine purpose; *and bound Jesus,* for he was bound by the moral law and the will of God, to which he freely submitted; *and carried him away, and delivered him to Pilate,* the deputy of the Roman government, which ruled the world by divine providence and prophetic appointment.[272] *And Pilate asked him, Art thou the King of the Jews?* for Pilate knew that they envied him. *And he answering said unto him, Thou sayest it.* The question admits the legitimacy of the claim, and the truth thereof follows. *And the chief priests accused him of many things: but he answered nothing.* He rested in the presumption of his innocence, and gave no place to his accusers, but patiently withstood all, whatsoever the Father imputed to him, according to his pleasure. *And Pilate asked him again, saying, Answerest thou nothing? behold how many things they witness against thee.* They sought to overwhelm him with a multitude of accusations, yet he bore them all, even the sins of the world, through his nonlegal righteousness. *But Jesus yet answered nothing; so that Pilate marvelled.* Jesus would not answer any charge besides that of his office, that he should be put to death for that only. *Now at that feast he released unto them one prisoner, whomsoever they desired,* mercy, and the fallibility of human justice, commending this custom. *And there was one named Barabbas, which lay bound with them that had made insurrection with him, who had committed murder in the insurrection. And the multitude crying aloud began to desire him to do as he had ever done unto them,* mercy commended by the unmerciful. *But Pilate answered them, saying, Will ye that I release unto you the King of the Jews?* He acknowledges his divine innocence. *For he knew that the chief priests had delivered him for envy,* for all men sinned to be like God, and behold, here is God manifest in the flesh. *But the chief priests moved the people, that he should rather release Barabbas unto them,* that through the judgment of Christ, mercy should come to those worthy of death. *And Pilate answered and said again unto them, What will ye then that I shall do unto him whom ye call the King of the Jews?* Whom they confessed to be king by putting him to the test. *And they cried out*

---

[272] Dan. 2:31-43.

again, Crucify him. Then Pilate said unto them, Why, what evil hath he done? And they cried out the more exceedingly, Crucify him. They condemned him unconditionally. *And so Pilate, willing to content the people, released Barabbas unto them, and delivered Jesus, when he had scourged him, to be crucified,* for by the justification of the Holy Ghost, Jesus is sanctified through sufferings and death, vindicating the condemnation of the Father.

Luke 22:54-23:25

Then took they him, and led him, and brought him into the high priest's house, to be judged privately, as by the Father. *And when they had kindled a fire in the midst of the hall, and were set down together, Peter sat down among them,* as a man out of place. *But a certain maid beheld him as he sat by the fire, and earnestly looked upon him,* because he was conspicuous among them, and she could tell by his spirit that he was a disciple; *and said, This man was also with him. And he denied him, saying, Woman,* he showed her respect; the sins of the elect are lined with grace; *I know him not. And after a little while another saw him, and said, Thou art also of them. And Peter said, Man, I am not. And about the space of one hour after,* the Lord giving Peter time to repent, and to work his mercy in his heart; *another confidently affirmed,* they were in no way deceived by him, that no harm should be done by his denials; *saying, Of a truth this fellow also was with him: for he is a Galilaean,* God using even ordinary characteristics to mark his own. *And Peter said, Man, I know not what thou sayest. And immediately, while he yet spake, the cock crew. And the Lord turned, and looked upon Peter,* correcting his error with no more than a look. *And Peter remembered the word of the Lord, how he had said unto him, Before the cock crow, thou shalt deny me thrice,* as Jesus had foretold him, that he should suffer alone, that his disciples might afterward suffer with him. *And Peter went out, and wept bitterly,* for the sinfulness of his sin. *And the men that held Jesus mocked him, and smote him. And when they had blindfolded him, they struck him on the face, and asked him, saying, Prophesy, who is it that smote thee?* They tempted him to judge, though he came not to judge, but to save.[273] *And many other things blasphemously spake*

---

[273] John 3:17.

they against him. They blasphemed him, acknowledging him Lord, as do the heathen. *And as soon as it was day*, the judgment of God fulfilled without delay, to bring to light his righteousness; *the elders of the people and the chief priests and the scribes came together, and led him into their council, saying, Art thou the Christ? tell us*, by which they acknowledged him to be the same. *And he said unto them, If I tell you, ye will not believe:* they asked in order to condemn; *And if I also ask you, ye will not answer me, nor let me go*, that he might not defend himself. *Hereafter shall the Son of man sit on the right hand of the power of God*, for he does not justify himself, but the Spirit of the Father. *Then said they all, Art thou then the Son of God? And he said unto them, Ye say that I am*, for they asked the question. *And they said, What need we any further witness? for we ourselves have heard of his own mouth.* They needed witnesses to bring him to trial, and to hold him in contempt, as though he had blasphemed in the legitimate presence of the court. *And the whole multitude of them arose, and led him unto Pilate. And they began to accuse him, saying, We found this fellow perverting the nation, and forbidding to give tribute to Caesar, saying that he himself is Christ a King*, they accused him of civil matters, not religious; *And Pilate asked him, saying, Art thou the King of the Jews? And he answered him and said, Thou sayest it*, Pilate confessed Jesus to be the Son of God the moment he acknowledged its possibility. *Then said Pilate to the chief priests and to the people, I find no fault in this man.* The religious leaders condemned Jesus, because the Father imputes to him the sins of the world, yet the civil power acquitted him before all, because he works righteousness on behalf of his people. *And they were the more fierce*, because of his innocence; *saying, He stirreth up the people, teaching throughout all Jewry, beginning from Galilee to this place.* They accuse him again after his acquittal. *When Pilate heard of Galilee, he asked whether the man were a Galilaean. And as soon as he knew that he belonged unto Herod's jurisdiction, he sent him to Herod*, who beheaded John the Baptist, for the head of John the Baptist is required of him, which is Christ; and whose father had condemned Jesus and slain the infants, that he, being judged by the father, might be shown nonlegally righteous by the son; *who himself also was at Jerusalem at that time*, Christ is righteous, not only under the law, but also above it; wherefore, Pilate sends him to Herod, to the jurisdiction of another outside his own. *And when*

Herod saw Jesus, he was exceeding glad: with an earthly joy; *for he was desirous to see him of a long season, because he had heard many things of him; and he hoped to have seen some miracle done by him.* He was curious, and sought wonder, but blind to the wonder before him, for the mystery of Christ lies in his obedience unto death. *Then he questioned with him in many words; but he answered him nothing,* for his righteousness is above the law. *And the chief priests and scribes stood and vehemently accused him.* He withstood all condemnation through his nonlegal righteousness. *And Herod with his men of war set him at nought,* for they made war against him, acknowledging him to be the conqueror; *and mocked him, and arrayed him in a gorgeous robe, and sent him again to Pilate.* Disappointed by the simplicity of his obedience, he disciplines him without any verdict. Pilate justifies Christ. Herod neither justifies nor condemns, showing forth the nonlegal righteousness of Christ. *And the same day Pilate and Herod were made friends together: for before they were at enmity between themselves,* for in the death of Christ, Jesus' innocence harmonizes with his nonlegal righteousness. *And Pilate, when he had called together the chief priests and the rulers and the people, Said unto them, Ye have brought this man unto me, as one that perverteth the people: and, behold, I, having examined him before you, have found no fault in this man touching those things whereof ye accuse him:* No, nor yet Herod: because the lack of a guilty verdict constitutes an acquittal; *for I sent you to him; and, lo, nothing worthy of death is done unto him. I will therefore chastise him, and release him.* He again acquits him, because it is the will of man that the righteous should live, but it is the will of God that Christ should be raised from the dead. *(For of necessity,* because Jesus is king; *he must release one unto them at the feast.),* according to the will of the people, through whom governments possess all their just power to punish; *And they cried out all at once, saying, Away with this man, and release unto us Barabbas: (Who for a certain sedition made in the city,* one not falsely accused, but known to have lead others astray; *and for murder,* one through whom comes death; *was cast into prison.) Pilate therefore, willing to release Jesus, spake again to them.* He sought to persuade them, to release Jesus by a custom, rather than to make good his acquittal. *But they cried, saying, Crucify him, crucify him. And he said unto them the third time,* fully and finally acquitted by all three divine persons; *Why, what evil hath he done? I have found no cause of death in him: I will therefore chastise him, and let him go.* Though he was weak to deliver him to their will, he did not veer from the judgment of his innocence. *And they were instant with loud voices, requiring* of necessity; *that he might be crucified,* according to the divine will. *And the voices of them and of the chief priests prevailed,* the mob exercising their tyranny over the true king. *And Pilate gave sentence that it should be as they required,* not according to law, but for the glory of the Father. *And he released unto them him that for sedition and murder was cast into prison, whom they had desired;* whom they took as it were for their head, which prophesied how the Jews would revolt against Rome, shedding blood, and be destroyed for their rejection of the Messiah;[274] *but he delivered Jesus to their will,* yet not he, but God, that Jesus might bear the sins of many rebels.

John 18:15-19:16

And Simon Peter followed Jesus, and so did another disciple: yet were they not arrested and tried by the multitude, because Jesus should, for their sakes, suffer alone; *that disciple was known unto the high priest, and went in with Jesus into the palace of the high priest,* into his home, the private dwelling place of the Lord's anointed, because Christ is put to death by divine privilege. *But Peter stood at the door without,* for they desired only the Lord, because he alone must be put to death for the sins of his people. *Then went out that other disciple, which was known unto the high priest, and spake unto her that kept the door, and brought in Peter,* God using the enemies of his Christ to be merciful to his people. *Then saith the damsel that kept the door unto Peter, Art not thou also one of this man's disciples? He saith, I am not,* whereby he denied not only the Lord, but fellowship with John, yet his lie was so plain to them as that no harm should be done by it. *And the servants and officers stood there, who had made a fire of coals; for it was cold:* for the love of God was not in that place;[275] *and they warmed themselves: and Peter stood with them, and warmed himself.* The whole world is comforted by the sacrifice of Christ, especially his disciples. *The high priest then asked Jesus of his disciples, and of his*

---

[274] Josephus, *The Jewish War.*
[275] Matt. 24:12.

doctrine, he asked unjustly, for he asked what he knew already. *Jesus answered him, I spake openly to the world; I ever taught in the synagogue, and in the temple, whither the Jews always resort; and in secret have I said nothing. Why askest thou me? ask them which heard me, what I have said unto them: behold, they know what I said.* All public, without dispute, neither subject to trial, much less in secret. *And when he had thus spoken, one of the officers which stood by struck Jesus with the palm of his hand,* for Jesus being righteous suffered by the Holy Spirit; *saying, Answerest thou the high priest so? Jesus answered him, If I have spoken evil, bear witness of the evil: but if well, why smitest thou me?* for he was smitten of God, and the high priest is bound by the law, and God gave up his own Son to fulfill all righteousness on our behalf. *Now Annas had sent him bound unto Caiaphas the high priest,* to be offered by his hand, as it were, a sacrifice for sins; *And Simon Peter stood and warmed himself. They said therefore unto him, Art not thou also one of his disciples?* They asked not to condemn him, but as a mere point of fact. *He denied it, and said, I am not. One of the servants of the high priest, being his kinsman whose ear Peter cut off, saith, Did not I see thee in the garden with him?* Not even that he should suffer with Christ because he defended him, for Christ must suffer alone for his people. *Peter then denied again: and immediately the cock crew. Then led they Jesus from Caiaphas unto the hall of judgment:* Having determined in secret to put Christ to death, they now put their plans into public execution, that he might be justified before all; *and it was early; and they themselves went not into the judgment hall, lest they should be defiled; but that they might eat the passover.* His accusers deprived him of the right to face them in person, because Christ is condemned by the invisible God, to be our passover. *Pilate then went out unto them, and said, What accusation bring ye against this man? They answered and said unto him, If he were not a malefactor, we would not have delivered him up unto thee.* The Father condemns the Son without any particular ground but that of his own pleasure.[276] *Then said Pilate unto them, Take ye him, and judge him according to your law.* The law of one nation, not of all; of limited jurisdiction, and not of the whole world. *The Jews therefore said unto him, It is not lawful for us to put any man to death:* They had no authority over criminal cases, but civil only. The phrase "put to death" refers

---

[276] Is. 53:10.

to the punishment of any criminal matter, for all such punishment is a form of death, whether of the whole or of a part only.[277] Thus David describes fourfold restitution: "*As* the LORD liveth, the man that hath done this *thing* shall surely die: And he shall restore the lamb fourfold, because he did this thing, and because he had no pity" (2 Samuel 12:5-6). Jesus Christ is not condemned in himself, but in relation to the Father. A civil case determines the relation of one person to another, and is judged privately, and not by all; but a criminal case judges a matter in itself, as good or evil, and so worthy of punishment or reward, and that by the whole community. So Christ is condemned by the Father, yet is he justified by the Spirit, who proceeds from the Father and the Son. *That the saying of Jesus might be fulfilled, which he spake, signifying what death he should die.* That he should die on the cross, in the sight of all men, at the hands of Jew and Gentile, to draw all men unto himself, and that he should ascend into heaven after he is raised from the dead. "And I, if I be lifted up from the earth, will draw all *men* unto me. This he said, signifying what death he should die" (John 12:32-33). *Then Pilate entered into the judgment hall again, and called Jesus, and said unto him, Art thou the King of the Jews? Jesus answered him, Sayest thou this thing of thyself, or did others tell it thee of me?* He ought to judge for himself, that he might be saved, for if not by mere repetition of words, but with understanding of the meaning, then Pilate should have understood the truth of the matter from the words themselves. *Pilate answered, Am I a Jew? Thine own nation and the chief priests have delivered thee unto me: what hast thou done? Jesus answered, My kingdom is not of this world: if my kingdom were of this world, then would my servants fight, that I should not be delivered to the Jews: but now is my kingdom not from hence.* Christ is a king, not by force of arms, but by an eternal priesthood. *Pilate therefore said unto him, Art thou a king then? Jesus answered, Thou sayest that I am a king. To this end was I born,* for the sake of practical reason; *and for this cause came I into the world,* begotten of the Father; *that I should bear witness unto the truth,* that by his witness we should keep the moral law. *Every one that is of the truth heareth my voice,* for it is of the essence. *Pilate saith unto him, What is truth?* By the very question he admitted the answer, though he understood it not, because he

---

[277] Matt. 5:29-30.

sought by theoretical reason what is given only through practical. *And when he had said this, he went out again unto the Jews, and saith unto them, I find in him no fault at all,* not only of the charges, but of any wrongdoing whatsoever. Pilate acquitted him for lack of any evidence whatsoever. Christ is condemned only by the Father, for the glory of his person, that he might be justified by his Spirit.[278] *But ye have a custom, that I should release unto you one at the passover:* an honorable custom to preserve the integrity of the law, and to show the benefits of Christ's blood; *will ye therefore that I release unto you the King of the Jews?* His duty under the law, which he sought to fulfill, not by means of judgment, but by a custom of the people, whereby he gave Christ up to their will. *Then cried they all again, saying, Not this man, but Barabbas. Now Barabbas was a robber.* Their wrath being so much more against Christ than against a notorious criminal, even as the condemnation of Christ encompasses all our sin, and overshadows all our guilt. *Then Pilate therefore took Jesus, and scourged him.* The Son is sanctified by the justification of his Spirit. *And the soldiers platted a crown of thorns, and put it on his head,* the king of suffering, a king by suffering, to sanctify those who suffer righteously; *and they put on him a purple robe, And said, Hail, King of the Jews! and they smote him with their hands.* A king who bore their sins, unwittingly confessed by his mockers. *Pilate therefore went forth again, and saith unto them, Behold, I bring him forth to you, that ye may know that I find no fault in him.* Pilate confesses his innocence. *Then came Jesus forth, wearing the crown of thorns, and the purple robe,* whereby the people also received him as such. *And Pilate saith unto them, Behold the man!* God manifest in the flesh, visible to all. *When the chief priests therefore and officers saw him,* for they despised his glory; *they cried out, saying, Crucify him, crucify him.* They would have Pilate crucify him, who found him without fault. *Pilate saith unto them, Take ye him, and crucify him: for I find no fault in him.* This transition is given only by John, to show the unity of sign and event. *The Jews answered him, We have a law, and by our law he ought to die,* not of the Jews—*our law*—but of the Holy Trinity; *because he made himself the Son of God,* for by the divine will he created himself in human nature. *When Pilate therefore heard that saying, he was the more afraid;* having impartially acquitted him, he now

____

[278] Ps. 51:4.

understands the significance of the title, "King of the Jews;" *And went again into the judgment hall, and saith unto Jesus, Whence art thou? But Jesus gave him no answer,* for he is from above. *Then saith Pilate unto him, Speakest thou not unto me? knowest thou not that I have power to crucify thee, and have power to release thee?* Having already acquitted him, Pilate now claimed a power not lawful. *Jesus answered, Thou couldest have no power at all against me, except it were given thee from above: therefore he that delivered me unto thee hath the greater sin.* Caiaphas, for the council of the Jews ruled Israel of old, and knew that Messiah would come. Christ said this to Pilate that he might repent, to show that all comes to pass for the glory of God, and the salvation of sinners. *And from thenceforth Pilate sought to release him:* he truly acknowledged his innocence; *but the Jews cried out, saying, If thou let this man go, thou art not Caesar's friend: whosoever maketh himself a king speaketh against Caesar.* He chose rather friendship with the world, and with the imperial authority, than with Christ, the king of kings. *When Pilate therefore heard that saying,* Pilate was persuaded by political motives; *he brought Jesus forth, and sat down in the judgment seat in a place that is called the Pavement, but in the Hebrew, Gabbatha,* in the sight of all men. *And it was the preparation of the passover, and about the sixth hour:* They rushed to judgment, to put him to death before the Sabbath, the will of God fulfilled without delay; *and he saith unto the Jews, Behold your King!* He confesses him by affirmation, giving him the official recognition of the Roman government. *But they cried out, Away with him, away with him, crucify him. Pilate saith unto them, Shall I crucify your King? The chief priests answered, We have no king but Caesar.* They denied God himself. *Then delivered he him therefore unto them to be crucified.* Pilate acquitted Jesus, confessing him king of the Jews; accordingly also, all those who through Pilate's judgment crucified him, showing forth in their sin the righteous judgment of God, who justifies Christ in his submission to condemnation.

The Burial of Christ

In death Christ fully satisfies the justice of God, not only for himself, but also for his people; yea, for all men, that they might live. Yet the church confesses that he descended into hell, and the Scriptures testify also:

> Wherefore he saith, When he ascended up on high, he led captivity captive, and gave gifts unto men. (Now that he ascended, what is it but that he also descended first into the lower parts of the earth? He that descended is the same also that ascended up far above all heavens, that he might fill all things.) Ephesians 4:8-10, cf. Phil. 2:10

The burial of Christ manifests his nonlegal righteousness. The divine nature is invisible, and the human nature, conformed to the divine, is hidden by death, and covered by burial. Nevertheless, the righteous in no way desire death, but life, and the righteousness of Christ remains the ground of his life. Wherefore, in death the body of Jesus lies in hell, and the soul, in the ground of its union with the body, lies there with the body also;[279] but as Christ ought to live, his flesh rests in hope, and his soul rejoices in paradise. Therefore, in all righteousness, *he descended into hell*, when he was buried in the grave, that he should be raised from the dead.[280]

> Therefore my heart is glad, and my glory rejoiceth: my flesh also shall rest in hope. For thou wilt not leave my soul in hell; neither wilt thou suffer thine holy one to see corruption. Psalm 16:9-10

> If I make my bed in hell, behold, thou *art there*. Psalm 139:8

---

[279] Aquinas, *Summa* 3.52.1-4.
[280] *Larger Catechism* Q.50.

Because in him remains the ground of life, yea, life itself and the Spirit of life, he is kept alive under the power of death, for in him death is life, and the dead live.

> O LORD, thou hast brought up my soul from the grave: thou hast kept me alive, that I should not go down to the pit. Psalm 30:3

> For he is not a God of the dead, but of the living: for all live unto him. Luke 20:38

The burial of Christ represents the transition from death to life, for if he lives while dead, then he must also be raised.

> What profit *is there* in my blood, when I go down to the pit? Shall the dust praise thee? Shall it declare thy truth? Hear, O LORD, and have mercy upon me: LORD, be thou my helper. Thou hast turned for me my mourning into dancing: thou hast put off my sackcloth, and girded me with gladness; To the end that *my* glory may sing praise to thee, and not be silent. O LORD my God, I will give thanks unto thee forever. Psalm 30:9-12

In death the body is separated from the soul, wherein it produces no intuition of the image of God. Though the form thereof remains, yet the matter is formless and void. Nevertheless Christ, resting in the grave, yet lived, showing forth the image of divine righteousness, that in his resurrection all sorrow may be transformed into joy. And by beholding his likeness, we all partake of the same, for he is God manifest in the flesh, yea, our divine head.

> For with thee *is* the fountain of life: in thy light shall we see light. Psalm 36:9

And every man that hath this hope in him purifieth himself, even as he is pure. 1 John 3:3

The old creation passes away in his death;[281] it is buried with him, that the resurrection of Christ should be the beginning of a new creation, "wherein dwelleth righteousness" (2 Peter 3:13).

Therefore if any man *be* in Christ, *he is* a new creature: old things are passed away; behold, all things are become new. 2 Corinthians 5:17

For in Christ Jesus neither circumcision availeth any thing, nor uncircumcision, but a new creature. Galatians 6:15

By burial I understand the means whereby the whole community consents to the death of a member, and the body is preserved for the glory of God, out of the continuing rights of the person in this world, and acknowledgement of his passage to the next, unto the resurrection of the dead. Wherefore, the burial of Christ is our entrance into a new life, whereby we are preserved to the end of the world, to the restoration of all things, and the new creation.

Christ rests in his suffering; sanctified and perfected, his work is complete, that those who sleep in Jesus may rest also. It is a work of his soul, united with his body, whereby he consents to death, and so brings forth life. Death truly is the separation of body and soul, permanent by reason of its ground, yet on the last day all shall be raised, their death encompassed by life renewed, death being swallowed up in victory.[282]

The burial of Christ is the work whereby men are consecrated to God in this life, in the body of death and the old creation. There must be a ground for the transition from the old creation to the new, that we may be saved in this present life, and not only in glory; that being saved in this life, we may be saved also in

---

[281] Rom. 6:6.
[282] Is. 25:8; 1 Cor. 15:54.

glory. And though we see him not, we yet live by faith, resting in his finished work.

> Know ye not, that so many of us as were baptized into Jesus Christ were baptized into his death? Therefore we are buried with him by baptism into death: that like as Christ was raised up from the dead by the glory of the Father, even so we also should walk in newness of life. Romans 6:3-4

> If ye then be risen with Christ, seek those things which are above, where Christ sitteth on the right hand of God. Set your affection on things above, not on things on the earth. For ye are dead, and your life is hid with Christ in God. When Christ, *who is* our life, shall appear, then shall ye also appear with him in glory. Colossians 3:1-4

Scripture Proofs

The law of God requires burial, not only of the righteous and honorable, but of the wicked and condemned. These are by diverse judgments united in Christ.

> And if a man have committed a sin worthy of death, and he be to be put to death, and thou hang him on a tree: His body shall not remain all night upon the tree, but thou shalt in any wise bury him that day; (for he that is hanged *is* accursed of God;) that thy land be not defiled, which the Lord thy God giveth thee *for* an inheritance. Deuteronomy 21:22-23

Thou shalt in any wise bury him that day. Though accursed of God, yet not of man, whose punishment extends only to this life, and not unto the next. They had no power to deprive him of burial, no, not for a single unit of time. Whether he be elect or reprobate, he must be preserved unto the resurrection. Not even Jezebel was regarded as wicked enough to be deprived of burial by men; she was deprived of that honor by God.[283] And not only that, but the place where Judas hanged himself became a place of burial. Nor should the curse remain in the land, for the sin purged by death is no more; the body must be buried. Lest therefore they should partake of his curse, he must be buried.

> Whoso sheddeth man's blood, by man shall his blood be shed: for in the image of God made he man. Genesis 9:6

> So ye shall not pollute the land wherein ye *are*: for blood it defileth the land: and the land cannot be cleansed of the blood that is shed therein, but by the blood of him that shed it. Defile not therefore the land which ye shall inhabit, wherein I dwell: for I the Lord dwell among the children of Israel. Numbers 35:33-34

The punishment of crime extends no further than death.[284] Bloodshed ought not to be prolonged unto rottenness and decay, nor ought men to presume upon the office of divine vengeance. They ought to put away the sin and curse of the dead by burial, to cleanse the land, to make it fit for the service of God.

How grievous is the sin of those mortal men, who after they have tortured and slain their enemy, defile even the body of the dead? How great is their wrath? But the wrath of God being satisfied in Christ, he is buried even with the consent of his enemies, for their wrath ceased in his death, because he drank it patiently to the end.[285]

Matthew 27:55-66

When the even was come, there came a rich man of Arimathaea, for in the burial of Christ are hidden riches of his grace; *named Joseph,* he bore the name of Jesus'

---

[283] 2 Kings 9:34-37.
[284] Rom 13:4.
[285] Aquinas, *Summa* 3.51.2 Reply to Objection 1.

father, to show the unity of Christ's birth and death, that his death might be the birth of a new creation; *who also himself was Jesus' disciple:* that Christ might be buried in love, even the love of the Father. *He went to Pilate, and begged the body of Jesus,* though rich, yet poor in spirit.[286] *Then Pilate commanded the body to be delivered,* to fulfill all righteousness by the man who judged him innocent. *And when Joseph had taken the body, he wrapped it in a clean linen cloth,* as the righteousness of Christ; *And laid it in his own new tomb,* for he loved him as himself, and Christ is buried unto the new creation; *which he had hewn out in the rock:* a place prepared for him in hell; *and he rolled a great stone to the door of the sepulchre,* holy, separated unto God, he lay under the power of death; *and departed,* for he had put him in the hand of the Almighty. *And there was Mary Magdalene, and the other Mary, sitting over against the sepulchre,* for the church by her life bears witness to his burial. *Now the next day, that followed the day of the preparation,* the Sabbath, wherein Christ rested from his work; *the chief priests and Pharisees came together unto Pilate, Saying, Sir, we remember that that deceiver said, while he was yet alive, After three days I will rise again,* one day for each judgment, to show forth the justification of the Holy Spirit, who proceeds from the Father and the Son. *Command therefore that the sepulchre be made sure until the third day,* the sepulchre was sealed by those who crucified him, as by the condemnation of the Father, until the time appointed; *lest his disciples come by night,* that all should be public; *and steal him away, and say unto the people, He is risen from the dead: so the last error shall be worse than the first.* They testified to his death and burial, that the resurrection might also be sure. *Pilate said unto them, Ye have a watch: go your way, make it as sure as ye can,* that only God himself should set him free from the grave. *So they went, and made the sepulchre sure, sealing the stone, and setting a watch,* that even his enemies should be witnesses, that all men might watch for his return.

---

[286] Matt. 5:3.

Mark 15:42-47

And now when the even was come, because it was the preparation, that is, the day before the sabbath, by his perfect sanctification in death, Jesus perfectly prepared for the sabbath, and in burial he perfectly kept the same; *Joseph of Arimathaea, an honourable counsellor,* with standing before God and man; *which also waited for the kingdom of God,* willing to set aside his own authority for the king of kings; *came, and went in boldly unto Pilate, and craved the body of Jesus,* in the humility of faith. *And Pilate marvelled if he were already dead:* Christ died, not through the slack hand of man, but of God, for he was quick unto sanctification, so that Pilate marvelled; *and calling unto him the centurion, he asked him whether he had been any while dead,* this one, who converted through Christ's death, became also a means to his burial, because the purpose is one. *And when he knew it of the centurion, he gave the body to Joseph. And he bought fine linen,* to show the riches of his grace;[287] *and took him down,* the curse removed in his death; *and wrapped him in the linen, and laid him in a sepulchre which was hewn out of a rock, and rolled a stone unto the door of the sepulchre,* that his body might be set apart to God, separate from sinners, as in the ascension.[288] *And Mary Magdalene and Mary the mother of Joses beheld where he was laid,* that they might return to his rest after the Sabbath, for in his resurrection that rest is renewed.

Luke 23:50-56

And, behold, there was a man named Joseph, a counsellor; and he was a good man, and a just: to bury Christ in righteousness; *(The same had not consented to the counsel and deed of them;)* He was of that body, but not of their spirit, for in righteousness the Father condemns the Son; *he was of Arimathaea, a city of the Jews: who also himself waited for the kingdom of God,* a true Jew.[289] *This man went unto Pilate, and begged the body of Jesus.* Though he had authority, he emptied

---

287 Eph. 1:7
288 Heb. 7:26.
289 Rom. 2:28-29.

himself.[290] *And he took it down, and wrapped it in linen, and laid it in a sepulchre that was hewn in stone, wherein never man before was laid,* that it might be wholly dedicated to the Lord. *And that day was the preparation, and the sabbath drew on,* for in his rest he perfectly fulfills the sabbath. *And the women also, which came with him from Galilee, followed after, and beheld the sepulchre, and how his body was laid,* even the manner, for it was divine, and they hallowed his burial in their hearts. *And they returned, and prepared spices and ointments;* to anoint him again after the Sabbath, to consecrate his rest; *and rested the sabbath day according to the commandment,* because the sabbath is perpetual, and endures after the death of Christ, to show forth the completion of his work.

John 19:38-42

And after this Joseph of Arimathaea, being a disciple of Jesus, but secretly for fear of the Jews, to show forth the secret righteousness of Christ; *besought Pilate that he might take away the body of Jesus: and Pilate gave him leave. He came therefore, and took the body of Jesus. And there came also Nicodemus, which at the first came to Jesus by night,* another who learned of him in secret;[291] *and brought a mixture of myrrh and aloes, about an hundred pound weight,* the great weight of Christ's righteousness, for a sweet-smelling savor. *Then took they the body of Jesus, and wound it in linen clothes with the spices, as the manner of the Jews is to bury,* because he gave up his life for his people. *Now in the place where he was crucified there was a garden;* for Christ is planted unto new life;[292] *and in the garden a new sepulchre, wherein was never man yet laid,* of the new creation, and holy. *There laid they Jesus therefore because of the Jews' preparation day,* to observe the Sabbath, because on that day Christ rested from his work; *for the sepulchre was nigh at hand.* The will of God being one, Christ is buried near the place of his crucifixion.

---

[290] Phil. 2:7.
[291] John 3:1-21.
[292] John 12:24.

The Anointing of Mary

Scripture plainly teaches the sign of Christ's burial: the anointing of Jesus by Mary. Jesus says that she did this for his burial, and that for this she shall be remembered everywhere in the preaching of the Gospel. Nor did the apostles understand the sign, but objected to it, and withal it has common elements with the burial itself.

Jesus Christ lives, even under the power of death. The life of man belongs to the spirit, and the spirit returns to God, but the life of Christ belongs to the Holy Ghost, through whom he is justified, that he should live again. Wherefore, Christ's burial is signified by an emblem of the Holy Spirit, bestowed on the blessedness of God by the image thereof, for by his blessedness he freely submits himself to condemnation.

This sign is omitted from Luke because it belongs not to the Son, but to the Holy Spirit, through whom Christ lives under death, yet Luke records the conspiracy of Judas, which is the part of this sign that pertains to the Son, to show forth the condemnation of the Father, and the necessity of sin for the glory of God.

Matthew 26:1-13

And it came to pass, when Jesus had finished all these sayings, having spoken of the final judgment, and the division between the righteous and the wicked, for as the end of the world and the beginning of the new, so is the death and resurrection of Christ; *he said unto his disciples, Ye know that after two days is the feast of the passover, and the Son of man is betrayed to be crucified.* The Lord Jesus Christ was slain by men, to be their passover. *Then assembled together the chief priests, and the scribes, and the elders of the people, unto the palace of the high priest, who was called Caiaphas, And consulted that they might take Jesus by subtilty, and kill him.* Christ is put to death by the foreknowledge of God, signified by his chosen instruments. *But they said, Not on the feast day, lest there be an uproar among the people.* The leaders of Israel took counsel privately, without the people. *Now when Jesus was in Bethany, in the house of Simon the leper*, he ate with outcasts to show that he has a righteousness outside the law, by which he bears their sins; *There came unto him a woman having an alabaster box of very precious ointment, and poured it on his head, as he sat at meat*, for he is our head, and our sins being forgiven make him more lovely to us.[293] *But when his disciples saw it, they had indignation, saying, To what purpose is this waste? For this ointment might have been sold for much, and given to the poor.* They did not understand the sign. *When Jesus understood it, he said unto them, Why trouble ye the woman? for she hath wrought a good work upon me*, to produce an intuition of the Holy Spirit, who proceeds from the Father and the Son. *For ye have the poor always with you; but me ye have not always.* The poor are ends in themselves, but the divine persons are supreme ends in themselves.[294] *For in that she hath poured this ointment on my body, she did it for my burial*, an intuition for the concept, for even the body of Christ is holy, and shows forth the divine nature in his death, giving forth the savor of life. *Verily I say unto you, Wheresoever this gospel shall be preached in the whole world, there shall also this, that this woman hath done, be told for a memorial of her.* Those who glorify Christ partake also of his glory. *Then one of the twelve, called Judas Iscariot, went unto the chief priests, And said unto them, What will ye give me, and I will deliver him unto you?* He conspired with them to put him to death, to show forth the condemnation of the Father. *And they covenanted with him for thirty pieces of silver*, because he minded earthly things, and understood not the mystery of God before him. *And from that time he sought opportunity to betray him*, that all the elements of his crime should be manifest for the glory of God.

Mark 14:1-9

After two days was the feast of the passover, and of unleavened bread: that is, of moral duties without the mixture of sensual motives;[295] *and the chief priests and the scribes sought how they might take him by craft*, like unto the serpent, whose

---

[293] Luke 7:36-50.
[294] Cf. Mark 15:40-41; Luke 8:2-3; 2 Cor. 8:9.
[295] 1 Cor. 5:8.

head should be bruised by the seed of the woman; *and put him to death. But they said, Not on the feast day, lest there be an uproar of the people,* they refrained only for the sake of the people, against whom they would put him to death. *And being in Bethany in the house of Simon the leper,* because to him all men are clean, devoted to the divine purpose; *as he sat at meat, there came a woman having an alabaster box of ointment of spikenard very precious;* for his innocence, to give forth the savor of life in death; *and she brake the box,* signifying the breaking of his body for us; *and poured it on his head,* because he is buried through the love of the Father, and through his burial he gives life to men. *And there were some that had indignation within themselves, and said, Why was this waste of the ointment made?* The riches of grace so greatly poured out upon him.[296] *For it might have been sold for more than three hundred pence, and have been given to the poor. And they murmured against her,* for they were contrary. *And Jesus said, Let her alone; why trouble ye her? she hath wrought a good work on me. For ye have the poor with you always, and whensoever ye will ye may do them good: but me ye have not always,* he affirmed; *She hath done what she could: she is come aforehand to anoint my body to the burying,* for she affirmed him in his death. *Verily I say unto you, Wheresoever this gospel shall be preached throughout the whole world, this also that she hath done shall be spoken of for a memorial of her.*

Luke 22:1-6

Now the feast of unleavened bread drew nigh, which is called the Passover, when the multitudes of Israel gathered to Jerusalem. *And the chief priests and scribes sought how they might kill him; for they feared the people,* who believed him a prophet. *Then entered Satan into Judas surnamed Iscariot, being of the number of the twelve,* it was not of him, but of the devil. *And he went his way, and communed with the chief priests and captains, how he might betray him unto them,* Luke omits the occasion, to show that it was not a sudden reaction, but a settled intent, grounded in his own person, as the unconditional condemnation of the Father, the anointing of Mary being the occasion of his offense, which drew out his

---

[296] Cant. 1:3.

sinful inclination. *And they were glad, and covenanted to give him money,* because he was a thief. *And he promised, and sought opportunity to betray him unto them in the absence of the multitude,* as of the will of the Father.

John 12:1-11

Then Jesus six days before the passover came to Bethany, where Lazarus was which had been dead, whom he raised from the dead, to show that Christ, here anointed for his burial, should also rise from the dead. *There they made him a supper; and Martha served: but Lazarus was one of them that sat at the table with him.* Lazarus here signifies the resurrection of Christ; Martha, in her service to God and the church, his death; and Mary, by the anointing, his burial.[297] *Then took Mary a pound of ointment of spikenard, very costly, and anointed the feet of Jesus, and wiped his feet with her hair: and the house was filled with the odour of the ointment.* Matthew and Mark say she anointed his head, but John says she anointed his feet, for she anointed both. Christ bears our sins in righteousness, and because he is our head, we also partake of his righteousness, and walk in his footsteps. *Then saith one of his disciples, Judas Iscariot, Simon's son, which should betray him,* Judas, a disciple and an apostle, to show the necessity of Christ's death; *Why was not this ointment sold for three hundred pence, and given to the poor?* A civil business of charity, not inherently religious, but consistent with pure religion. *This he said, not that he cared for the poor; but because he was a thief, and had the bag, and bare what was put therein.* He minded not the things of God, neither had he any regard to moral duties on earth. *Then said Jesus, Let her alone: against the day of my burying hath she kept this.* Judas did not understand the burial of Christ, nor the resurrection, because he understood not the death of Christ, but became the instrument thereof. *For the poor always ye have with you; but me ye have not always,* that Christ, being raised and ascended to the Father, should be met with in the poor.[298] *Much people of the Jews therefore knew that he was there: and they came not for Jesus' sake only, but that they might see Lazarus also, whom he had raised from the*

---

[297] Luke 10:38-42.
[298] Prov. 14:31, 17:5, 19:17; Matt. 25:37-40.

dead, to foretell the resurrection of Jesus. *But the chief priests consulted that they might put Lazarus also to death; Because that by reason of him many of the Jews went away, and believed on Jesus.* They willfully resisted the truth, that even his enemies should testify that Jesus is the Christ, the Son of God.

The missions of Christ yield intuitions of the divine relations:[1] in the virgin birth, of the Father to the Son; in the ascension, of the Son to the Father; and in the second coming, of the Father and the Son to one another in the Holy Spirit.

The relations belong to the persons, but the persons are intuited in their judgments, and the judgments in the atonement. Therefore, the missions of Christ are intuitions of intuitions. The missions are not intuited directly, but indirectly, as grounds of the lawfulness of the atonement, and the persons themselves represented therein. They glorify the atonement, showing forth the divine persons, through whom it comes to pass that Christ is crucified, buried, and raised from the dead.

Thus in the death of Christ his virgin birth appears, for he could not suffer for men's sins, unless he himself is the only begotten Son of God.[2] And so the Scriptures represent these events under a common conception.

> He was taken from prison and from judgment: and who shall declare his generation? For he was cut off out of the land of the living: for the transgression of my people was he stricken. Isaiah 53:8

God gave his Son to the world, that he should give his life for the world.

> For God so loved the world, that he gave his only begotten Son, that whosoever believeth in him should not perish, but have everlasting life. For God sent not his Son into the world to condemn the world; but that the world through him might be saved. John 3:16-17, cf. Rom. 8:32, Gal. 4:4-6, Eph. 5:1-2, Col. 1:19-20, 1 Tim. 1:15

The burial of Christ represents his perfect sanctification in death. This comes to pass through the invisible righteousness he has from the Father.

---

[1] Augustine, *On The Trinity* 2.2, 4.5.
[2] Matt. 27:54; Mark 15:39.

And no man hath ascended up to heaven, but he that came down from heaven, *even* the Son of man which is in heaven. And as Moses lifted up the serpent in the wilderness, even so must the Son of man be lifted up: That whosoever believeth in him should not perish, but have eternal life. John 3:13-15

Likewise, in his resurrection his perfect righteousness shines forth, to be revealed on the last day, but the revelation of his coming cannot be received by us through any sensible intuition; therefore, it must be represented to us through his resurrection, as the necessary end of his life.

Therefore we are buried with him by baptism into death: that like as Christ was raised up from the dead by the glory of the Father, even so we also should walk in newness of life. Romans 6:4

Raised up from the dead, even into heaven, as he says,

If ye then be risen with Christ, seek those things which are above, where Christ sitteth on the right hand of God. Set your affection on things above, not on things on the earth. For ye are dead, and your life is hid with Christ in God. When Christ, who is our life, shall appear, then shall ye also appear with him in glory. Colossians 3:1-4, cf. Acts 17:31

Your life is hid with Christ in God, for we are buried with Christ in his ascension, and raised with him in his return, that we might be glorified with him; *When Christ, who is our life*, because he not only lived, but rose from the dead; *then shall ye also appear with him in glory*.

The order of the atonement follows the order of the persons. Therefore, the order of the missions begins with the virgin birth, because the ground of his death lies in his life. The life of Christ must be thought prior to his death: he is born of a virgin, to die for the sins of men. Likewise, he is buried to ascend, and raised to return in glory. Nevertheless, in the resurrection his death is also the ground of his life, and also follows from the virgin birth, and therefore the whole atonement precedes the ascension and second coming, to glorify the life of Christ.

The Virgin Birth

Jesus Christ is the Son of God, both as God and as man,[3] for he is the blessedness of God, identical in distinction to his righteousness; identical in nature, distinct in person. As identical, Jesus is God begotten of the Father; as distinct, he is a man conceived in the womb of the virgin Mary by the Holy Ghost, for that in him lies distinction, there subsists an intuition of the Son distinct from the concept, sensible and outwardly lawful, and this belongs to man.[4] The identity thereof belongs to God, but the distinction to man, and this distinction is ever enveloped in identity by the Holy Ghost who dwells within him.[5] Wherefore, the Scripture says,

> I will declare the decree: the LORD hath said unto me, Thou *art* my Son; this day have I begotten thee. Psalm 2:7

This day, not in eternity, but in history, not as God, but as man, for as he is eternally begotten of the Father, so also he is born of a virgin.

> Behold, a virgin shall conceive, and bear a son, and shall call his name Immanuel. Isaiah 7:14

> For unto us a child is born, unto us a son is given: and the government shall be upon his shoulder: and his name shall be called Wonderful, Counsellor, The Mighty God, The everlasting Father, the Prince of Peace. Isaiah 9:6

> For in him dwelleth all the fulness of the Godhead bodily. Colossians 2:9

---

[3] Aquinas, *Summa* 3.23.4.
[4] *Summa*, 3.28.1-2.
[5] *Summa* 3.32.1-2.

Jesus Christ is the blessedness of God, born of God the Father.[6] He is begotten of God, both as God and as man, one person with two natures, and that by the Holy Spirit, in whom lies the identity in distinction of God's righteousness and blessedness, whereby God manifests himself in the flesh.

> Then said Mary unto the angel, How shall this be, seeing I know not a man? And the angel answered and said unto her, The Holy Ghost shall come upon thee, and the power of the Highest shall overshadow thee: therefore also that holy thing which shall be born of thee shall be called the Son of God. Luke 1:34-35

Jesus Christ is the blessedness of God, distinct from his righteousness. He has the righteousness of his birth, not from the image of God's righteousness, but from the Father alone, for he is the very image of God, and of his righteousness. The blessedness of his birth he has from his mother alone, in distinction from the image of his righteousness, because Christ is the very blessedness of God, in distinction from his righteousness. Every child is born of the mother, the blessedness distinguished in the image, together in union with the husband, to glorify God in his holiness. Jesus Christ is born of a virgin, because in him the blessedness of God is distinguished from his righteousness. His conception and birth lie not in his mother's union with a man, but in the holiness of the Godhead.

Nevertheless, the identity of God's righteousness and blessedness must also be represented in Christ's humanity. Wherefore, though Christ is born of a virgin, he is not born of a damsel, but conceived of a woman espoused,[7] and born of a woman married, though a virgin.[8] Jesus is conceived in the womb of the virgin Mary by the Holy Spirit, and born of the union of Mary and Joseph, because he is a distinct person, yet one God with the Father. As he is conceived by the Holy Spirit, so also he is born of the image of God's holiness, not of the

---

[6] Aquinas, *Summa* 3.28.1.

[7] *Summa* 3.29.1.

[8] Matt. 1:24-25.

act itself, but of union with separation, to show forth identity in distinction. This is necessary also for the sake of Mary, to give birth to the Lord according to the image of God's righteousness, and for Joseph to take a son not of his own flesh.

Children represent the objects of man's happiness. Happiness may never be willed for its own sake, but only for the law. What is willed for its own sake is holiness, that is, the image thereof, to which the image of happiness is joined. The objects of marital bliss ought not to be willed directly by husband and wife, but through the pure sensible representation of God's holiness, whereby he brings all things into being.

Conception and birth are not direct purposes of men, to be willed in themselves, but the consummation of marriage, that particular act wherein the joy of holiness is manifest. Conception and birth are indirect purposes of man's will, to be hoped for through the fulfillment of one's duty.[9] God did not ask Mary for her permission, yet because her consent was required beforehand, God authored it through his own commandment, signified by his angel Gabriel.[10]

Gabriel is the Holy Spirit.

> But I will shew thee that which is noted in the scripture of truth: and *there is* none that holdeth with me in these things, but Michael your prince. Daniel 10:21

Your prince, the Messiah.

The Holy Spirit comes to Mary as an angel to reveal what must come to pass through himself in a sign. Because the conception of children must never be a direct object of man's will, Mary could not give her consent as a condition of the act itself. If her consent is necessary, it must be grounded in the very thing to which she must consent. It is therefore revealed to Mary by the one through whom it came to pass, who appeared to her in the form of an angel, that she might freely consent to it beforehand, and yield her body to God by faith in the

---

[9] Gen. 1:28, 25:21, 30:1-2, 38:8-10; 1 Samuel 1.
[10] Luke 1:38.

promise[11]—not by compulsion of duty, but by the message of promise—which by believing, she might also discover that the angel who spoke to her is none other than the Holy Ghost. To Joseph God revealed it afterward, because with him lay not the ground of Christ's conception, but the legitimacy of his birth.

Herein lies the difference between conception and birth. As God conceives all things, and wills them into being, so also the children of men are conceived by the wife known by her husband, and brought into the appearance of being.[12] Conception is as conception. Birth is as creation; it is the appearance of the transition from non-being to being.[13] Conception is the beginning of life, birth is the beginning of the appearance of life.

The beginning of life is a transition from non-existence to existence, but conception and birth are not of themselves, but of the parents. Adam is not born, but made, neither Eve, but made of Adam—yet are they born of God in Christ— and the children are conceived and born of their parents, because through them they have their life in this world.

The world has a beginning, and a person in the world. Neither a human person nor an angelic has his existence within himself, but in God, the supreme end of all things, even of persons. Therefore, all men are made of God and born of their parents, according to the divine perfections distributed to them.[14]

Nevertheless, the Son of God has his existence within himself; yea, he has his existence within himself from the Father: "For as the Father hath life in himself; so hath he given to the Son to have life in himself" (John 5:26). Wherefore, it comes to pass that he is not begotten by man, but conceived by the Holy Ghost in the womb of the virgin Mary.[15] This is the blessed woman, and her husband, a just man, for to Joseph belongs the birthright, that is, the right of Jesus' birth,[16] and even Joseph's father is called by the name of Jacob.

---

[11] Aquinas, *Summa* 3.30.1.

[12] Gen. 4:1.

[13] Ps. 139:13-16.

[14] Ps. 90:1-2, 100:3.

[15] John 1:4, 14-15.

[16] Gen. 48:15-16, 22, 49:26; 2 Chron. 5:2.

Christ is born into the world through the unconditional condemnation of the Father, and by his submission to condemnation, he bears the guilt of original sin in righteousness.

> Against thee, thee only, have I sinned, and done this evil in thy sight: that thou mightest be justified when thou speakest, and be clear when thou judgest. Behold, I was shapen in iniquity; and in sin did my mother conceive me. Psalm 51:4-5

He bears that guilt through the woman alone, without the man, that he may submit to God in righteousness, to bear the sin of Adam in his body with the righteousness of the head, for he has the righteousness of Adam, yea, a greater righteousness. Jesus Christ bears the guilt of Adam's sin without partaking of his headship, and by persevering in Adam's original righteousness, Jesus ever is, and so becomes, the rightful head of the human race. All men indeed are made in original righteousness,[17] but the Lord Jesus Christ only perseveres therein. Original righteousness is conveyed from the father to the children; not actual righteousness, but original; else men are inherently evil, but rather they are fallen. Nevertheless, the Lord Jesus Christ inherits the original righteousness of Adam, and perseveres therein. He inherits the righteousness of the one through his mother, because he is the author and preserver of it. In Christ man is righteous, still and again.

> But when the fulness of time was come, God sent forth his Son, made of a woman, made under the law, To redeem them that were under the law, that we might receive the adoption of sons. And because ye are sons, God hath sent forth the Spirit of his Son into your hearts, crying, Abba, Father. Wherefore thou art no more a servant, but a son; and if a son, then an heir of God through Christ. Galatians 4:4-7

---

[17] Eccl. 7:29.

Made of a woman, not only born of a woman, but made of a woman, that is, born of a virgin.[18]

> Who his own self bare our sins in his own body on the tree, that we, being dead to sins, should live unto righteousness: by whose stripes ye were healed. For ye were as sheep going astray; but are now returned unto the Shepherd and Bishop of your souls. 1 Peter 2:24-25

Returned to their creator, though they knew him not in the act of creation.

> I Jesus have sent mine angel to testify unto you these things in the churches. I am the root and the offspring of David, *and* the bright and morning star. Revelation 22:16

I am the root and the offspring of David, born of him to be his head; *the bright and morning star,* one and the same as the evening star.

Guilt must follow sin, but not sin guilt; sin is a free choice of the thinking subject. Nevertheless, guilt may be imputed if it agrees with freedom of choice. The devil, having tempted Adam, and in him all of humanity, with the promise of the divine likeness, brought guilt upon all his descendants, who sin with him and in him for the same. The Lord Jesus Christ, "who being in the form of God, thought it not robbery to be equal with God," consented to bear our guilt, and persevering in Adam's original righteousness, ever is, and so became,[19] the rightful head of the human race, by whom grace reigns "through righteousness unto eternal life" (Philippians 2:6, Romans 5:21).

For this reason also he is called the Son of man, because he is born of the whole human race, to bear their sins.[20]

----

[18] Cf. Matt. 11:11.
[19] John 1:15; Acts 2:36; Rev. 22:16.
[20] Is. 9:6.

Scripture Proofs

Matthew gives the genealogy of Joseph; therefore, Luke's genealogy must belong to Mary. Matthew proves Christ's legal right to the throne of David, the fulfillment of the promises made to the fathers. He begins with Abraham, the founder of the nation, proceeding to David the king, and to the end of the monarchy until the Messiah, the true king.[21]

Luke's genealogy begins with Jesus, tracing his origin to Adam, even to God, for by the virgin birth, Christ is given to us in intuition, and his genealogy must be traced back to the Father.[22] Hence it is of Mary, to show forth the biological right of Christ, the fulfillment of the promises made to the fathers, that of David's seed he would set on his throne forever,[23] that Abraham's seed should inherit the earth,[24] that the seed of the woman should bruise the head of the serpent.[25]

There is a difficulty ascribed to the genealogy of Luke in these words, "And Jesus himself began to be about thirty years of age, being (as was supposed) the son of Joseph, which was *the son* of Heli, which was *the son* of Levi..." (Luke 1:23-24). It is claimed that the Evangelist's differ as to the identity of Joseph's father. This I resolve as follows: the subject of each entry in the genealogy of Luke is Christ. "Jesus... being (as was supposed) the son of Joseph, which [Jesus] was *the son* of Heli, which [Jesus] was *the son* of Levi..." This is the only reading consistent with the final entry, "which was *the son* of God." It also resolves the addition of a second Cainan, the brother of Salah who died childless.[26] Salah then married his wife and called his firstborn after the name of his brother.[27] Jesus is the son of both, but not one of the other. Lastly, by marriage with Mary,

---

[21] Cf. Ezek. 21:27.

[22] Isaiah 53:8.

[23] 2 Sam. 7:8-17; 1 Chron. 17:7-15; Ps. 89:18-37, 132:11-12; Aquinas, *Summa* 3.31.2.

[24] Gen. 15:18-21, 17:1-8, 22:15-18; cf. Gen. 11, Ps. 2; Aquinas, *Summa* 3.31.2.

[25] Gen. 3:15.

[26] Gen. 11:12.

[27] Gen. 38:1-11; Deut. 25:5-10.

Joseph is as much the son of Heli as he is the father of Jesus, for both are true by affinity. [28]

Joseph is the husband of Mary, the father of God, not by the flesh but by the law, yet not contrary to the flesh, as though some other man were his father by the flesh, for the Father of Jesus according to the flesh is outside the flesh. There is no flesh that begets Christ's flesh, but God who is spirit, yea, the Father of spirits.[29]

It is necessary that Christ be born into sin, that he be born of Adam, and inherit the guilt of original sin through his mother. Though he is not begotten of Joseph, nevertheless, he is the son of Joseph by his union with Mary. And therefore, as he is the son of Mary, he is also the son of Joseph, a just man, the son of David, the king of Israel.[30]

Joseph legitimizes the birth of Jesus. Through him Christ inherits the kingdom of Israel; yea, through Joseph he inherits the kingdom by Mary, through the promise of God to David.

Herein lies the promise of the virgin birth:

> Thus saith the LORD, Write ye this man childless, a man *that* shall not prosper in his days: for no man of his seed shall prosper, sitting upon the throne of David, and ruling any more in Judah. Jeremiah 22:30

Though he is the son of the kings, yet is he not of their seed, but of David through Mary.

Abram married his sister Sarai, who according to Abraham had the same father but not the same mother, yet Moses calls her Abraham's wife, which the law forbids.[31] Nevertheless, Adam's children being neither near nor far of kin, the nearest being also the farthest, likewise Abraham was lawfully married to his sister, because he is the first of the nation, the father of many nations, and of all who are justified by faith. A man's wife symbolizes his blessedness; a man's

---

[28] Ezra 2:61.
[29] John 4:24; Heb. 12:9.
[30] 2 Sam. 23:3.
[31] Gen. 11:29, 20:12; Lev. 18.

sister signifies a blessedness distinct. Therefore, the marriage of Abraham to Sarah signifies identity in distinction. Abraham married his sister, yet Moses calls her his wife, because Sarah was Abraham's sister by flesh, but his wife by law, for the promise of the law is that Jesus Christ should come by her flesh.

Matthew 1:1-25

The book of the generation of Jesus Christ, the son of David, the son of Abraham, to whom the promises are made; *Abraham begat Isaac;* the child of promise, whose name means *laughter,* because through the birth of Jesus Christ the dreadful punishment of sin is unexpectedly transformed into the reward of perfect righteousness;[32] *and Isaac begat Jacob;* who supplanted Esau, the firstborn;[33] *and Jacob begat Judas and his brethren,* the twelve, who reveal the fullness of the doctrine of the nation; *And Judas begat Phares and Zara of Thamar; and Phares,* who broke forth before his brother;[34] *begat Esrom; and Esrom begat Aram; And Aram begat Aminadab; and Aminadab begat Naasson;* the head of Judah who wandered in the wilderness;[35] *and Naasson begat Salmon; And Salmon begat Boaz of Rachab;* the harlot, because Jesus Christ bore the idolatry of his people; *and Boaz begat Obed of Ruth;* the Moabitess, for he bears the sins of the stranger; *and Obed begat Jesse; And Jesse begat David the king;* his seventh son, the shepherd of Israel; *and David the king begat Solomon of her that had been the wife of Urias;* David's first child by Bathsheba, the child of adultery and murder, perished according to the word of the Lord, but the second, the legitimate son of their union, became the instrument of God's grace to his people, and a type of our Lord Jesus Christ; *And Solomon begat Roboam;* from whom the kingdom was rent; *and Roboam begat Abia; and Abia begat Asa; And Asa begat Josaphat; and Josaphat begat Joram; and Joram begat Ozias; And Ozias begat Joatham; and Joatham begat Achaz; and Achaz begat Ezekias; And Ezekias begat Manasses; and Manasses begat Amon; and Amon begat Josias; And Josias begat Jechonias and his brethren, about the*

---

[32] Cf. Gen. 17:15-19, 18:12, 21:6.
[33] Gen. 25:19-34, 27:1-40.
[34] Gen. 38:27-30.
[35] Num. 1:7.

time they were carried away to Babylon: The kings of Judah, sometimes righteous, sometimes wicked, and the wicked sometimes repentant, and the people idolatrous, God fulfills the promise to David, not by taking away the crown of Judah, but by limiting it to the righteous one.[36] These kings were disciplined, and the throne of David was perpetuated, not by their righteousness, but by the righteousness of Christ, and the kingdom was taken away from them, that the captivity of God's people might be delivered by Jesus.[37] *And after they were brought to Babylon,* that he might also cleanse the abomination of desolation set up in this time;[38] *Jechonias begat Salathiel; and Salathiel begat Zorobabel; And Zorobabel begat Abiud; and Abiud begat Eliakim; and Eliakim begat Azor; And Azor begat Sadoc; and Sadoc begat Achim; and Achim begat Eliud; And Eliud begat Eleazar; and Eleazar begat Matthan; and Matthan begat Jacob; And Jacob begat Joseph,* to whom belongs the birthright; *the husband of Mary, of whom was born Jesus,* though the vision was cut off, God preserved his people for the sake of his Son; *who is called Christ.* Matthew proves the legitimacy of Christ's claim to the throne of David to establish its apodictic truth, to show that he who is alone called Christ is the very same. *So all the generations from Abraham to David are fourteen generations; and from David until the carrying away into Babylon are fourteen generations; and from the carrying away into Babylon unto Christ are fourteen generations.* Jesus came in the fullness of time. He is born of the fathers, and of the kings, and of the sons of captivity, because he is begotten of the Father, to bear the sins of his people, and to redeem them from captivity.[39] *Now the birth of Jesus Christ was on this wise: When as his mother Mary was espoused to Joseph, before they came together,* the son of their union, without proceeding from its consummation; *she was found with child of the Holy Ghost,* not through the image of holiness, but through holiness itself. *Then Joseph her husband, being a just man,* to legitimize the birth of Christ; *and not willing to make her a public example,* for she was innocent; *was minded to put her away privily,* according to the law of Moses concerning divorce, that Joseph should not be tempted to sin, either to punish the innocent, or marry one

---

[36] Ezek. 21:25-27.
[37] 2 Sam. 7:12-16; 1 Chron. 17:11-14; Ps. 89:29-37; Is. 7:1-16, 9:1-7.
[38] Dan. 9:25-27.
[39] Is. 8:6-8, 9:4-7.

whom he suspected of adultery. *But while he thought on these things,* God provided for his righteousness, even the inward thought of his heart, but that he should not act thereon: *behold, the angel of the Lord appeared unto him in a dream,* for he contemplated a mystery that reason may not discover, yet once revealed may certainly believe; *saying, Joseph, thou son of David, fear not to take unto thee Mary thy wife:* that as he had promised, so he should do, and with the proper feeling; *for that which is conceived in her is of the Holy Ghost. And she shall bring forth a son, and thou shalt call his name Jesus: for he shall save his people from their sins,* for because he is born of a virgin, he bears the guilt of original sin in righteousness. *Now all this was done, that it might be fulfilled which was spoken of the Lord by the prophet,* for Jesus is the true prophet, and the end of all prophecy; *saying, Behold, a virgin shall be with child, and shall bring forth a son, and they shall call his name Emmanuel, which being interpreted is, God with us. Then Joseph being raised from sleep,* as Adam, for it was a special act of creation; *did as the angel of the Lord had bidden him, and took unto him his wife:* Christ is born of their union, to show forth the holiness of God in his birth, that he might have right to the throne of David; *And knew her not till she had brought forth her firstborn son:* that it might not only be but also appear that he is conceived and born of a virgin,[40] and afterward they knew each other, and bore fruit, that the birth of Christ might be abundantly legitimated by the consummation of their lawful union;[41] *and he called his name Jesus.* So called of both man and God, because he is both man and God in one person.

Luke 1:1-2:41

It is the peculiar purpose of Luke's Gospel to prove that Jesus Christ is the Son of God; wherefore, he writes of the virgin birth more than any other evangelist, and even of the birth of John, because John is the forerunner of Christ, not only in his ministry, but also in his birth. How greatly honored is this

---

[40] Aquinas, *Summa* 3.28.1-2.
[41] *Summa* 3.28.3 Objection 2.

man, whom Jesus calls more than a prophet, and the greatest of those born of women![42]

Forasmuch as many have taken in hand to set forth in order a declaration of those things which are most surely believed among us, being apodictically certain and necessary for practical reason; *Even as they delivered them unto us, which from the beginning were eyewitnesses,* because the Spirit testifies through the history; *and ministers of the word;* even those who believed the same, and were changed by it; *It seemed good to me also, having had perfect understanding of all things from the very first, to write unto thee in order,* from the very beginning; *most excellent Theophilus, That thou mightest know the certainty of those things, wherein thou hast been instructed,* for the true doctrine follows after concepts. *There was in the days of Herod, the king of Judaea, a certain priest named Zacharias,* John is born of a priest, that he, being a prophet, might anoint the Lord to his priesthood; *of the course of Abia:* of the eighth course appointed by lot before David, a son of Zadok, or of Abiathar;[43] *and his wife was of the daughters of Aaron, and her name was Elisabeth.* John is born of the legitimate, ceremonial[44] union of Zacharias and Elisabeth[45], to fulfill the Levitical priesthood by proclaiming Christ come in the flesh. *And they were both righteous before God, walking in all the commandments and ordinances of the Lord blameless,* the Levitical priesthood is nothing but obedience to God.[46] *And they had no child,* from the Levitical priesthood nothing comes, but the coming of our Lord Jesus Christ; *because that Elisabeth was barren, and they both were now well stricken in years,* that priesthood of old had not born fruit unto righteousness. *And it came to pass, that while he executed the priest's office before God in the order of his course,* he continued in that duty of his, as God had commanded of old, of ancient times, that the prophesied son might partake of his priesthood, to proclaim the coming of the Lord; *According to the custom of the priest's office, his lot was to burn incense when he went into the temple of the Lord,* according to the

---

[42] Matt. 11:11.
[43] 1 Chron. 24:1-19; Ezek. 44:15.
[44] Lev. 21:7.
[45] Ex. 6:23.
[46] 1 Cor. 7:19.

prayer of all God's people, who precede the one who is before them. *And the whole multitude of the people were praying without at the time of incense,* the many represented by the one. *And there appeared unto him an angel of the Lord standing on the right side of the altar of incense,* that he should beget an anointed one, to be seated beside the Lord, as it is written by the prophet who shares his name.[47] *And when Zacharias saw him, he was troubled, and fear fell upon him,* to remember his sins. *But the angel said unto him, Fear not, Zacharias: for thy prayer is heard;* prayers offered, as incense, through the Spirit; *and thy wife Elisabeth shall bear thee a son, and thou shalt call his name John,* for God of his grace gives us a Savior. *And thou shalt have joy and gladness; and many shall rejoice at his birth,* because he is the forerunner of Christ, even in his birth. *For he shall be great in the sight of the Lord, and shall drink neither wine nor strong drink;* a Nazarite, specially dedicated to the service of the Lord;[48] *and he shall be filled with the Holy Ghost, even from his mother's womb,* his whole life appointed to proclaim the Lord's coming. *And many of the children of Israel shall he turn to the Lord their God,* the many through the one. *And he shall go before him in the spirit and power of Elias,* of the message of eternal life; *to turn the hearts of the fathers to the children, and the disobedient to the wisdom of the just; to make ready a people prepared for the Lord,* to preach repentance before the faith of Jesus. *And Zacharias said unto the angel, Whereby shall I know this?* He ought to have believed for the sake of Christ come, whereof John himself is the sign; *for I am an old man, and my wife well stricken in years.* He ought to have believed for the fullness of time. *And the angel answering said unto him, I am Gabriel, that stand in the presence of God;* for because John is the messenger of the Lord,[49] he is also born by the promise of the Spirit in the form of an angel; *and am sent to speak unto thee, and to shew thee these glad tidings,* he ought to have believed for the joy revealed; *And, behold, thou shalt be dumb, and not able to speak,* that the proclamation should belong to John, for although the Levitical priesthood proclaimed Christ to come, yet the proclamation of Christ come belongs to another, specially devoted to that purpose; *until the day that these*

---

[47] Zechariah 4:11-14.
[48] Numbers 6:1-3.
[49] Mal. 3:1, 4:5-6.

things shall be performed, because thou believest not my words, which shall be fulfilled in their season, for the time was at hand. *And the people waited for Zacharias, and marvelled that he tarried so long in the temple.* He was a faithful priest, who performed his duties without affecting prolongment.[50] *And when he came out, he could not speak unto them: and they perceived that he had seen a vision in the temple: for he beckoned unto them, and remained speechless,* they knew that he had seen a vision, but not what he had seen, because the substance pertained to John. *And it came to pass, that, as soon as the days of his ministration were accomplished, he departed to his own house.* Though dumb, he continued in his duty, and received his reward. *And after those days his wife Elisabeth conceived, and hid herself five months,* the secret to be revealed in his birth; *saying, Thus hath the Lord dealt with me in the days wherein he looked on me, to take away my reproach among men.* The priesthood of Aaron is honored through Christ come in the flesh. *And in the sixth month the angel Gabriel was sent from God unto a city of Galilee, named Nazareth,* the same angel appearing to both, because the purpose is one; *To a virgin espoused to a man whose name was Joseph,* to whom belongs the birthright; *of the house of David; and the virgin's name was Mary,* from the bitterness of sin and guilt comes the beloved Son. *And the angel came in unto her, and said, Hail, thou that art highly favoured,* for the church of old is precious to God for the sake of his Son; *the Lord is with thee: blessed art thou among women,* from whom should come the very blessedness of God. *And when she saw him, she was troubled at his saying, and cast in her mind what manner of salutation this should be.* She contemplated the mystery, for reason indeed seeks, but it cannot find; it is fearful at first for sin, until it understands the grace revealed. *And the angel said unto her, Fear not, Mary: for thou hast found favour with God,* that grace of God foretold by John. *And, behold, thou shalt conceive in thy womb,* without intimacy, immediately to the birth of him who is the beginning and the end; *and bring forth a son, and shalt call his name Jesus,* the Savior. *He shall be great,* like John,[51] bringing repentance to the people. How great is John that Jesus is compared to him! For howsoever great John is, yet is Jesus greater than he; *and shall be called the Son of the Highest: and the Lord*

---

50 Prov. 17:27; Matt. 6:7.
51 Luke 1:15.

God shall give unto him the throne of his father David: by an act of restoration through his father Joseph; *And he shall reign over the house of Jacob for ever; and of his kingdom there shall be no end.* This is the inheritance of the Son of God. *Then said Mary unto the angel, How shall this be, seeing I know not a man?* Wherein is the lawfulness of his birth? — "And who shall declare his generation?" (Isaiah 53:8)—for the lawfulness of his birth is not made in the image thereof. *And the angel answered and said unto her, The Holy Ghost shall come upon thee,* but in the thing itself, revealed in the flesh, the very image of God;[52] *and the power of the Highest shall overshadow thee:* known by feeling; *therefore also that holy thing which shall be born of thee shall be called the Son of God,* for that which is born of the Spirit is holy. *And, behold, thy cousin Elisabeth,* for they are close of kin, even as Jesus and John are close in essence; *she hath also conceived a son in her old age: and this is the sixth month with her, who was called barren.* This is told Mary after the promise of Christ, because the coming of Christ is the end sought for, whereof the birth of John gives assurance. *For with God nothing shall be impossible.* All things are possible with the Father, and he works all things through Jesus Christ his Son. *And Mary said, Behold the handmaid of the Lord;* a servant of the Lord, that the Lord should be born under the law; *be it unto me according to thy word.* He did not ask for her permission, but commanded it by promise. *And the angel departed from her,* that she might be visited by the Son.[53] *And Mary arose in those days, and went into the hill country with haste, into a city of Juda; And entered into the house of Zacharias, and saluted Elisabeth. And it came to pass, that, when Elisabeth heard the salutation of Mary, the babe leaped in her womb;* that he should proclaim Christ come, even from the womb; *and Elisabeth was filled with the Holy Ghost: And she spake out with a loud voice, and said, Blessed art thou among women, and blessed is the fruit of thy womb,* the blessedness of God from the image thereof. *And whence is this to me, that the mother of my Lord should come to me? For, lo, as soon as the voice of thy salutation sounded in mine ears,* the will of God fulfilled without delay; *the babe leaped in my womb for joy. And blessed is she that believed: for there shall be a performance of those things which were told her from the Lord,* for the blessedness of

---

[52] Col. 1:15; Heb. 1:3.
[53] John 16:7.

Christ comes to us by faith. *And Mary said, My soul doth magnify the Lord, And my spirit hath rejoiced in God my Saviour.* She glorified God in her soul, even in her spirit, that she might bear the Lord in her body. *For he hath regarded the low estate of his handmaiden:* to bring forth the heavenly from the earthly; *for, behold, from henceforth all generations shall call me blessed,* for the blessedness of the Son born of her. *For he that is mighty,* the Father; *hath done to me great things; and holy is his name,* for the Spirit necessarily proceeds from them both. *And his mercy is on them that fear him from generation to generation,* the line of the godly preserved for the sake of the Son. *He hath shewed strength with his arm;* his Spirit; *he hath scattered the proud in the imagination of their hearts,* who sought the glory of God beyond what they could see or think. *He hath put down the mighty from their seats, and exalted them of low degree,* by revealing himself in the form of a servant. *He hath filled the hungry with good things; and the rich he hath sent empty away,* dividing between the reprobate and the elect. *He hath holpen his servant Israel, in remembrance of his mercy; As he spake to our fathers, to Abraham, and to his seed for ever,* the promises fulfilled in the virgin birth. *And Mary abode with her about three months,* until about the birth of John; *and returned to her own house. Now Elisabeth's full time came that she should be delivered; and she brought forth a son,* through whom the old law is fulfilled unto Christ. *And her neighbours and her cousins heard how the Lord had shewed great mercy upon her;* because the old is fulfilled in the new, and the law is exalted by mercy; *and they rejoiced with her,* for the joy of one is the joy of all.[54] *And it came to pass, that on the eighth day they came to circumcise the child; and they called him Zacharias, after the name of his father,* that he should follow after him, as a priest, and after the prophet who spake of him. *And his mother answered and said, Not so; but he shall be called John,* to distinguish the new from the old, for John is intermediate between them. *And they said unto her, There is none of thy kindred that is called by this name,* they gave him a new name. *And they made signs to his father, how he would have him called. And he asked for a writing table, and wrote, saying, His name is John,* the written word of God. *And they marvelled all,* the righteousness of God revealed in his birth. *And his mouth was opened immediately, and his tongue loosed, and he spake, and praised God.* He is set free from

---

[54] 1 Cor. 12:26.

bondage to prophesy of faith. *And fear came on all that dwelt round about them: and all these sayings were noised abroad throughout all the hill country of Judaea. And all they that heard them laid them up in their hearts,* the seed of the Gospel sown about thirty years before its preaching; *saying, What manner of child shall this be! And the hand of the Lord was with him,* the Spirit. *And his father Zacharias was filled with the Holy Ghost, and prophesied,* for after the birth of John, the old also testifies to the new; *saying, Blessed be the Lord God of Israel; for he hath visited and redeemed his people, And hath raised up an horn of salvation for us in the house of his servant David;* not John, but the one whom John proclaimed; *As he spake by the mouth of his holy prophets, which have been since the world began:* of whom John is the last; *That we should be saved from our enemies, and from the hand of all that hate us;* that the righteous should have their reward, and not be brought down by the wicked; *To perform the mercy promised to our fathers, and to remember his holy covenant; The oath which he sware to our father Abraham,* whereby he saved his people of old; *That he would grant unto us, that we being delivered out of the hand of our enemies might serve him without fear, In holiness and righteousness before him,* through the blessedness of his Son; *all the days of our life,* even in this world, and in the world to come. *And thou, child, shalt be called the prophet of the Highest:* the peculiar prophet of Christ; *for thou shalt go before the face of the Lord to prepare his ways; To give knowledge of salvation unto his people by the remission of their sins, Through the tender mercy of our God;* the Spirit; *whereby the dayspring from on high hath visited us,* the Son. *To give light to them that sit in darkness and in the shadow of death, to guide our feet into the way of peace.* Zacharias now testifies after the women to the same things, for that Jesus is the blessedness of God, identical in distinction to his righteousness. *And the child grew, and waxed strong in spirit, and was in the deserts till the day of his shewing unto Israel.* Though he is born of a priest, yet he should not be of the old order, but of the new, to baptize Christ to his ministry. *And it came to pass in those days, that there went out a decree from Caesar Augustus, that all the world should be taxed,* because Christ came to free men from Roman bondage, yea, from slavery to sin, and from death, and from war;[55] *(And this taxing was first made when Cyrenius was governor of Syria.) And all went to be taxed,*

---

[55] Is. 9:4-7; Ex. 30:11-16.

every one into his own city. And Joseph also went up from Galilee, out of the city of Nazareth, into Judaea, unto the city of David, which is called Bethlehem; (because he was of the house and lineage of David:), to show that Jesus is the promised seed and the rightful king; *To be taxed with Mary his espoused wife, being great with child.* Christ is born under the oppression of Rome, that his people should be delivered therefrom.[56] *And so it was, that, while they were there, the days were accomplished that she should be delivered,* as in the fullness of time Christ came to free men from slavery. *And she brought forth her firstborn son, and wrapped him in swaddling clothes, and laid him in a manger;* humble in his birth, born a servant under the law; *because there was no room for them in the inn,* a man over and above those born of men. *And there were in the same country shepherds abiding in the field, keeping watch over their flock by night,* visited by God in the course of their ordinary duty. *And, lo, the angel of the Lord came upon them, and the glory of the Lord shone round about them:* the glory of God appearing to men of humble estate, who signify the work of Christ; *and they were sore afraid,* for the glory of God brings to mind our many sins, that we should lay hold of his forgiveness. *And the angel said unto them, Fear not: for, behold, I bring you good tidings of great joy, which shall be to all people.* Christ is born not only for the nation and people of Israel, but also for the whole world. *For unto you is born this day in the city of David a Saviour, which is Christ the Lord. And this shall be a sign unto you; Ye shall find the babe wrapped in swaddling clothes, lying in a manger.* The exceeding glory of God manifest in the humble things of this world, through the inward glory of the moral law. *And suddenly there was with the angel a multitude of the heavenly host praising God, and saying,* neither is it wanting in any outward glory, but in him the invisible is made visible; *Glory to God in the highest, and on earth peace, good will toward men,* the will of God accomplished through the Son. *And it came to pass, as the angels were gone away from them into heaven, the shepherds said one to another, Let us now go even unto Bethlehem, and see this thing which is come to pass, which the Lord hath made known unto us,* they sought the fulfillment of the vision, because they believed with all their heart. *And they came with haste,* in the joy of faith; *and found Mary, and Joseph, and the babe lying in a manger. And when they had seen it, they*

---

[56] Cf. Gen. 35:16-20.

made known abroad the saying which was told them concerning this child, that the birth of Christ might be a fact of history, known to the community. *And all they that heard it wondered at those things which were told them by the shepherds,* the seed of the Gospel sown among them. *But Mary kept all these things, and pondered them in her heart,* that seed having taken root within her. *And the shepherds returned, glorifying and praising God for all the things that they had heard and seen, as it was told unto them,* for as they believed it with their ears, so they saw it with their eyes. *And when eight days were accomplished for the circumcising of the child,* because he was of the seed of Abraham; *his name was called Jesus, which was so named of the angel before he was conceived in the womb,* the name given him by the promise of the Father.[57] *And when the days of her purification according to the law of Moses were accomplished,* for she bore him in the guilt of original sin; *they brought him to Jerusalem, to present him to the Lord; (As it is written in the law of the Lord, Every male that openeth the womb shall be called holy to the Lord;),* for he must be redeemed from the Levitical priesthood, that he should be a priest upon his throne, "the firstborn of every creature" (Col. 1:15). *And to offer a sacrifice according to that which is said in the law of the Lord, A pair of turtledoves, or two young pigeons.* He is sanctified even by his own offering of himself to God, signified by the ancient sacrifices. *And, behold, there was a man in Jerusalem, whose name was Simeon;* who believed by hearing, that he might also see;[58] *and the same man was just and devout,* to show the redemption of sinners, and the gathering together of God's people; *waiting for the consolation of Israel:* He waited for Christ, having learned from the prophets that the time was near; *and the Holy Ghost was upon him,* not of himself, but of God. *And it was revealed unto him by the Holy Ghost, that he should not see death,* that he should die in hope; *before he had seen the Lord's Christ,* that he might be a witness to the birth of the savior. *And he came by the Spirit into the temple: and when the parents brought in the child Jesus, to do for him after the custom of the law,* a custom of men, obligatory for the commandment of God; *Then took he him up in his arms, and blessed God, and said, Lord, now lettest thou thy servant depart in peace, according to thy word: For mine eyes have seen thy salvation, Which thou hast prepared*

---

[57] Gen. 17:19; Rom. 9:6-9.
[58] Gen. 29:31-33.

before the face of all people; through the establishment of the ancient church, and the temple renowned throughout the world;[59] *A light to lighten the Gentiles, and the glory of thy people Israel,* the peculiar people, for "salvation is of the Jews" (John 4:22). *And Joseph and his mother marvelled at those things which were spoken of him.* The secret of God revealed to men, and understood, detracts not from his glory, but fills them with wonder. *And Simeon blessed them, and said unto Mary his mother, Behold, this child is set for the fall and rising again of many in Israel;* the division between the righteous and the wicked, and the apostasy of the Jews, together with their restoration;[60] *and for a sign which shall be spoken against; (Yea, a sword shall pierce through thy own soul also,)* as a sinner who gave birth to the righteous; *that the thoughts of many hearts may be revealed,* by the preaching of the Gospel from heaven, and his return to judge the living and the dead. *And there was one Anna,* as having life again from death; *a prophetess,* a holy woman; *the daughter of Phanuel,* to see the face of God in his blessedness; *of the tribe of Aser:* to speak of the blessedness of Christ;[61] *she was of a great age, and had lived with an husband seven years from her virginity;* having performed the ordinary duties of marriage for a sufficient time, to signify the blessedness of the church in all ages; *And she was a widow of about fourscore and four years,* the greater part of her life spent in devotion to God; *which departed not from the temple, but served God with fastings and prayers night and day,* of eminent piety. *And she coming in that instant gave thanks likewise unto the Lord,* for he is at once both righteous before God, and blessed; a babe honored of ancients, the ancient one; *and spake of him to all them that looked for redemption in Jerusalem,* that it might be a fact of history.[62] *And when they had performed all things according to the law of the Lord,* that Christ might not only be perfect in his own obedience, but in the obedience of his parents for his sake, as of the Father; *they returned into Galilee, to their own city Nazareth,* in the ancient land of Israel, for "all Israel shall be saved" (Romans 11:26).[63] *And the*

---

[59] Ps. 68:29; Is. 2:1-4; Josephus, *The Jewish War*, trans. by G.A. Williamson, rev. by E. Mary Smallwood (Penguin Books, 1981), 164.

[60] Rom. 11.

[61] Gen. 30:12-13.

[62] Aquinas, *Summa* 3.36.

[63] 2 Kings 15:29.

child grew, and waxed strong in spirit, filled with wisdom: and the grace of God was upon him, sanctified as a Son, receiving the Holy Spirit without measure.[64]

The Baptism of Christ

Baptism is the application of water to the flesh, to cleanse it, a sign of the transition from sin to righteousness. This transition has two elements, repentance and faith. There is therefore a baptism of repentance and a baptism of faith. The sign of the new covenant symbolizes faith, but before the ministry of Christ, John preached a baptism of repentance, because repentance requires faith, and faith repentance.[65] No man can repent except unto faith in Christ revealed; neither has any man believed if he has not repented of his unbelief. Repentance comes before faith: it is the means to faith, whereby any man may be saved. Thus Jesus is baptized by John, "that all men through him might believe" (John 1:7).

Water symbolizes the plurality of sensation. The waters above are divided from the waters below. The waters below symbolize sensation without any purpose; the waters above symbolize the purpose of the sensible world, to give grace from heaven.[66]

There is therefore a baptism, either of immersion into the depths, or of pouring and sprinkling from above. The former is the punishment of the wicked, the latter is the salvation of the righteous, for we indeed are dipped into the waters above when they are poured out upon our heads.

> And God said, Let there be a firmament in the midst of the waters, and let it divide the waters from the waters. And God made the firmament, and divided the waters which were under the firmament from the waters which were above the firmament: and it was so. And God called

---

[64] John 3:34.
[65] Matt. 3:2, 4:17; Mark 1:15; Jas. 2:26.
[66] Is. 55:8-11; Eph. 5:26; 2 Pet. 3:5-6; Rev. 12:15, 21:1.

the firmament Heaven. And the evening and the morning were the second day. Genesis 1:6-8

Which sometime were disobedient, when once the longsuffering of God waited in the days of Noah, while the ark was a preparing, wherein few, that is, eight souls were saved by water. The like figure whereunto *even* baptism doth also now save us (not the putting away of the filth of the flesh, but the answer of a good conscience toward God,) by the resurrection of Jesus Christ. 1 Peter 3:20-21, cf. Rev. 16:3

The old world was cleansed, *first*, by the immersion of the wicked in judgment; *second*, by the sprinkling of the righteous with grace. Likewise, the children of Israel crossed the red sea on foot, but the Egyptians were drowned.

Moreover, brethren, I would not that ye should be ignorant, how that all our fathers were under the cloud, and all passed through the sea; And were all baptized unto Moses in the cloud and in the sea. 1 Corinthians 10:1-2

God saves his anointed through his Holy Spirit, and Christ is baptized into the flesh, born of a virgin, to bear our sins.[67] Water symbolizes the flesh, because the plurality of sensation belongs to the body.[68] Jesus is dipped into the flesh by the Father, born of a virgin to bear the sins of his people, and that by the Holy Spirit. Likewise, his people are baptized into his headship, yea, into his flesh,[69] by sprinkling from above.[70] Though he has no sin, yet he repents of the sins of his people, and works faith on their behalf.[71] Accordingly, he is baptized into Jordan by John, a prophet and a priest, an anointed one, to anoint the Lord.[72]

---

[67] 1 John 5:6-8.
[68] John 3:5-6; 1 John 5:6-8.
[69] Eph. 5:30.
[70] Is. 44:3; Rom. 6:3; 1 Cor. 11:3.
[71] Ps. 40:12; Heb. 12:2.
[72] Aquinas, *Summa* 3.38.1, 39.1-4.

Matthew 3:13-17

Then cometh Jesus from Galilee to Jordan unto John, to be baptized of him. Christ bears the sins of many with the original righteousness of the one, and he is sanctified through repentance, not for his sins, but for ours: "then I restored *that which I took not away*" (Psalm 69:4). *But John forbad him*, he understood not the mystery of God, until it was revealed to him for righteousness; *saying, I have need to be baptized of thee, and comest thou to me?* Because Jesus is one of the many.[73] *And Jesus answering said unto him, Suffer it to be so now:* it is a sign; *for thus it becometh us to fulfil all righteousness*, even of repentance from sin on behalf of his people. *Then he suffered him. And Jesus, when he was baptized, went up straightway out of the water:* he stood in the water to show that he partook of the body of Israel, and of the divine judgment; *and, lo, the heavens were opened unto him,* as the glory of God; *and he saw the Spirit of God descending like a dove,* grace and truth to bear the sins of his people; *and lighting upon him:* as his peculiar dwelling place. Jesus was first baptized by John in water, then immediately after on earth by the Holy Ghost; the first, after the multitude of sensation, the second, after the obedience of holiness. *And lo a voice from heaven, saying, This is my beloved Son, in whom I am well pleased.* Baptized by man and by God, the Son of man and the Son of God, set apart for his ministry.

Mark 1:9-11

And it came to pass in those days, that Jesus came from Nazareth of Galilee, and was baptized of John in Jordan. And straightway coming up out of the water, he saw the heavens opened, and the Spirit like a dove descending upon him: And there came a voice from heaven, saying, Thou art my beloved Son, in whom I am well pleased. Mark shows briefly that by the baptism of John and that of the Holy Spirit, the Son of God is set apart for the preaching of the Gospel.

---

[73] Ps. 22:22; Heb. 2:11-12.

But Herod the tetrarch, being reproved by him for Herodias his brother Philip's wife, and for all the evils which Herod had done, Added yet this above all, that he shut up John in prison. John proclaimed the coming of the Lord; when therefore the Lord was come, John was shut up into prison. *Now when all the people were baptized, it came to pass, that Jesus also being baptized,* as one of them; *and praying,* by faith; *the heaven was opened, And the Holy Ghost descended in a bodily shape,* for the Holy Ghost appears to us bodily in the body of Jesus Christ; *like a dove,* of innocence and grace; *upon him,* from above; *and a voice came from heaven, which said, Thou art my beloved Son;* born of a virgin, baptized into the flesh;[74] *in thee I am well pleased,* not only with him, but also in him with all things. *And Jesus himself began to be about thirty years of age,* three decades for the ordinary sanctification of his life, that he might serve in the temple;[75] *being (as was supposed) the son of Joseph,* Luke now gives the genealogy of Christ through Mary, to show the affinity of his baptism with the doctrine of his birth; *which,* Jesus; *was the son of Heli, Which was the son of Matthat, which was the son of Levi, which was the son of Melchi, which was the son of Janna, which was the son of Joseph, Which was the son of Mattathias, which was the son of Amos, which was the son of Naum, which was the son of Esli, which was the son of Nagge, Which was the son of Maath, which was the son of Mattathias, which was the son of Semei, which was the son of Joseph, which was the son of Juda, Which was the son of Joanna, which was the son of Rhesa, which was the son of Zorobabel, which was the son of Salathiel, which was the son of Neri, Which was the son of Melchi, which was the son of Addi, which was the son of Cosam, which was the son of Elmodam, which was the son of Er, Which was the son of Jose, which was the son of Eliezer, which was the son of Jorim, which was the son of Matthat, which was the son of Levi, Which was the son of Simeon, which was the son of Juda, which was the son of Joseph, which was the son of Jonan, which was the son of Eliakim, Which was the son of Melea, which was the son of Menan, which was the son of Mattatha, which was the son of Nathan, which was the son of David, Which was the*

---

74 Ps. 85:10-11; Is. 45:8.
75 Num. 4:3, 23, 30, 35, 39, 43, 47.

son of Jesse, which was the son of Obed, which was the son of Booz, which was the son of Salmon, which was the son of Naasson, Which was the son of Aminadab, which was the son of Aram, which was the son of Esrom, which was the son of Phares, which was the son of Juda, Which was the son of Jacob, which was the son of Isaac, which was the son of Abraham, which was the son of Thara, which was the son of Nachor, Which was the son of Saruch, which was the son of Ragau, which was the son of Phalec, which was the son of Heber, which was the son of Sala, Which was the son of Cainan, which was the son of Arphaxad, which was the son of Sem, which was the son of Noe, which was the son of Lamech, Which was the son of Mathusala, which was the son of Enoch, which was the son of Jared, which was the son of Maleleel, which was the son of Cainan, Which was the son of Enos, which was the son of Seth, which was the son of Adam, which was the son of God. Luke traces the genealogy of Jesus to Adam, yea, to God, to show that he is the seed of the woman promised to Adam. The genealogy of Christ is here put together with his baptism, to identify the one of whom the Father spake, *Thou art my beloved Son; in thee I am well pleased;* and all these names are given to establish the legitimacy of Jesus' claim to be the Messiah, the apodictic truth thereof following.

John 1:29-34

The next day John seeth Jesus coming unto him, and saith, Behold the Lamb of God, which taketh away the sin of the world, whose blood washes away all our sins, and whose righteousness covers all our shame. *This is he of whom I said, After me cometh a man which is preferred before me: for he was before me.* Jesus preceded him even as man, because the ground of Christ's humanity lies in his eternal person, together with the rightful headship of the human race. *And I knew him not: but that he should be made manifest to Israel, therefore am I come baptizing with water,* to show forth in a sign repentance unto faith in Jesus Christ. *And John bare record, saying, I saw the Spirit descending from heaven like a dove,* full of grace and truth; *and it abode upon him.* John omits the baptism of John to show the Son in his blessedness, which Jesus possesses in himself from the Father; yet the testimony of John is recorded, because the blessedness of Christ encompasses all things within itself. *And I knew him not: but he that sent me to baptize with water,* that all men should be cleansed through repentance; *the same said unto me, Upon whom thou shalt see the Spirit descending, and remaining on him, the same is he which baptizeth with the Holy Ghost.* Those forgiven by faith in Christ also partake of his Spirit. *And I saw, and bare record that this is the Son of God,* the testimony of his baptism.

The Ascension

In righteousness Jesus submits himself to the condemnation of the Father; wherefore, to show forth the invisible righteousness he has with the Father, he afterward ascends into heaven. As the Father reveals himself in the Son, so also the Father hides the Son with himself. In burial the righteousness of Christ exceeds the old creation; wherefore, after he rises from the dead, he ascends into heaven until the last day, when all things shall be made new. And because he is seated at the right hand of the throne of God, he sends forth the Holy Spirit, whereby he is known through the promise of salvation, and reigns in the midst of his enemies.

Life is the causality of the thinking subject to produce an intuition of itself. The intuition produced in agreement with the moral law is blessed, and on account of this causality, which is original, man is called free.[76]

The life of Christ is divine; his life, once conformed to the divine, belongs in heaven,[77] to fulfill his blessedness, accomplishing all his purposes by his Spirit, for because he is known through the apodictic certainty of the Gospel preached from heaven, men see him crucified before their very eyes, that they might be reconciled to God and receive eternal life.[78]

> And no man hath ascended up to heaven, but he that came down from heaven, even the Son of man which is in heaven. And as Moses lifted up the serpent in the wilderness, even so must the Son of man be lifted up: That whosoever believeth in him should not perish, but have eternal life. John 3:13-15, cf. Isaiah 6:1

> For I came down from heaven, not to do mine own will, but the will of him that sent me. And this is the Father's will which hath sent me, that of all which he hath given me I should lose nothing, but should raise it

---

[76] Jas. 1:22-25.
[77] Aquinas, *Summa* 3.57.1.
[78] 2 Cor. 4:4-6; Gal. 3:1; 1 John 5:7-8.

up again at the last day. And this is the will of him that sent me, that every one which seeth the Son, and believeth on him, may have everlasting life: and I will raise him up at the last day. John 6:38-40

Jesus Christ is both God and man, visibly invisible, invisibly visible. His invisible righteousness must be represented visibly, and his visible righteousness once conformed to the divine, must be taken up into the invisible, until the day that the invisible appears.

Appearances are distinct from things in themselves; their combination consists of a transition from one to the other. Jesus Christ is born of a virgin, to reveal his divinity in his humanity; wherefore, he also ascends into heaven, to show forth the perfect sanctification of his human nature; whence he shall return, to manifest both natures perfectly united in himself.

The transition into heaven occurs after his work on earth is complete, for he submits to condemnation in the flesh, but his nonlegal righteousness remains forever invisible. Therefore, after he fulfills the pleasure of the Father in the work of submission, God also exalts him to heaven, to show forth his invisible righteousness forevermore, which he has with the Father from eternity past.

Lord, thou hast been our dwelling place in all generations. Before the mountains were brought forth, or ever thou hadst formed the earth and the world, even from everlasting to everlasting, thou *art* God. Psalm 90:1-2

Verily, verily, I say unto thee, We speak that we do know, and testify that we have seen; and ye receive not our witness. If I have told you earthly things, and ye believe not, how shall ye believe, if I tell you *of* heavenly things? And no man hath ascended up to heaven, but he that came down from heaven, even the Son of man which is in heaven. John 3:11-13

We, the Holy Trinity; *speak that we do know, and testify that we have seen,* for the Son of man came down from heaven to reveal divine mysteries. *If I have told you earthly things,* even the necessity of repentance; *how shall ye believe, if I tell you of heavenly things?* even of the way of repentance through faith in Jesus Christ.

> I have glorified thee on the earth: I have finished the work which thou gavest me to do. And now, O Father, glorify thou me with thine own self with the glory which I had with thee before the world was. John 17:4-5

If his burial represents his perfect righteousness, which in the body transcends the body, then the ascension glorifies the blessedness of his person, which in the soul transcends the soul, even unto the divine nature. In death his soul ascends to God,[79] but his body descends into hell; in the ascension, body and soul united are lifted up to God, that he may be glorified in the body even as in the soul. Having humbled himself unto death, he is exalted to the highest heaven, far above kings and nations.

> Behold, my servant shall deal prudently, he shall be exalted and extolled, and be very high. As many were astonied at thee; his visage was so marred more than any man, and his form more than the sons of men: So shall he sprinkle many nations; the kings shall shut their mouths at him: for *that* which had not been told them shall they see; and *that* which they had not heard shall they consider. Isaiah 52:13-15

> Wherefore he saith, When he ascended up on high, he led captivity captive, and gave gifts unto men. (Now that he ascended, what is it but that he also descended first into the lower parts of the earth? He that descended is the same also that ascended up far above all heavens, that he might fill all things.) Ephesians 4:8-10

---

[79] Ps. 25:1-2, 86:4, 14, 143:7-8.

The possibility of salvation depends upon the divine persons; therefore, the divine persons must be glorified in the work of redemption, that men might see the possibility of salvation, and repent unto life. The ascension works salvation because therein God glorifies his Son. It is not the work of atonement, whereby men are saved, but the work of glorification, whereby the righteousness of the atonement is revealed to men, that they might trust therein.

> Verily thou *art* a God that hidest thyself, O God of Israel, the Saviour. They shall be ashamed, and also confounded, all of them: they shall go to confusion together *that are* makers of idols. *But* Israel shall be saved in the LORD with an everlasting salvation: ye shall not be ashamed nor confounded world without end. Isaiah 45:15-17

> Ought not Christ to have suffered these things, and to enter into his glory? Luke 24:24, cf. 46-53

Christ ascends into heaven to be glorified with the Father, but the Father is invisible; therefore, to make known his union with the Father, he sends forth the Holy Spirit, who justifies him, who also rewards him with the salvation of his people, applying his redemption to the church, that Christ may rest in his work until the application is complete.

> The Lord said unto my Lord, Sit thou at my right hand, until I make thine enemies thy footstool. The Lord shall send the rod of thy strength out of Zion: rule thou in the midst of thine enemies. Psalm 110:1-2

The rod of thy strength, the actuality of potentiality, which lies in the holiness of the Spirit.

> My sheep hear my voice, and I know them, and they follow me: And I give unto them eternal life; and they shall never perish, neither shall any *man* pluck them out of my hand. My Father, which gave *them* me,

is greater than all; and no *man* is able to pluck *them* out of my Father's hand. I and *my* Father are one. John 10:27-30

My hand, the Holy Spirit; *my Father's hand*, the same, because he says, *I and my Father are one.*

Jesus reveals himself from heaven through the necessity of practical reason for a solution to the problem of sin, and that by the Holy Spirit, who applies the work of redemption to believers, in whom lies the apodictic certainty of identity in distinction, whereby they are comforted with mercy and truth.

> If ye love me, keep my commandments. And I will pray the Father, and he shall give you another Comforter, that he may abide with you for ever; *Even* the Spirit of truth; whom the world cannot receive, because it seeth him not, neither knoweth him: but ye know him; for he dwelleth with you, and shall be in you. I will not leave you comfortless: I will come to you. Yet a little while, and the world seeth me no more; but ye see me: because I live, ye shall live also. At that day ye shall know that I *am* in my Father, and ye in me, and I in you. He that hath my commandments, and keepeth them, he it is that loveth me: and he that loveth me shall be loved of my Father, and I will love him, and will manifest myself to him. Judas saith unto him, not Iscariot, Lord, how is it that thou wilt manifest thyself unto us, and not unto the world? Jesus answered and said unto him, If a man love me, he will keep my words: and my Father will love him, and we will come unto him, and make our abode with him. He that loveth me not keepeth not my sayings: and the word which ye hear is not mine, but the Father's which sent me. These things have I spoken unto you, being *yet* present with you. But the Comforter, *which is* the Holy Ghost, whom the Father will send in my name, he shall teach you all things, and bring all things to your remembrance, whatsoever I have said unto you. Peace I leave with you, my peace I give unto you: not as the world giveth, give I unto you. Let not your heart be troubled, neither let it be afraid. Ye have

heard how I said unto you, I go away, and come *again* unto you. If ye loved me, ye would rejoice, because I said, I go unto the Father: for my Father is greater than I. And now I have told you before it come to pass, that, when it is come to pass, ye might believe. Hereafter I will not talk much with you: for the prince of this world cometh, and hath nothing in me. But that the world may know that I love the Father; and as the Father gave me commandment, even so I do. Arise, let us go hence. John 14:15-31

For my Father is greater than I, though equal in nature, yet is he greater in relation; wherefore, Jesus must have ascended to the Father, to be glorified with him.

The Holy Spirit contains the identity in distinction of God's righteousness and blessedness. In the virgin birth, the Son is distinguished from the Father; in the ascension, he is united together with the Father; and to show forth that union in distinction, he sends forth the Holy Spirit, the Spirit of the Father and of the Son.

But now I go my way to him that sent me; and none of you asketh me, Whither goest thou? But because I have said these things unto you, sorrow hath filled your heart. Nevertheless I tell you the truth; It is expedient for you that I go away: for if I go not away, the Comforter will not come unto you; but if I depart, I will send him unto you. And when he is come, he will reprove the world of sin, and of righteousness, and of judgment: Of sin, because they believe not on me; Of righteousness, because I go to my Father, and ye see me no more; Of judgment, because the prince of this world is judged. I have yet many things to say unto you, but ye cannot bear them now. Howbeit when he, the Spirit of truth, is come, he will guide you into all truth: for he shall not speak of himself; but whatsoever he shall hear, *that* shall he speak: and he will shew you things to come. He shall glorify me: for he shall receive of mine, and shall shew *it* unto you. All things that the Father hath are mine: therefore said I, that he shall take of mine, and shall shew *it* unto you. A little while, and ye shall not see me: and again, a little while, and ye shall see me, because I go to the Father. John 16:5-16

And because ye are sons, God hath sent forth the Spirit of his Son into your hearts, crying, Abba, Father. Galatians 4:6

Christ manifests himself from heaven, not by a sensible intuition, but by the proclamation of the word. The world lies in sin, but the Gospel is known by righteousness, unto righteousness. The perfect righteousness of Christ, once manifested in the flesh, seen and testified by men saved by it, is that whereby men know that he dwells in heaven; by the very doctrine of Christ ascended, God reveals his righteousness to men, and the Holy Spirit testifies through its apodictic truth; for to heaven belong those things thought through pure concepts.

Forever, O Lord, thy word is settled in the heaven. Psalm 119:89

Even the Word of God, who is known by his word.[80]

For after that in the wisdom of God the world by wisdom knew not God, it pleased God by the foolishness of preaching to save them that believe. 1 Corinthians 1:21

This is he that came by water and blood, *even* Jesus Christ; not by water only, but by water and blood. And it is the Spirit that beareth witness, because the Spirit is truth. For there are three that bear record in heaven, the Father, the Word, and the Holy Ghost: and these three are one. And there are three that bear witness in earth, the Spirit, and the water, and the blood: and these three agree in one. 1 John 5:6-8

---

[80] Heb. 4:12-13.

For this reason the apostles watched him ascend until they saw him no more, that they might receive of his Spirit; and they waited for the promise of the Father, that they might preach Christ from heaven; yea, to persuade men to believe in himself, Christ himself preaches from heaven,[81] that by union with him, men might partake of the divine nature.

> And, lo, I am with you alway, *even* unto the end of the world. Amen. Matthew 28:20

> Now then we are ambassadors for Christ, as though God did beseech *you* by us: we pray *you* in Christ's stead, be ye reconciled to God. For he hath made him *to be* sin for us, who knew no sin; that we might be made the righteousness of God in him. 2 Corinthians 5:20-21

> And hath raised *us* up together, and made *us* sit together in heavenly *places* in Christ Jesus: That in the ages to come he might shew the exceeding riches of his grace in *his* kindness toward us through Christ Jesus. Ephesians 2:6-7

The ascension of Christ is a glorious form of an earthly phenomenon. Death forms no part of the original creation. There must have been a way for men to depart from this temporal abode into their eternal habitation, after they had proved themselves righteous many days. Accordingly, it is written,

> And Enoch lived sixty and five years, and begat Methuselah: And Enoch walked with God after he begat Methuselah three hundred years, and begat sons and daughters: And all the days of Enoch were three hundred sixty five years: And Enoch walked with God: and he *was* not: for God took him. Genesis 5:21-24

---

[81] Heb. 12:25.

Of the fathers it is written that they lived, but of Enoch it is written that he walked with God after the birth of his son. A marvelous alteration manifested itself in him through the Son of God, who would come from his loins. Though man had fallen, Enoch testifies that man might yet be righteous with God, because for his obedience he did not die, but was taken into heaven, having the invisible righteousness of Christ, through the forgiveness of sins.[82]

Elijah ascended into heaven; Elisha watched him ascend, that he might receive a double portion of his spirit, for after Christ ascends into heaven, he sends forth the Holy Spirit from the Father. This Elijah, sanctified to God and separate from sinners, by his life eternal continually testifies of repentance, and of the sinfulness of man sold into slavery, and the necessity of faith in Christ to come. He prophesied during the time of Ahab and Jezebel, to bring the kingdom of Israel to repentance, that they might be reunited under the crown of Judah.[83] His ministry failed to convert the kingdom to God, because the time of Christ had not yet come. Yet that Messiah would come and restore all things, Elijah ascended into heaven, for he would come again in the person of John.[84] Thereafter the kingdom of Israel was taken into captivity, that the dominion might be confirmed to Judah, from whom sprang our Lord.[85]

John the Baptist comes in the name and power of Elijah, to turn the kingdom to Christ, to prepare the way of the Lord.[86] John turned the hearts of the people to God, for that Christ was now come in the flesh. He is Elijah, whose testimony complete, remains forever: the message of repentance settled in heaven, that all should believe in Christ come. As Elijah suffered of Jezebel, so also John the Baptist suffered of Herodias. John did not ascend into heaven, but Christ who comes after him, to testify of faith until the end of the world.

---

[82] Heb. 11:5.
[83] Ezek. 37:15-28; Zech. 11:14.
[84] Mal. 4:5-6.
[85] Heb. 7:14.
[86] Is. 40:3.

Scripture Proof

Christ ascended into heaven in the sight of his apostles. The apostles are witnesses of his resurrection, therefore also of his ascension, for it is the afterward condition of the atonement. Christ must ascend to have completed his work. The apostles are witnesses by office of his resurrection; wherefore, they also saw him ascend, until they saw him no more.

Though they saw him ascend, yet they did not see him sit down on the right hand of God, for he was taken out of their sight by a cloud. To this only the angels in heaven are witnesses, and the souls of just men made perfect; to two men only is it given to bear witness of Jesus seated on his throne. The resurrection is a fact of the church, known to the whole community.[87] The ascension is a transition from the visible to the invisible, whereof only the apostles are witnesses, because it is manifest in the preaching of the Gospel. Yet only Stephen and Paul have seen Christ on his throne: Stephen in his death, and Paul in his life, for Paul is brought to life in Christ after Stephen is slain, even with the consent of Paul. This Paul was before called Saul, to show in him the united kingdom of Judah and Benjamin,[88] because the death of Christ issues forth in new life. One believer dies, another is raised. This is the work of Christ on his throne, the application of the atonement to his people, that all who die in Christ, and all who live in Christ, may look to him on his throne in heaven.[89]

> For none of us liveth to himself, and no man dieth to himself. For whether we live, we live unto the Lord; and whether we die, we die unto the Lord: whether we live therefore, or die, we are the Lord's. For to this end Christ both died, and rose, and revived, that he might be Lord both of the dead and living. Romans 14:7-9

---

[87] 1 Cor. 15:1-8.
[88] Gen. 49:27; Rom. 11:1; Phil. 3:5.
[89] Aquinas, *Summa* 3.58.1, 4.

And rose, and revived, for in his ascension he is raised up, as in his resurrection; he is raised up into heaven, to live forever to God, who raised him from the dead.[90]

The ascension is the transition from the visible to the invisible. Though a historical truth, testified by the apostles, yet is it not known through the word of witnesses, but by the faith of his people, who seek him in those heavenly places.

> *When thou saidst*, Seek ye my face; my heart said unto thee, Thy face, Lord, will I seek. Hide not thy face *far* from me; put not thy servant away in anger: thou hast been my help; leave me not, neither forsake me, O God of my salvation. Psalm 27:8-9

> Seek the Lord, and his strength: seek his face evermore. Psalm 105:4

Therefore he is also manifest to the world through his children.

> Bind up the testimony, seal the law among my disciples. And I will wait upon the Lord, that hideth his face from the house of Jacob, and I will look for him. Behold, I and the children whom the Lord hath given me *are* for signs and for wonders in Israel from the Lord of hosts, which dwelleth in mount Zion. Isaiah 8:16-18

The children whom God hath given me, not his children, but the children of the Father, whom the Father gives to the Son, for they are one.

The ascension has a peculiar relation to the preaching of the Gospel and the person of the Son. It is therefore spoken of by Mark and Luke. The Gospel is preached from heaven through the Holy Spirit, and it belongs to Christ to be seated at the right hand of the throne of God, because he is his Son. Luke writes of it a second time in Acts, because it is through the ascension that he sends forth

---

[90] Rom. 6:4, 10; Col. 3:1.

the Holy Spirit from heaven, to work salvation in his people and preach the Gospel to the world.

Mark 16:15-20

And he said unto them, Go ye into all the world, and preach the gospel to every creature, for Christ is preached from heaven over all the earth. *He that believeth and is baptized shall be saved; but he that believeth not shall be damned.* Men know Christ by faith in the word preached. *And these signs shall follow them that believe; In my name shall they cast out devils; they shall speak with new tongues; They shall take up serpents; and if they drink any deadly thing, it shall not hurt them; they shall lay hands on the sick, and they shall recover.* Heavenly works performed in his name testify to Christ ascended, above all the conversion of sinners to righteousness. Miracles belong chiefly to the transition; once the church is established, Christ is known by the preaching of the Gospel and the good works of his people. *So then after the Lord had spoken unto them, he was received up into heaven, and sat on the right hand of God,* which they knew by faith. *And they went forth, and preached every where, the Lord working with them, and confirming the word with signs following,* Christ preaching from heaven by his Spirit. *Amen.*

Luke 24:50-53

And he led them out as far as to Bethany, and he lifted up his hands, and blessed them, for by his ascension he pours out heavenly blessings upon the church. *And it came to pass, while he blessed them,* for he is the blessed one; *he was parted from them,* for he is holy; *and carried up into heaven,* even by angels, for in his human nature he was subject to them,[91] but in his divine nature he rules over them; therefore, when his humanity ascended into heaven, to be glorified with the Father, he was carried up by angels, exalted by their submission to God manifest

---

[91] Gal. 4:4, cf. 3:19; Heb. 2:9.

in the flesh, even as they shall be revealed with him at the end.[92] *And they worshipped him, and returned to Jerusalem with great joy: And were continually in the temple, praising and blessing God,* for his people are with him in heaven, as he is with them on earth.[93] *Amen.*

Acts 1

The former treatise have I made, Luke distinguishes between the Gospel and its preaching; *O Theophilus,* which he wrote to a single person, as it is fit for all, and for each one individually; *of all that Jesus began both to do and teach,* both of the moral law and of the doctrine of righteousness; *Until the day in which he was taken up,* to be unto God forever, as before the world was made; *after that he through the Holy Ghost had given commandments unto the apostles whom he had chosen:* that they should obey the moral law; *To whom also he shewed himself alive after his passion,* to assure them of the doctrine of righteousness; *by many infallible proofs,* the Spirit testifying through the evidence of history; *being seen of them,* for he is the image; *forty days,* as the constitution of the law; *and speaking of the things pertaining to the kingdom of God:* whose foundation he laid in person, that they should build upon it.[94] *And, being assembled together with them, commanded them that they should not depart from Jerusalem,* that the work might not be of men; *but wait for the promise of the Father,* that Christ himself should be with them; *which, saith he, ye have heard of me,* for the Spirit proceeds from both. *For John truly baptized with water;* a sign of repentance unto faith in Christ; *but ye shall be baptized with the Holy Ghost not many days hence,* John taught repentance; Jesus Christ preaches faith; the Spirit works holiness. *When they therefore were come together, they asked of him, saying, Lord, wilt thou at this time restore again the kingdom to Israel?* To remove the yoke of Roman bondage and restore the independence of

---

[92] Ps. 68:17-18, 91:11-16; Matt. 13:41, 16:27, 24:31, 25:31; Mark 8:38, 13:27; Luke 9:26, 16:22; John 1:51; 2 Thess. 1:7; 1 Tim. 3:16; 1 Pet. 3:22; Aquinas, *Summa* Supp. 76.3; *Jamieson-Fausset-Brown Bible Commentary* and *Gill's Exposition of the Entire Bible* on Luke 24:51, (https://biblehub.com/commentaries/luke/24-51.htm).
[93] John 14:18; Eph. 2:6; Col. 3:3.
[94] 1 Cor. 3:9-23.

their nation. *And he said unto them, It is not for you to know the times or the seasons, which the Father hath put in his own power,* for although it belongs equally to the three divine persons, yet has the Father reserved this unto himself, that we should mind the things revealed, to keep the law.[95] The history of the world unto the end Jesus did not fully reveal to his disciples until the end of the apostles' ministry, by the word of his servant John.[96] *But ye shall receive power, after that the Holy Ghost is come upon you:* the power of God's holiness through prayer; *and ye shall be witnesses unto me both in Jerusalem, and in all Judaea,* to all the Jews; *and in Samaria,* even to the rejected people, the false Jews; *and unto the uttermost part of the earth,* to the Jews in every corner of the world, and to the Gentiles, that they may be gathered into one, for he reigns from heaven over all. *And when he had spoken these things, while they beheld, he was taken up;* they are witnesses of his ascension; *and a cloud received him out of their sight,* as seeing the invisible Son of God through his Spirit giving them life. *And while they looked stedfastly toward heaven as he went up,* that they might receive of his Spirit; *behold, two men stood by them in white apparel;* angels, who henceforth see him in heaven, to worship him in truth, by whom he also ascended;[97] *Which also said, Ye men of Galilee, why stand ye gazing up into heaven?* For the word was in their hearts, and they must be about his will;[98] *this same Jesus, which is taken up from you into heaven, shall so come in like manner as ye have seen him go into heaven,* through the preaching of the Gospel to the world and the sanctification of the church, wherein also the angels are fellow laborers, to be revealed with him at the end of the world.[99] *Then returned they unto Jerusalem from the mount called Olivet,* where Jesus in holiness ascended, having finished the work he was sent to do;[100] *which is from Jerusalem a sabbath day's journey,* that rest being the measure of the foundation of the church, united with him in heaven. *And when they were come in, they went up into an upper room, where abode both Peter, and James, and John, and Andrew, Philip,*

---

[95] Deut. 29:29.
[96] John 16:12-13; Rev. 1:1-3.
[97] Ps. 91:11-16; 1 Tim. 3:16.
[98] Deut. 30:11-14.
[99] Matthew 13:41, 49, 16:27, 24:31; Mark 13:27.
[100] John 17:4-5.

and Thomas, Bartholomew, and Matthew, James the son of Alphaeus, and Simon Zelotes, and Judas the brother of James. These all continued with one accord in prayer and supplication, to receive the Spirit; *with the women, and Mary the mother of Jesus,* who ministered to him and to them, that they might partake of his blessedness; *and with his brethren,* to testify of his righteousness in all things. *And in those days Peter stood up in the midst of the disciples, and said, (the number of names together were about an hundred and twenty,),* in the fullness of the doctrine of righteousness; *Men and brethren, this scripture must needs have been fulfilled,* for the sake of the moral law; *which the Holy Ghost by the mouth of David spake before concerning Judas, which was guide to them that took Jesus,* Peter calls him "guide" to show what he has in common with the Spirit, for the Spirit is guide to the Father and the Son, to justify Jesus in his submission to condemnation.[101] *For he was numbered with us, and had obtained part of this ministry,* to teach the necessity of sin for the glory of God. *Now this man purchased a field with the reward of iniquity;* of necessity providing for his own body after death; *and falling headlong, he burst asunder in the midst, and all his bowels gushed out,* the secrets of his heart revealed, and the sin of his inward part punished. *And it was known unto all the dwellers at Jerusalem;* a fact of history; *insomuch as that field is called in their proper tongue, Aceldama,* corroborated even by unbelievers; *that is to say, The field of blood,* for he is the son of perdition. *For it is written in the book of Psalms, Let his habitation be desolate, and let no man dwell therein: and his bishoprick let another take. Wherefore of these men which have companied with us all the time that the Lord Jesus went in and out among us,* with whom all was fact; *Beginning from the baptism of John, unto that same day that he was taken up from us, must one be ordained to be a witness with us of his resurrection,* for that is the office of an apostle. *And they appointed two, Joseph called Barsabas, who was surnamed Justus, and Matthias,* as far as their wisdom could tell. *And they prayed, and said, Thou, Lord, which knowest the hearts of all men, shew whether of these two thou hast chosen,* for the calling is of the essence; *That he may take part of this ministry and apostleship, from which Judas by transgression fell,* as the devil and his angels fell from their offices; *that he might go to his own place,* which is his by essence, according to which he had transgressed. *And they gave forth*

---

[101] John 16:13.

their lots; and the lot fell upon Matthias; and he was numbered with the eleven apostles. That there might be one among them taken out of necessity, without foreknowledge of his calling, that all Christians might be assured of their eternal inheritance.

The Lord's Supper

Men know Christ ascended, not by an intuition given, but to be produced. Though he is not in the world, yet he appears to us in his flesh and blood, not sensibly but by faith, more necessary than bread, and finer than wine. Men know Christ by their need of him, and by his blessedness.

> Then Jesus said unto them, Verily, verily, I say unto you, Except ye eat the flesh of the Son of man, and drink his blood, ye have no life in you. Whoso eateth my flesh, and drinketh my blood, hath eternal life; and I will raise him up at the last day. For my flesh is meat indeed, and my blood is drink indeed. He that eateth my flesh, and drinketh my blood, dwelleth in me, and I in him. As the living Father hath sent me, and I live by the Father: so he that eateth me, even he shall live by me. This is that bread which came down from heaven: not as your fathers did eat manna, and are dead: he that eateth of this bread shall live for ever. These things said he in the synagogue, as he taught in Capernaum. Many therefore of his disciples, when they had heard *this*, said, This is an hard saying; who can hear it? When Jesus knew in himself that his disciples murmured at it, he said unto them, Doth this offend you? *What* and if ye shall see the Son of man ascend up where he was before? It is the spirit that quickeneth; the flesh profiteth nothing: the words that I speak unto you, *they* are spirit, and *they* are life. John 6:53-63, cf. 1 Cor. 11:17-34

That the body of Christ may benefit his disciples, he ascends up into heaven, and sends forth his Spirit, appointing the Lord's Supper in remembrance of himself, whereof he also partook, because God redeemed him by his Spirit.[102]

This sign is divided into the passover and the Lord's supper. The ascension represents the completeness of the atonement, and so marks the beginning of the new church, distinguished from the old.[103] The passover signifies the unconditional condemnation of the Father, whereby he gives his only begotten Son for the sins of men. Christ bore the condemnation of the Father, and being justified therein, fully satisfied the justice of God on behalf of his people, so that they also partake of his life in heaven; and this is what is represented to us in the Lord's Supper. Thus, the ground of this division lies in the succession from the old to the new, as from condemnation to justification.[104]

John omits the Passover and the Lord's supper, saying only that "supper being ended," Jesus washed the feet of his disciples, and sent out Judas from their midst (John 13:2). Jesus then gave them of the Lord's supper, for Luke calls the passover supper,[105] which John says, "being ended," he washed the feet of his disciples.[106]

Nevertheless, John omits both the passover and the Lord's Supper, because Christ in his blessedness is not far from us, but always near. For by these signs we draw near to the one who is invisible, but his blessedness is always with us.[107]

Matthew 26:17-35

Now the first day of the feast of unleavened bread, when they slew the passover;[108] *he disciples came to Jesus, saying unto him, Where wilt thou that we prepare for thee to eat the passover?* according to the commandment of God, which he kept, even unto death. *And he said, Go into the city to such a man, and say unto*

---

102 Ps. 20:6.
103 Acts 1:8-2:47; Eph. 4:7-16.
104 Gal. 3:10-14.
105 Luke 22:20.
106 John 13:2.
107 Deut. 30:11-14.
108 Ex. 12:18-20; Lev. 23:4-8.

him, The Master saith, My time is at hand; the time appointed of the Father in the hand of the Holy Ghost; *I will keep the passover at thy house with my disciples.* The Lord has servants for himself in every time and place. *And the disciples did as Jesus had appointed them; and they made ready the passover,* God effectually works in his people to accomplish his purposes. *Now when the even was come,* when they should eat the passover, because the old creation passes away in the sacrifice of Christ;[109] *he sat down with the twelve,* who represent the whole church;[110] *And as they did eat,* of the Passover; *he said, Verily I say unto you, that one of you shall betray me,* to signify the condemnation of the Father, and the necessity of sin for the glory of God. *And they were exceeding sorrowful, and began every one of them to say unto him, Lord, is it I?* for he would save them from their sins. *And he answered and said, He that dippeth his hand with me in the dish, the same shall betray me,* one who joined him in earthly things, though his heart was not with him. *The Son of man goeth as it is written of him:* for Jesus must be put to death for sin, that God may be glorified in the redemption of sinners; *but woe unto that man by whom the Son of man is betrayed! it had been good for that man if he had not been born,* though he fulfills the prophecy, yet is he alone to blame for his sin. *Then Judas, which betrayed him, answered and said, Master, is it I? He said unto him, Thou hast said,* he at once confessed his sin, and Christ the Lord. *And as they were eating,* of the Lord's Supper; *Jesus took bread, and blessed it, and brake it, and gave it to the disciples, and said, Take, eat; this is my body,* for the body of the Lord is broken for the church, and his perfections are distributed to his disciples.[111] *And he took the cup, and gave thanks, and gave it to them, saying, Drink ye all of it;* they ought to partake of it by faith, that it might be applied to them; *For this is my blood of the new testament, which is shed for many for the remission of sins,* that they might be united with him in his life eternal, whereby he rises from the dead. *But I say unto you, I will not drink henceforth of this fruit of the vine, until that day when I drink it new with you in my Father's kingdom,* when after he had suffered, his soul ascended into heaven.[112] *And when they had sung an hymn, they went out into the mount of Olives,*

---

[109] Gen. 1:5; Lev. 23:5; Deut. 16:6.
[110] Luke 22:29-30.
[111] Eph. 4:7-10.
[112] Luke 23:43.

for by his afterward ascension into heaven in that place, he bore all the wrath of the Father, "who for the joy that was set before him endured the cross, despising the shame, and is set down at the right hand of the throne of God" (Hebrews 12:2). *Then saith Jesus unto them, All ye shall be offended because of me this night: for it is written, I will smite the shepherd, and the sheep of the flock shall be scattered abroad,* that Christ alone should be glorified therein. *But after I am risen again, I will go before you,* to restore them by his righteousness, that they might partake of his glory; *into Galilee,* to affirm his life. *Peter answered and said unto him, Though all men shall be offended because of thee, yet will I never be offended.* He boasted. *Jesus said unto him, Verily I say unto thee, That this night, before the cock crow, thou shalt deny me thrice,* that he should afterward boast in Christ his Savior. *Peter said unto him, Though I should die with thee, yet will I not deny thee. Likewise also said all the disciples.* The disciples resolved, yet they did not bear out their resolution, for this belongs to Christ, and in him only do men persevere until the end.

Mark 14:12-31

And Judas Iscariot, one of the twelve, went unto the chief priests, to betray him unto them, in the same act both to affirm and negate. *And when they heard it, they were glad, and promised to give him money. And he sought how he might conveniently betray him. And the first day of unleavened bread, when they killed the passover, his disciples said unto him, Where wilt thou that we go and prepare that thou mayest eat the passover?* They knew that he would keep the feast appointed by God, but not the means. *And he sendeth forth two of his disciples, and saith unto them, Go ye into the city, and there shall meet you a man bearing a pitcher of water:* to give drink to his people; *follow him,* for the disciples of the Lord are met with in their ordinary duties. *And wheresoever he shall go in, say ye to the goodman of the house,* good, as the Father;[113] *The Master saith, Where is the guestchamber, where I shall eat the passover with my disciples? And he will shew you a large upper room furnished and prepared:* because the Lord prepares a place for us in heaven;[114] *there make ready*

---

113 Matt. 19:17.
114 John 14:1-4.

for us. And his disciples went forth, and came into the city, and found as he had said unto them: and they made ready the passover. They prepared his way, as the church of old. *And in the evening he cometh with the twelve. And as they sat and did eat, Jesus said, Verily I say unto you, One of you which eateth with me shall betray me.* He knew it beforehand, that he might submit to the condemnation of the Father, to bring forth affirmation out of negation. *And they began to be sorrowful, and to say unto him one by one, Is it I? and another said, Is it I? And he answered and said unto them, It is one of the twelve, that dippeth with me in the dish,* who partook of his baptism, and ate the bread of the covenant. *The Son of man indeed goeth, as it is written of him: but woe to that man by whom the Son of man is betrayed! good were it for that man if he had never been born,* for by his very birth, however lawful, yet according to his essence, he transgressed. *And as they did eat, Jesus took bread, and blessed, and brake it, and gave to them, and said, Take, eat: this is my body,* his own blessed body broken for the church. *And he took the cup, and when he had given thanks, he gave it to them: and they all drank of it. And he said unto them, This is my blood of the new testament, which is shed for many,* for the blood of Christ gives life to the dead. *Verily I say unto you, I will drink no more of the fruit of the vine, until that day that I drink it new in the kingdom of God,* because torments had been prepared for him until that time. *And when they had sung an hymn, they went out into the mount of Olives,* where he also ascended, that he might give peace.[115] *And Jesus saith unto them, All ye shall be offended because of me this night: for it is written, I will smite the shepherd, and the sheep shall be scattered,* because for their sins he is given up to death. *But after that I am risen, I will go before you into Galilee. But Peter said unto him, Although all shall be offended, yet will not I. And Jesus saith unto him, Verily I say unto thee, That this day, even in this night, before the cock crow twice, thou shalt deny me thrice. But he spake the more vehemently, If I should die with thee, I will not deny thee in any wise. Likewise also said they all.* They had the seed of faith, but not yet its perfection, for they had need of historical doctrine.

---

[115] John 14:27.

Now the feast of unleavened bread drew nigh, which is called the Passover, the time of remembrance, when the Lord slew the firstborn of the Egyptians, but spared the firstborn of Israel, and dedicated them to himself, even "the firstborn of every creature" (Colossians 1:15). *And the chief priests and scribes sought how they might kill him; for they feared the people.* They sought to sacrifice him to themselves, but accomplished nothing but the will of God. *Then entered Satan into Judas surnamed Iscariot,* the head of the serpent to be bruised in the person of the betrayer; *being of the number of the twelve,* showing the necessity of sin for the glory of God. *And he went his way, and communed with the chief priests and captains, how he might betray him unto them,* he conspired with those who condemned and crucified the Lord. *And they were glad, and covenanted to give him money,* for he was a thief. *And he promised, and sought opportunity to betray him unto them in the absence of the multitude,* that Christ in his death should be alone, the only begotten Son of God. *Then came the day of unleavened bread, when the passover must be killed.* Jesus, condemned by the Father, must be sacrificed to God. *And he sent Peter and John,* the apostles of unity and affirmation, to show forth Christ come in the flesh;[116] *saying, Go and prepare us the passover, that we may eat,* because he was the seed of Abraham. *And they said unto him, Where wilt thou that we prepare?* He provides a place for us in heaven, as we provide a place for him in our hearts.[117] *And he said unto them, Behold, when ye are entered into the city, there shall a man meet you, bearing a pitcher of water;* to give drink to the thirsty; *follow him into the house where he entereth in. And ye shall say unto the goodman of the house, The Master saith unto thee, Where is the guestchamber, where I shall eat the passover with my disciples? And he shall shew you a large upper room furnished:* a place prepared for us in heaven; *there make ready. And they went, and found as he had said unto them: and they made ready the passover. And when the hour was come,* the events that follow being spoken of a single time, and not in order; *he sat down, and the twelve apostles with him,* he enjoyed fellowship with them, in

---

[116] Matt. 16:13-19; 1 John 2:22, 4:2-3, 5:6.
[117] John 14:2-3; 15-23.

preparation for his sacrifice of himself for their sins. *And he said unto them, With desire I have desired to eat this passover with you before I suffer:* By the fruit of his suffering he is prepared for the torments of hell. *For I say unto you, I will not any more eat thereof, until it be fulfilled in the kingdom of God,* when his soul ascended into heaven. *And he took the cup, and gave thanks, and said, Take this, and divide it among yourselves: For I say unto you, I will not drink of the fruit of the vine, until the kingdom of God shall come,* when he shall have been perfectly sanctified in death. He gave them first of the passover, then of his own supper. Though he drank again thereof immediately thereafter, yet for the unity of the sacrament he says, "I will not drink of the fruit of the vine, until the kingdom of God shall come" (vs. 18). *And he took bread, and gave thanks, and brake it, and gave unto them, saying, This is my body which is given for you: this do in remembrance of me,* the Lord's Supper. *Likewise also the cup after supper,* that is, passover; *saying, This cup is the new testament in my blood, which is shed for you.* Luke first shows the succession from the Passover to the Lord's Supper, and only then writes of the betrayal, to demonstrate the unity of the sacrament and the distinction of the signs, for the new is identical in distinction to the old. *But, behold, the hand of him that betrayeth me is with me on the table,* which he said in that hour. *And truly the Son of man goeth, as it was determined: but woe unto that man by whom he is betrayed!* All men by their essences do serve the king, even in their sin, for they are made in his image, and he rests in his work.[118] *And they began to enquire among themselves, which of them it was that should do this thing,* they sought to understand the sign. *And there was also a strife among them, which of them should be accounted the greatest,* here told to show forth the greatness of Christ's service shortly to be accomplished. *And he said unto them, The kings of the Gentiles exercise lordship over them;* lording it over them, treating them as servants; *and they that exercise authority upon them are called benefactors,* even in the just use of their powers, they are honored above others; *But ye shall not be so: but he that is greatest among you, let him be as the younger; and he that is chief, as he that doth serve.* "Let this mind be in you, which was also in Christ Jesus: Who, being in the form of God, thought it not robbery to be equal with God: But made himself of no reputation, and took

---

[118] Genesis 1:26-28, 2:1-3.

upon him the form of a servant, and was made in the likeness of men: And being found in fashion as a man, he humbled himself, and became obedient unto death, even the death of the cross" (Philippians 2:5-8). *For whether is greater, he that sitteth at meat, or he that serveth? is not he that sitteth at meat? but I am among you as he that serveth,* the greatest glory from the lowest service. "Wherefore God also hath highly exalted him, and given him a name which is above every name: That at the name of Jesus every knee should bow, of things in heaven, and things in earth, and things under the earth; And that every tongue should confess that Jesus Christ is Lord, to the glory of God the Father" (Philippians 2:9-11). *Ye are they which have continued with me in my temptations,* they served him immediately in his sanctification. *And I appoint unto you a kingdom, as my Father hath appointed unto me;* because they would serve his people, and express the several virtues of his person; *That ye may eat and drink at my table in my kingdom,* blessed with him; *and sit on thrones judging the twelve tribes of Israel,* ruling both in this world and in the world to come. *And the Lord said, Simon, Simon, behold, Satan hath desired to have you, that he may sift you as wheat:* yet were they subject to temptation and sin; *But I have prayed for thee, that thy faith fail not:* upheld by the priesthood of Christ; *and when thou art converted, strengthen thy brethren,* that grace poured out on us for the sake of others also. *And he said unto him, Lord, I am ready to go with thee, both into prison, and to death,* for he had the resolve of faith, but not yet the fullness of devotion; nor should he as yet obey unto death, but after Christ. Wherefore, after Jesus rose from the dead, he corrected his denials and set him apart for the service of the church: "So when they had dined, Jesus saith to Simon Peter, Simon, *son* of Jonas, lovest thou me more than these? He saith unto him, Yea, Lord; thou knowest that I love thee. He saith unto him, Feed my lambs. He saith to him again the second time, Simon, *son* of Jonas, lovest thou me? He saith unto him, Yea, Lord; thou knowest that I love thee. He saith unto him, Feed my sheep. He saith unto him the third time, Simon, *son* of Jonas, lovest thou me? Peter was grieved because he said unto him the third time, Lovest thou me? And he said unto him, Lord, thou knowest all things; thou knowest that I love thee. Jesus saith unto him, Feed my sheep. Verily, verily, I say unto thee, When thou wast young, thou girdedst thyself, and walkedst whither thou wouldest: but when thou shalt be old, thou shalt stretch forth thy hands, and another shall gird thee, and carry *thee* whither thou wouldest not. This spake he, signifying by what death he should glorify God. And when he had spoken this, he saith unto him, Follow me" (John 21:15-19). *And he said, I tell thee, Peter, the cock shall not crow this day, before that thou shalt thrice deny that thou knowest me,* for before Peter should suffer for Jesus, Jesus must first suffer alone for his people. *And he said unto them, When I sent you without purse, and scrip, and shoes, lacked ye any thing? And they said, Nothing.* God provided all. *Then said he unto them, But now, he that hath a purse, let him take it, and likewise his scrip: and he that hath no sword, let him sell his garment, and buy one,* that they should provide for themselves. *For I say unto you, that this that is written must yet be accomplished in me, And he was reckoned among the transgressors: for the things concerning me have an end.* They must fend for themselves while Christ is tried and put to death. *And they said, Lord, behold, here are two swords. And he said unto them, It is enough.* Even in such a time as this, God upheld them. *And he came out, and went, as he was wont, to the mount of Olives;* to give peace in his holy mountain; *and his disciples also followed him,* they followed him as far as they could for the present.

The Second Coming

That the world has a beginning comes to pass through the eternal purpose of God; therefore, to fulfill that purpose, the world must also have end.[119] If the beginning of time represents a ground preceding time itself, then the end of time represents an effect beyond it, and remaining afterwards. An infinite progress of time, on the other hand, represents a purpose never achieved, always remaining within the world itself. Yet because the purpose of the world lies outside the world, in the divine will, according to which all things come to pass, the world has both a beginning and an end.

The world exists for the glory of God; Jesus Christ is the image and glory of God. Wherefore, at the end of time, the Lord Jesus Christ manifests himself in the flesh, his glorious body perfectly conformed to the divine nature, and shining forth, for the redemption and glorification of his people, and the consecration of a new creation.

> That in the dispensation of the fulness of times he might gather together in one all things in Christ, both which are in heaven, and which are on earth; *even* in him. Ephesians 1:10

Having proved himself by the law, righteous above the law, he is taken up into heaven, whence he shall return unto the full manifestation of the invisible God.

> I give thee charge in the sight of God, who quickeneth all things, and *before* Christ Jesus, who before Pontius Pilate witnessed a good confession; That thou keep *this* commandment without spot, unrebukeable, until the appearing of our Lord Jesus Christ: Which in his times he shall shew, *who* is the blessed and only Potentate, the King of kings, and Lord of lords; Who only hath immortality, dwelling in the light which no man can approach unto; whom no man hath seen,

---

[119] Aquinas, *Summa* 3.74.1, 91.1.

nor can see: to whom *be* honour and power everlasting. Amen. 1
Timothy 6:13-16

The divine purpose is to save sinners from their sin. God rewards Christ
with the salvation of those for whom he died. Wherefore, the Holy Spirit, who
justifies Christ, also applies the work of redemption to the church, sanctifying
them until the last day, when the application shall have been complete.

> The Lord shall send the rod of thy strength out of Zion: rule thou in the
> midst of thine enemies. Thy people *shall be* willing in the day of thy
> power, in the beauties of holiness from the womb of the morning: thou
> hast the dew of thy youth. Psalm 110:2-3

> Being confident of this very thing, that he which hath begun a good
> work in you will perform *it* until the day of Jesus Christ. Philippians
> 1:6

On that day, the divine nature shall be fully manifest in his flesh, even his
body, the church, and he shall raise all men unto judgment, for his resurrection
testifies to the judgment, that men might fear God until he returns.

> Marvel not at this: for the hour is coming, in the which all that are in
> the graves shall hear his voice, And shall come forth; they that have
> done good, unto the resurrection of life; and they that have done evil,
> unto the resurrection of damnation. John 5:28-29, cf. 19-27

> Because he hath appointed a day, in the which he will judge the world
> in righteousness by *that* man whom he hath ordained; *whereof* he hath
> given assurance unto all *men,* in that he hath raised him from the dead.
> Acts 17:31

And to wait for his Son from heaven, whom he raised from the dead, *even* Jesus, which delivered us from the wrath to come. 1 Thessalonians 1:10

Christ is truly God, and shall judge all men by the revelation he has given them, for sin lies in the conception thereof, and is judged accordingly.

Then answered Jesus and said unto them, Verily, verily, I say unto you, The Son can do nothing of himself, but what he seeth the Father do: for what things soever he doeth, these also doeth the Son likewise. For the Father loveth the Son, and sheweth him all things that himself doeth: and he will shew him greater works than these, that ye may marvel. For as the Father raiseth up the dead, and quickeneth *them*; even so the Son quickeneth whom he will. For the Father judgeth no man, but hath committed all judgment unto the Son: That *all* men should honour the Son, even as they honour the Father. He that honoureth not the Son honoureth not the Father which hath sent him. John 5:19-23

Jesus cried and said, He that believeth on me, believeth not on me, but on him that sent me. And he that seeth me seeth him that sent me. I am come a light into the world, that whosoever believeth on me should not abide in darkness. And if any man hear my words, and believe not, I judge him not: for I came not to judge the world, but to save the world. He that rejecteth me, and receiveth not my words, hath one that judgeth him: the word that I have spoken, the same shall judge him in the last day. For I have not spoken of myself; but the Father which sent me, he gave me a commandment, what I should say, and what I should speak. And I know that his commandment is life everlasting: whatsoever I speak therefore, even as the Father said unto me, so I speak. John 12:44-50, cf. Luke 12:41-48

Those who believe in Christ will be glorified with him, because in him they see the identity in distinction of righteousness and blessedness, whereby they partake of the same, not only because he is God, but also because he is man, yea, God manifest in the flesh, our divine head.

> When Christ, *who* is our life, shall appear, then shall ye also appear with him in glory. Colossians 3:4

And by their hopeful expectation of the same, they are sanctified unto that day.

> Beloved, now are we the sons of God, and it doth not yet appear what we shall be: but we know that, when he shall appear, we shall be like him; for we shall see him as he is. And every man that hath this hope in him purifieth himself, even as he is pure. 1 John 3:2-3

The second coming reveals the identity in distinction of God's righteousness and blessedness; therefore also of God's visibility and invisibility, to reveal the invisible visibly. God is the ground of all that is. When therefore the invisible God appears to men, the world shall be remade according to the image thereof. The new creation is the beauty of holiness, the invisible made visible, heaven on earth, redemption from sin.

> For, behold, I create new heavens and a new earth: and the former shall not be remembered, nor come into mind. But be ye glad and rejoice for ever *in that* which I create: for, behold, I create Jerusalem a rejoicing, and her people a joy. And I will rejoice in Jerusalem, and joy in my people: and the voice of weeping shall be no more heard in her, nor the voice of crying. Isaiah 65:17-19

Behold, in Christ, the image and glory of God, that in him the divine persons may be fully known.

Christ returns to reveal the identity in distinction of his righteousness and blessedness. In him they are distinct, in the Holy Spirit they are identical. Wherefore, he returns only after the Holy Spirit has applied the work of redemption to his people; he returns to finish that work and bring it to glory.

When he returns, he shows forth the glory of God in his body. Having been once perfected in righteousness, his perfect righteousness shall then appear to all. Thus John depicts his glory at the beginning of the Apocalypse, because the prophecies of that book fill the history of the world until the end of time.

> And I turned to see the voice that spake with me. And being turned, I saw seven golden candlesticks; And in the midst of the seven candlesticks *one* like unto the Son of man, clothed with a garment down to the foot, and girt about the paps with a golden girdle. His head and *his* hairs *were* white like wool, as white as snow; and his eyes *were* as a flame of fire; And his feet like unto fine brass, as if they burned in a furnace; and his voice as the sound of many waters. And he had in his right hand seven stars: and out of his mouth went a sharp twoedged sword: and his countenance *was* as the sun shineth in his strength. And when I saw him, I fell at his feet as dead. Revelation 1:12-17

He has not left the world without his presence; he is always with the church, even unto the end of the age; and he often visits the sons of men in mercy and in judgment. The destruction of the temple in Jerusalem he depicts under his second coming,[120] and all his holy judgments upon the earth are visitations of the Lord, though not yet the fullness of that day. Prophetic history typifies that day, that men should not be ignorant of the final judgment, that they may repent themselves beforehand, and the Lord be gracious to them.[121]

Christ saves not only individuals, but also nations, even the world. He comes to establish a kingdom on earth, not an earthly kingdom, but a heavenly kingdom on earth, for after God has destroyed the imperial body prophesied by

---

[120] Matt. 24:14, 29-51; Mark 13:24-37; Luke 21:24-36.
[121] Joel 2:12-14.

Daniel, the kingdom of Christ shall be established forever, first on earth, then after his return, forevermore.[122]

Jesus Christ shall come again. Though he has finished his work and ascended into heaven, that work has not yet been fully applied to his people. Even now the Holy Ghost works in the hearts of men, to sanctify them unto the end, but when Christ returns, the application shall have been finished, and God will be glorified in Christ. If God is glorified in Christ, and Christ is glorified in his people, then when he returns the work of redemption shall have been fully applied to his people. This event encompasses, not only the perfection of the just on earth, but also the resurrection of the righteous and the wicked—the righteous perfected, and their perfection manifested, and the glory of Christ perfected in his church.

But no man, not even the Son, knows the hour of his return, for the times of things belong to the Father.[123] Time is the form of inner sense:[124] one's position in time cannot be determined absolutely, except in relation to a person who is absolute. And the end of time is the transition to eternity. Not even the Son knows the end of time; though he has theoretical knowledge of the end, he does not have practical cognition to constitute a ground of action. The Father alone, who sees all things unconditionally, initiates and accomplishes the transition into eternity.

The transition from the temporal to the eternal takes place in a moment that combines them both. Between any two successive nonhomogeneous quantities there must lie an intermediate state. The moment before is temporal, the moment after is eternal; therefore, the moment itself must be both temporal and eternal, a period of time that is itself momentary, a day, and the last day. The moment before represents the end of the temporal; the moment after represents the beginning of the eternal. These are identical in distinction. God therefore calls it a day wherein all men shall be raised unto judgment, "in a moment, in the twinkling of an eye, at the last trump: for the trumpet shall sound, and the

---

[122] Dan. 2:31-45; Rev. 20:1-10.
[123] Ps. 31:5; Matt. 24:36; Mark 13:32; Luke 7:1-14; Acts 1:7.
[124] Kant, *Critique*, B46-73.

dead shall be raised incorruptible, and we shall be changed" (1 Corinthians 15:52). The old earth is, at the beginning of that day, destroyed, but at the end of the day, renewed. Thus Scripture depicts both events in harmony.[125]

Jesus is righteous under condemnation; wherefore, he has the right to condemn by the word that he has spoken, and to cause all condemnation and suffering in hell to be for the glory of God, who gave up his Son for the sins of the world; for as in him the old creation is put to death and buried, in his resurrection the world is renewed in righteousness, and dedicated to holiness. Death and hell are destroyed, cast into the lake of fire, together with the bodies and souls of the wicked. Hell is the place of damned souls; the lake of fire is prepared for the wicked, their bodies and souls reunited, that God may be glorified in their destruction.

Jesus is nonlegally righteous in his submission to condemnation; wherefore, he has the right to cause all to submit to condemnation: the wicked, for the glory of God in their damnation; the elect, to their own salvation. All will confess that Jesus is Lord, to the glory of God the Father, even the wicked. The justice of their damnation they shall acknowledge, the glory of God obtained therein, the grace offered and rejected, and the sovereign rights of God to ordain, and the wisdom of God to pass over, unto judgment. And to cause the elect to submit to unconditional condemnation in himself, that in him they may also be justified.

Jesus is justified, justified in his submission to condemnation, and in exercising all the divine rights given him by the Father, to hold all men accountable to innocence, and to save his elect by imputing his innocence to them; for he has the right to make the elect partakers with his condemnation, that they may also be glorified with him.

> And this is the Father's will which hath sent me, that of all which he hath given me I should lose nothing, but should raise it up again at the last day. And this is the will of him that sent me, that every one which

---

[125] Ps. 102:25-26; Rom. 8:19-21; 2 Pet. 3:10-13; Aquinas, *Summa* 3.74.1, 91.1.

seeth the Son, and believeth on him, may have everlasting life: and I
will raise him up at the last day. John 6:39-40

Let not your heart be troubled: ye believe in God, believe also in me. In
my Father's house are many mansions: if *it were* not *so,* I would have
told you. I go to prepare a place for you. And if I go and prepare a place
for you, I will come again, and receive you unto myself; that where I
am, *there* ye may be also. And whither I go ye know, and the way ye
know. John 14:1-4

Howbeit when he, the Spirit of truth, is come, he will guide you into
all truth: for he shall not speak of himself; but whatsoever he shall hear,
that shall he speak: and he will shew you things to come. He shall
glorify me: for he shall receive of mine, and shall shew *it* unto you. All
things that the Father hath are mine: therefore said I, that he shall take
of mine, and shall shew it unto you. A little while, and ye shall not see
me: and again, a little while, and ye shall see me, because I go to the
Father. John 16:13-16

Father, I will that they also, whom thou hast given me, be with me
where I am; that they may behold my glory, which thou hast given me:
for thou lovedst me before the foundation of the world. John 17:24

Scripture Proof

The second coming cannot be intuited as an appearance, for it is the
transition to the eternal; neither can it be intuited as a past event, for it is future.
The narrative of Scripture therefore consists of prophecy. The Old Testament
speaks of it prior to the Lord's coming, as to men unacquainted with historical
doctrine. I shall therefore restrict myself to those accounts given after the Lord
ascended into heaven. I might indeed have commented on those accounts
contained in the prophecy of Jesus, but these are given in the context of

prophetic history, not historical doctrine. It is the purpose of this book to illuminate those Scriptures specially dedicated to the narrative of events, and these are found in the epistles of Paul and Peter.

Peter is the first apostle, Paul is the last. The beginning of the world is its creation; in the end of the world, that creation is destroyed, and renewed. This occurs when Jesus Christ returns in the flesh, who is "Alpha and Omega, the beginning and the end, the first and the last" (Revelation 22:13). It is therefore fitting that the second coming should be narrated by these men, and not rather by John, who speaks of the history of the world until the end.

Mark is the Gospel of Peter;[126] Luke is the Gospel of Paul.[127] The second coming has a peculiar relation to the preaching of the Gospel and the person of the Son of God. The good news should be declared in preparation of the day when the Son of God shall be revealed. In view of that day, men ought to sanctify themselves through faith in the death and resurrection of Christ, who is in heaven.

1 Corinthians 15

Moreover, brethren, I declare unto you the gospel which I preached unto you, an expression indicative of the apodictic truth of the Gospel preached, whereby the matter of divine truth is clothed with the form; *which also ye have received,* by faith, that is, consent; *and wherein ye stand;* even before God; *By which also ye are saved, if ye keep in memory what I preached unto you,* for true faith continues therein; *unless ye have believed in vain,* according to mere theoretical reason, and not to fulfill the moral law. *For I delivered unto you first of all that which I also received,* being saved by the same that saves those who hear; *how that Christ died for our sins,* not the death of any ordinary man, but the death of an innocent, for the sins of others; *according to the scriptures;* according to that which is written, the word

---

[126] Mark 1:1; 1 Pet. 5:13; Eusebius, *Ecclesiastical History*, 2.15, 3.39, 6.14 (https://www.catholic-resources.org/Bible/Eusebius_Gospels.htm).
[127] Acts; 2 Tim. 4:11; Eusebius, *Ecclesiastical History*, 3.24 and Irenaeus of Lyon, *On the Composition of the Four Gospels* (https://www.catholic-resources.org/Bible/Eusebius_Gospels.htm).

to all mankind. *And that he was buried,* the wrath of God ceasing in his death; *and that he rose again the third day according to the scriptures:* because he bore our sins in righteousness; *And that he was seen of Cephas,* the first of the apostles, who denied these things beforehand;[128] *then of the twelve:* as ministers of the church, and representatives of his person; *After that, he was seen of above five hundred brethren at once;* of the whole church in obedience to his commandments; *of whom the greater part remain unto this present,* testifying not for a moment, but for their lives, even a generation; *but some are fallen asleep,* because they live in Jesus. *After that, he was seen of James; then of all the apostles,* when he ascended in their sight. *And last of all he was seen of me also, as of one born out of due time,* who not only saw him raised, but also seated at the right hand of God, for as the last of the apostles, he represents the church overspreading the world.[129] *For I am the least of the apostles, that am not meet to be called an apostle, because I persecuted the church of God,* by which he should have been disqualified. *But by the grace of God I am what I am:* to bring the word of salvation to the Gentiles; *and his grace which was bestowed upon me was not in vain; but I laboured more abundantly than they all:* "Benjamin shall ravin *as* a wolf: in the morning he shall devour the prey, and at night he shall divide the spoil" (Genesis 49:27); *yet not I, but the grace of God which was with me,* the Holy Spirit. *Therefore whether it were I or they, so we preach, and so ye believed.* The work of salvation is told us of sinful men who partake of the same, because its certainty lies in its power to save sinners. *Now if Christ be preached that he rose from the dead, how say some among you that there is no resurrection of the dead?* Either possibly, that there is no such thing, or actually, that there is no resurrection at the end of the world. *But if there be no resurrection of the dead, then is Christ not risen:* which follows either analytically or synthetically, because if Christ is risen, then are all raised in him. *And if Christ be not risen, then is our preaching vain, and your faith is also vain.* If Christ is not risen, how does it appear that he died for our sins? For if he died in innocence, then he should also live. *Yea, and we are found false witnesses of God;* the Spirit testifying through the history; *because we have testified of God that he raised up Christ:* the history agreeing

---

128 Matt. 16:21-22; Mark 8:31-32.
129 Gal. 2:7-8; 2 Cor. 10:14-16; Phil. 3:5.

with the doctrine; *whom he raised not up, if so be that the dead rise not. For if the dead rise not, then is not Christ raised: And if Christ be not raised, your faith is vain; ye are yet in your sins.* It is necessary that Jesus Christ rise from the dead, to save us from our sins: "for if ye believe not that I am *he*, ye shall die in your sins" (John 8:24). It is a truth of practical reason, confirmed by aesthetic judgment through the word of truth. *Then they also which are fallen asleep in Christ are perished,* that the dead should live to God.[130] *If in this life only we have hope in Christ, we are of all men most miserable,* for then we seek righteousness without reward. *But now is Christ risen from the dead, and become the firstfruits of them that slept.* In that he died for sin, he is the head of all who die therein. *For since by man came death, by man came also the resurrection of the dead.* As there is a head unto death, so also must there be a head unto life, that men might repent, to which they are free as long as they live. *For as in Adam all die, even so in Christ shall all be made alive,* for he is the rightful head of all, through whom any man may be saved. *But every man in his own order: Christ the firstfruits; afterward they that are Christ's at his coming,* and the wicked also, deduced from the foregoing, and confirmed by what follows. *Then cometh the end,* wherein the purpose of the world is accomplished; *when he shall have delivered up the kingdom to God, even the Father;* having applied his work by the Spirit, he gives to the Father what he also received from the Father;[131] *when he shall have put down all rule and all authority and power,* the wicked on earth, and the fallen angels. *For he must reign, till he hath put all enemies under his feet,* to bring them in subjection to the moral law. *The last enemy that shall be destroyed is death,* for if death is the wages of sin, then the end of death is the end of sin.[132] *For he hath put all things under his feet,* in the earth, his footstool.[133] *But when he saith all things are put under him, it is manifest that he is excepted, which did put all things under him,* for he is above him, "for my Father is greater than I" (John 14:28). *And when all things shall be subdued unto him, then shall the Son also himself be subject unto him that put all things under him,* for as God he depends upon the Father, so also as man he submits to God in the flesh; *that*

---

130 Luke 20:27-38.
131 John 17:1-5.
132 Rom. 6:23.
133 Is. 66:1-3.

God may be all in all, "For of him, and through him, and to him, *are* all things: to whom *be* glory for ever. Amen" (Romans 11:36). *Else what shall they do which are baptized for the dead,* for those who have died in faith, and for martyrs, as follows; *if the dead rise not at all? why are they then baptized for the dead? And why stand we in jeopardy every hour? I protest by your rejoicing which I have in Christ Jesus our Lord, I die daily. If after the manner of men I have fought with beasts at Ephesus, what advantageth it me, if the dead rise not? let us eat and drink; for to morrow we die.* If happiness be cut off from the law, and there is no reward for our obedience, shall we not rather be happy? So also through obedience from the heart, we prove the reality of those doctrines necessary to keep the law.[134] *Be not deceived: evil communications corrupt good manners.* To seek happiness, though not contrary to the law, is yet not blameless, if it be sought without it. *Awake to righteousness,* as unto new life; *and sin not;* but repent; *for some,* of whose ignorance we ought not to partake; *have not the knowledge of God:* which is to do his will in Christ, and be happy for it;[135] *I speak this to your shame. But some man will say, How are the dead raised up? and with what body do they come? Thou fool,* because he, being earthly, cannot imagine the heavenly, and seeks out things too high for him;[136] *that which thou sowest is not quickened, except it die:* we must first cast off this body before we can receive the next; *And that which thou sowest, thou sowest not that body that shall be, but bare grain, it may chance of wheat, or of some other grain:* unto a new body, which we do not know. *But God giveth it a body as it hath pleased him,* in wisdom and righteousness; *and to every seed his own body,* as the intuition in agreement with the concept. *All flesh is not the same flesh: but there is one kind of flesh of men, another flesh of beasts, another of fishes, and another of birds.* The matter being particular, is particular to the kind, and admits of genus, species, difference, and individual, for the matter is conceptualized in the intuition. *There are also celestial bodies, and bodies terrestrial: but the glory of the celestial is one, and the glory of the terrestrial is another. There is one glory of the sun, and another glory of the moon, and another glory of the stars: for one star differeth from another star in glory,* difference

---

[134] Kant, *Practical Reason,* 5:3.
[135] Jer. 22:15-16
[136] Ps. 131.

of essence yields difference of intuition. *So also is the resurrection of the dead,* wherein every man glorifies God through the particular distribution of divine virtues. *It is sown in corruption; it is raised in incorruption: It is sown in dishonour; it is raised in glory: it is sown in weakness; it is raised in power: It is sown a natural body; it is raised a spiritual body. There is a natural body, and there is a spiritual body.* According as there is body and soul, visible and invisible. *And so it is written, The first man Adam was made a living soul;* a soul giving life to the body; *the last Adam was made a quickening spirit,* a body giving life to souls. *Howbeit that was not first which is spiritual, but that which is natural;* the glory of God given us by his grace, and not by our own nature; *and afterward that which is spiritual. The first man is of the earth, earthy: the second man is the Lord from heaven,*[137] in whom the human race forms a totality. *As is the earthy, such are they also that are earthy: and as is the heavenly, such are they also that are heavenly,* the nature inhering in persons. *And as we have borne,* that is, in righteousness; *the image of the earthy, we shall also bear the image of the heavenly,* the intuition distinct from the concept, yet identified therewith. *Now this I say, brethren, that flesh and blood cannot inherit the kingdom of God; neither doth corruption inherit incorruption,* for it must be transformed. *Behold, I shew you a mystery; We shall not all sleep, but we shall all be changed,* for those at the end are perfectly sanctified with Christ when he returns; *In a moment,* the transition from the temporal to the eternal; *in the twinkling of an eye,* as from darkness to light, in the subject's mode of apprehension;[138] *at the last trump:* whereby all are called to appear before God; *for the trumpet shall sound, and the dead shall be raised incorruptible,* to die no more; *and we shall be changed,* to receive the eternal. *For this corruptible must put on incorruption,* as a garment; *and this mortal must put on immortality. So when this corruptible shall have put on incorruption, and this mortal shall have put on immortality, then shall be brought to pass the saying that is written, Death is swallowed up in victory,* by a new and greater life brought forth from the jaws of death.[139] *O death, where is thy sting? O grave, where is thy victory? The sting of death is sin;* for death has no power over the just;

---

[137] John 3:31-36.
[138] Ps. 17:15; Kant, *Critique*, A98-100, 120.
[139] Judg. 14:5-9, 14, 18.

and the strength of sin is the law, by which the slaves of sin are punished. *But thanks be to God, which giveth us the victory through our Lord Jesus Christ*, the righteous one. *Therefore, my beloved brethren, be ye stedfast, unmoveable, always abounding in the work of the Lord, forasmuch as ye know that your labour is not in vain in the Lord.* "Let us hear the conclusion of the whole matter: Fear God, and keep his commandments: for this *is* the whole *duty* of man. For God shall bring every work into judgment, with every secret thing, whether *it be* good, or whether *it be* evil" (Ecclesiastes 12:13-14).

1 Thessalonians 4:13-18

But I would not have you to be ignorant, brethren, that they might be comforted; *concerning them which are asleep, that ye sorrow not, even as others which have no hope,* sorrowing in sin; *For if we believe that Jesus died and rose again, even so them also which sleep in Jesus will God bring with him,* to raise them up. *For this we say unto you by the word of the Lord, that we which are alive and remain unto the coming of the Lord shall not prevent them which are asleep,* who shall not die, because the Lord died to preserve the life of man; *For the Lord himself shall descend from heaven with a shout,* to execute judgment in person; *with the voice of the archangel,* to raise all men from the dead by his word,[140] and gather them together through his angels;[141] *and with the trump of God:* even the Spirit of glory, to summon all to appear before God; *and the dead in Christ shall rise first:* to be one body with the rest; *Then we which are alive and remain shall be caught up together with them in the clouds,* together with all the angels of God; *to meet the Lord in the air:* to see him face to face, and so be made like him; *and so shall we ever be with the Lord. Wherefore comfort one another with these words,* because those who sorrow for sin shall be comforted with holiness.[142] *But of the times and the seasons,* for the history of the world is divided into such; *brethren, ye have no need that I write unto you. For yourselves know perfectly that the day of the Lord so cometh as a thief in the night,* for

---

[140] John 5:28-29.
[141] Matt. 13:24-30, 36-43, 47-49, 16:27, 24:31, 25:31; Mark. 8:38, 13:27; Luke 9:26.
[142] Matt. 5:3.

that day is the transition to eternity, known only to the Father. *For when they shall say, Peace and safety; then sudden destruction cometh upon them,* that the majesty of God might never depart from before the eyes of men, and the utmost misery to those who look away from his fear; *as travail upon a woman with child;* their suffering is not for themselves, but for the glory of God's mercy to the church; *and they shall not escape,* for the judgment of God is certified through the preaching of the Gospel. *But ye, brethren, are not in darkness,* in sinful ignorance; *that that day should overtake you as a thief,* for we watch for it by faith. *Ye are all the children of light, and the children of the day:* born of the church afflicted; *we are not of the night, nor of darkness,* without form or purpose. *Therefore let us not sleep, as do others; but let us watch and be sober. For they that sleep sleep in the night;* as those who are ignorant; *and they that be drunken are drunken in the night,* as those who revel. *But let us, who are of the day, be sober, putting on the breastplate of faith and love;* to guard the heart; *and for an helmet, the hope of salvation,* to guard the mind, taking knowledge of his coming by righteousness. *For God hath not appointed us to wrath, but to obtain salvation by our Lord Jesus Christ, Who died for us, that, whether we wake or sleep, we should live together with him,* for in him the dead live. *Wherefore comfort yourselves together, and edify one another, even as also ye do,* sanctifying ourselves unto the Lord's return.

2 Thessalonians 1-2

Paul, and Silvanus, and Timotheus, unto the church of the Thessalonians in God our Father and the Lord Jesus Christ: Grace unto you, and peace, in the Holy Spirit who proceeds from the Father and the Son; *from God our Father and the Lord Jesus Christ,* to those who hold the fundamentals, namely, the Incarnation and the Trinity. *We are bound to thank God always for you, brethren, as it is meet, because that your faith groweth exceedingly, and the charity of every one of you all toward each other aboundeth;* as unto the last day; *So that we ourselves glory in you in the churches of God for your patience and faith in all your persecutions and tribulations that ye endure:* being sanctified therein; *Which is a manifest token of the righteous judgment of God,* not of men, but of God; *that ye may be counted worthy of the kingdom of God,* as

Christ before us; *for which ye also suffer:* as Christ suffered; *Seeing it is a righteous thing with God,* a practical necessity; *to recompense tribulation to them that trouble you;* to put a difference between the righteous and the wicked; *And to you who are troubled rest with us,* relief from suffering through the perfection of holiness; *when the Lord Jesus shall be revealed from heaven with his mighty angels,* the invisible made visible, and the church glorified; *In flaming fire taking vengeance on them that know not God, and that obey not the gospel of our Lord Jesus Christ:* for this is to know God: to do his will in Christ; *Who shall be punished with everlasting destruction,* because they sinned for all time, and rejected their hope of salvation; *from the presence of the Lord, and from the glory of his power;* the instrument of his will, and the actuality of his potentiality, two expressions for the Holy Spirit, because he proceeds from the Father and the Son; *When he shall come to be glorified in his saints, and to be admired in all them that believe (because our testimony among you was believed) in that day,* when the perfect end of the law shall have been fulfilled. *Wherefore also we pray always for you,* as fellow partakers of that end; *that our God would count you worthy of this calling, and fulfil all the good pleasure of his goodness,* which is of himself, in the sanctification of the righteous through the unconditional condemnation of Christ; *and the work of faith with power:* by the Holy Spirit; *That the name of our Lord Jesus Christ may be glorified in you,* in perfect fulfillment of the moral law; *and ye in him,* even to the divine likeness; *according to the grace of our God and the Lord Jesus Christ,* for it is the work of the divine persons. *Now we beseech you, brethren, by the coming of our Lord Jesus Christ, and by our gathering together unto him,* in observance of that day, signified by the Sabbath, when the whole church shall be made perfect in Christ; *That ye be not soon shaken in mind, or be troubled, neither by spirit, nor by word, nor by letter as from us, as that the day of Christ is at hand. Let no man deceive you by any means: for that day shall not come, except there come a falling away first,* to show forth those who are approved;[143] *and that man of sin be revealed, the son of perdition;* the Pope, who being with the Lord is against him; *Who opposeth and exalteth himself above all that is called God, or that is worshipped;* making himself to be head of the church; *so that he as God sitteth in the temple of God, shewing himself that he is God,* both in the

___

143 1 Cor. 11:19.

church, and in an earthly temple as an image. *Remember ye not, that, when I was yet with you, I told you these things?* for we are slow to understand, even those things that are necessary and good for us. *And now ye know what withholdeth that he might be revealed in his time,* for the roman empire must reign until the kingdom of Christ is established on the earth.[144] *For the mystery of iniquity doth already work:* that is, the empire of Rome; *only he who now letteth will let, until he be taken out of the way,* the emperor. *And then shall that Wicked be revealed,* the Pope, who takes his place, and revives the empire, and crowns the Holy Roman Emperor; *whom the Lord shall consume with the spirit of his mouth,* the Holy Spirit; *and shall destroy with the brightness of his coming:* the same, for he proceeds from the Father and the Son; not in his own person, but in the person of the Holy Spirit, even as he himself shall come at the last;[145] *Even him, whose coming is after the working of Satan with all power and signs and lying wonders,* who speaks not in the name of the Lord;[146] *And with all deceivableness of unrighteousness in them that perish;* for he teaches the doctrine of sin; *because they received not the love of the truth, that they might be saved,* for out of God's kindness he gave them time to repent.[147] *And for this cause God shall send them strong delusion, that they should believe a lie:* he suffers them to fulfill their own wickedness, in order to sanctify his church. *That they all might be damned who believed not the truth, but had pleasure in unrighteousness.* God suffers them to sin as they will, even as he foreordained, that he might be true and just in judgment.[148] *But we are bound to give thanks alway to God for you, brethren beloved of the Lord, because God hath from the beginning,* according to his eternal purpose; *chosen you to salvation through sanctification of the Spirit and belief of the truth:* for that is the final end of all things; *Whereunto he called you by our gospel, to the obtaining of the glory of our Lord Jesus Christ,* to be like God. *Therefore, brethren, stand fast, and hold the traditions which ye have been taught, whether by word, or our epistle,* the apostolic tradition, and the teaching of the church, according to the word of God. *Now our Lord Jesus Christ himself, and*

---

144 Dan. 2:44-45.
145 Cf. Rev. 19:11-16.
146 Deut. 13:1-5; Rev. 13:11-17.
147 Rev. 2:21.
148 Ps. 51:4; Rom. 3:4.

God, even our Father, which hath loved us, and hath given us everlasting consolation, even now unto eternity; *and good hope through grace,* through the comfort of the promises; *Comfort your hearts, and stablish you in every good word and work,* that we may delight to do his will.[149]

2 Peter 3

This second epistle, beloved, I now write unto you; in both which I stir up your pure minds by way of remembrance: practical reason being confirmed by aesthetic judgment; *That ye may be mindful of the words which were spoken before by the holy prophets,* who testify before; *and of the commandment of us the apostles of the Lord and Saviour:* who testify after; *Knowing this first, that there shall come in the last days scoffers, walking after their own lusts,* who for the pleasures of sin deny the doctrine of righteousness; *And saying, Where is the promise of his coming?* Not the coming itself, but the promise thereof, for coming of Christ is signified by the times and seasons; *for since the fathers fell asleep, all things continue as they were from the beginning of the creation,* as though there were no distinction of times. *For this they willingly are ignorant of,* the knowledge of God being blotted out by wickedness; *that by the word of God the heavens were of old,* extending far beyond what men can imagine, not by their own nature, but by the will of God; *and the earth standing out of the water and in the water:* being brought forth on the second day; *Whereby the world that then was, being overflowed with water, perished:* it perished after a manner, reverting to its primeval state, as on the second day; *But the heavens and the earth, which are now,* renewed by the recession of the waters, as on the third day; *by the same word are kept in store, reserved unto fire against the day of judgment and perdition of ungodly men.* Water symbolizes the plurality of sensation, the lusts of the flesh in which sinners drown, but fire signifies the destruction of the sensible world itself, to reveal the things in themselves, and the contradiction of sinners against their own nature, which is their lot in the lake of fire. *But, beloved, be not ignorant of this one thing, that one day is with the Lord as a thousand years, and a thousand years as one day,* for in those

---

[149] Ps. 40:8.

first seven days lies the whole pattern of history. *The Lord is not slack concerning his promise,* as though he delayed his coming; *as some men count slackness; but is longsuffering to us-ward, not willing that any should perish, but that all should come to repentance,* because of his great love for every creature, the one principle outweighing the other.[150] *But the day of the Lord will come as a thief in the night;* for the transition from time to eternity, being unimaginable, is also unforeseen, especially to those who look not to things eternal, but temporal,[151] that they should be taken by surprise and destroyed; *in the which the heavens shall pass away with a great noise,* overwhelming to the senses; *and the elements shall melt with fervent heat,* the intensity of the judgment reaching even to the least part, even to things in themselves;[152] *the earth also and the works that are therein shall be burned up,* the old things passing away. *Seeing then that all these things shall be dissolved, what manner of persons ought ye to be in all holy conversation and godliness,* not cleaving to things destructible, but to things that remain forever; *Looking for,* by faith, *and hasting,* by works, *unto the coming of the day of God,* when Christ, "the Sun of righteousness," shall appear (Mal. 4:2); *wherein the heavens being on fire shall be dissolved, and the elements shall melt with fervent heat?* The judgment of hell, transcending all earthly pain, now made visible in the world. *Nevertheless we, according to his promise, look for new heavens and a new earth, wherein dwelleth righteousness,* as in a habitation, an intuition for the concept. *Wherefore, beloved, seeing that ye look for such things,* by faith; *be diligent that ye may be found of him in peace,* for his warfare is unimaginable; *without spot,* having within us a disposition to uproot the least sin, which should separate us from God; *and blameless,* through the blood of Christ. *And account that the longsuffering of our Lord is salvation;* that we should have time to repent, and to sanctify ourselves against that day, to work out our salvation "with fear and trembling" (Philippians 2:12); *even as our beloved brother Paul also according to the wisdom given unto him hath written unto you;* the last agrees with the first, the end with the beginning; *As also in all his epistles, speaking in them of these things; in which are*

---

[150] Jas. 2:13.

[151] 2 Cor. 4:18.

[152] Kant, *Critique*, B462-472, B518-543.

some things hard to be understood, for they must be understood in righteousness, and in the fullness of reason, and in the increase of the church;[153] *which they that are unlearned and unstable wrest, as they do also the other scriptures, unto their own destruction,* for they seek wisdom sinfully, and in sin.[154] *Ye therefore, beloved, seeing ye know these things before,* to prepare us for what lies ahead; *beware lest ye also, being led away with the error of the wicked,* the doctrine of unrighteousness; *fall from your own stedfastness,* as men preserved by the grace of God. *But grow in grace, and in the knowledge of our Lord and Saviour Jesus Christ,* for the truth is known by righteousness unto righteousness. *To him be glory both now and for ever,* both in this world and in the world to come. *Amen.*

The Transfiguration

Christ shows forth the new creation in the body of his resurrection; wherefore, the second coming is signified by his transfiguration on the mount. Herein God transforms the earthly visage of Christ into the glorious appearance of the Son of God, his invisible righteousness shining forth in the flesh, as on the last day. Christ shows this sign to three of his apostles: Peter, James, and John, the apostles of unity, totality, and affirmation, to show his disciples that he returns as God manifest in the flesh, the rightful head of the human race, to be glorified in all its members.

> For we have not followed cunningly devised fables, when we made known unto you the power and coming of our Lord Jesus Christ, but were eyewitnesses of his majesty. For he received from God the Father honour and glory, when there came such a voice to him from the excellent glory, This is my beloved Son, in whom I am well pleased. And this voice which came from heaven we heard, when we were with him in the holy mount. 2 Peter 1:16-18

---

[153] Eph. 4:11-16; Col. 2:19.
[154] Prov. 17:16, 18:2, 24:7.

This is my beloved Son, in whom I am well pleased, the same words spoken by the Father in his baptism, for this is the end of his ministry unto which he is born.

John omits the transfiguration, because it is a peculiar manifestation of his blessedness, which Christ has in the whole of his life, death, and resurrection.

Matthew 17:1-13

And after six days Jesus taketh Peter, James, and John his brother, and bringeth them up into an high mountain apart, as the holiness of God, nigh unto heaven; *And was transfigured before them:* in his glory; *and his face did shine as the sun, and his raiment was white as the light,* his divine righteousness manifest in the flesh, as on the last day; twofold, as the glory of the Holy Spirit. *And, behold, there appeared unto them Moses and Elias talking with him,* the law and the prophets, to be fulfilled on the last day. *Then answered Peter, and said unto Jesus, Lord, it is good for us to be here: if thou wilt, let us make here three tabernacles; one for thee, and one for Moses, and one for Elias,* for he understood not the sign. *While he yet spake, behold, a bright cloud overshadowed them:* as the Holy Ghost, in whom the darkness shines as the light;[155] as when he ascends, and when he returns;[156] *and behold a voice out of the cloud,* the Father speaking through his Spirit; *which said, This is my beloved Son, in whom I am well pleased; hear ye him,* that they should listen to the Son, as to the law and the prophets, which speak of him. *And when the disciples heard it, they fell on their face, and were sore afraid,* for the coming of Jesus inspires fear in the hearts of sinners. *And Jesus came and touched them, and said, Arise, and be not afraid,* yet we ought not to be afraid, but trust in his grace for remission of sins. *And when they had lifted up their eyes,* to see God face to face; *they saw no man, save Jesus only,* for there is one God, and one mediator between God and man.[157] *And as they came down from the mountain,* as he should return from heaven at the last; *Jesus charged them, saying, Tell the vision to no man, until the Son of man be risen again from the dead,* for it is a sign. The second coming is the end of his

---

[155] Ps. 139:7-12.
[156] Acts 1:9, 11; Rev. 1:7.
[157] 1 Tim. 2:5.

resurrection; wherefore, they must first learn of his death, burial, and resurrection, before they understand his second coming. Mark adds, "And they kept that saying with themselves, questioning one with another what the rising from the dead should mean," because the fruit of their reasoning depended on revelation (9:10). *And his disciples asked him, saying, Why then say the scribes that Elias must first come?* for in the second coming no man precedes him. *And Jesus answered and said unto them, Elias truly shall first come, and restore all things*, that is, Elias shall come before the millennium, just as he came before Christ, for before Jesus comes he calls men to repent through a prophet. Wherefore, Mark says, "Elias verily cometh first," because the Lord is ever preceded by his prophets, save on the last day when there is no repentance (Mark 9:12). *But I say unto you, That Elias is come already, and they knew him not,* for John is a sign of Christ to come; *but have done unto him whatsoever they listed.* The scribes who spoke of Elias did not recognize John come in his power. There is much that may be known through theoretical reason without the consent of practical. *Likewise shall also the Son of man suffer of them,* for John comes before him in all things, in birth, life, and death; and the head of John the Baptist is required of him, which is Christ. *Then the disciples understood that he spake unto them of John the Baptist,* for he is a sign.

Luke 9:28-36

Jesus Christ proves himself to be the Son of God chiefly by his death, burial, and resurrection. Wherefore, Luke also includes many sayings from the end of his ministry, when his hour is nigh. This is why the transfiguration comes so early in his Gospel. The substance of Christ's ministry he summarizes thus:

> And it came to pass afterward, that he went throughout every city and village, preaching and showing the glad tidings of the kingdom of God: and the twelve *were* with him. Luke 8:1

Then he called his twelve disciples together, and gave them power and authority over all devils, and to cure diseases. And he sent them to preach the kingdom of God, and to heal the sick. Luke 9:1-2

And it came to pass about an eight days after these sayings, he took Peter and John and James, and went up into a mountain to pray, for he must first ascend into heaven to make intercession for the saints, before he returns to his inheritance as a king. *And as he prayed, the fashion of his countenance was altered,* for by prayer, even unto death, he is both sanctified and glorified; *and his raiment was white and glistering,* for his fleshed clothed with divinity, shone with glory. *And, behold, there talked with him two men, which were Moses and Elias: Who appeared in glory,* because they are glorified in him and with him, both the law and the prophets, and all the saints and holy martyrs; *and spake of his decease which he should accomplish at Jerusalem,* Christ himself is instructed in the law and the prophets, and compassed by the souls of just men made perfect, and by the church before, and by his seed after, and by the living and the dead, and by the holy angels.[158] *But Peter and they that were with him were heavy with sleep:* as in the garden of Gethsemane, for they understood not what they saw; *and when they were awake, they saw his glory, and the two men that stood with him,* for the church shall stand with him in glory. *And it came to pass, as they departed from him,* that he alone should be glorified; *Peter said unto Jesus, Master, it is good for us to be here: and let us make three tabernacles; one for thee, and one for Moses, and one for Elias: not knowing what he said,* for he prophesied, for there are three tabernacles: Christ came in the tabernacle of his body, to ascend to the temple of God in heaven, to establish the temple of God on earth. *While he thus spake, there came a cloud, and overshadowed them:* as the glory of the Holy Spirit; *and they feared as they entered into the cloud,* because the grace of God calls to mind our sins. *And there came a voice out of the cloud, saying, This is my beloved Son: hear him,* beloved in the Spirit. *And when the voice was past,* in all things instructed by God; *Jesus was found alone,* the only begotten Son of God. *And they kept it close, and told no man in those days*

---

[158] Jer. 31:22; Heb. 12:22-24.

any of those things which they had seen, even the secret of his righteousness, to be
revealed through his resurrection from the dead.

255

A modality is the relation of an object to the thinking subject, whereby the concept of the object refers to the object itself. Historical doctrines pertain not to the concept, but to the intuition produced. Accordingly, the modalities represent the divine nature manifest in the flesh, the person of Christ in his relation to mankind. These are called *offices*.

The judgments are lawful for the divine persons revealed, and the persons subsist in the divine nature through their essences, but a judgment consists in the relation of one person to another, and the judgments are subjective intuitions of the persons. Thus, for the glory of the divine persons, there must also be objective intuitions; these are the missions of Christ. These are grounded in his divine nature, but they are intuited in his humanity;[1] therefore, the modalities are necessary to refer these intuitions to the divinity manifest in his flesh, as the bodily indwelling thereof,[2] that the persons may be glorified in Christ's human nature.

The divine persons may indeed be known through their conception, but this conception can only be acquired through the revelation of Jesus Christ. Furthermore, Christ's humanity refers to this headship, and within his headship divine lies the concept of his offices; therefore, the modalities are not only concepts of the divine nature manifest in the flesh, but also relations of his person to the sinners for whom he died. Lastly, in him must be visible the righteousness and holiness of the divine nature, whereby a man may be happy in obedience to the moral law; and the mission of Christ must be understood in relation to the thinking subject, that Christ might be glorified in every man.[3] Thus, Jesus must be a prophet, to reveal the divine persons; a priest, to save men by his sacrifice; and a king, to make men partakers of the divine nature.

As a prophet, Jesus reveals the righteousness of God to men, the possibility of their salvation, for because he is born of a virgin, he bears the guilt of original

---

[1] Aquinas, *Summa* 3.35.1, 57.2.
[2] Col. 2:9-10.
[3] Col. 1:28.

sin in righteousness, whereby a transition from condemnation to justification is possible.

As a priest, Christ communicates the blessedness of God to men, for because he has ascended into heaven, he shows forth the completeness of his work, and God's acceptance thereof, whereby those who believe in him are not only forgiven their sins and justified, but also made partakers of the divine nature.[4] Therefore, by the life of Christ in heaven, sinners are not only free and able by faith to repent, but persuaded and enticed to believe, for that they sought to be like God, they fell into sin, but in Christ they are saved from their sin, and conformed to the image of the Son.[5] That salvation revealed by Jesus' prophetic ministry is made actual in his priesthood: Christ brings forth life from death by standing before God on behalf of men.

As a king, Jesus Christ shows forth the holiness of God to men in the work of salvation. The end of the work is the application thereof, to save sinners from their sins, and bestow upon them the glory of God. In the second coming of Christ, men see the end of their salvation, and are sanctified unto the last day. Christ rules over his people, making his righteousness theirs. The salvation of the soul begins with repentance, proceeds to faith, and ends in sanctification and glory.

He is a prophet, who reveals; a priest, who saves; and a king, who rules; for he is the blessedness of God, identical to his righteousness, distinct therefrom, identical in distinction.

The righteousness of Christ is the ground of his headship; the guilt of original sin imputed to him contains the ground of the transition from Adam to Christ, whereby his headship is made actual; and his divine nature is the ground of their union, that the work of Christ might be effectually applied to those for whom he died.

The offices of Christ do not manifest themselves in particular events, but in various states of the life of Christ. The modalities add nothing to the concept of the object, but solely its relation to the thinking faculty. This relation is not a

---

[4] 2 Pet. 1:4.
[5] Rom. 8:29.

historical event, but the way in which a historical event receives objective validity. The modalities are inversions of the relations, and are therefore universal historical truths of his person, that is, successive states of his life, accomplished through transitional events, wherein they find their grounds. The office of prophet manifests itself in his virgin birth and life on earth; after he ascends, he sits as a priest upon his throne; and as king, he shall return from heaven, to be forever glorified in the new creation.[6]

The offices are conditions of the lawfulness of the work, not as concepts for intuitions, but as intuitions produced through concepts. The intuitions contain within themselves the concepts that prescribe them; without the intuitions produced, the concepts would not have been conceived. Therefore, the offices are necessary for the lawful conception of the divine persons through intuition, that each person may be glorified.

As God is in himself, so he appears to us in Jesus Christ. "He that hath seen me hath seen the Father" (John 14:9). And being glorified in the work of salvation, that work is also lawful, being first righteous, then blessed, and finally holy, because he also performs that work in his people; for the mind of man reaches unto God thereby, first understanding the righteousness of God in his salvation, then seeing blessedness of God in performing the work, and lastly feeling the holiness of God working in his own heart.

> For God, who commanded the light to shine out of darkness, hath shined in our hearts, to *give* the light of the knowledge of the glory of God in the face of Jesus Christ. 2 Corinthians 4:6

---

6 Zech. 6:12-13; Luke 24:19-21; 1 Cor. 15:24-28; Heb. 8:4; Rev. 22:3-5.

Prophet

Possibility consists of the formal agreement between substance and inherence. To the possibility of unconditional condemnation, which is thought in the Father, historical doctrine adds the intuition in the person of the Son. Jesus is condemned by God, to show forth the righteousness of God; in him lies the appearance of the divine righteousness, by which a transition from condemnation to justification is possible, and by revealing the righteousness of God in the flesh, he makes men able to repent through faith in himself. This is his prophetic office.

The moral law requires agreement between the person and his legal state. Christ is condemned, though righteous; this legal state cannot be thought in agreement with his person through his human righteousness, but through the revelation of the righteousness of God, and this revelation must be intuited within the very person of Jesus, as the way in which his person is conceived.

The prophetic office thinks the possibility of the virgin birth through the divine nature manifest in the flesh. The virgin birth shows forth Jesus' relation to the Father, whereby he bears the guilt of original sin in divine righteousness; for because he is his Son, he submits himself to the wrath of the Father, wherein the possibility of salvation is revealed to men.

The virgin birth reveals the righteousness of God in saving sinners through the condemnation of his only begotten Son. In this revelation consists all prophecy, and the person who reveals it is a prophet.[7] The whole life of Christ reveals the Father to us because he is his Son, and he is not only a prophet, but the true prophet, and the object of all prophecy, through whom mankind originally acquires the knowledge of salvation.

Jesus Christ is the blessedness of God, his only begotten Son. The essence of the Son consists of the union of a universal with a particular, for he is particular in relation to the Father, who is universal.[8] Within the Son lies the divine blessedness, identical in distinction to the Father's righteousness. And as

---

[7] Rev. 19:10.

[8] Gress, *Christ Condemned*, 51.

he is one God with the Father, so also he became man, to reveal the righteousness of God in sensible intuition.[9]

As Jesus is God, the infinite is thought in identity with affirmation, but as Jesus is man, it is thought with distinction. Therefore, his essence is that of unity and totality, or of affirmation and limitation, because the form and the matter are united in his divinity. The union of a universal and a particular is the singular, but these are identical in God, distinct in man. As identical, Jesus Christ is God; as distinct, Jesus Christ also became man.

Because he is God, affirmation and infinity are thought, not as distinct, but as identical in distinction, and the infinite is, in identity with affirmation, particular to it; for this reason also infinity takes the place of limitation. Therefore, to show forth his divine nature, he takes on the flesh and body of a male, for a male is the union of a universal and a particular, wherein the singular is identified with the universal. Again, the blessedness of God is the very image of God's righteousness; wherefore, he is also made in the image of God's righteousness, male.

God possesses all his perfections, even his blessedness, within his righteousness, in identity therewith;[10] he is therefore referred to by the masculine gender, without the loss of any female perfection;[11] wherefore, he also has creative power, and even begets a Son, his very image and likeness.

Jesus is the blessedness of God; his essence is to be both God and man, two natures in one person. Through Jesus the essences of all other creatures are thought, especially those of the church, for as within him lies the divine bliss, through him all the objects of God's will are brought into being and sustained.[12]

Jesus is the blessedness of God, identical in distinction to his righteousness. So far as these are distinguished, he may subsist in the human nature as a sensible representation of the identity, because the distinction thought in his person also contains the ground of a sensible intuition in agreement therewith. And this distinction is ever enveloped in identity. Wherefore, although the Holy

---

[9] Aquinas, *Summa* 3.1.1-2.
[10] *Summa* 1.3.7.
[11] Is. 46:3-4.
[12] Jer. 10:12; Col. 1:15-18; Heb. 1:2-3.

Spirit proceeds from him, yet is he conceived by the Spirit, and the Spirit is bestowed upon him prior to his ministry.[13]

> Come ye near unto me, hear ye this: I have not spoken in secret from the beginning; from the time that it was, there *am* I: and now the Lord GOD, and his Spirit, hath sent me. Isaiah 48:16, cf. 61:1

> The Spirit of the Lord GOD *is* upon me; because the LORD hath anointed me to preach good tidings unto the meek; he hath sent me to bind up the brokenhearted, to proclaim liberty to the captives, and the opening of the prison to *them that are* bound; To proclaim the acceptable year of the LORD, and the day of vengeance of our God; to comfort all that mourn; To appoint unto them that mourn in Zion, to give unto them beauty for ashes, the oil of joy for mourning, the garment of praise for the spirit of heaviness, that they might be called trees of righteousness, the planting of the LORD, that he might be glorified. Isaiah 6:1-3

The ground of Christ's prophetic office also lies in the virgin birth, for he bears the guilt of original sin in righteousness through the unconditional condemnation of the Father, wherein he reveals the righteousness of God in the imputation of guilt.

> Pilate therefore said unto him, Art thou a king then? Jesus answered, Thou sayest that I am a king. To this end was I born, and for this cause came I into the world, that I should bear witness unto the truth. Every one that is of the truth heareth my voice. John 18:37

The possibility of the virgin birth consists of the formal agreement between his divine and human dependence. Christ is begotten of the Father in eternity, yet is he conceived in the womb of Mary, and born of her virginity. Wherefore, John says,

---

[13] Aquinas, *Summa* 3.39.5-6, 8.

And the Word was made flesh, and dwelt among us, (and we beheld his glory, the glory as of the only begotten of the Father,) full of grace and truth. John 1:14

For that glory subsists in his humanity.

For in him dwelleth all the fulness of the Godhead bodily. Colossians 2:9

The formal agreement of the divine and human nature of Christ contains the manifestation of the Father in the Son; wherefore, the possibility of the virgin birth lies in the office he thereby receives, appointed of God a prophet.

Sacrifice and offering thou didst not desire; mine ears hast thou opened: burnt offering and sin offering hast thou not required. Then said I, Lo, I come: in the volume of the book *it is* written of me, I delight to do thy will, O my God: yea, thy law *is* within my heart. I have preached righteousness in the great congregation: lo, I have not refrained my lips, O LORD, thou knowest. I have not hid thy righteousness within my heart; I have declared thy faithfulness and thy salvation: I have not concealed thy lovingkindness and thy truth from the great congregation. Psalm 40:6-10

Who hath saved us, and called *us* with an holy calling, not according to our works, but according to his own purpose and grace, which was given us in Christ Jesus before the world began, But is now made manifest by the appearing of our Saviour Jesus Christ, who hath abolished death, and hath brought life and immortality to light through the gospel. 2 Timothy 1:9-10

For the grace of God that bringeth salvation hath appeared to all men, Teaching us that, denying ungodliness and worldly lusts, we should live soberly, righteously, and godly, in this present world; Looking for that blessed hope, and the glorious appearing of the great God and our Saviour Jesus Christ; Who gave himself for us, that he might redeem us from all iniquity, and purify unto himself a peculiar people, zealous of good works. Titus 2:11-14

The Son subsists in the divine nature as his blessedness, so also in the human nature, as the blessedness of the Father, the image of the invisible God. The Father is invisible, yet is he manifested by the virgin birth. By his generation Jesus reveals unto us the Father, whom we knew not, and the power of God to save sinners.[14]

The possibility of the virgin birth consists in the revelation of God the Father, yea, of the moral law itself in his flesh, for the lawfulness of his birth belongs to the intuition produced of a person, and as he is both God and man in dependence on the Father, so also his human nature reveals the divine.

Wherefore also, not only in his birth, but in his whole life, he reveals the Father who sent him, for he obeys the Father, even unto death. That is to say, Christ is the prophet of God, for a prophet speaks the word of God, but Jesus is the Word of God.

And he said unto them, What things? And they said unto him, Concerning Jesus of Nazareth, which was a prophet mighty in deed and word before God and all the people: And how the chief priests and our rulers delivered him to be condemned to death, and have crucified him. But we trusted that it had been he which should have redeemed Israel: and beside all this, to day is the third day since these things were done. Luke 24:19-21

Jesus Christ is born into the world to testify of the Father, for he has the righteousness of his Father, and glorifies the Father by speaking his words and performing his works.

---

[14] Matt. 11:25-27; Luke 10:21-22; Rom. 1:16-17; 1 Cor. 1:18.

For he whom God hath sent speaketh the words of God: for God giveth not the Spirit by measure *unto him*. The Father loveth the Son, and hath given all things into his hand. John 3:34-35

But Jesus answered them, My Father worketh hitherto, and I work. Therefore the Jews sought the more to kill him, because he not only had broken the sabbath, but said also that God was his Father, making himself equal with God. Then answered Jesus and said unto them, Verily, verily, I say unto you, The Son can do nothing of himself, but what he seeth the Father do: for what things soever he doeth, these also doeth the Son likewise. For the Father loveth the Son, and sheweth him all things that himself doeth: and he will shew him greater works than these, that ye may marvel. John 5:17-20

I can of mine own self do nothing: as I hear, I judge: and my judgment is just; because I seek not mine own will, but the will of the Father which hath sent me. If I bear witness of myself, my witness is not true. There is another that beareth witness of me; and I know that the witness which he witnesseth of me is true. Ye sent unto John, and he bare witness unto the truth. But I receive not testimony from man: but these things I say, that ye might be saved. He was a burning and a shining light: and ye were willing for a season to rejoice in his light. But I have greater witness than *that* of John: for the works which the Father hath given me to finish, the same works that I do, bear witness of me, that the Father hath sent me. And the Father himself, which hath sent me, hath borne witness of me. Ye have neither heard his voice at any time, nor seen his shape. And ye have not his word abiding in you: for whom he hath sent, him ye believe not. John 5:30-38

Jesus saith unto him, Have I been so long time with you, and yet hast thou not known me, Philip? he that hath seen me hath seen the Father; and how sayest thou *then*, Shew us the Father? Believest thou not that

I am in the Father, and the Father in me? the words that I speak unto
you I speak not of myself: but the Father that dwelleth in me, he doeth
the works. Believe me that I am in the Father, and the Father in me: or
else believe me for the very works' sake. John 14:9-11

So far as in him the possibility of salvation is revealed to men, whosoever
receives this revelation may repent of his sins and be saved. Through the
modalities, the relations are thought of as subsisting, not only in our conception
of the object, but in the object itself. God reveals the righteousness of his
salvation by a prophet he sends into the world, whereby there is not only an
intuition for the concept, but the object thought thereby pertains to us, being
substantiated through an office. Wherefore, man's salvation harmonizes with
the supreme end of all things.

Help us, O God of our salvation, for the glory of thy name: and deliver
us, and purge away our sins, for thy name's sake. Psalm 79:9

I, *even* I, *am* he that blotteth out thy transgressions for mine own sake,
and will not remember thy sins. Isaiah 43:25

The historical doctrines manifest the possibility of salvation in sensible
intuition, whereby man knows and understands that he may be saved. This only
is required of him, that he repent and believe. "Believe on the Lord Jesus Christ,
and thou shalt be saved, and thy house" (Acts 16:31). If a man lawfully consents
to salvation through Jesus Christ, then he will be saved; for that consent, if it be
lawful, finds its ground in repentance from sin, in which the transition to
righteousness actually consists.

The law of God declares that the man who repents of his sin shall live.[15]
This is not a promise of the Gospel, but of the moral law of God, that whosoever

---

[15] Deut. 31:15-20; Ez. 18, 33:1-20.

does righteousness shall live thereby.[16] Nevertheless, it is proved already that no man repents of his sin by the mere conception of the law.[17] The possibility of repentance lies in the Lord Jesus Christ. Through faith in his name men are enabled to repent, and according to the law of God, whosoever turns again shall live. Thus, whosoever believes in Christ shall be saved from death.

In Christ there is life from death, justification from condemnation, righteousness from sin. The condition of his application to us is faith. He is our rightful head, the savior of all men; his work ought indeed to be applied to us, but God will not save anyone without their consent. Those who believe that God is able to save them from their sins, have repented of their sins, and walk in the righteousness of faith. If then any man believe, he will be saved.

> Verily, verily, I say unto you, He that heareth my word, and believeth on him that sent me, hath everlasting life, and shall not come into condemnation; but is passed from death unto life. John 5:24

> How much more shall the blood of Christ, who through the eternal spirit offered himself without spot to God, purge your conscience from dead works to serve the living God? Hebrews 9:14

Indeed, all men would be saved by Christ, if only they would let him.

> For thus saith the Lord GOD, the Holy One of Israel; In returning and rest shall ye be saved; in quietness and in confidence shall be your strength: and ye would not. Isaiah 30:15

> O Jerusalem, Jerusalem, *thou* that killest the prophets, and stonest them which are sent unto thee, how often would I have gathered thy

---

[16] Lev. 18:5; Deut. 5:33. 8:1, 30:16; Matt. 19:16-17; Mark 10:17-19; Luke 10:25-28, 18:18-20; Rom. 10:5.

[17] Gress, *Christ Condemned*, 18.

children together, even as a hen gathereth her chickens under *her* wings, and ye would not! Matthew 23:37

The work of Christ's prophetic ministry is to call men to repent and believe in himself, that they may be saved, and to verify his divine mission, he performs miracles in the name of the Father. And because those who believe are members of the kingdom of God, he speaks of that kingdom in parables. Likewise, he prophesies of the destruction of Jerusalem and the establishment of the church, and of the history of the church to the end of the world. The last of these he more fully reveals by his servant John, the exposition of which belongs to a history of the world.

The ministry of Christ is the empirical manifestation of his prophetic office. The signs are sensible intuitions, to manifest the person of the Son in history. Therefore, all the signs occur during the time of his ministry on earth, to prophesy of him.

Scripture Proof

The prophets lived during the time of the kingdom: Samuel the first,[18] Elijah and Elisha, and the authors of Scripture, and those in Scripture, and those omitted, for there are many prophets, not only among the ancient Jews, but even among the Gentiles, and many things have been lost by the wisdom of divine providence, which is evident not only from external sources, but from the Scriptures themselves, yea, not only common sayings, but whole books.[19] Above all there is Moses, a prophet and more than a prophet, for he is lawgiver and king, and Aaron is his priest, though God would not withhold even this from Moses, but gave it to his own brother, and that at his own behest.[20] And before Moses are the fathers, who are not less than prophets, but not distinctly so

---

[18] Acts 3:24, 13:20.

[19] Num. 21:14; Josh. 10:13; 1 Sam. 10:25; 2 Sam. 1:18; 1 Kings 11:41; 14:19; 1 Chron. 29:29; 2 Chron. 9:29, 20:34, 26:22, 33:18, 33:19-20, 34:14-28; 1 Cor. 5:9; Col. 4:16; Eph. 3:3; Amos 3:7; Augustine, *City of God* 18.23; Josephus, *The Jewish War*, 265.

[20] Ex. 4:10-17; Deut. 33:4-5; Ps. 99:6.

called.[21] And after the Babylonian captivity there are prophets unto the second temple, then is the vision cut off until John the Baptist.[22]

By the mere subsistence of a prophet, Christ is prophesied, for that there is not only a command to repent, but a person who commands, there is a revelation of a person by faith in whom men are enabled to repent. Yet to some belongs the work of prophesying certain doctrines or events, according as the excellencies of Christ and the gifts of the Holy Spirit are distributed to his people.

What is required of a prophet is that his message consists with what is already known, both from pure reason and prior revelation.

> If there arise among you a prophet, or a dreamer of dreams, and giveth thee a sign or a wonder, And the sign or the wonder come to pass, whereof he spake unto thee, saying, Let us go after other gods, which thou hast not known, and let us serve them; Thou shalt not hearken unto the words of that prophet, or that dreamer of dreams: for the LORD your God proveth you, to know whether ye love the LORD your God with all your heart and with all your soul. Ye shall walk after the LORD your God, and fear him, and keep his commandments, and obey his voice, and ye shall serve him, and cleave unto him. And that prophet, or that dreamer of dreams, shall be put to death; because he hath spoken to turn *you* away from the LORD your God, which brought you out of the land of Egypt, and redeemed you out of the house of bondage, to thrust thee out of the way which the LORD thy God commanded thee to walk in. So shalt thou put the evil away from the midst of thee. Deuteronomy 13:1-5

> The LORD thy God will raise up unto thee a Prophet from the midst of thee, of thy brethren, like unto me; unto him ye shall hearken; According to all that thou desiredst of the LORD thy God in Horeb in

---

[21] Gen. 20:7; Ps. 105:15.

[22] Mic. 3:5-7; Mal. 3:1, 4:4-6; Matt. 11:12-14.

the day of the assembly, saying, Let me not hear again the voice of the LORD my God, neither let me see this great fire any more, that I die not. And the LORD said unto me, They have well *spoken that* which they have spoken. I will raise them up a Prophet from among their brethren, like unto thee, and will put my words in his mouth; and he shall speak unto them all that I shall command him. And it shall come to pass, *that* whosoever will not hearken unto my words which he shall speak in my name, I will require *it* of him. But the prophet, which shall presume to speak a word in my name, which I have not commanded him to speak, or that shall speak in the name of other gods, even that prophet shall die. And if thou say in thine heart, How shall we know the word which the LORD hath not spoken? When a prophet speaketh in the name of the LORD, if the thing follow not, nor come to pass, that *is* the thing which the LORD hath not spoken, *but* the prophet hath spoken it presumptuously: thou shalt not be afraid of him. Deuteronomy 18:15-22

A Prophet like unto thee, a greater than Moses, for Moses is the greatest of all the prophets,[23] but Jesus Christ is the true prophet, who not only reveals the law, but also fulfills it.[24]

Only those prophets who speak in the name of the Lord, and whose signs come to pass, are prophets indeed. Those who do not speak in the name of the Lord are not to be trusted, though they perform signs and wonders; they must be put to death. Nor ought men to fear those who speak in the name of the Lord, but their words fall to the ground, and bear no fruit unto righteousness.[25]

The message of salvation must therefore agree with the fundamental doctrines of the law. The doctrine of Christ, as the object of all prophecy, harmonizes with pure moral religion. The demonstration thereof is the work of a prophet who is not a prophet, because it is not a work of revelation, but of

---

[23] Deut. 34:10-12; Aquinas, *Summa* 2.2.174.4.
[24] John 1:17.
[25] Matt. 7:15-20.

reason in accordance with revelation. This must come after the revelation, because reason only has insight into things revealed after they are revealed. This is perhaps the work of the least in the kingdom of heaven, who is not alone therein, but is preceded by all the saints and martyrs of the first resurrection, as John came before.

> And I will give *power* unto my two witnesses, and they shall prophesy a thousand two hundred *and* threescore days, clothed in sackcloth. These are the two olive trees standing before the God of the earth. Revelation 11:3-4

And when they shall have finished their testimony (vs. 7), because the testimony begins with one and ends with the other, and they encompass all the saints and martyrs of the first resurrection, who shall live and reign with Christ a thousand years, all who through John believed, repenting of their sins, to be like Christ their Lord.[26]

The whole of Christ's life on earth, and especially his ministry, shows forth his prophetic office. This narrative is given to us by John, for as the blessedness of God, Jesus shows forth the righteousness of the Father.

John 1:1-18

In the beginning was the Word, and the Word was with God, before God and unto God—πϱὸς, unto—a sacrifice of righteousness; *and the Word was God,* revealing his righteousness because he possesses it within himself. *The same was in the beginning with God,* united, though distinct. *All things were made by him;* for he is his blessedness; *and without him was not any thing made that was made,* the spirit of affirmation, which rules over all things negation. *In him was life; and the life was the light of men,* the light of a person, giving life. *And the light shineth in darkness; and the darkness comprehended it not,* divine mysteries being understood only through righteousness. *There was a man sent from God,* a prophet; *whose name*

---

[26] John 1:7; Rev. 20:4-6.

was John, of grace. *The same came for a witness, to bear witness of the Light, that all men through him might believe,* the many through the one. *He was not that Light, but was sent to bear witness of that Light,* like him in essence, though only a man, yet so like him that it must be said, "He was not that light." *That was the true Light, which lighteth every man that cometh into the world,* the one in whom all are gathered. *He was in the world, and the world was made by him, and the world knew him not,* because of sin. *He came unto his own, and his own received him not,* of the seed of Abraham. *But as many as received him,* consenting by faith; *to them gave he power to become the sons of God,* to be like Christ; *even to them that believe on his name:* through whom comes repentance; *Which were born, not of blood, nor of the will of the flesh, nor of the will of man, but of God.* They were born of God, that they might repent and believe, that they might be adopted, conformed to the image of his Son.[27] *And the Word was made flesh, and dwelt among us, (and we beheld his glory, the glory as of the only begotten of the Father,) full of grace and truth,* for he was born of a virgin, to testify of the Father. *John bare witness of him, and cried, saying, This was he of whom I spake, He that cometh after me is preferred before me: for he was before me,* a prophet, and the end of all prophecy. *And of his fulness have all we received,* the one in whom all are gathered; *and grace for grace,* κάριν ἀντὶ κάρις, grace for grace against: grace to condemn him for our sins, grace to justify him in bearing our sins, that we should be forgiven our sins and justified. *For the law was given by Moses,* according to which all things must done; *but grace and truth came by Jesus Christ,* the perfect fulfillment of the law through the diversity of judgments executed upon him, whereby iniquity is purged.[28] *No man hath seen God at any time; the only begotten Son, which is in the bosom of the Father,* that is, the Spirit; *he hath declared him.* He showed the way into the bosom of the Father, that his people might partake of his holiness.

---

[27] Rom. 8:12-23.
[28] Prov. 16:6.

John the Baptist

To represent the formal possibility of repentance through the concept of the law, together with a promise of life, repentance must first be manifested in a person distinct from Christ. In Christ lies both repentance and faith, but before Jesus is revealed to men, they are free to repent, though not able. If then Christ is a prophet, there must also be a prophet for the possibility of repentance, which is made actual in Christ. If the one is found in a person, then the other also. And because possibility precedes actuality, this prophet comes before the Lord, to prepare his way.

> The voice of him that crieth in the wilderness, Prepare ye the way of the LORD, make straight in the desert a highway for our God. Every valley shall be exalted, and every mountain and hill shall be made low: and the crooked shall be made straight, and the rough places plain: And the glory of the LORD shall be revealed, and all flesh shall see *it* together: for the mouth of the Lord hath spoken *it*. Isaiah 40:3-5

> Behold, I will send my messenger, and he shall prepare the way before me: and the Lord, whom ye seek, shall suddenly come to his temple, even the messenger of the covenant, whom ye delight in: behold, he shall come, saith the LORD of hosts. Malachi 3:1

> Remember ye the law of Moses my servant, which I commanded unto him in Horeb for all Israel, *with* the statutes and judgments. Behold, I will send you Elijah the prophet before the coming of the great and dreadful day of the LORD: And he shall turn the heart of the fathers to the children, and the heart of the children to their fathers, lest I come and smite the earth with a curse. Malachi 4:4-6

John the Baptist is a sign of repentance, which is only possible through faith in Christ, who comes after him. Thus, the ministry of John is not fully understood until Christ appears.[29]

All the Gospels speak of John the Baptist, because each one narrates the prophetic ministry of Christ, and the ministry of John comes before, to prepare his way.

Matthew 3:1-12

In those days came John the Baptist, the first to baptize, an anointed one, to baptize the anointed one and set him apart for his ministry; *preaching in the wilderness of Judaea,* uncultivated by men, to avoid the pollutions of the city and temple, and the abomination of desolation spoken of by the prophet Daniel.[30] *And saying, Repent ye:* the word of a prophet; *for the kingdom of heaven is at hand,* the church, whose king is near; *For this is he that was spoken of by the prophet Esaias,* as required by the moral law; *saying, The voice of one crying in the wilderness, Prepare ye the way of the Lord, make his paths straight,* that the savior might appear to a willing people. *And the same John had his raiment of camel's hair, and a leathern girdle about his loins;* a rough man, bearing a burden; *and his meat was locusts,* as the many; *and wild honey,* as the one. *Then went out to him Jerusalem, and all Judaea, and all the region round about Jordan,* because Christ came to minister "unto the lost sheep of the house of Israel" (Matt. 10:6).[31] *And were baptized of him in Jordan, confessing their sins,* for by confession men repent,[32] and through faith they are cleansed. *But when he saw many of the Pharisees and Sadducees come to his baptism,* John preached in the wilderness because Christ is not of men, nor of the rulers, but from heaven above; *he said unto them, O generation of vipers, who hath warned you to flee from the wrath to come?* Because God corrects the wicked that they might repent. *Bring forth therefore fruits meet for repentance:* for there is no true

---

[29] Matt. 17:10-13; John 1:19-28.
[30] Is. 40:3-5; Dan. 8-9; Mal. 4:5-6; Matt. 24:15-21; Mark 13:14-19; Luke 21:20-24; 1 Macc. 2:27-30; 2 Macc. 4:27.
[31] Matt. 15:24; John 1:11.
[32] 1 John 1:9.

repentance without good works that follow. *And think not to say within yourselves,* for even the thoughts of our hearts are governed by the moral law; *We have Abraham to our father:* because the seed of Abraham is Christ; *for I say unto you, that God is able of these stones to raise up children unto Abraham.* By the rejection of the Jews, the Gentiles are made children by faith. *And now also the axe is laid unto the root of the trees:* for judgment is upon every one who does not believe in the name of the only begotten Son of God;[33] *therefore every tree which bringeth not forth good fruit is hewn down, and cast into the fire,* to be baptized therein. *I indeed baptize you with water unto repentance:* that they should believe in Christ to come, in whom there is repentance through faith in his name; *but he that cometh after me is mightier than I, whose shoes I am not worthy to bear:* he is not worthy even to serve him who came to serve, though he is Lord of all; *he shall baptize you with the Holy Ghost, and with fire:* those not baptized with the one are baptized with the other, for Christ is the head of all, whether unto life or death.[34] *Whose fan is in his hand,* the Spirit of God; *and he will throughly purge his floor,* sanctifying his people; *and gather his wheat into the garner;* bringing them to glory; *but he will burn up the chaff with unquenchable fire,* which shall continue to burn even after it consumes.

Mark 1:1-15

The beginning of the gospel of Jesus Christ, the Son of God; that is, the beginning of its preaching, for the gospel is the good news; *As it is written in the prophets,* preached beforehand; *Behold, I send my messenger before thy face,* for men should not see the face of God without repentance;[35] *which shall prepare thy way before thee,* that is, repentance unto faith in Christ revealed. *The voice of one crying in the wilderness,* to avoid the pollution of the city and temple; *Prepare ye the way of the Lord, make his paths straight,* to show himself to a willing people.[36] *John did baptize in the wilderness, and preach the baptism of repentance for the remission of sins,* to

---

[33] John 3:18.
[34] Aquinas, *Summa* 3.8.1-4.
[35] Ge. 32:30, 33:10; Ex. 33:20.
[36] Psalm 110:3.

cleanse the conscience through faith in Christ come. *And there went out unto him all the land of Judaea, and they of Jerusalem, and were all baptized of him in the river of Jordan,* as leaving this promised land to enter into the true promised land;[37] *confessing their sins,* for therein lies true repentance. *And John was clothed with camel's hair, and with a girdle of a skin about his loins; and he did eat locusts and wild honey;* John represents the righteousness of the one and the guilt of many, which are joined together in Christ. *And preached, saying, There cometh one mightier than I after me,* who entering therein should cleanse even the city and the temple by his presence;[38] *the latchet of whose shoes I am not worthy to stoop down and unloose,* not even to serve the one who came to serve, though he is Lord of all. *I indeed have baptized you with water: but he shall baptize you with the Holy Ghost,* the breath of God, by which the Gospel is preached from heaven. *And it came to pass in those days, that Jesus came from Nazareth of Galilee, and was baptized of John in Jordan.* Christ did not ordain himself to serve, but John who came before him, because Christ is sent by God to bear the sins of his people. *And straightway coming up out of the water,* standing on dry land; *he saw the heavens opened, and the Spirit like a dove descending upon him:* set apart by the Father; *And there came a voice from heaven, saying, Thou art my beloved Son, in whom I am well pleased,* the Word revealed in the flesh through his perfect obedience, by whom all things being made are also reconciled to God. *And immediately the Spirit driveth him into the wilderness,* to sanctify him, to show forth his nonlegal righteousness in repenting of our sins;[39] *And he was there in the wilderness forty days, tempted of Satan;* he is tempted, not of himself, nor of God, but of the devil, by whom sin enters into the world; *and was with the wild beasts;* his animal desires he kept in subjection to reason, for they represent the many virtues of his person; *and the angels ministered unto him,* not only the symbols of things, but also the things in themselves. *Now after that John was put in prison, Jesus came into Galilee, preaching the gospel of the kingdom of God, And saying, The time is fulfilled, and the kingdom of*

---

[37] John 1:28, 10:40.
[38] Dan. 9:27.
[39] Lev. 16:20-22.

God is at hand: repent ye, and believe the gospel. To repentance, Jesus adds faith;
when then Jesus comes, John is taken away.

Luke 3:1-20

Now in the fifteenth year of the reign of Tiberius Caesar, reckoned from Imperial
Rome, because the Son of God inherits the whole world; *Pontius Pilate being
governor of Judaea, and Herod being tetrarch of Galilee, and his brother Philip tetrarch
of Ituraea and of the region of Trachonitis, and Lysanias the tetrarch of Abilene, Annas
and Caiaphas being the high priests,* Christ, being the true high priest, came to free
men from Roman bondage;[40] *the word of God came unto John the son of Zacharias in
the wilderness,* for the temple was not yet cleansed.[41] *And he came into all the
country about Jordan, preaching the baptism of repentance for the remission of sins; As
it is written in the book of the words,* for the Word reveals himself in words; *of Esaias
the prophet, saying, The voice of one crying in the wilderness, Prepare ye the way of the
Lord, make his paths straight. Every valley shall be filled, and every mountain and hill
shall be brought low; and the crooked shall be made straight, and the rough ways shall
be made smooth; And all flesh shall see the salvation of God,* for in him lies every
perfection united. *Then said he to the multitude that came forth to be baptized of him,
O generation of vipers, who hath warned you to flee from the wrath to come?* Because
that generation would reject Christ, for whose sake Jerusalem and her temple
would be destroyed.[42] *Bring forth therefore fruits worthy of repentance, and begin not
to say within yourselves,* not even to think thereon; *We have Abraham to our father:
for I say unto you, That God is able of these stones to raise up children unto Abraham,*
for the seed promised to Abraham is Christ, and whosoever believes in him shall
be saved. *And now also the axe,* the empire of Rome, through whom the land of
Israel was laid waste, her city and temple destroyed, and her people slaughtered
and sold into slavery;[43] *is laid unto the root of the trees: every tree therefore which
bringeth not forth good fruit is hewn down, and cast into the fire. And the people asked*

---

[40] Is. 9:4-7; Dan. 22:31-45.
[41] Dan. 8:13-14.
[42] Dan. 9:24-27.
[43] Is. 10:15; Dan. 9:26; Josephus, *The Jewish War,* 371-372.

him, saying, What shall we do then? He answereth and saith unto them, He that hath two coats, let him impart to him that hath none; and he that hath meat, let him do likewise, to love one another. *Then came also publicans to be baptized, and said unto him, Master, what shall we do? And he said unto them, Exact no more than that which is appointed you. And the soldiers likewise demanded of him, saying, And what shall we do? And he said unto them, Do violence to no man, neither accuse any falsely; and be content with your wages.* The glory of the Gospel lies not in outward show, but in the ordinary duties of the moral law. *And as the people were in expectation,* which they ought to be of Christ; *and all men mused in their hearts of John,* they wondered without ground, they thought but said nothing; *whether he were the Christ, or not;* for he is near in essence to him; *John answered, saying unto them all, I indeed baptize you with water; but one mightier than I cometh, the latchet of whose shoes I am not worthy to unloose:* not even to be his servant, for Jesus came to serve, though he is Lord of all; *he shall baptize you with the Holy Ghost and with fire:* both the righteous and the wicked in the resurrection;[44] *Whose fan is in his hand, and he will throughly purge his floor,* sanctifying his people by his Spirit, and putting away the wickedness of the wicked; "Break thou the arm of the wicked and the evil *man:* seek out his wickedness *till* thou find none" (Psalm 10:15); *and will gather the wheat into his garner;* unto eternal glory; *but the chaff he will burn with fire unquenchable,* to show forth the divine nature in his wrath. *And many other things in his exhortation preached he unto the people,* of the purity of the law, and of Christ come in the flesh, that men should repent of their sins and believe that Jesus is the Messiah. *But Herod the tetrarch, being reproved by him for Herodias his brother Philip's wife,* whom he ought not to have married for that cause, for John kept the whole law, even those things that are lost in our day;[45] *and for all the evils which Herod had done, Added yet this above all, that he shut up John in prison,* that Jesus Christ, whom John proclaimed, might be shown to be the only begotten Son of God.

---

[44] Eph. 1:13-14; 1 Cor. 3:12-15.
[45] Rev. 3:2.

And this is the record of John, when the Jews sent priests and Levites from Jerusalem to ask him, Who art thou? Christ came not from any of the great men of the time, but after the manner of John preaching in the wilderness. *And he confessed, and denied not; but confessed, I am not the Christ.* He confessed Christ by denying himself. *And they asked him, What then? Art thou Elias?* For they knew the Scriptures, yet they thought that Elijah would come in his own person. *And he saith, I am not. Art thou that prophet? And he answered, No. Then said they unto him, Who art thou? that we may give an answer to them that sent us. What sayest thou of thyself?* That he should testify of himself. *He said, I am the voice of one crying in the wilderness, Make straight the way of the Lord, as said the prophet Esaias.* He testifies not of himself,[46] but Isaiah of him, and he of Christ. *And they which were sent were of the Pharisees. And they asked him, and said unto him, Why baptizest thou then, if thou be not that Christ, nor Elias, neither that prophet?* For he should baptize the Lord, and the people to his coming. *John answered them, saying, I baptize with water: but there standeth one among you, whom ye know not; He it is, who coming after me is preferred before me, whose shoe's latchet I am not worthy to unloose. These things were done in Bethabara beyond Jordan, where John was baptizing,* that through Jesus we should enter the land of promise.

---

[46] Prov. 27:2.

Priest

Actuality consists of the material agreement between cause and effect. Jesus Christ is nonlegally righteous in his submission to condemnation; his nonlegal righteousness is actual, because by it he bears the guilt of original sin in righteousness. To this blessedness, historical doctrine adds the office of his priesthood, whereby his nonlegal righteousness is intuited in the flesh, and his blessedness communicated to his people.

Christ is nonlegally righteous in his submission to condemnation. This legal state does not agree with the condemnation of his person, but through the intuition produced of his blessedness. And the blessedness of Christ lies in the actuality of his will; therefore, the nonlegal righteousness of Christ is intuited in the effects of his work.

By his ascension into heaven Christ produces an intuition of his unity with the Father. His nonlegal righteousness, whereby he submits to the condemnation of the Father, also contains the ground of his headship of the human race, whereby he bears the guilt of original sin in righteousness. And the righteousness of the head is the righteousness of all the members. Therefore, in him the whole of humanity forms an image of the divine nature, and the elect are raised up into heaven with him. The actuality of the ascension, the objective condition whereby the ascension is grounded in the very person of Christ, consists in his priesthood,[47] whereby he stands before God on behalf of his people, and makes them partakers of his joy.[48]

> For if, when we were enemies, we were reconciled to God by the death
> of his Son, much more, being reconciled, we shall be saved by his life.
> And not only *so*, but we also joy in God through our Lord Jesus Christ,
> by whom we have now received the atonement. Romans 5:10-11, cf. 12-
> 21

---

[47] Heb. 8:4.
[48] Aquinas, *Summa* 3.22.1-6, 57.6.

He is the blessedness of God, and his blessedness lies in his people.

> *O my soul,* thou hast said unto the Lord, Thou *art* my Lord: my
> goodness *extendeth* not to thee; *But* to the saints that *are* in the earth,
> and *to* the excellent, in whom *is* all my delight. Psalm 16:2-3

> For, behold, I create new heavens and a new earth: and the former shall
> not be remembered, nor come into mind. But be ye glad and rejoice for
> ever *in that* which I create: for, behold, I create Jerusalem a rejoicing,
> and her people a joy. And I will rejoice in Jerusalem, and joy in my
> people: and the voice of weeping shall be no more heard in her, nor the
> voice of crying. Isaiah 65:17-19

In the virgin birth Christ is known distinctly from the Father; in the
ascension he is known together with the Father. Though we see him not, yet is
he known through the preaching of the Gospel,[49] whereby men are brought to
faith in himself. Wherefore, he not only reveals the possibility of salvation to
men, but also effectually persuades them to believe, that they might be partakers
of his bliss. As a prophet, he reveals the way of salvation; as a priest, he
accomplishes it. As a prophet, he offers salvation to all who believe; as a priest,
he works faith in his people unto glory.

> Now then we are ambassadors for Christ, as though God did beseech
> *you* by us: we pray *you* in Christ's stead, be ye reconciled to God. For
> he hath made him *to be* sin for us, who knew no sin; that we might be
> made the righteousness of God in him. 2 Corinthians 5:20-21

> Wherefore seeing we also are compassed about with so great a cloud
> of witnesses, let us lay aside every weight, and the sin which doth so
> easily beset *us,* and let us run with patience the race that is set before
> us, Looking unto Jesus the author and finisher of *our* faith; who for the

---

[49] 2 Cor. 5:20-21; 1 John 5:7-8.

joy that was set before him endured the cross, despising the shame, and is set down at the right hand of the throne of God. Hebrews 12:1-2

Christ died for sinners; he died righteously, and therefore he is also exalted. And because he died, not for his own sin, but for the sins of others, God rewards him with their salvation, and glorifies them with himself. Wherefore, to make known his righteousness and their acceptance in the beloved, he ever stands before God in the heavenly places.

But God, who is rich in mercy, for his great love wherewith he loved us, Even when we were dead in sins, hath quickened us together with Christ, (by grace ye are saved;) And hath raised *us* up together, and made *us* sit together in heavenly *places* in Christ Jesus: That in the ages to come he might shew the exceeding riches of his grace in *his* kindness toward us through Christ Jesus. Ephesians 2:4-7

The causality and actuality of the will are ends of the moral law. The sixth commandment requires the preservation of life, while the ninth protects the manifestation of life in word. Thus, Christ's priesthood consists in his continuing life for his people and intercession on their behalf. His life is the life of his resurrection; he continually stands before God in heaven, an offering of worship for all time, as in the beginning,[50] pleading with God his sacrifice for sins, that those who believe in him may partake of his life eternal.

Who *is* he that condemneth? It *is* Christ that died, yea rather, that is risen again, who is even at the right hand of God, who also maketh intercession for us. Romans 8:34

A priest offers sacrifices according to the law and intercedes for the people. It is required of a priest that he stand before God in the holy place, that he goes

---

[50] John 1:1-2, 17:5.

before the people, and leads them thither. Neither is he appointed by himself, but by God, for Jesus sent not himself into the world, but the Father.

The LORD said unto my Lord, Sit thou at my right hand, until I make thine enemies thy footstool. The Lord shall send the rod of thy strength out of Zion: rule thou in the midst of thine enemies. Thy people *shall be* willing in the day of thy power, in the beauties of holiness from the womb of the morning: thou hast the dew of thy youth. The Lord hath sworn, and will not repent, Thou *art* a priest for ever after the order of Melchizedek. The Lord at thy right hand shall strike through kings in the day of his wrath. He shall judge among the heathen, he shall fill *the places* with the dead bodies; he shall wound the heads over many countries. He shall drink of the brook in the way: therefore shall he lift up the head. Psalm 110

Let not your heart be troubled: ye believe in God, believe also in me. In my Father's house are many mansions: if *it were* not *so*, I would have told you. I go to prepare a place for you. And if I go and prepare a place for you, I will come again, and receive you unto myself; that where I am, *there* ye may be also. And whither I go ye know, and the way ye know. John 14:1-4

Jesus, having ascended into heaven, sits at the right hand of God, "a priest upon his throne;" resting in his work he pleads for his people, and they, being united to him in his death, partake also of his life; so he builds the temple of the Lord, until "he shall have delivered the kingdom up to God, even the Father" (1 Corinthians 15:24).

Behold, my servant shall deal prudently, he shall be exalted and extolled, and be very high. As many were astonied at thee; his visage was so marred more than any man, and his form more than the sons of men: So shall he sprinkle many nations; the kings shall shut their mouths at him: for *that* which had not been told them shall they see; and *that* which they had not heard shall they consider. Isaiah 52:13-15

Behold the man whose name *is* The Branch; and he shall grow up out of his place, and he shall build the temple of the Lord: Even he shall build the temple of the Lord; and he shall bear the glory, and shall sit and rule upon his throne; and he shall be a priest upon his throne: and the counsel of peace shall be between them both. Zechariah 6:12-13

Jesus Christ ascends into heaven to be glorified with the Father, and being blessed on behalf of his people, he lives to intercede for them, and to be glorified in their salvation.

These words spake Jesus, and lifted up his eyes to heaven, and said, Father, the hour is come; glorify thy Son, that thy Son also may glorify thee: As thou hast given him power over all flesh, that he should give eternal life to as many as thou hast given him. And this is life eternal, that they might know thee the only true God, and Jesus Christ, whom thou hast sent. I have glorified thee on the earth: I have finished the work which thou gavest me to do. And now, O Father, glorify thou me with thine own self with the glory which I had with thee before the world was. I have manifested thy name unto the men which thou gavest me out of the world: thine they were, and thou gavest them me; and they have kept thy word. Now they have known that all things whatsoever thou hast given me are of thee. For I have given unto them the words which thou gavest me; and they have received *them*, and have known surely that I came out from thee, and they have believed that thou didst send me. I pray for them: I pray not for the world, but for them which thou hast given me; for they are thine. And all mine are thine, and thine are mine; and I am glorified in them. And now I am no more in the world, but these are in the world, and I come to thee. Holy Father, keep through thine own name those whom thou hast given me, that they may be one, as we *are*. While I was with them in the world, I kept them in thy name: those that thou gavest me I have kept, and none of them is lost, but the son of perdition; that the scripture might be fulfilled. And now come I to thee; and these things I speak in the world, that they might have my joy fulfilled in themselves. I have given them thy word; and the world hath hated them, because they are not of the world, even as I am not of the world. I pray not that thou shouldest take them out of the world, but that thou shouldest keep them from the evil. They are not of the world, even as I am not of the world. Sanctify them through thy truth: thy word is truth. As thou hast sent me into the world, even so have I also sent them into the world. And for their sakes I sanctify myself, that they also might be sanctified through the truth. Neither pray I for these alone, but for them also which shall believe on me through their word; That they all may be one; as thou, Father, *art* in me, and I in thee, that they also may be one in us: that the world may believe that thou hast sent me. And the glory which thou gavest me I have given them; that they may be one, even as we are one: I in them, and thou in me, that they may be made perfect in one; and that the world may know that thou hast sent me, and hast loved them, as thou hast loved me. Father, I will that they also, whom thou hast given me, be with me where I am; that they may behold my glory, which thou hast given me: for thou lovedst me before the foundation of the world. O righteous Father, the world hath not known thee: but I have known thee, and these have known that thou hast sent me. And I have declared unto them thy name, and will declare *it*: that the love wherewith thou hast loved me may be in them, and I in them. John 17

Scripture Proof

The priesthood belongs to Christ as the Son of God; therefore, the story that belongs peculiarly to his priesthood is given by Luke, during his childhood, for in childhood especially are persons conceived as sons and daughters.

Luke 2:41-52

Now his parents went to Jerusalem every year at the feast of the passover, to obey the commandment of God, which Jesus continued his whole life even unto death, to be our Passover. *And when he was twelve years old, they went up to Jerusalem after the custom of the feast. And when they had fulfilled the days, as they returned, the child Jesus tarried behind in Jerusalem;* he served yet more than the feast; *and Joseph and his mother knew not of it,* it was not of them, but of the Father. *But they, supposing him to have been in the company,* as their own son; *went a day's journey; and they sought him among their kinsfolk and acquaintance,* as a relation. *And when they found him not, they turned back again to Jerusalem, seeking him,* in that place where he should suffer and die. *And it came to pass, that after three days they found him in the temple, sitting in the midst of the doctors, both hearing them, and asking them questions,* as a priest. *And all that heard him were astonished at his understanding and answers,* as God. *And when they saw him, they were amazed: and his mother said unto him, Son, why hast thou thus dealt with us? behold, thy father and I have sought thee sorrowing.* They dared not rebuke him, but entreated. *And he said unto them, How is it that ye sought me?* Nor did he answer roughly, but in kind; *wist ye not that I must be about my Father's business?* He served the temple of the Lord always, ever before he began his ministry. *And they understood not the saying which he spake unto them,* a sign of things to come. *And he went down with them, and came to Nazareth, and was subject unto them:* according to his duty under the law; *but his mother kept all these sayings in her heart,* for she knew that he was born of God. *And Jesus increased in wisdom and stature, and in favour with God and man,* continually sanctified in his ordinary life.

This story shows us that Jesus Christ is the Son of both God and man; that he took his calling not from his parents, but from the Father; so likewise in good conscience he, knowing the grief of his parents, not only subjected himself to them, but corrected their mistake; and that under their parentage he both grew and was sanctified to his office, his whole life being dedicated to the service of the Lord.

Hebrews 1-3:6

God, the author of this book withholds his name, because the message is not of men or of angels, but of Christ; *who at sundry times and in divers manners spake in time past unto the fathers by the prophets,* for he is manifest in all, to whom his virtue is distributed, specially by those persons appointed to foretell his coming; *Hath in these last days spoken unto us by his Son,* the true prophet; *whom he hath appointed heir of all things,* the Son of God and the Son of man, appointed to inherit what is his by birth; *by whom also he made the worlds;* for his own holy purpose; *Who being the brightness of his glory, and the express image of his person,* the blessedness of God, revealing the Father; *and upholding all things by the word of his power,* through his perfect righteousness from the Father; *when he had by himself,* without the help of any creature; *purged our sins,* a priest unto God; *sat down on the right hand of the Majesty on high;* a king, to apply the work to his people; *Being made so much better than the angels,* perfectly sanctified by sufferings and death; *as he hath by inheritance obtained a more excellent name than they,* begotten with every divine perfection. *For unto which of the angels,* who are many; *said he at any time, Thou art my Son,* the only begotten; *this day have I begotten thee?* Born of a virgin, as of eternity. *And again, I will be to him a Father, and he shall be to me a Son?* Born of a virgin, dedicated to the Lord, a priest unto God. *And again, when he bringeth in the firstbegotten into the world,* according to his eternal generation from the Father; *he saith, And let all the angels of God worship him,* God manifest in the flesh. *And of the angels he saith, Who maketh his angels spirits, and his ministers a flame of fire,* who bear in distinction the many virtues of the divine nature, and administer his perfections to men; *But unto the Son he saith, Thy throne, O God, is for ever and ever:* in whom all divine perfections are united; *a sceptre of righteousness is the sceptre of thy kingdom,* an inwardly lawful being, reigning in righteousness. *Thou hast loved righteousness, and hated iniquity;* his happiness lying in the moral law; *therefore God, even thy God, hath anointed thee with the oil of gladness above thy fellows,* set apart for divine offices. *And, Thou, Lord, in the beginning hast laid the foundation of the earth; and the heavens are the works of thine hands: They shall perish;* being destroyed; *but thou remainest; and they all shall wax old as doth a garment; And as a vesture shalt thou fold them up, and they shall be changed:* yet renewed; *but thou art the same, and thy years shall not fail,* even his flesh clothed with eternity. *But to which of the angels said he at any time, Sit on my right hand, until I make thine enemies thy footstool?* To await the full application of his work, both to the righteous and the wicked. *Are they not all ministering spirits, sent forth to minister for them who shall be heirs of salvation?* The angels take part in the work, to minister the manifold grace of God to men. *Therefore we ought to give the more earnest heed to the things which we have heard,* to the things revealed unto us for repentance from sin; *lest at any time we should let them slip,* to fall back to sin the second time. *For if the word spoken by angels was stedfast, and every transgression and disobedience received a just recompence of reward;* the law testifying to the righteous judgment of God; *How shall we escape, if we neglect so great salvation;* how much more just is the damnation of those who refuse salvation in Christ! *which at the first began to be spoken by the Lord, and was confirmed unto us by them that heard him;* by the Lord himself, and by his disciples, and by the testimony of the church throughout all ages; *God also bearing them witness, both with signs and wonders, and with divers miracles, and gifts of the Holy Ghost,* to establish the church, for once the word has been confirmed, the extraordinary things cease;[51] *according to his own will?* because he is ever with them in heaven. *For unto the angels hath he not put in subjection the world to come, whereof we speak.* The angels rule over the concept of things, but not the totality. *But one in a certain place testified, saying, What is man, that thou art mindful of him? or the son of man, that thou visitest him? Thou madest him a little lower than the angels;* for men would shortly be taken into heaven, and in his human nature Christ was subject to

---

[51] 1 Cor. 2:22-24, 12:31, 13:8-13; 14:22; Eph. 4:7-16.

them; *thou crownedst him with glory and honour, and didst set him over the works of thy hands: Thou hast put all things in subjection under his feet.* Because man is nothing, it pleased God to bring forth from him the glory of perfect obedience. *For in that he put all in subjection under him, he left nothing that is not put under him,* affirmation ruling over all things negation. *But now we see not yet all things put under him.* The decree being given, is not yet executed. *But we see Jesus,* in heaven, through the preaching of the Gospel, whereby he is crucified and raised before our very eyes;[52] *who was made a little lower than the angels for the suffering of death,* for angels neither suffer nor die; *crowned with glory and honour;* a crown of unconditional condemnation; *that he by the grace of God should taste death for every man,* for he is justified by the Spirit, and rewarded with the salvation of those for whom he died. *For it became him, for whom are all things, and by whom are all things, in bringing many sons unto glory, to make the captain of their salvation,* the rightful head of humanity, because he bore their sins in righteousness; *perfect through sufferings,* to raise up his delight in the law above all earthly things.[53] *For both he that sanctifieth and they who are sanctified are all of one:* because they belong to the Father in Christ, and are foreknown by essence; *for which cause he is not ashamed to call them brethren, Saying, I will declare thy name unto my brethren,* for through him they are such; *in the midst of the church will I sing praise unto thee,* for he is ever with his people in spirit; *And again, I will put my trust in him. And again, Behold I and the children which God hath given me. Forasmuch then as the children are partakers of flesh and blood, he also himself likewise took part of the same;* he has affinity with them by essence, that he might inherit their guilt and pay the penalty of their sins; *that through death he might destroy him that had the power of death, that is, the devil;* who lost the power of his office by putting to death an innocent; *And deliver them who through fear of death were all their lifetime subject to bondage,* to pay the debt of sin, and take away the fear of punishment, that they might lift up their eyes to God. *For verily he took not on him the nature of angels;* the person of an angel cannot bear variety of judgment, nor show forth identity in distinction; *but he took on him the seed of Abraham,* to whom the promise is made. *Wherefore in*

---

[52] 1 Cor. 2:1-5; Gal. 3:1.
[53] Ps. 40:6-8; 73:25-26.

all things it behoved him to be made like unto his brethren, that he might be a merciful and faithful high priest in things pertaining to God, to make reconciliation for the sins of the people. He partakes of the common lot of humanity, that he might stand before God on their behalf. *For in that he himself hath suffered being tempted,* for temptation is suffering to the righteous; *he is able to succour them that are tempted,* because he bestows on them the very blessedness by which he overcame all temptation. *Wherefore, holy brethren, partakers of the heavenly calling, consider the Apostle and High Priest of our profession, Christ Jesus;* for by the consideration of faith, we also partake of his righteousness; *Who was faithful to him that appointed him, as also Moses was faithful in all his house,* as the perfect fulfillment of the law; *For this man was counted worthy of more glory than Moses,* because he is not only under the law, but also above it; *inasmuch as he who hath builded the house hath more honour than the house,* for he built the house. *For every house is builded by some man;* because Jesus is man; *but he that built all things is God,* because Jesus is God. *And Moses verily was faithful in all his house, as a servant, for a testimony of those things which were to be spoken after;* to fulfill the law in Christ; *But Christ as a son over his own house;* which house having built, he also rules; *whose house are we, if we hold fast the confidence and the rejoicing of the hope firm unto the end.*

The author then exhorts the saints to remain faithful, that they may enter into the rest of God, to be partakers of his holiness, for many who ought to have entered therein have fallen short through lack of faith, and there is nothing wanting in the work of Christ but that it should be applied to us, except there be found in us a heart of unbelief.

Hebrews 4:14-5:11

Seeing then, not by sight, but by faith in the word preached; *that we have a great high priest,* for that is the ground of his ascension; *that is passed into the heavens,* the visible into the invisible; *Jesus the Son of God,* a priest by birth; *let us hold fast our profession,* that we might partake of his holiness. *For we have not an high priest which cannot be touched with the feeling of our infirmities,* to give us his Spirit; *but was in all points tempted like as we are, yet without sin,* to be our head; *Let us therefore come boldly,* with confident assurance, because he became like us; *unto the throne of grace, that we may obtain mercy, and find grace to help in time of need.* Though he suffered temptation, yet he overcame it, and was sanctified, and because he bore our sins, we also bear his righteousness. *For every high priest taken from among men is ordained for men,* the one from the many, to represent them all; *in things pertaining to God, that he may offer both gifts and sacrifices for sins:* a person in whom lies not only the law, but also its more perfect fulfillment on their behalf; *Who can have compassion on the ignorant, and on them that are out of the way;* for that they sinned not contemptuously, nor perpetually, but in ignorance and weakness and wandering, so that they may also be forgiven and restored; *for that he himself also is compassed with infirmity,* because he knows whence he is redeemed, and may lead others in the way. *And by reason hereof he ought, as for the people, so also for himself, to offer for sins,* to show them their need of Christ, for he himself is a sinner, redeemed by God. *And no man taketh this honour unto himself, but he that is called of God, as was Aaron,* for nothing pleases God besides obedience to his commandments. *So also Christ glorified not himself to be made an high priest,* for the persons glorify one another;[54] *but he that said unto him, Thou art my Son, to day have I begotten thee,* as God begets him in righteousness, so also he makes him the righteousness of the children of God. *As he saith also in another place, Thou art a priest for ever after the order of Melchisedec,* a priest and a king. *Who in the days of his flesh, when he had offered up prayers and supplications with strong crying and tears unto him that was able to save him from death,* being sanctified therein; *and was heard in that he feared;* for he was justified; *Though he were a Son, yet learned he obedience by the things which he suffered;* because he endured; *And being made perfect,* through death; *he became the author of eternal salvation unto all them that obey him;* the rightful head of humanity; *Called of God an high priest after the order of Melchisedec,* both to save and to rule in righteousness and peace. *Of whom we have many things to say, and hard to be uttered, seeing ye are dull of hearing.*

The author then exhorts the people to continue in the doctrine of righteousness, not only persevering in their current state, but advancing to

---

[54] Prov. 27:2; John 17:1.

higher degrees, that they might not be found unprofitable servants.[55] To that end, he shows forth the strong assurance of the promise to Abraham when God swears by himself, that is, one divine person swears by another, to produce an intuition of the apodictic certainty of the Gospel.[56]

Hebrews 6:19-10:25

Which hope we have as an anchor of the soul, both sure and stedfast, and which entereth into that within the veil; for by that hope we are sanctified and made partakers of the divine nature;[57] *Whither the forerunner is for us entered, even Jesus, made an high priest for ever after the order of Melchisedec,* there to appear before God on our behalf, that we may be with him in heaven henceforth forever; *For this Melchisedec, king of Salem, priest of the most high God, who met Abraham returning from the slaughter of the kings, and blessed him;* for the blessing is of Christ; *To whom also Abraham gave a tenth part of all;* that all should be done in obedience to the moral law; *first being by interpretation King of righteousness, and after that also King of Salem, which is, King of peace; Without father, without mother, without descent, having neither beginning of days, nor end of life;* whose birth and death are not recorded in the book of generations; *but made like unto the Son of God; abideth a priest continually,* for there comes another after him, who is before him, to whom the office of Melchizedek belongs. *Now consider how great this man was, unto whom even the patriarch Abraham gave the tenth of the spoils,* for Abraham is blessed on account of his seed, and there is a greater than he, who comes through his loins. *And verily they that are of the sons of Levi, who receive the office of the priesthood, have a commandment to take tithes of the people according to the law,* that is, of their brethren, their equals; *though they come out of the loins of Abraham:* for though Christ is our brother, yet is he much greater; *But he whose descent is not counted from them received tithes of Abraham, and blessed him that had the promises,* having a priesthood not from men, but from God. *And without all contradiction the less is blessed of the*

---

[55] Matt. 25:14-30.

[56] Ps. 89:35: Amos 4:2.

[57] 1 John 3:2-3.

better, for Abraham is blessed by Melchizedek on account of his seed; yea, Abraham is blessed by his seed. *And here men that die receive tithes; but there he receiveth them, of whom it is witnessed that he liveth*, it is not said of Melchizedek that he died, but that he lived. *And as I may so say, Levi also, who receiveth tithes, payed tithes in Abraham*, the one priesthood paid tithes to the other. *For he was yet in the loins of his father, when Melchisedec met him*, yet not Christ, who is a priest ever before he was born of a virgin.[58] *If therefore perfection were by the Levitical priesthood, (for under it the people received the law,)*, the law of Moses administered by persons, to show forth the need for a divine person in whom the law is fulfilled; *what further need was there that another priest should rise after the order of Melchisedec, and not be called after the order of Aaron?* for the Levitical priesthood is put away by Christ. *For the priesthood being changed, there is made of necessity a change also of the law*, the one to show forth our need, the other to satisfy it. *For he of whom these things are spoken pertaineth to another tribe, of which no man gave attendance at the altar.* Those offices before joined in Melchizedek, and afterward divided to Levi and Judah, are reunited in Christ, to whom they belong. *For it is evident that our Lord sprang out of Juda;* because the office of king combines both the prophetic and priestly offices of Christ; *of which tribe Moses spake nothing concerning priesthood*, to reserve the true priesthood to the true king. *And it is yet far more evident: for that after the similitude of Melchisedec there ariseth another priest,* according to the need revealed, and the apodictic truth of the Gospel; *Who is made, not after the law of a carnal commandment, but after the power of an endless life,* which must necessarily be for our salvation, to which all the law and the prophets testify. *For he testifieth, Thou art a priest for ever after the order of Melchisedec*, in that he lives forever, he gives them eternal life, not through the law, but through a person in whom it dwells. *For there is verily a disannulling of the commandment going before for the weakness and unprofitableness thereof*, which is weak through the separation of offices. *For the law made nothing perfect*, for with the commandment of the law comes the possibility of sin, and the law of Moses testifies of our own failure to keep it, and the separation of offices shows forth the necessity of their union; *but the bringing in of a better hope did;* whereby the

---

[58] Aquinas, *Summa* 3.22.5, 31.8.

people of God partake of the divine nature; *by the which we draw nigh unto God.* The law of Moses upholds the moral law, but Jesus Christ fulfills the law, both for himself and for us, that all who believe in him may be saved and made like him. *And inasmuch as not without an oath he was made priest: (For those priests were made without an oath;* an oath is a word of promise to the duties enjoined, and the Lord's name is holy; therefore, the Levitical priests, though they were blessed, were not holy, save in obedience to God's commandments, but Jesus is holy; *but this with an oath by him that said unto him, The Lord sware and will not repent, Thou art a priest for ever after the order of Melchisedec:) By so much was Jesus made a surety of a better testament,* wherein the blessedness of God is revealed, identical in distinction to his righteousness. *And they truly were many priests,* according to the guilt of original sin; *because they were not suffered to continue by reason of death:* according to the curse; *But this man, because he continueth ever,* by his resurrection from the dead; *hath an unchangeable priesthood,* for the priesthood belongs to him by generation and birth. *Wherefore he is able also to save them to the uttermost,* not only to restore them to righteousness, but also to bestow upon them the righteousness of God, which they sought by sin; *that come unto God by him, seeing he ever liveth to make intercession for them,* for that he is innocent, God hears his prayers, and the pleading of his sacrifice for them, not only by his death but also by his life, because his life gives worth to his death: "For the life of the flesh *is* in the blood: and I have given it to you upon the altar to make an atonement for your souls: for it *is* the blood *that* maketh an atonement for the soul" (Leviticus 17:11); "Much more then, being now justified by his blood, we shall be saved from wrath through him. For if, when we were enemies, we were reconciled to God by the death of his Son, much more, being reconciled, we shall be saved by his life" (Romans 5:9-10). *For such an high priest became us,* who are foreknown by the Father his children; *who is holy, harmless, undefiled, separate from sinners, and made higher than the heavens;* who sits in glory, to bestow upon us every spiritual blessing;[59] *Who needeth not daily, as those high priests, to offer up sacrifice, first for his own sins,* for he is the righteous one; *and then for the people's:* of whom he is the head; *for this he did once,* because he bore our sins; *when he offered up*

---

[59] Eph. 1:3, 2:6.

himself, that is, his own obedience. *For the law maketh men high priests which have infirmity;* being earthly, sinful; *but the word of the oath,* which is not of the law, but of the divine persons; *which was since the law,* to come after it, and to magnify it;[60] *maketh the Son, who is consecrated for evermore,* wholly set apart for divine service. *Now of the things which we have spoken this is the sum: We have such an high priest, who is set on the right hand of the throne of the Majesty in the heavens;* a priest and a king, both to work salvation and to apply that work to his people by the Spirit; *A minister of the sanctuary, and of the true tabernacle, which the Lord pitched, and not man,* of the invisible things, and of heaven, and of the moral law, and of the angels, and of the just. *For every high priest is ordained to offer gifts and sacrifices:* gifts of righteousness and sacrifices for sin; *wherefore it is of necessity that this man have somewhat also to offer.* Because it pertains to the Son to be a priest, he must also offer himself for his people. *For if he were on earth, he should not be a priest, seeing that there are priests that offer gifts according to the law:* many priests, according to the sensible intuition, wherein lies distinction; *Who serve unto the example and shadow of heavenly things, as Moses was admonished of God when he was about to make the tabernacle:* for these are symbols of the heavenly, wherein there is identity; *for, See, saith he, that thou make all things according to the pattern shewed to thee in the mount,* revealed by God. *But now hath he obtained a more excellent ministry, by how much also he is the mediator of a better covenant, which was established upon better promises,* not of righteousness only, or of the law, but of participation in the divine joy. *For if that first covenant had been faultless,* not only for sin, but also for righteousness; *then should no place have been sought for the second. For finding fault with them,* not only to remove sin, but also its possibility. "Behold, he put no trust in his servants; and his angels he charged with folly," not because they sinned, but because they might (Job 4:18). And so, *he saith, Behold, the days come, saith the Lord, when I will make a new covenant with the house of Israel and with the house of Judah: Not according to the covenant that I made with their fathers in the day when I took them by the hand to lead them out of the land of Egypt;* to give them a temporal habitation in the land of Canaan; *because they continued not in my covenant,* they did not persevere in the moral law, neither

---

their first father;[61] *and I regarded them not, saith the Lord.* The law of Moses upholds the moral law and foretells its fulfillment in Christ; the old covenant passes away through its fulfillment. *For this is the covenant that I will make with the house of Israel after those days, saith the Lord; I will put my laws into their mind, and write them in their hearts:* to put his own perfect righteousness within them; *and I will be to them a God, and they shall be to me a people: And they shall not teach every man his neighbour, and every man his brother, saying, Know the Lord: for all shall know me,* not in the symbols of things, but in the things themselves; *from the least to the greatest,* each one according to his essence. *For I will be merciful to their unrighteousness, and their sins and their iniquities will I remember no more.* They will know him perfectly by the forgiveness of sins, for salvation lies in the knowledge of the Trinity. *In that he saith, A new covenant, he hath made the first old,* by showing in history its inability to save sinners, for although they enjoyed every advantage, yet went they astray.[62] *Now that which decayeth and waxeth old is ready to vanish away,* to be buried in Christ. *Then verily the first covenant had also ordinances of divine service, and a worldly sanctuary,* for it is a covenant of grace. *For there was a tabernacle made; the first, wherein was the candlestick,* symbolizing the Spirit of God, who illuminates our darkness; *and the table,* the Holy Spirit, who administers to us the bread of life; *and the shewbread;* the bread that by its appearance feeds the tribes of Israel; *which is called the sanctuary,* wherein God dwells with men. *And after the second veil, the tabernacle which is called the Holiest of all;* in heaven; *Which had the golden censer,* the offering of prayer; *and the ark of the covenant overlaid round about with gold,* Christ, weak in the flesh, but strong in spirit,[63] and glorious in heaven;[64] *wherein was the golden pot that had manna,* as the body of Christ;[65] *and Aaron's rod that budded,* the rod of his priesthood, which is the Holy Spirit; *and the tables of the covenant;* the law itself within his heart;[66] *And over it the cherubims of glory shadowing the mercyseat;* the Holy Spirit, who

---

[61] Is. 43:27-28.
[62] Is. 5:1-7.
[63] Matt. 26:41.
[64] John 3:13.
[65] John 6:31-58.
[66] Ps. 40:8.

proceeding from the Father and the Son, justifies Christ in his submission to condemnation; *of which we cannot now speak particularly.* The author focuses on the Gospel, yet should others arise to discuss these matters particularly. *Now when these things were thus ordained, the priests,* who were many; *went always into the first tabernacle, accomplishing the service of God. But into the second went the high priest,* who is one; *alone once every year,* the measure of the times; *not without blood,* for we know Christ by his sacrifice for us; *which he offered for himself, and for the errors of the people:* After Christ offered himself for sins, he entered into heaven, there to plead for us his sacrifice; *The Holy Ghost this signifying, that the way into the holiest of all was not yet made manifest, while as the first tabernacle was yet standing:* that Christ should come in the flesh; *Which was a figure for the time then present, in which were offered both gifts and sacrifices, that could not make him that did the service perfect, as pertaining to the conscience;* which only awaken the conscience with the symbols of things in themselves, to show forth our need of a savior; *Which stood only in meats and drinks, and divers washings, and carnal ordinances, imposed on them until the time of reformation,* until Christ should come in the flesh. *But Christ being come an high priest of good things to come, by a greater and more perfect tabernacle, not made with hands, that is to say, not of this building;* that is, his body, for he is born of a virgin; *Neither by the blood of goats and calves, but by his own blood he entered in once into the holy place, having obtained eternal redemption for us.* By the perfection of his death he enters into heaven, and because he died for our sins, he ever lives to intercede for us; *For if the blood of bulls and of goats, and the ashes of an heifer sprinkling the unclean, sanctifieth to the purifying of the flesh:* in the outward appearance, speaking of our need of Christ, not to cleanse the conscience, but to awaken moral feeling; *How much more shall the blood of Christ, who through the eternal Spirit offered himself without spot to God, purge your conscience from dead works to serve the living God?* The justice of God being satisfied in his death, and how much more in his life? *And for this cause he is the mediator of the new testament, that by means of death, for the redemption of the transgressions that were under the first testament, they which are called might receive the promise of eternal inheritance,* even the divine likeness, together with angelic offices. *For where a testament is, there must also of necessity be the death of the testator.*

The inheritance being lost to the parents, is given to the children, the life of Christ being no benefit to us without the shedding of his blood. *For a testament is of force after men are dead: otherwise it is of no strength at all while the testator liveth,* the benefits of Christ come to us, not through his innocence alone, but through his obedience unto death. *Whereupon neither the first testament was dedicated without blood. For when Moses had spoken every precept to all the people according to the law,* that all might be fulfilled by Christ; *he took the blood of calves and of goats, with water, and scarlet wool, and hyssop, and sprinkled both the book,* even the revelation of God, which comes to us through the sacrifice of Christ; *and all the people, Saying, This is the blood of the testament which God hath enjoined unto you. Moreover he sprinkled with blood both the tabernacle, and all the vessels of the ministry,* for all speak of him. *And almost all things are by the law purged with blood; and without shedding of blood is no remission. It was therefore necessary,* for the glory of God in the sacrifice of Christ; *that the patterns of things in the heavens should be purified with these;* to speak of him to come; *but the heavenly things themselves with better sacrifices than these,* for in Christ the whole church is sacrificed to God, to cleanse the temple in heaven, and give the offices of fallen angels to the elect. *For Christ is not entered into the holy places made with hands, which are the figures of the true; but into heaven itself, now to appear in the presence of God for us:* lifted up for the salvation of his people.[67] *Nor yet that he should offer himself often, as the high priest entereth into the holy place every year with blood of others;* as of many; *For then must he often have suffered since the foundation of the world:* as a sinner; *but now once,* for God is one; *in the end of the world,* to bring forth the new; *hath he appeared to put away sin by the sacrifice of himself,* who is righteous under condemnation. *And as it is appointed unto men once to die, but after this the judgment:* because then is the appearance taken away, and the thing in itself revealed; *So Christ was once offered to bear the sins of many;* to bear the whole punishment of sin; *and unto them that look for him shall he appear the second time without sin unto salvation,* when the work shall have been perfectly applied by the Holy Spirit. *For the law having a shadow of good things to come,* the symbol of the appearance only; *and not the very image of the things,* identical in distinction to the concept; *can never with those sacrifices*

---

[67] Is. 52:13-15.

which they offered year by year continually make the comers thereunto perfect. For then would they not have ceased to be offered? because that the worshippers once purged should have had no more conscience of sins, for the law is one. *But in those sacrifices there is a remembrance again made of sins every year. For it is not possible that the blood of bulls and of goats should take away sins.* Wherefore, they are neither buried nor raised, because they signify the need for a better sacrifice. *Wherefore when he cometh into the world, he saith, Sacrifice and offering thou wouldest not, but a body hast thou prepared me:* not a sacrifice of things, but of a person; "Mine ears hast thou opened," a sacrifice of obedience in the flesh (Psalm 40:6); *In burnt offerings and sacrifices for sin thou hast had no pleasure,* but in obedience to the law. *Then said I, Lo, I come (in the volume of the book it is written of me,),* as of the apodictic truth of the moral law; *to do thy will, O God. Above when he said, Sacrifice and offering and burnt offerings and offering for sin thou wouldest not, neither hadst pleasure therein; which are offered by the law; Then said he, Lo, I come to do thy will, O God. He taketh away the first, that he may establish the second.* He offered up his obedience to God, even unto death. *By the which will we are sanctified through the offering of the body of Jesus Christ once for all,* his inward lawfulness manifest in the flesh through the bearing of our sins. *And every priest standeth,* that is, before God and accepted by law; *daily ministering and offering oftentimes the same sacrifices, which can never take away sins:* the death of Christ symbolized by the beast, but the life of him by the priest, and that outside him, because these judgments are not lawful for men, but in different objects; *But this man, after he had offered one sacrifice for sins for ever, sat down on the right hand of God;* as a king, to fulfill the work of his priesthood; *From henceforth expecting till his enemies be made his footstool,* to apply the work to his people. *For by one offering he hath perfected for ever them that are sanctified,* for the work is one, yet the Spirit applies the work to the church from the beginning of the world to the end, for which reason he is sometimes called by the number seven.[68] *Whereof the Holy Ghost also is a witness to us:* from heaven in our hearts; *for after that he had said before, This is the covenant that I will make with them after those days, saith the Lord, I will put my laws into their hearts, and in their minds will I write them; And their sins and iniquities will I remember no more. Now where remission*

---

[68] Rev. 1:4-5, 3:1, 4:5, 5:6.

of these is, there is no more offering for sin. Having therefore, brethren, boldness to enter into the holiest by the blood of Jesus, for he is our head, to persuade us to believe, to partake of his holiness, that we might forsake the sin whereby we fall short of his glory;[69] *By a new and living way, which he hath consecrated for us, through the veil, that is to say, his flesh;* through the object of sensible intuition revealing the Father; *And having an high priest over the house of God; Let us draw near with a true heart in full assurance of faith,* through the absolute certainty of the moral law fulfilled in Christ; *having our hearts sprinkled from an evil conscience,* the judgment poured out on Christ being applied to us by his Spirit; *and our bodies washed with pure water,* that even the flesh may be cleansed, yea, the whole person. *Let us hold fast the profession of our faith without wavering;* by doing good; *(for he is faithful that promised;)* because there is a great reward; *And let us consider one another to provoke unto love and to good works:* wherein lies the end of our salvation, the ground of faith and its perfection; *Not forsaking the assembling of ourselves together,* even as we are together sacrificed in Christ, as members of his body; *as the manner of some is; but exhorting one another: and so much the more, as ye see the day approaching,* the day of his coming, which we see by the sanctification of our faith.

The author then expounds on faith as the condition of Christ's application to us, and exhorts to the people to obedience, through which faith is proven and perfected.[70]

Washing the Feet of the Disciples

Christ stands before God on behalf of his people, to plead the benefits of his sacrifice for them.[71] By his priesthood, the church is cleansed of her sins, even as they walk upon the earth, that they should love one another. Wherefore, the sign of his priesthood consists of his washing the feet of his disciples. That men might partake of his flesh and blood, Jesus continually cleanses them for their service on earth, and is ever with them in heaven, daily forgiving their sins.

---

[69] Rom. 3:23.
[70] Jas. 2:14-26.
[71] 1 John 2:1-2.

This sign is given only by John, for the work of his priesthood reveals his blessedness.

John 13:1-17

Now before the feast of the passover, when Jesus knew that his hour was come that he should depart out of this world unto the Father, first invisibly in his death, and afterward visibly in his ascension; *having loved his own which were in the world, he loved them unto the end,* even to death, and to the last day. *And supper being ended, the devil having now put into the heart of Judas Iscariot, Simon's son, to betray him;* that the devil himself might be bruised in the head; *Jesus knowing that the Father had given all things into his hands, and that he was come from God, and went to God;* for he is his blessedness; *He riseth from supper, and laid aside his garments; and took a towel, and girded himself,* not to work for himself, but to work on others behalf, that through him they might be cleansed. *After that he poureth water into a bason, and began to wash the disciples' feet,* that they might be purified for their work; *and to wipe them with the towel wherewith he was girded,* to take away their sins by the imputation of his righteousness. *Then cometh he to Simon Peter: and Peter saith unto him, Lord, dost thou wash my feet?* as a servant. *Jesus answered and said unto him, What I do thou knowest not now; but thou shalt know hereafter,* a sign of his priesthood. *Peter saith unto him, Thou shalt never wash my feet. Jesus answered him, If I wash thee not, thou hast no part with me,* for because he bears our sins, we also bear his righteousness. *Simon Peter saith unto him, Lord, not my feet only, but also my hands and my head. Jesus saith to him, He that is washed needeth not save to wash his feet, but is clean every whit:* Once cleansed by the blood of Christ, there is need only of daily repentance; *and ye are clean, but not all. For he knew who should betray him;* who should repent of righteousness; *therefore said he, Ye are not all clean,* for there must be sin in the world, that God should be glorified in the salvation of sinners. *So after he had washed their feet, and had taken his garments,* to fulfill his own work on their behalf; *and was set down again, he said unto them, Know ye what I have done to you? Ye call me Master and Lord: and ye say well; for so I am. If I then, your Lord and Master, have washed your feet;* forgiving our sins, that we might walk in righteousness; *ye also ought to wash one another's feet,* that we might walk together. *For I have given you an example, that ye should do as I have done to you.* We ought to forgive one another, even as God in Christ has forgiven us.[72] *Verily, verily, I say unto you, The servant is not greater than his lord; neither he that is sent greater than he that sent him. If ye know these things, happy are ye if ye do them.* That is, blessed.

---

[72] Eph. 5:1-2; Col. 3:13.

King

Necessity thinks the material agreement of cause and effect as lying within the formal agreement of substance and inherence. Christ reveals the righteousness of God to men and satisfies the justice of God on their behalf; wherefore, he also imputes his righteousness to men, so that his obedience is made theirs. Jesus rules over his people, obeying the law on their behalf, and working his righteousness in their hearts. This is his kingly office.

Jesus Christ is justified in his submission to condemnation. This legal state does not agree with either condemnation or nonlegal righteousness, except as these reciprocally produce justification. Therefore, the justification of Christ must be thought in his person through the community produced, and this lies in the kingdom of God.

Necessity thinks the communal agreement of substances through their reciprocal causality. Jesus Christ is justified in his submission to condemnation by the Holy Spirit. This legal state does not agree with the condemnation of his person or his nonlegal righteousness, but as the mutual effect of both. Therefore, having revealed the righteousness of God to men, and communicated his blessedness to his people, he is also glorified in his church, and his church is glorified in him, because they partake of his righteousness, and by their voluntary submission they glorify him as king.

It is necessary that Christ be justified in his submission to condemnation, and that by the Holy Spirit. To this necessity, historical doctrine adds the necessary effect of his work in his own person, for in that he died for sinners, he is rewarded with the salvation of those for whom he died, who are united with him in his righteousness.[73] And because he shall return in righteousness to judge the living and the dead, he himself is glorified as a king in his holiness, and his people are glorified with him. By his Spirit Christ reigns in the world until his return, when he shall raise all men to judgment by his voice, to rule over the new creation forevermore.

---

[73] Aquinas, *Summa* 3.48.1.

Thou wilt prolong the king's life: *and* his years as many generations. He shall abide before God for ever: O prepare mercy and truth, *which* may preserve him. So will I sing praise unto thy name for ever, that I may daily perform my vows. Psalm 61:6-8

But the king shall rejoice in God; every one that sweareth by him shall glory: but the mouth of them that speak lies shall be stopped. Psalm 63:11

For God *is* my King of old, working salvation in the midst of the earth. Psalm 74:12

He must be a king, to fulfill the reward of his work. Christ died for the sins of his people, that they might be saved; those whose sins are imputed to Christ are personally united with him; and because he partakes of their sin, they also partake of his righteousness.

He shall see of the travail of his soul, *and* shall be satisfied: by his knowledge shall my righteous servant justify many; for he shall bear their iniquities. Isaiah 53:11

In those days, and at that time, will I cause the Branch of righteousness to grow up unto David; and he shall execute judgment and righteousness in the land. In those days shall Judah be saved, and Jerusalem shall dwell safely: and this *is the name* wherewith she shall be called, The LORD our righteousness. Jeremiah 33:15-16

This work is executed by the Holy Spirit, who rewards Christ with the salvation of his people. A king rules over his people by word and deed, both in the execution of the law and the leadership of the army.[74] Christ has fulfilled the law on our behalf, but the law of God requires that it be fulfilled in every

---

[74] 1 Samuel 8.

individual person, who is an end in himself. Therefore, the obedience of Christ must be applied to the elect, his obedience made theirs. And because this is the desired effect of his work, and the Holy Spirit justifies him therein, it also belongs to the Holy Spirit to apply the work to his people.

> My heart is inditing a good matter: I speak of the things which I have made touching the king: my tongue *is* the pen of a ready writer. Thou art fairer than the children of men: grace is poured into thy lips: therefore God hath blessed thee for ever. Gird thy sword upon *thy* thigh, O *most* mighty, with thy glory and thy majesty. And in thy majesty ride prosperously because of truth and meekness *and* righteousness; and thy right hand shall teach thee terrible things. Thine arrows *are* sharp in the heart of the king's enemies; *whereby* the people fall under thee. Thy throne, O God, *is* for ever and ever: the sceptre of thy kingdom *is* a right sceptre. Thou lovest righteousness, and hatest wickedness: therefore God, thy God, hath anointed thee with the oil of gladness above thy fellows. All thy garments *smell* of myrrh, and aloes, *and* cassia, out of the ivory palaces, whereby they have made thee glad. Kings' daughters *were* among thy honourable women: upon thy right hand did stand the queen in gold of Ophir. Hearken, O daughter, and consider, and incline thine ear; forget also thine own people, and thy father's house; So shall the king greatly desire thy beauty: for he *is* thy Lord; and worship thou him. And the daughter of Tyre *shall be there* with a gift; *even* the rich among the people shall intreat thy favour. The king's daughter *is* all glorious within: her clothing *is* of wrought gold. She shall be brought unto the king in raiment of needlework: the virgins her companions that follow her shall be brought unto thee. With gladness and rejoicing shall they be brought: they shall enter into the king's palace. Instead of thy fathers shall be thy children, whom thou mayest make princes in all the earth. I will make thy name to be remembered in all generations: therefore shall the people praise thee for ever and ever. Psalm 45:1-17

Although the possibility of salvation is apodictically certain, the concept thereof may only be received through revelation. Salvation must be revealed to men for them to comprehend its possibility and exercise faith. Thus, the transition from sin to righteousness depends upon the revelation of the Son. And the end of salvation is charity. The elect are sanctified by the sight of Christ, whereby they partake of his righteousness in heaven, but this vision is not perfect, but imperfect. Therefore, the perfection of Christ in them rests on the full sight of Christ, which they have of him in his return.

> For with thee *is* the fountain of life: in thy light shall we see light. Psalm 36:9

Light makes all things visible, yet itself is not seen, but the light of God is seen in the brightness of our Lord Jesus Christ,[75] for in him men find their blessedness identical in distinction to their righteousness.

> If ye then be risen with Christ, seek those things which are above, where Christ sitteth on the right hand of God. Set your affection on things above, not on things on the earth. For ye are dead, and your life is hid with Christ in God. When Christ, *who is* our life, shall appear, then shall ye also appear with him in glory. Colossians 3:1-4

> Behold, what manner of love the Father hath bestowed upon us, that we should be called the sons of God: therefore the world knoweth us not, because it knew him not. Beloved, now are we the sons of God, and it doth not yet appear what we shall be: but we know that, when he shall appear, we shall be like him; for we shall see him as he is. And every man that hath this hope in him purifieth himself, even as he is pure. 1 John 3:1-3

---

[75] John 1:4, 8:12; Heb. 1:3.

This perfect vision is twofold, which the soul has in heaven after death, and in the body on the last day. Those who sleep in Christ are buried with him, and their souls ascending into heaven are made perfect, and they dwell with him in paradise;[76] and on the last day, those who sleep in Christ shall be raised with him, ascending to meet him in the clouds, that the whole life of Christ may be visible in his church, even in those who neither die nor sleep, but are changed, as in the transfiguration.[77] Although the church is yet laden with many sins, nevertheless, by the hope of his coming she is sanctified, and through his Spirit Christ reigns unto the last day, when the church shall be made perfect.

> Being confident of this very thing, that he which hath begun a good work in you will perform *it* until the day of Jesus Christ. Philippians 1:6

That time is appointed by the Father; it cannot be changed. Nevertheless, the people of God hasten that day by their sanctification, preparing themselves for the heavenly kingdom.[78] The hope of his return is the means whereby Christ rules over his church, and by consideration thereof she obeys the law of God, waging war against her own sins, and against the powers of darkness.[79]

Christ, having completed his work, ascends into heaven. Likewise, when the Spirit of God shall have fully applied the redemption to his people, he returns from heaven to earth to bring forth the new creation, to show forth the invisible in the visible, the full manifestation of his righteousness in the world: the bride of Christ, the new Jerusalem.[80]

Jesus manifests the blessedness of God in his ascension, and the holiness of God in his second coming, for because he is the blessedness of God, he is holy, and the Holy Spirit justifies him, and all his people in him, because the Spirit

---

[76] Heb. 12:22-24; Luke 23:42-43.
[77] 1 Cor. 15:51-52; 1 Thes. 4:15-17.
[78] 2 Peter 3:10-14.
[79] Matt. 24:36-25:30.
[80] Rev. 21:9-27.

dwells within him and within them, and he is a king. Those who are saved by Christ, by him fulfill the law, the end of their salvation.

> In whom ye also *trusted*, after that ye heard the word of truth, the gospel of your salvation: in whom also after that ye believed, ye were sealed with that holy Spirit of promise, Which is the earnest of our inheritance until the redemption of the purchased possession, unto the praise of his glory. Ephesians 1:13-14

> And because ye are sons, God hath sent forth the Spirit of his Son into your hearts, crying, Abba, Father. Wherefore thou art no more a servant, but a son; and if a son, then an heir of God through Christ. Galatians 4:6-7

In Christ dwells the fullness of the divine nature; all the divine persons are glorified in him, in his work, even in his body, for all the offices of Christ are modalities of his divine nature manifest in his flesh.

> The king shall joy in thy strength, O LORD; and in thy salvation how greatly shall he rejoice! Thou hast given him his heart's desire, and hast not withholden the request of his lips. Selah. For thou preventest him with the blessings of goodness: thou settest a crown of pure gold on his head. He asked life of thee, *and* thou gavest it him, *even* length of days for ever and ever. His glory *is* great in thy salvation: honour and majesty hast thou laid upon him. For thou hast made him most blessed for ever: thou hast made him exceeding glad with thy countenance. For the king trusteth in the LORD, and through the mercy of the most High he shall not be moved. Psalm 21:1-7

Jesus Christ returns to glorify the Father in himself. He is a king because he is holy; he rules over his people by his law, subduing their sins and enemies, to glorify the Holy Spirit in the application of the work, who is given to them until his return, when he shall glorify them in himself.

If ye love me, keep my commandments. And I will pray the Father, and he shall give you another Comforter, that he may abide with you for ever; *Even* the Spirit of truth; whom the world cannot receive, because it seeth him not, neither knoweth him: but ye know him; for he dwelleth with you, and shall be in you. I will not leave you comfortless: I will come to you. Yet a little while, and the world seeth me no more; but ye see me: because I live, ye shall live also. At that day ye shall know that I *am* in my Father, and ye in me, and I in you. He that hath my commandments, and keepeth them, he it is that loveth me: and he that loveth me shall be loved of my Father, and I will love him, and will manifest myself to him. Judas saith unto him, not Iscariot, Lord, how is it that thou wilt manifest thyself unto us, and not unto the world? Jesus answered and said unto him, If a man love me, he will keep my words: and my Father will love him, and we will come unto him, and make our abode with him. He that loveth me not keepeth not my sayings: and the word which ye hear is not mine, but the Father's which sent me. These things have I spoken unto you, being *yet* present with you. But the Comforter, *which is* the Holy Ghost, whom the Father will send in my name, he shall teach you all things, and bring all things to your remembrance, whatsoever I have said unto you. Peace I leave with you, my peace I give unto you: not as the world giveth, give I unto you. Let not your heart be troubled, neither let it be afraid. Ye have heard how I said unto you, I go away, and come *again* unto you. If ye loved me, ye would rejoice, because I said, I go unto the Father: for my Father is greater than I. And now I have told you before it come to pass, that, when it is come to pass, ye might believe. Hereafter I will not talk much with you: for the prince of this world cometh, and hath nothing in me. But that the world may know that I love the Father; and as the

Father gave me commandment, even so I do. Arise, let us go hence. John 14:15-31

These things have I spoken unto you, that ye should not be offended. They shall put you out of the synagogues: yea, the time cometh, that whosoever killeth you will think that he doeth God service. And these things will they do unto you, because they have not known the Father, nor me. But these things have I told you, that when the time shall come, ye may remember that I told you of them. And these things I said not unto you at the beginning, because I was with you. But now I go my way to him that sent me; and none of you asketh me, Whither goest thou? But because I have said these things unto you, sorrow hath filled your heart. Nevertheless I tell you the truth; It is expedient for you that I go away: for if I go not away, the Comforter will not come unto you; but if I depart, I will send him unto you. And when he is come, he will reprove the world of sin, and of righteousness, and of judgment: Of sin, because they believe not on me; Of righteousness, because I go to my Father, and ye see me no more; Of judgment, because the prince of this world is judged. I have yet many things to say unto you, but ye cannot bear them now. Howbeit when he, the Spirit of truth, is come, he will guide you into all truth: for he shall not speak of himself; but whatsoever he shall hear, *that* shall he speak: and he will shew you things to come. He shall glorify me: for he shall receive of mine, and shall shew *it* unto you. All things that the Father hath are mine: therefore said I, that he shall take of mine, and shall shew *it* unto you. A little while, and ye shall not see me: and again, a little while, and ye shall see me, because I go to the Father. John 16:1-16

The kingdom of Christ is threefold: King of the Jews, King of Kings, and King of the Church. Likewise, there is a threefold law: ceremonial, judicial, and moral.[81]

---

[81] *Westminster* 19.

King of the Jews

"King of the Jews" is an earthly office that is not an earthly office, but a heavenly one. The king of the Jews is anointed of God to lead his people Israel. Israel of old is the church of God, a nation;[82] therefore, the king of the Jews is head both of the nation and of the church; not of the many, but of the one, "for salvation is of the Jews" (John 4:22). This office pertains not to men, but to God, for so the Lord calls his anointed one by the name of his father David.

> Alas! for that day *is* great, so that none *is* like it: it *is* even the time of Jacob's trouble; but he shall be saved out of it. For it shall come to pass in that day, saith the LORD of hosts, *that* I will break his yoke from off thy neck, and will burst thy bonds, and strangers shall no more serve themselves of him: But they shall serve the LORD their God, and David their king, whom I will raise up unto them. Jeremiah 30:7-9

> And thou, profane wicked prince of Israel, whose day is come, when iniquity *shall have* an end, Thus saith the Lord GOD; Remove the diadem, and take off the crown: this *shall* not *be* the same: exalt *him that is* low, and abase *him that is* high. I will overturn, overturn, overturn, it: and it shall be no *more*, until he come whose right it is; and I will give it *him*. Ezekiel 21:25-27

> Nathanael answered and saith unto him, Rabbi, thou art the Son of God; thou art the King of Israel. John 1:49

Before Christ comes in the flesh, there must be a sensible intuition of his person, that all men might believe on him for salvation. Those who come before Christ, though he is before them, are his people; to them the promises are given, and in types and sacrifices he is figured, and in the law commanded his perfect obedience is foretold. By him Israel of old was a people whose church and state

---

[82] Ex. 19:5-6.

were identical in distinction[83], a visible manifestation of the church's eternal state, to show forth Christ to come, her king.

When therefore the king was come, in whom every perfection dwells, church and state were disjoined, and the Gentiles received into the household of God. Israel of old is constituted a holy people, but the church is regulated so; the outward glory has ceased, and the inward glory is nigh.[84]

The fundamental doctrines contain within themselves the ground of our salvation, yea, the historicals themselves, identical in distinction; therefore, the historical doctrines, grounded in the fundamentals, are eternal, and men may be saved prior to the coming of Christ through the work God accomplished before the world began.

> And all that dwell upon the earth shall worship him, whose names are not written in the book of life of the Lamb slain from the foundation of the world. Revelation 13:8

Nevertheless, to make known the fundamentals prior to the history that reveals them, they are manifested in types and shadows, even in the offices of church and state.[85] And because he is their king, this people he shall save and restore.

> And so all Israel shall be saved. Romans 11:26

King of Kings

Christ is king of kings, for he is God, and he conquers, not by force of arms, but by the preaching of the Gospel.

---

[83] Ex. 19:6, cf. 1 Pet. 2:9; 2 Sam. 7:23; 1 Chron. 17:21; Ps. 106:4-5.
[84] Eph. 2:11-22; Col. 2:16-23; Heb. 8:7-12.
[85] Heb. 10:1.

Yet have I set my king upon my holy hill of Zion. I will declare the decree: the Lord hath said unto me, Thou *art* my Son; this day have I begotten thee. Ask of me, and I shall give *thee* the heathen *for* thine inheritance, and the uttermost parts of the earth *for* thy possession. Thou shalt break them with a rod of iron; thou shalt dash them in pieces like a potter's vessel. Psalm 2:6-9

Yet have I set my king upon my holy hill of Zion, through justification of his submission to unconditional condemnation. *Ask of me,* by prayer. *Thou shalt break them with a rod of iron,* the Holy Spirit, who is just to the wicked, but gracious to the elect.

But ye shall receive power, after that the Holy Ghost is come upon you: and ye shall be witnesses unto me both in Jerusalem, and in all Judaea, and in Samaria, and unto the uttermost part of the earth. Acts 1:8

And I saw when the Lamb opened one of the seals, and I heard, as it were the noise of thunder, one of the four beasts saying, Come and see. And I saw, and behold a white horse: and he that sat on him had a bow; and a crown was given unto him: and he went forth conquering, and to conquer. Revelation 6:1-2, cf. Ps. 45:4-5

A white horse, innocent, to give peace; *and he that sat on him had a bow,* the Holy Spirit, who strikes from afar;[86] *and he went forth conquering, and to conquer,* to conquer and subdue, to civilize and unite, for his rule shall be established "in earth, as *it is* in heaven" (Matthew 6:10).

---

[86] Ps. 45:5.

King of the Church

Jesus is king of a peculiar people, the church, made up of all those who profess faith in him, and their children.[87] These are distinguished from the nation of Israel, and the nations of the world, without identity. This is the kingdom of God preached by John the Baptist, and by the Lord in parables.

> Wherefore remember, that ye *being* in time past Gentiles in the flesh, who are called Uncircumcision by that which is called the Circumcision in the flesh made by hands; That at that time ye were without Christ, being aliens from the commonwealth of Israel, and strangers from the covenants of promise, having no hope, and without God in the world: But now in Christ Jesus ye who sometimes were far off are made nigh by the blood of Christ. For he is our peace, who hath made both one, and hath broken down the middle wall of partition *between us*; Having abolished in his flesh the enmity, *even* the law of commandments *contained* in ordinances; for to make in himself of twain one new man, *so* making peace; And that he might reconcile both unto God in one body by the cross, having slain the enmity thereby: And came and preached peace to you which were afar off, and to them that were nigh. For through him we both have access by one Spirit unto the Father. Now therefore ye are no more strangers and foreigners, but fellowcitizens with the saints, and of the household of God; And are built upon the foundation of the apostles and prophets, Jesus Christ himself being the chief corner *stone*; In whom all the building fitly framed together groweth unto an holy temple in the Lord: In whom ye also are builded together for an habitation of God through the Spirit. Ephesians 2:11-22, cf. Col. 2:11-19

This kingdom he rules by laws, officers, ordinances, and sacraments, to sanctify them unto the end. His people he commands to obey the moral law,

---

[87] Ezek. 16:20-21; Matt. 19:14; 1 Cor. 7:14.

and by his Spirit he teaches them how. And these three things in particular: to teach and to preach, to worship him in truth, and to govern his people in righteousness.[88]

The doctrine of the church belongs to the application of the work by the Holy Spirit. This is the doctrine of her king. He is the only head of his church, visible and invisible; he will establish her, destroying all her enemies, even the son of perdition, the Antichrist, who pretends to his place as head of the church after the cessation of the imperial line; yea, not only the enemies in this world, but also the fallen angels, whose offices he gives to his own people.

> *And* having spoiled principalities and powers, he made a shew of them openly, triumphing over them in it. Colossians 2:15

> And there was war in heaven: Michael and his angels fought against the dragon; and the dragon fought and his angels, And prevailed not; neither was their place found any more in heaven. And the great dragon was cast out, that old serpent, called the Devil, and Satan, which deceiveth the whole world: he was cast out into the earth, and his angels were cast out with him. Revelation 12:7-9, cf. 2 Cor. 10:3-5; Eph. 6:12

The Ceremonial Law[89]

The ceremonial law prescribed the conditions under which a sinful people might draw near to God, to serve the Lord and worship him in truth. It was necessary for the law of Moses to show forth, not only the letter of law, to be obeyed out of respect, but also the spirit thereof, to be kept in love. The moral law requires subjection of the heart; the judicial law, only outward conformity; but the ceremonial law enjoins love for duty, and shows the supreme benefit of Christ's sacrifice. It divided the people of God from the heathen, and by the

---

[88] Matt. 18:15-20; John 4:23-24; Eph. 4:1-16; *Westminster* 25.4; *Larger Catechism* Q.45.
[89] Lev. 5:15, 17.

appearance of the Son of God, removed the boundary between Jew and Gentile. Christ is therefore a king, to delight his people in the law, and to unite them from every corner of the earth.[90]

> For I *am* the LORD your God: ye shall therefore sanctify yourselves, and ye shall be holy; for I *am* holy: neither shall ye defile yourselves with any manner of creeping thing that creepeth upon the earth. For I *am* the LORD that bringeth you up out of the land of Egypt, to be your God: ye shall therefore be holy, for I *am* holy. Leviticus 11:44-45

> And ye shall be holy unto me: for I the Lord *am* holy, and have severed you from *other* people, that ye should be mine. Leviticus 20:26

Love for righteousness comes to men through the sacrifice of Christ, whereby they perceive the love of the divine persons, and so partake of the same. Wherefore, before he comes, his offering of himself is typified by a multitude of sacrifices, to show forth the manifold glory of his life, death, and resurrection.

The diverse virtues united in man are elsewhere distributed to animals. Clean animals were fit for food, by whose dead body a Jew was not defiled, signifying the excellencies of Christ's death.[91] The unclean animals were in no way virtuous in death, but only in life; therefore, they signify the glory of his resurrection.[92]

The Judicial Law[93]

The certain punishment of death assured every man of the continuing obligation of the law given to man in the day of his creation, and by the threat

---

[90] Lev. 10:8-11, 11:44-47; John 11:52; Eph. 2:11-22.
[91] John 1:29, Rev. 5:6.
[92] Rev. 5:5; cf. Lev. 11:1-8.
[93] Lev. 6:2-3, Deut. 16:18, 17:8-13.

of death to all who have sinned, men are taught to hope for salvation through the one who bore the curse.[94]

The law of Moses tolerated what it could not reform: divorce, polygamy, and slavery.[95] The letter of the law was weak to extinguish these sins from the hearts of men, but with the coming of Christ men are left without excuse. Their legality served only so far as the means of sanctification was lacking, and prophesied of the coming king.

The toleration of divorce prophesied of the virgin birth, that Joseph might not think to make Mary a public example, for God tempts no man, not even to think an evil thing.[96] The toleration of slavery foretold the voluntary subjection of the Son of God, not only to the law, but to the condemnation of the Father, to liberate all the children of God, even the Gentiles.[97] The toleration of polygamy served to show the wondrous diversity of the bride of Christ, upon whom the Spirit bestows every perfection.[98]

Christ come in the flesh now commands the full obedience of nations to the moral law, and by his sacrifice he works the same in the hearts of men.

> A bruised reed shall he not break, and the smoking flax shall he not quench: he shall bring forth judgment unto truth. He shall not fail nor be discouraged, till he have set judgment in the earth: and the isles shall wait for his law. Isaiah 42:3-4

> And Jesus came and spake unto them, saying, All power is given unto me in heaven and in earth. Go ye therefore, and teach all nations, baptizing them in the name of the Father, and of the Son, and of the Holy Ghost: Teaching them to observe all things whatsoever I have commanded you: and, lo, I am with you alway, even unto the end of the world. Amen. Matthew 28:18-20

---

[94] Gen. 9:5-6.
[95] Deut. 24:1-4; Lev. 18:18, 25:44-46.
[96] Matt. 1:19.
[97] Gal. 4:1-7.
[98] Gen. 29:31- 30:24; Kings 11:1; Cant. 1:4, 4:1-7; Gal. 4:21-31.

The Moral Law[99]

The law of Christ is the moral law, and he not only commands its execution out of respect, but works in his people performance from love. He is the moral law in the flesh; he loves the law, and imbues that same love to all the members of his kingdom.

> But now we are delivered from the law, that being dead wherein we were held; that we should serve in newness of spirit, and not *in* the oldness of the letter. Romans 7:6, Ps. 119

The moral law prescribes the world to exist. God created the world to be inhabited.

> For thus saith the LORD that created the heavens; God himself that formed the earth and made it; he hath established it, he created it not in vain, he formed it to be inhabited: I *am* the Lord; and *there is* none else. Isaiah 45:18

The devil sought to destroy mankind and ruin all creation. By sin, the world reverts to its original state of chaos.

> For my people *is* foolish, they have not known me; they *are* sottish children, and they have none understanding: they *are* wise to do evil, but to do good they have no knowledge. I beheld the earth, and, lo, *it was* without form, and void; and the heavens, and they *had* no light. Jeremiah 4:22-23

Nevertheless, the purpose of God stands.

---

[99] Lev. 4:2, 13, 22, 27.

I have not spoken in secret, in a dark place of the earth: I said not unto
the seed of Jacob, Seek ye me in vain: I the LORD speak righteousness,
I declare things that are right. Isaiah 45:19

For thus hath the LORD said, The whole land shall be desolate; yet will
I not make a full end. Jeremiah 4:27

The Lord Jesus Christ restores the law and fulfills it, having preserved it.[100]
He saves the world, keeps it, and uplifts it. Through his work men are not only
made righteous, but holy, as God is holy,[101] for Jesus is a king: he keeps the law
not only for himself, but also for others.

The Lord is well pleased for his righteousness' sake; he will magnify
the law, and make *it* honourable. Isaiah 42:21

Behold, the days come, saith the LORD, that I will raise unto David a
righteous Branch, and a King shall reign and prosper, and shall execute
judgment and justice in the earth. In his days Judah shall be saved, and
Israel shall dwell safely: and this *is* his name whereby he shall be called,
THE LORD OUR RIGHTEOUSNESS. Jeremiah 23:5-6

Typology

The excellency of our Lord Jesus Christ is typified by the lives his saints,
and even the wicked, but his virtues are distributed amongst several persons
according to their essences, no one type embodying them all.

Reuben, the firstborn son of Jacob, "the excellency of dignity, and the
excellency of power," to whom the priesthood and the kingdom belonged, and
the birthright also, lost these privileges by lying with his father's wife (Genesis

---

[100] Matt. 5:17-18.
[101] Lev. 11:44-45, 19:2, 20:26, 22:32-33.

49:3). God then gave the priesthood to the firstborn sons of Israel, and afterward to Levi; the scepter he gave to Judah, and to Joseph the birthright.[102]

> Now the sons of Reuben the firstborn of Israel, (for he *was* the firstborn; but, forasmuch as he defiled his father's bed, his birthright was given unto the sons of Joseph the son of Israel: and the genealogy is not to be reckoned after the birthright. For Judah prevailed above his brethren, and of him *came* the chief ruler; but the birthright *was* Joseph's:). 1 Chronicles 5:1-2

The Lord Jesus Christ possesses all things from the Father, for by the promise of God to Abraham, they were all to dwell within one person. Nevertheless, every type must be distinguished from the antitype. Wherefore, although these privileges were all intended for Reuben, they were taken away from him for the sin he committed, because he is not the Lord Jesus Christ, but a type only; yea, rather a type of Adam, whom Jesus supplants. And the excellencies of Reuben God gave to divers of his brethren, for that the same original sin that corrupted the firstborn corrupted all his brethren.

Simeon and Levi slaughtered the men of Shechem for the sake of their sister Dinah, whom Shechem the son of Hamor defiled. For this sin Jacob scatters them in Israel. And when the Lord slew the firstborn of Egypt, he kept alive the firstborn of Israel, and sanctified them to himself, to minister to him.[103] But when the Israelites made a golden calf, the Levites took up arms against their brethren, God turning his anger on behalf of his sister into zeal for the purity of Christ's bride, and for this righteous deed God gave them the priesthood, because the true priesthood belongs to Christ not by the flesh, but by righteousness. Moreover, God commanded that every firstborn son be redeemed, that the true priesthood might be sure to the firstborn of every creature.[104] And even Adam

---

[102] Gen. 48:22-49:28.
[103] Ex. 13:1-2.
[104] Num. 3:5-13, 40-51; Col. 1:15.

in Christ is blessed, and of Reuben he says, "Let Reuben live, and not die; and let not his men be few" (Deuteronomy 33:6).

Reuben sought to rule over his brethren by interceding for the life of Joseph,[105] and to persuade their father to send Benjamin with them into Egypt.[106] He failed. It was Judah who persuaded his brethren to sell Joseph to the Ishmaelites;[107] it was Judah who became surety for Benjamin to his father;[108] and it was Judah who persuaded Joseph to have mercy on him and his brethren.[109]

Joseph bore Manasseh and Ephraim in Egypt, but Jacob put Ephraim before Manasseh, and called them his own,[110] for Jesus Christ comes after Adam, yet is he before him,[111] and though Jesus is the son of Joseph, he is rather the Son of God.

A king came first from Benjamin, beloved of his father Jacob, for whom Judah is surety. When therefore Saul by sin fell from the kingdom, Judah inherited the scepter. Saul is condemned; David had a part with Saul, whom he served, and whose son in law he became, but he also had a part with God, to be king in place of Saul. Wherefore, as Jacob and Esau, and Pharez and Zerah, so also David and Saul. David submitted to the condemnation of the Father in the person of Saul, and by his strength he subdued kingdoms. Yet he sinned in the matter of Bathsheba, for that he is not the chosen one; nevertheless, through his union with Bathsheba came our Lord and Savior, not by flesh but by law, not as from the son of David's sin, who died nameless, but from the son of his repentance, for that our savior inherits the guilt of original sin in righteousness, whereof he speaks in the psalm of repentance, "To the chief Musician, A Psalm of David, when Nathan the prophet came unto him, after he had gone in to Bathsheba" (Psalm 51). Solomon built the temple of God, having received wisdom from God to bring peace and prosperity to Israel. Yet even Solomon fell astray to idols by the influence of strange wives, for he is not the Lord Jesus

---

[105] Gen. 37:21-22, 29-30.
[106] Gen. 42:37-38.
[107] Gen. 37:26-28.
[108] Gen. 43:1-14.
[109] Gen. 44:14-34.
[110] Gen. 48:1-22.
[111] John 1:15.

Christ, but a type only, a type of the one who redeems for himself a singular bride from every nation and tongue, with many sons and daughters.

And what more shall I tell of all the types of Jesus Christ? For in him every virtue and blessing is united.[112]

Scripture Proof

The office of king combines the prophetic and priestly offices of Christ, yea, therein lies the totality of historical doctrine. Every event of Jesus' life pertains to his kingship, nothing is excluded: above all his trial and death, itself the sum of the signs, wherein he is crowned king of the Jews. Yet one event belongs uniquely to his kingship, the visitation of the Magi, showing that he is born king of the Jews. As a king Jesus both fulfills the law, and causes his people to fulfill it, an inwardly lawful being; wherefore, this event is recorded only by Matthew, whose genealogy is given for that purpose, for once the true king has been born, the false king is taken away. The diadem was thrice overthrown; first by exile, then by the Hasmonean dynasty, and lastly by the Herodian line of kings, when came the true king.[113]

> Therefore the Lord himself shall give you a sign; Behold, a virgin shall conceive, and bear a son, and shall call his name Immanuel. Butter and honey shall he eat, that he may know to refuse the evil, and choose the good. For before the child shall know to refuse the evil, and choose the good, the land that thou abhorrest shall be forsaken of both her kings. Isaiah 7:14-16, cf. vs. 1-13; 2 Kings 8:19; 2 Chron. 21:7

After the birth of Christ, Herod slew his own heir, and himself perished in great pains. His son, Herod Archelaus, was deposed by the Romans after nine

---

[112] John 3:34-35.
[113] Ezek. 21:27.

years, so that the land was "forsaken of both her kings" before the child came of age, or ever had attained knowledge of good and evil.[114]

Now when Jesus was born in Bethlehem of Judaea in the days of Herod the king, behold, there came wise men from the east to Jerusalem, for the king of the Jews inherits all nations; *Saying, Where is he that is born King of the Jews?* Born of a virgin; *for we have seen his star in the east,* according to a prophecy given to the Gentiles;[115] *and are come to worship him,* who is God manifest in the flesh. *When Herod the king had heard these things, he was troubled,* for he was envious of the true king; *and all Jerusalem with him,* because they knew the prophecies. *And when he had gathered all the chief priests and scribes of the people together, he demanded of them where Christ should be born,* he acknowledged the truth of the holy oracles, and consulted them vainly to strive against them.[116] *And they said unto him, In Bethlehem of Judaea: for thus it is written by the prophet, And thou Bethlehem, in the land of Juda, art not the least among the princes of Juda:* where Rachel died giving birth to Joseph, because in many afflictions the church gives birth to her children;[117] *for out of thee shall come a Governor, that shall rule my people Israel.* What was faintly revealed to the Magi, God particularly foretold by the Holy Scriptures given to Israel, whereunto God directed the Magi, that they might seek him in his holy place. *Then Herod, when he had privily called the wise men, enquired of them diligently what time the star appeared.* He showed himself a student of the word. *And he sent them to Bethlehem, and said, Go and search diligently for the young child; and when ye have found him, bring me word again, that I may come and worship him also.* He also confessed him king. *When they had heard the king, they departed; and, lo, the star, which they saw in the east, went before them, till it came and stood over where the young child was,* the sign was with them from first to last. *When they saw the star, they rejoiced with exceeding great joy,* they had faith through the means given to them, for they were called. *And when they were come into the house, they saw the young child with Mary his mother, and fell down, and worshipped*

---

[114] Deut. 1:39; Josephus, *The Jewish War,* 103-132.
[115] Cf. Num. 24:17.
[116] Cf. Ps. 2:1-3.
[117] Gen. 30:24, 35:16-20; 1 Samuel 16:1; Gal. 4:19; Rev. 12:1-2.

him: as God; and when they had opened their treasures, they presented unto him gifts; gold, and frankincense, and myrrh, for the glory of the king. *And being warned of God in a dream that they should not return to Herod,* the one who led them there did not suffer them any harm; *they departed into their own country another way,* for they were changed men. *And when they were departed, behold, the angel of the Lord appeareth to Joseph in a dream, saying, Arise, and take the young child and his mother, and flee into Egypt, and be thou there until I bring thee word: for Herod will seek the young child to destroy him,* nor did he suffer any harm to his anointed child, or his parents. *When he arose, he took the young child and his mother by night, and departed into Egypt: And was there until the death of Herod: that it might be fulfilled which was spoken of the Lord by the prophet, saying, Out of Egypt have I called my son,* out of the hard bondage of sin he called his only begotten. *Then Herod, when he saw that he was mocked of the wise men, was exceeding wroth, and sent forth, and slew all the children that were in Bethlehem, and in all the coasts thereof, from two years old and under,* that it should appear that there is no other besides Jesus who is called Christ; *according to the time which he had diligently enquired of the wise men, Then was fulfilled that which was spoken by Jeremiah the prophet,* Herod, who sought knowledge from the Scriptures to frustrate their purpose, instead became the instrument of their fulfillment; *saying, In Rama was there a voice heard, lamentation, and weeping, and great mourning, Rachel weeping for her children, and would not be comforted, because they are not,* Jesus is born near where Rachel died, because through many labors the church gives birth to her king, and is conformed to his image.[118] *But when Herod was dead,* he makes no comment on the death of that wicked man, except that it was the occasion for Jesus' return to Israel; *behold, an angel of the Lord appeareth in a dream to Joseph in Egypt, Saying, Arise, and take the young child and his mother, and go into the land of Israel:* because in him are fulfilled the generations of Abraham;[119] *for they are dead which sought the young child's life,* a prophet like unto Moses, a king.[120] *And he arose, and took the young child and his mother, and came into the land of Israel. But when he heard that Archelaus did reign in*

---

118 Rev. 11:7.
119 Gen. 12:10-13:1, 15:13-14.
120 Deut. 18:15-19, 33:4-5.

Judaea in the room of his father Herod, he was afraid to go thither: notwithstanding, being warned of God in a dream, he turned aside into the parts of Galilee: the king, not only of Judah, but also of all Israel;[121] *And he came and dwelt in a city called Nazareth: that it might be fulfilled which was spoken by the prophets, He shall be called a Nazarene,* a saying not in Scripture, but known to the Jews, because God reveals himself to whomsoever he pleases, howsoever he pleases, as this story abundantly proves.

The Triumphal Entry

The sign of his kingly office is plain, the triumphal entry into Jerusalem, wherein he is worshipped as king, according to the prophecy cited by the evangelists,[122] and the 24th and 118th psalms. This sign is recorded in every Gospel, because Christ's kingship contains within itself the whole, for the last of all must have within itself the completeness of the system.

Matthew 21:1-11

And when they drew nigh unto Jerusalem, the ancient city of Melchizedek; *and were come to Bethphage, unto the mount of Olives,* a king in his holiness, to give peace; *then sent Jesus two disciples, Saying unto them, Go into the village over against you, and straightway ye shall find an ass tied, and a colt with her:* beasts of burden, for the church bears Christ to his throne, as he also bears their sins; *loose them, and bring them unto me,* to set them free for the Lord's service. *And if any man say ought unto you, ye shall say, The Lord hath need of them;* for he is a king of necessity; *and straightway he will send them,* that the Lord should rule with the consent of his people, and by their voluntary contributions. *All this was done, that it might be fulfilled which was spoken by the prophet,* for as a prophet, he is also a king; *saying, Tell ye the daughter of Sion, Behold, thy King cometh unto thee, meek, and sitting upon an ass, and a colt the foal of an ass.* He comes humbly, not to rule, but

---

[121] 2 Kings 15:29; Isaiah 9:1-2.
[122] Zech. 9:9.

to serve, and by serving rule; not to conquer, but to liberate, and by liberating conquer; not to lay on them burdens, but to bear the burden of their sins, and lay on them the burden of his righteousness. *And the disciples went, and did as Jesus commanded them, And brought the ass, and the colt, and put on them their clothes, and they set him thereon.* He is a king by the consent of his people, by the very consent he works in them. *And a very great multitude spread their garments in the way;* his way paved by the righteousness of his people; *others cut down branches from the trees, and strawed them in the way.* He came roughly, with inward glory, to make the high things low and the low things high, to dedicate earthly things to divine service. *And the multitudes that went before, and that followed,* both the ancient church, and the new; *cried, saying, Hosanna to the Son of David: Blessed is he that cometh in the name of the Lord; Hosanna in the highest,* the blessedness of God. *And when he was come into Jerusalem, all the city was moved,* in feeling, as by the testimony of the Holy Ghost; *saying, Who is this?* For he is wonderful, and his name is secret, as the psalm foretells: "Who is this King of glory? The LORD of hosts, he *is* the King of glory. Selah" (Psalms 24:10). *And the multitude said, This is Jesus the prophet of Nazareth of Galilee,* that secret now apparent: a prophet, revealing the Father; a priest, bearing men's sins; a king, ruling them by his Spirit.

Mark 11:1-11

And when they came nigh to Jerusalem, the city of the great king;[123] *unto Bethphage and Bethany, at the mount of Olives,* from the mountain of his holiness, to be perfectly happy in his perfect obedience, whereby he ascended into heaven;[124] *he sendeth forth two of his disciples, And saith unto them, Go your way into the village over against you: and as soon as ye be entered into it,* for all things are unto his glory, without intermission or delay; *ye shall find a colt tied, whereon never man sat;* that is, holy; *loose him, and bring him. And if any man say unto you, Why do ye this? say ye that the Lord hath need of him;* for his kingship is a matter of necessity;

---

123 Matt. 5:35.
124 Luke 24:50-51; Acts 1:12.

and straightway he will send him hither, to fulfill his will without delay. *And they went their way, and found the colt tied by the door without in a place where two ways met;* as heaven and earth meet in Christ;[125] *and they loose him. And certain of them that stood there said unto them, What do ye, loosing the colt?* They did not judge them. *And they said unto them even as Jesus had commanded: and they let them go. And they brought the colt to Jesus, and cast their garments on him;* their righteousness, which they wrought in him, because he is their king; *and he sat upon him. And many spread their garments in the way: and others cut down branches off the trees, and strawed them in the way,* the high trees being humbled before his humility. *And they that went before, and they that followed, cried, saying, Hosanna; Blessed is he that cometh in the name of the Lord: Blessed be the kingdom of our father David, that cometh in the name of the Lord: Hosanna in the highest,* for because he is the blessed Son of God, he inherits the throne of his father David. *And Jesus entered into Jerusalem, and into the temple: and when he had looked round about upon all things, and now the eventide was come, he went out unto Bethany with the twelve,* for his reign is not of earth below, but of heaven above.

Luke 19:28-40

And when he had thus spoken, he went before, ascending up to Jerusalem, as a servant, to be king.[126] *And it came to pass, when he was come nigh to Bethphage and Bethany, at the mount called the mount of Olives, he sent two of his disciples, Saying, Go ye into the village over against you; in the which at your entering,* immediately to his service; *ye shall find a colt tied, whereon yet never man sat: loose him, and bring him hither. And if any man ask you, Why do ye loose him? thus shall ye say unto him, Because the Lord hath need of him. And they that were sent went their way, and found even as he had said unto them. And as they were loosing the colt, the owners thereof said unto them, Why loose ye the colt? And they said, The Lord hath need of him. And they brought him to Jesus: and they cast their garments upon the colt, and they set Jesus thereon. And as he went, they spread their clothes in the way. And when he was come*

---

[125] Ps. 85:9-11; Eph. 1:10.
[126] Prov. 30:21-22.

nigh, even now at the descent of the mount of Olives, for he humbled himself from heaven; *the whole multitude of the disciples began to rejoice and praise God with a loud voice for all the mighty works that they had seen; Saying, Blessed be the King that cometh in the name of the Lord: peace in heaven,* through the filling of the offices of fallen angels; *and glory in the highest,* the greatest glory from the lowest service. *And some of the Pharisees from among the multitude said unto him, Master, rebuke thy disciples. And he answered and said unto them, I tell you that, if these should hold their peace, the stones would immediately cry out,* because the glory of God is the necessary end of creation.

John 12:12-19

On the next day much people that were come to the feast, all Israel gathered together to keep the passover, that they might receive their true king; *when they heard that Jesus was coming to Jerusalem, Took branches of palm trees, and went forth to meet him, and cried, Hosanna: Blessed is the King of Israel that cometh in the name of the Lord. And Jesus, when he had found a young ass, sat thereon;* a beast of burden, to bear the burdens of his people; not to conquer, but to serve; *as it is written, Fear not, daughter of Sion: behold, thy King cometh, sitting on an ass's colt. These things understood not his disciples at the first:* a sign; *but when Jesus was glorified, then remembered they that these things were written of him, and that they had done these things unto him,* that they had accepted him as king. *The people therefore that was with him when he called Lazarus out of his grave, and raised him from the dead, bare record,* a king in his resurrection. *For this cause the people also met him, for that they heard that he had done this miracle,* for through his resurrection from the dead, he gives life to his people, because he bore their sins. *The Pharisees therefore said among themselves, Perceive ye how ye prevail nothing? behold, the world is gone after him.* King of the Jews, king of the world. Amen.

The New Creation

Christ sits as a priest upon his throne, and rules over his kingdom by his Spirit, but the fullness of his kingdom is realized in the new creation, when he shall reign in person, for this is the end of his work, the eternal sabbath rest of the people of God.[127]

The author of Hebrews describes this eternal rest, because through the priesthood of Christ the world both passes away, and is made new.[128] And John narrates the new creation itself, because therein the blessedness of Christ is fully manifest in his people.

Hebrews 4:1-13

Let us therefore fear, lest, a promise being left us of entering into his rest, any of you should seem to come short of it. For unto us was the gospel preached, even from heaven; *as well as unto them: but the word preached did not profit them, not being mixed with faith in them that heard it,* faith in Christ, who dwells in heaven. *For we which have believed do enter into rest,* even now, and in eternity; *as he said, As I have sworn in my wrath, if they shall enter into my rest: although the works were finished from the foundation of the world,* for God makes a new work through the resurrection of Christ. *For he spake in a certain place of the seventh day on this wise, And God did rest the seventh day from all his works,* the sabbath of the old creation. *And in this place again, If they shall enter into my rest. Seeing therefore it remaineth that some must enter therein,* for that the old creation brought forth no fruit unto righteousness; *and they to whom it was first preached entered not in because of unbelief:* a sign that these things spoke not of the land of Israel, but of the new creation; *Again, he limiteth a certain day,* even the first, whereon Christ rose from the dead, and the church gathers to hear the word of God; *saying in David, To day, after so long a time; as it is said, To day if ye will hear his voice, harden not your hearts. For if Jesus had given them rest, then would he not afterward have spoken of*

---

[127] 1 Cor. 15:24.
[128] Is. 65:17-25; Ps. 110; 1 John 2:17.

another day, even the eighth, which is the dawn of a new creation. *There remaineth therefore a rest to the people of God,* signified by the sabbath of the new creation; *For he that is entered into his rest, he also hath ceased from his own works,* being justified by the work of Christ;[129] *as God did from his,* his work finished in Christ. *Let us labour therefore to enter into that rest,* for we must work in faith, that we might rest in glory; *lest any man fall after the same example of unbelief,* looking to Christ in heaven, and to his glorious return. *For the word of God is quick, and powerful,* to raise the dead; *and sharper than any twoedged sword, piercing even to the dividing asunder of soul and spirit,* to slay by the word of his mouth; *and of the joints and marrow,* even the dissolution of the parts of the body; *and is a discerner of the thoughts and intents of the heart,* that we should obey with our whole selves. *Neither is there any creature that is not manifest in his sight:* the word to all mankind; *but all things are naked,* that we should be clothed with his righteousness; *and opened unto the eyes of him with whom we have to do.*

Revelation 20-22

And I saw an angel come down from heaven, having the key of the bottomless pit and a great chain in his hand, because God rules over the powers of darkness. *And he laid hold on the dragon,* the spirit of Imperial Rome;[130] *that old serpent,* who for the sake of the divine likeness, induced our first parents to sin; *which is the Devil, and Satan,* the spirit of negation and contradiction; *and bound him a thousand years,* the fullness of time, to show forth Christ's righteousness in the earth; *And cast him into the bottomless pit, and shut him up, and set a seal upon him,* by force and by the moral law; *that he should deceive the nations no more, till the thousand years should be fulfilled:* The devil having been bound, all shall know that salvation comes through Jesus Christ, together with the divine likeness;[131] *and after that he must be loosed a little season,* to test the hearts of men.[132] *And I saw thrones,* angelic offices, "the powers of the world to come" (Hebrews 6:5); *and they sat upon them,*

---

129 Rom. 3:21-26.
130 Rev. 13:1-8.
131 2 Cor. 4:3-4.
132 Deut. 13:1-3.

the elect, as follows; *and judgment was given unto them: and I saw the souls of them,* for as yet they were dead; *that were beheaded for the witness of Jesus, and for the word of God, and which had not worshipped the beast, neither his image, neither had received his mark upon their foreheads, or in their hands; and they lived and reigned with Christ a thousand years,* for he is the king, and in him his people live. *But the rest of the dead lived not again until the thousand years were finished.* They neither lived while dead, nor shall they live when they are alive. *This is the first resurrection. Blessed and holy is he that hath part in the first resurrection:* for they have the righteousness of Christ; *on such the second death hath no power, but they shall be priests of God and of Christ, and shall reign with him a thousand years.* The kingdom of heaven established on earth, as prophesied by Daniel the prophet.[133] *And when the thousand years are expired, Satan shall be loosed out of his prison, And shall go out to deceive the nations which are in the four quarters of the earth,* throughout the whole earth; *Gog and Magog, to gather them together to battle:* gathered to judgment; *the number of whom is as the sand of the sea,* a great sacrifice to God.[134] *And they went up on the breadth of the earth, and compassed the camp of the saints about, and the beloved city:* the saints everywhere, and in their peculiar dwelling place; *and fire came down from God out of heaven, and devoured them,* destroyed not by man, but by God, together with the old world. *And the devil that deceived them was cast into the lake of fire and brimstone, where the beast and the false prophet are, and shall be tormented day and night for ever and ever. And I saw a great white throne,* innocent; *and him that sat on it, from whose face the earth and the heaven fled away;* who fills all and is not contained by any; *and there was found no place for them,* for his glory shall be fully manifest alone. *And I saw the dead, small and great,* each according to his essence; *stand before God; and the books were opened:* all their works recorded and revealed; *and another book was opened,* as of grace; *which is the book of life: and the dead were judged out of those things which were written in the books, according to their works,* whereby the elect show their faith. *And the sea gave up the dead which were in it;* all those who perished in the flood, and in their love of the world; *and death and hell delivered up the dead which were in them:*

---

[133] Dan. 2:44-45.
[134] Jer. 46:10.

their bodies reunited to their souls, being raised to judgment; *and they were judged every man according to their works*, according to the moral law. *And death and hell were cast into the lake of fire*, death and hell themselves are cast into the lake of fire, to be tormented therein, their purpose being totally overthrown, because death is no more, and in the destruction of the wicked God glorifies his Son. *This is the second death. And whosoever was not found written in the book of life was cast into the lake of fire*, set apart for that end by the condemnation of Christ. *And I saw a new heaven and a new earth:* for angels and men; *for the first heaven and the first earth were passed away; and there was no more sea*, that is, sensible intuition. *And I John saw the holy city, new Jerusalem, coming down from God out of heaven*, they are first gathered to the Lord in the sky, and thence descend to the earth;[135] *prepared as a bride adorned for her husband*, the blessedness of Christ. *And I heard a great voice out of heaven saying, Behold, the tabernacle of God is with men, and he will dwell with them, and they shall be his people, and God himself shall be with them*, in person; *and be their God. And God shall wipe away all tears from their eyes; and there shall be no more death, neither sorrow, nor crying, neither shall there be any more pain: for the former things are passed away.* They are made perfectly holy through the forgiveness of sins; wherefore, they are also made infinitely happy through the transformation of misery into joy. *And he that sat upon the throne said, Behold, I make all things new,* new things, even the same things made new. *And he said unto me, Write: for these words are true and faithful,* a testimony to all men. *And he said unto me, It is done. I am Alpha and Omega, the beginning and the end,* in whom the world finds both its beginning and its end. *I will give unto him that is athirst of the fountain of the water of life freely,* open to all. *He that overcometh shall inherit all things; and I will be his God, and he shall be my son,* having his righteousness. *But the fearful, and unbelieving, and the abominable, and murderers, and whoremongers, and sorcerers, and idolaters, and all liars, shall have their part in the lake which burneth with fire and brimstone: which is the second death,* a death greater than hell. *And there came unto me one of the seven angels which had the seven vials full of the seven last plagues,* for among them the church is made glorious;[136] *and talked with me,*

---

[135] 1 Thess. 4:17.
[136] Rev. 16:8-9, cf. Rev. 12:1-2, 5, 7-9.

saying, Come hither, I will shew thee the bride, the Lamb's wife. And he carried me away in the spirit to a great and high mountain, as of holiness reaching unto heaven; *and shewed me that great city, the holy Jerusalem, descending out of heaven from God,* heaven on earth; *Having the glory of God:* the divine likeness; *and her light was like unto a stone most precious,* as of pure light embodied in an earthly substance; *even like a jasper stone, clear as crystal;* seeing through it all things pure, and in her all divine perfections united. *And had a wall great and high,* that no sin or sinner could penetrate; *and had twelve gates,* as the true doctrine by which any man may enter therein; *and at the gates twelve angels,* and persons for the doctrines; *and names written thereon, which are the names of the twelve tribes of the children of Israel:* persons both of men and angels, for the elect become as angels; *On the east three gates; on the north three gates; on the south three gates; and on the west three gates,* four headings with three moments each. *And the wall of the city had twelve foundations, and in them the names of the twelve apostles of the Lamb,* as of the ancient church, so also of the new. *And he that talked with me,* the angel; *had a golden reed,* a glorious measure; *to measure the city, and the gates thereof, and the wall thereof,* to measure the limit and boundary, because it is established and complete. *And the city lieth foursquare, and the length is as large as the breadth: and he measured the city with the reed, twelve thousand furlongs,* the doctrine of holiness on each side. *The length and the breadth and the height of it are equal,* the perfections of God equally distributed to three classes of angels, according to the three divine persons. *And he measured the wall thereof, an hundred and forty and four cubits,* twelve by twelve, the union both of doctrines and of things; *according to the measure of a man, that is, of the angel,* for in the new creation men attain to the sight of things in themselves. *And the building of the wall of it was of jasper:* as the light of the city; *and the city was pure gold, like unto clear glass,* with inward glory. *And the foundations of the wall of the city were garnished with all manner of precious stones,* as of every essence subject to God, and every precious doctrine.[137] *The first foundation was jasper;* as the light of the city, and as the wall, so also the foundation thereof, which is the moral law of God;[138] *the second, sapphire; the*

---

[137] Ex. 28:15-21; Is. 28:16; Ezek. 28:13.
[138] Prov. 6:23, 10:25; Is. 8:20, 28:16-17, 51:4; Matt. 7:24-27; Luke 6:47-49.

third, a chalcedony; the fourth, an emerald; The fifth, sardonyx; the sixth, sardius; the seventh, chrysolite; the eighth, beryl; the ninth, a topaz; the tenth, a chrysoprasus; the eleventh, a jacinth; the twelfth, an amethyst, the perfect righteousness of the church through the doctrine of Christ.[139] *And the twelve gates were twelve pearls;* brought up from the sea, redeemed from the old creation; *every several gate was of one pearl:* perfectly united; *and the street of the city was pure gold,* as the glory of God; *as it were transparent glass,* all things visible in themselves through righteousness. *And I saw no temple therein: for the Lord God Almighty and the Lamb are the temple of it. And the city had no need of the sun, neither of the moon, to shine in it: for the glory of God did lighten it, and the Lamb is the light thereof,* not the symbols of things, but the things in themselves. *And the nations of them which are saved shall walk in the light of it:* the virtues and honors of this world preserved therein; *and the kings of the earth do bring their glory and honour into it,* unto the king of kings. *And the gates of it shall not be shut at all by day: for there shall be no night there,* perpetually open. *And they shall bring the glory and honour of the nations into it,* the diverse virtues of men. *And there shall in no wise enter into it any thing that defileth, neither whatsoever worketh abomination, or maketh a lie:* being held back by their sin; *but they which are written in the Lamb's book of life,* who are saved from their sin. *And he shewed me a pure river of water of life, clear as crystal, proceeding out of the throne of God and of the Lamb,* the Holy Spirit, containing the intuition identical in distinction to the concept, whereby men and angels are made holy, as God is holy.[140] *In the midst of the street of it, and on either side of the river, was there the tree of life,* as a vine spread throughout; *which bare twelve manner of fruits, and yielded her fruit every month: and the leaves of the tree were for the healing of the nations. And there shall be no more curse:* that curse put away through the sacrifice of Christ; *but the throne of God and of the Lamb shall be in it; and his servants shall serve him: And they shall see his face;* and so be like him; *and his name shall be in their foreheads. And there shall be no night there; and they need no candle, neither light of the sun; for the Lord God giveth them light: and they shall reign for ever and ever,* perfectly holy, like unto angels. *And he said unto me, These sayings are faithful and true: and the Lord God of*

---

[139] Is. 54:11-14.
[140] Lev. 11:44-45, 19:2, 20:26.

the holy prophets sent his angel to shew unto his servants the things which must shortly be done. Behold, I come quickly: for his work is ever nigh; *blessed is he that keepeth the sayings of the prophecy of this book,* these things being revealed to us for our obedience. *And I John saw these things, and heard them,* the vision of prophecy. *And when I had heard and seen, I fell down to worship before the feet of the angel which shewed me these things,* for the glory revealed. *Then saith he unto me, See thou do it not: for I am thy fellowservant, and of thy brethren the prophets,* an angel, a brother; *and of them which keep the sayings of this book: worship God,* who shall make us like himself. *And he saith unto me, Seal not the sayings of the prophecy of this book: for the time is at hand,* the things foretold beginning shortly afterward, and particular things fulfilled in every generation. *He that is unjust, let him be unjust still: and he which is filthy, let him be filthy still: and he that is righteous, let him be righteous still: and he that is holy, let him be holy still,* that each one should be righteous for himself, and not for others. *And, behold, I come quickly; and my reward is with me, to give every man according as his work shall be,* as at the first. *I am Alpha and Omega, the beginning and the end, the first and the last,* the image and glory of God. *Blessed are they that do his commandments, that they may have right to the tree of life,* as at the first; *and may enter in through the gates into the city,* to be holy, as God is holy, if any will obey the doctrine of righteousness. *For without are dogs, and sorcerers, and whoremongers, and murderers, and idolaters, and whosoever loveth and maketh a lie,* to those who do not embrace righteousness there remains only sin and its curse. *I Jesus have sent mine angel to testify unto you these things in the churches,* even the Holy Spirit in a sign, who shows us things to come.[141] *I am the root and the offspring of David, and the bright and morning star,* God and man in one person, before and after, beginning and end. *And the Spirit and the bride say, Come,* for the Spirit speaks through the church in whom he works. *And let him that heareth say, Come. And let him that is athirst come,* whoever finds in himself a desire for righteousness. *And whosoever will, let him take the water of life freely,* for in Christ men are free to live forever, even as Adam was free to eat of the tree of life. *For I testify unto every man that heareth the words of the prophecy of this book, If any man shall add unto these things, God shall add unto him the plagues that are written in this*

---

141 Dan. 8:15-17, 9:20-23; John 16:12-15.

book: And if any man shall take away from the words of the book of this prophecy, God shall take away his part out of the book of life, and out of the holy city, and from the things which are written in this book, for he has a part by his freedom, if he chooses. *He which testifieth these things saith, Surely I come quickly. Amen. Even so, come, Lord Jesus,* to fulfill the end of our salvation. *The grace of our Lord Jesus Christ be with you all. Amen.*

The Order of Events

There are six events of historical doctrine: virgin birth, death, burial, resurrection, ascension, and second coming.

The order of doctrine follows the categories, but the order of events follows the relations. Creation in six days represents the whole purpose of the moral law, but moral purposes begin with the concept thereof, and proceed to the persons in whom those concepts are fulfilled. Historical doctrine glorifies the Son of God; it represents a particular purpose of the law, the knowledge of the Son, beginning with his own person, and proceeding to those events through which he is known and glorified.

The three doctrines of the atonement together think the quality of his person, itself ordered by the relations. Therefore, they all come after the virgin birth, after his ministry on earth, and the signs, but before the ascension and second coming, for once his person is thought, his qualities must follow, and after that his causality and reciprocity.

The order of events is determined by the rule of the prequel. In the doctrine of the Son, the subject is constant and the predicate varies; therefore, the understanding proceeds from particular to universal. That particular event that thinks Christ's person is the virgin birth; the intuition pertaining to his person contains the negation of any prior condition, that is, the unconditional condemnation of the Father, through which he is born into the world. Therefore, the virgin birth is followed by his death. And because he lives even while dead, his burial follows his death, and his resurrection follows his burial. And the life of his resurrection he lives to God; wherefore, he also ascends into heaven, to be glorified with the Father, whence he shall return to glorify the Father in himself.

These six events reveal the life of Christ in time, and so follow the order of aesthetic judgments. Thus, the unity and reality of his person lies in the virgin birth; his plurality and negation, in his death, which yields an intuition of the diverse judgments executed upon him; his totality and limitation, whereby he shows forth in himself a righteousness exceeding the flesh, in his burial; his substance and inherence in his resurrection, because he has eternal life; his causality and dependence in his ascension, because he gives eternal life to his people; and his community and reciprocity in his second coming, because he gathers his people to himself.

However, because the object of intuition is not beyond sensation, but given to us in the very person of the Son, there is no seventh event expressing the completeness of the system, for the completeness thereof is always present in the Son himself.

The Order of the Signs

The signs are intuitions of the historical doctrines of Christ. The work of redemption consists of the whole life of Christ; nevertheless, the empirical representation thereof occurs during the three and a half years of his ministry, wherein his glory is made manifest on earth.[142] It therefore begins with the preaching of the Gospel by John the Baptist to the completion of Christ's work in his death.

There are twelve signs, one for each historical doctrine. Their chronology is more difficult to explain, yet clearly laid down in Scripture. Besides the twelve are certain repetitions; the temple is twice cleansed; the Lord's Supper is preceded by the Passover; and the Betrayal is divided into intention and act. Lastly, the trial of Christ comes directly before his death, and issues forth immediately in his crucifixion; therefore, in the division of signs I have joined it together with his death, in a place of its own.

Four of these signs occur at the beginning of his ministry; the remaining ten at the end. Therefore, the most natural division of the signs is into two groups, one representing the headings of concepts, the other representing the moral law of God fulfilled in Christ.

There are twelve signs according to doctrine, but these must be thought chronologically. The signs are intuitions for intuitions conceived, and may be thought of as lying within a single time, because they represent the whole system of historical doctrine. A moment in time has before, during, and after.

---

[142] John 17:4.

The beginning of historical doctrine lies in the headings of the categories, of which there are four signs; the ministry of Christ consists of his fulfillment of the law, for which there are ten; lastly, there is one sign for the end of his ministry, because the purpose is one.

The order of signs follows the rule of the prequel. Every sign thinks a universal concept that contains the ground of an intuition. The universal concept thought in each sign is the historical doctrine, and each historical doctrine is intuited in another, whose signs come to pass in order of intuition.

The order of the signs is comprehended in this table.

Key: *Doctrine — Sign*

Beginning

    Prophet — John the Baptist

    Virgin Birth — Baptism

    Plurality of Man — Temptation

    Resurrection — Cleansing

Act

    Second Coming — Transfiguration[143]

    Burial — Anointing[144]

    King — Triumph[145]

    Resurrection — Cleansing[146]

    Ascension — Passover

    Priest — Washing the Disciples' Feet[147]

    Totality of Man — Betrayal[148]

---

[143] Matt. 17:1, 24, 19:1, 20:29, 21:1; Mark 9:30, 33, 10:1, 32-34, 46, 11:1; Luke 9:51, 10:38, 22:1.

[144] John 12:1.

[145] Matt. 26:1-2, 6; John 12:12.

[146] Matt. 21:12; Mark 11:15.

[147] John 13:2.

[148] John 13:12-31.

Ascension—The Lord's Supper[149]

Unity of Man—Agony

Totality of Man—Betrayal

<u>End</u>

Death—Trial

The beginning of Jesus' ministry lies in his prophetic office; wherefore, the sign of Christ's prophetic office comes first: the preaching of John the Baptist in the wilderness. John represents the unity of the many, gathered together in Christ.

John the Baptist preached Christ come in the flesh. When therefore the Lord began his ministry, he came to John to be baptized by him, to be set apart for his work. And afterward is he baptized by the Holy Spirit, because the baptism of Christ represents the divine nature manifest in his flesh.

After Jesus is baptized by the Holy Spirit, he is also by the Spirit driven into the wilderness to be tempted by the devil, that he might be perfectly sanctified for his ministry. The temptation of Christ represents his union with his people, because he partook of their nature, that they might partake of his righteousness.

He sanctifies himself on behalf of his people, that they might be forgiven their sins and cleansed, that they might be holy, as he is holy. Wherefore, at the beginning of his ministry, he cleanses the temple on the earth, devoting it to the divine purpose. The cleansing of the temple represents the application of his work to his people.

This is the beginning and foundation of the ministry of Jesus Christ. Jesus, being foretold of the prophets, is born of a virgin, to bear our sins, to cleanse us from all unrighteousness and make us partakers of the divine nature.[150]

Christ saves sinners by his fulfillment of the moral law on their behalf. Whereas the beginning of Jesus' ministry consists of his perfect sanctification on behalf of his people, the ministry itself lies in his perfect righteousness manifest

---

[149] Luke 22:20.
[150] 1 John 1:9; 2 Pet. 1:4.

in the flesh. This is revealed to us in his second coming. Wherefore, the end of his ministry begins with his transfiguration on the mount, about the time he began to speak of his death and resurrection in Jerusalem.[151] The transfiguration signifies the perfect righteousness of Christ, the one true God, revealed to men.

The burial of Christ shows forth his perfect sanctification in the flesh, for that he must first be perfectly sanctified in death to show forth his perfect righteousness. Wherefore, the sign of his burial follows, the anointing by Mary. By resting in his obedience unto death, Christ shows forth in himself the image of God to men.

Christ sanctifies himself for his people, that they might be sanctified through the truth, even through the sight of Christ.[152] Therefore, the intuition of his perfect sanctification lies in his kingly office, and the sign thereof follows. In the triumphal entry of Christ into Jerusalem, the name of God is affirmed and exalted.[153]

His triumph consists of the perfect sanctification of his people in himself by their participation in his life, for the intuition of his kingdom lies in his rule over his people. On the last day he shall raise all men unto himself through the power of his resurrection, his people to be glorified with himself. Wherefore, the sign of his resurrection follows, that is, the second cleansing of the temple.

These four signs are distinguished from the following six by a short time before Jesus enters Jerusalem for the passover,[154] because they answer to the first four commandments.

God, being glorified in the work of redemption, and his people to be glorified with him, it remains only to show his working toward that end in his people.

Christ ascends into heaven to show forth the completeness of his work, that he might be glorified, and that his work might be applied to his people. Wherefore, after he cleanses the temple the second time, he gives his disciples

---

[151] Matt. 16:21; Mark 8:31.
[152] John 17:19.
[153] Ps. 24.
[154] Matt. 21:17, 26:17-18; Mark 14:12-13; Luke 22:7-10; John 11:54.

of the Passover, to signify the glory of his person in heaven, whereby men receive eternal life.

Those who believe in Christ are forgiven their sins and cleansed for their service on earth. Wherefore, the sign of his priesthood follows: the washing of the feet of his disciples, for in Christ men are enabled to live godly in this world, offering up good works to God.

Forgiveness comes to men through the headship of Christ, whereby the human race forms an image of the divine nature. It is necessary that there be sin in the world, that it might be forgiven in Christ, for so he bears the condemnation of the Father, that his people might be delivered from sin. Wherefore, after he washes the feet of his disciples, he sends Judas out from their midst, that he might be united with his true bride.

The intuition of Christ ascended lies in the application of the atonement to his people, for that there is sin in the world, it is washed away through faith in the blood of Christ. Wherefore, his true bride he gives to eat of his flesh and blood, that she might have a part with him in heaven.

The application of the work belongs to the unity of the human race, for that there is one rightful head in whom all the righteous are gathered, and this is signified by his agony in the garden, that they might be sanctified by the truth.[155]

This unity is itself intuited in the whole human race, the righteous divided from the wicked. Wherefore, his betrayal before indicated comes to pass, because in Christ God makes his people partakers of the divine nature, whereby they delight to obey his law, and for which they are envied and hated by the world.[156]

Lastly comes his trial, to show the end of the signs in the work of atonement, wherein the divine judgments executed upon him are especially manifest.

---

[155] John 17:17-26.
[156] John 17:14.

Conclusion

History is replete with characters vicious and virtuous, but none more sanctified than the Lord Jesus Christ, whose divine example shows us the way of salvation. To be happy in obedience is human; to be blessed in sufferings is divine. The beautiful and sublime character of this singular individual stands above every other as the most perfect example of moral excellence, and the righteousness of his person is worthy not only of sincere emulation, but also solemn worship.

He who alone has a legitimate claim to be the Christ must be the very same. Jesus fulfilled the prophecies of the Old Testament, taught the moral law of God, performed miracles in abundance, revealed the doctrine of righteousness, lived and died innocently before man and God, and it is he alone of whom these things are even spoken of. Wherefore, he alone has a legitimate claim to be the Messiah, and he alone is the very same, through whom men must be saved.

> Neither is there salvation in any other: for there is none other name under heaven given among men, whereby we must be saved. Acts 4:12

Because the historical doctrines are grounded in the fundamentals, they contain within themselves the apodictic certainty of the former, and their absolute necessity for salvation; yet because they are present in sensible intuition, they are also testified by the historical witness of the church. To this end men are called to preach the word and to hear it preached, that they might believe on Christ for salvation.

Men ought therefore to trust in the truth of God to convince sinners, and the power of God to convert them to himself. The minister of the word must rely on the word. The light of the word must shine through him, and by his life and ministry he ought to testify to the grace of God. Those who hear him ought not to hear fanciful tales or speculative myths, but the power and wisdom of God to save sinners, with reverence and obedience.

And I, brethren, when I came to you, came not with excellency of speech or of wisdom, declaring unto you the testimony of God. For I determined not to know any thing among you, save Jesus Christ, and him crucified. And I was with you in weakness, and in fear, and in much trembling. And my speech and my preaching *was* not with enticing words of man's wisdom, but in demonstration of the Spirit and of power: That your faith should not stand in the wisdom of men, but in the power of God. 1 Corinthians 2:1-5

Therefore seeing we have this ministry, as we have received mercy, we faint not; But have renounced the hidden things of dishonesty, not walking in craftiness, nor handling the word of God deceitfully; but by manifestation of the truth commending ourselves to every man's conscience in the sight of God. 2 Cor. 4:2, cf. James 1:21-25

This truth may indeed be illuminated by arguments of philosophy and history, but neither discipline is equal to the full assurance of the word, wherein lies both the form and matter of divine truth. Nevertheless, insofar as the arguments of philosophy shed light on the apodictic truth of the Gospel, they form a natural successor to the argument of the prequel. If the former may be called the ontotrinitarian argument, the latter may be called the cosmotrinitarian argument. By this I understand the full assurance of salvation arising from the historical intuition given to us in the preaching of the Gospel.[157] If the fundamentals are absolutely certain, and the historicals follow from the fundamentals, then the historicals are also absolutely certain. The work is not only possible, but actual; men are actually saved through faith in Christ, and receive eternal life, and are conformed to the image of the Son, and God is glorified in their salvation, so that men are without excuse, for therein lies the ground of its application to men. Through the sensible intuition thereof, men receive the comfort and assurance of the whole system of doctrine, wherein lies

---

[157] Col. 2:1-3.

not only the concept of things spoken before, but the image and likeness that fills the heart and mind.

> For God, who commanded the light to shine out of darkness, hath shined in our hearts, to *give* the light of the knowledge of the glory of God in the face of Jesus Christ. 2 Corinthians 4:6

> That their hearts might be comforted, being knit together in love, and unto all riches of the full assurance of understanding, to the acknowledgement of the mystery of God, and of the Father, and of Christ; In whom are hid all the treasures of wisdom and knowledge. Colossians 2:2-3

The fundamentals indeed show forth the possibility of salvation, but not the means whereby it comes to pass. The historicals reveal the fundamentals, that men might repent through faith in Christ, and also contain the ground of their application to men, that they might partake of his righteousness.

Men ought to be totally assured of his grace because they are wholly dependent upon it. Through the historical doctrine of the Son, men receive an intuition wherein lies the apodictic certainty of the fundamentals, and through the fundamentals, the work itself is made absolutely certain to the senses, that men might wholly trust in Christ for their salvation and receive the perfect consolation of apodictic truth.

The church ought to add her voice, not by subtle arguments or clever words, but by obedient subjection and humble preaching. The study of truth is to be commended withal, joined to its practice, wherein lies the purpose of the whole, but once separated from the fountain of truth, it becomes empty, and loses its vigor, and strays from its mark.

Therefore, it is necessary, not only to show forth the work of salvation, but its application to the church by the Holy Spirit, which I call *derivative* doctrine. This is the occupation of the sequel. There is, however, another study opened to us by the doctrine of Christ, in whom all things in heaven and earth are gathered into one: the history of the world.[158] This I call *prophetic history*, because its aim is not history as such, but the history of redemption in Christ. This is a great work, and I will endeavor to lay its foundation, if God wills it.

[158] Rev. 5.

Historical doctrine is the system of intuition whereby the divine persons are glorified in the appearance of the Son. The glory of the divine persons is the supreme end of salvation; therefore, these doctrines are necessary for salvation, to glorify the persons in the salvation of sinners. If God, in saving sinners, follows all the rules of his own law, then a man may lawfully consent to his own salvation, having turned from sin to righteousness.[159]

Fundamental doctrine prescribes the intuition to be produced. This intuition is made actual in the life of Christ, whereby it is also made actual for us through faith. By the manifestation of God in the flesh, a man is enabled to repent of his sins through faith in Christ.

The fundamental doctrines are grounds of the possibility of salvation. Through the divine persons salvation is lawfully conceived. However, this conception must itself be given through an intuition, and this intuition is given in the Son. Therefore, the historical doctrines are absolutely necessary for salvation, not for its possibility, but for the knowledge of its possibility, that men might be saved through faith in the power of God.

Peter denied the death and resurrection of our Lord, yet Jesus pronounced him blessed, because he confessed Jesus to be the Christ, the Son of the living God.[160] Therefore, the church ought to hold them blessed who together with them profess the one true God in three persons, notwithstanding their ignorance of historical doctrine. This peculiar blessing belongs to the ancient church. Yet insofar as this doctrine has been revealed in history, and testified by the church in all ages, it ought to be the ordinary measure of saving faith. "Whosoever denieth the Son, the same hath not the Father: *but* he that acknowledgeth the Son hath the Father also" (1 John 2:23).

Faith is only possible through knowledge of the Lord Jesus Christ. This knowledge is given in a sensible intuition, and this intuition may have any degree, greater or less. Therefore, the absolute standard of Christian faith cannot

---

[159] 1 Tim. 1:18; 2 Tim. 2:5.
[160] Matt. 16:13-23.

rest in the degree of faith, but solely in the conception of the divine persons revealed in Jesus Christ. Nevertheless, wherever there is true faith, there is also an understanding and knowledge of historicals, which shall not reject anything proper to true faith, and which may be increased through the teaching of the Word.

> Another parable put he forth unto them, saying, The kingdom of heaven is like to a grain of mustard seed, which a man took, and sowed in his field: Which indeed is the least of all seeds: but when it is grown, it is the greatest among herbs, and becometh a tree, so that the birds of the air come and lodge in the branches thereof. Matthew 13:31-32, cf. Eph. 4:1-16

In this sensible intuition lies, not only the possibility of salvation, but the actual end of our sin, to attain the divine likeness. Hence, the transition from sin to righteousness is possible through the common end to be realized in them. Sin distinguishes man's blessedness from his righteousness. All men desire happiness, and not otherwise than by law, that it might be assured to them according to a rule. The law annexes happiness, attaching it to itself, such that without law no one may be happy. Both are ends of our rational nature, but the law is our necessary duty, happiness is only an actual desire. Therefore, the law joins happiness to itself, and every man consenting thereunto, even in his sin, desires to be happy lawfully, that is blessed, though he sins. Sin is therefore the distinction in the will of righteousness and blessedness, rejecting the holiness of God, willing the latter but not by means of the former.

Nevertheless, those who see the blessedness of God in Christ, having willed the same end by their sin, and continually in their sin, are turned from sin to righteousness, if only within them lies the possibility of representing that identity in distinction; for in Christ, God's righteousness and blessedness are identical in distinction, and by desiring the blessedness of Christ, a man may turn from their distinction to their identity, and partake of the same in righteousness, which they at the first sought by sin.

The desire to be like God is the first motive to sin, and God's desire to make men like himself is the final end of redemption. No one will be as happy as God unless he is as holy as Christ.[161] When men see the divine likeness offered to them in Christ, they ought not to repent for the sake of their happiness, but out of conscientious duty, recognizing their unworthiness to that end, and willing only to be as his servants, that God might make them like his Son.[162] Nevertheless, even in their sin, they are enabled to see their true happiness joined to the law, and so from the one they may lawfully will the other, because the blessedness they desire is also righteous, and therefore holy, identical in distinction. When then a man sees the Lord Jesus Christ,[163] if within himself lies the possibility of representing this identity in distinction, he turns from distinction to identity, and by faith in the promise, he shall be made as holy and happy as Jesus Christ, being sanctified unto the last day. Thus men are persuaded to repent of their sins and believe in Jesus Christ, that they may be conformed to the image of the Son.[164]

> Verily, verily, I say unto thee, We speak that we do know, and testify that we have seen; and ye receive not our witness. If I have told you earthly things, and ye believe not, how shall ye believe, if I tell you *of* heavenly things? And no man hath ascended up to heaven, but he that came down from heaven, *even* the Son of man which is in heaven. And as Moses lifted up the serpent in the wilderness, even so must the Son of man be lifted up: That whosoever believeth in him should not perish, but have eternal life. For God so loved the world, that he gave his only begotten Son, that whosoever believeth in him should not perish, but have everlasting life. For God sent not his Son into the world to condemn the world; but that the world through him might be saved. He that believeth on him is not condemned: but he that believeth not is condemned already, because he hath not believed in

---

161 Heb. 12:14.
162 Luke 15:17-24.
163 John 6:40.
164 Rom. 8:28-30.

the name of the only begotten Son of God. And this is the condemnation, that light is come into the world, and men loved darkness rather than light, because their deeds were evil. For every one that doeth evil hateth the light, neither cometh to the light, lest his deeds should be reproved. But he that doeth truth cometh to the light, that his deeds may be made manifest, that they are wrought in God. John 3:11-21

And so testifies the church.

Now then we are ambassadors for Christ, as though God did beseech *you* by us: we pray *you* in Christ's stead, be ye reconciled to God. For he hath made him *to be* sin for us, who knew no sin; that we might be made the righteousness of God in him. 2 Corinthians 5:20-21

And the Spirit and the bride say, Come. And let him that heareth say, Come. And let him that is athirst come. And whosoever will, let him take the water of life freely. Revelation 22:17

WORKS CITED

Gress, Julian. 2019. *Christ Condemned: On the Incarnation and the Trinity*.
    Lynnwood, WA: Julian Gress.

—. 2018. *The Harmony of Reason and the Possibility of Man's Final
    End in Kant's Critique of Judgment*. B.A. thesis, St. John's College, Santa
    Fe, NM, 2010, revised 2017. https://juliangress.mywriting.network/
    https://juliangress.mywriting.network/essay-on-kant/.

Gill, John. Gill's Exposition of the Entire Bible. https://biblehub.com/
    https://biblehub.com/commentaries/gill/genesis/1.htm

Jamieson, Robert; Fausset, A.R.; Brown, David. *Jamieson-Fausset-Brown Bible
    Commentary*. https://biblehub.com/
    https://biblehub.com/commentaries/jfb/genesis/1.htm.

Kant, Immanuel. 1987. *Critique of Judgment*. Translated by Werner S. Pluhar.
    Indianapolis: Hackett Publishing Company.

—. 1997. *Critique of Practical Reason*. Edited by Mary Gregor. Translated by
    Mary Gregor. Cambridge: Cambridge University Press.

—. 1996. *Critique of Pure Reason*. Translated by Werner S. Pluhar. Indianapolis:
    Hackett Publishing Company.

—. 1998. *Groundwork of the Metaphysics of Morals*. Edited by Mary Gregor.
    Translated by Mary Gregor. Cambridge: Cambridge University Press.

—. 1996. *Metaphysics of Morals*. Edited by Mary Gregor. Translated by Mary
    Gregor. Cambridge: Cambridge University Press.

—. 1996. "Religion within the boundaries of mere reason." *In Religion and
    Rational Theology*, edited by Allen W. Wood and George di Giovanni,
    translated by George di Giovanni. New York: Cambridge University
    Press.